Indiana University Uralic and Altaic Series
Denis Sinor, Editor
Volume 167

Studies on Central Asian History in Honor of Yuri Bregel

Yuri Bregel

STUDIES ON

Central Asian History

IN HONOR OF

YURI BREGEL

EDITED BY

Devin DeWeese

Indiana University
Research Institute for Inner Asian Studies
Bloomington, Indiana
2001

Library of Congress Control Number: 2001088031
ISBN: 0-933070-48-9

Printed in the United States of America

Contents

Preface

It is an honor and a pleasure to be able to have a hand in putting together this volume in honor of Yuri Bregel. Planning for the volume began in earnest already in the summer of 1997, and all contributions were received between the spring of 1999 and the summer of 2000; numerous delays, some of my own making and others unforeseeable, postponed the appearance of the volume to the spring of 2001.

The individual contributions, it is hoped, will speak for themselves; in soliciting contributions I asked only that authors treat some important aspect of the history and civilization of Central Asia, and affirmed my conviction that the goal of honoring Yuri through the work of his colleagues would be better served by asking them to set their own agenda than by restricting them to a single, more narrowly defined theme. I was also loath to insist on arbitrary length restrictions, believing that scholars are better judges of the space their topics require than are editors or publishers. I have standardized the transliteration system employed in the various contributions, but have been content to avoid strict consistency where it would needlessly interfere with the author's aims (as in the philological discussions of Richard Frye and Peter Golden); I have also sought, where possible, not so much to standardize citations as to ensure that readers will face as little trouble as possible in tracking down cited sources and studies. The translations into English of the contributions of Elena Davidovich and G. E. Markov, which were submitted in Russian, are my own; the Russian versions have not been published elsewhere. I have sought to minimize any possible misrepresentations of these authors' views and arguments resulting from my translations, but I must acknowledge my regret, and my responsibility, should any remain.

The result of these efforts is a collection of articles, of varied length, each of which marks an original contribution to historical scholarship on Central Asia. They range in subject from slavery to intellectual history, from *vaqf* to political tract, and from dynastic history to the business correspondence of Sufis; they range in period and place from Bukhara on the eve of the Islamic era to Astrakhan on the eve of the Soviet era, encompassing nomadic communities of Central Asia while focusing primarily on sedentary and urban environments; and they range in discipline from philology and numismatics to ethnography, with the historical analysis of written sources predominating. I have arranged most of the contributions roughly in order of their chronological 'center of gravity,' with two more wide-ranging articles, devoted respectively to ethnography and history, placed outside this sequence, at the end.

I would like to take this opportunity to thank all the authors, both for their fine contributions and for their helpfulness, from beginning to end, in making my task as editor much easier than it might have been. The contributors form a truly stellar group of specialists on the history of Central Asia, and I am grateful to them for entrusting their work to me, and for their patience through the process of seeing the volume into print.! Thanks are due also to the series editor, Denis Sinor, both for his eagerness to publish this *Festschrift* for Yuri, and for his help in the final stages of the work.

Lastly, though I have expressed them elsewhere as well, my heartfelt thanks go again to Yuri Bregel; from the very day we first met—in the library of the Research Institute for Inner Asian Studies in Bloomington, in January, 1981—he has been a wonderful teacher, colleague, and friend. I knew of his scholarly talents and prestige twenty years ago; since then I have come to appreciate what a rare privilege, and joy, it has been to know him and to work with him. My fondest hope for my part in preparing this volume is that it might serve as a tangible substitute for the elusive words, which I consistently fail to find, that might adequately express to him my admiration, respect, gratitude, and affection.

DEVIN DEWEESE
Bloomington, Indiana
January 2001

Studies on Central Asian History in Honor of Yuri Bregel

INTRODUCTION

Devin DeWeese

The twelve articles presented here are offered in honor of Yuri Bregel by scholars from Europe and North America who share his devotion to the study of Central Asian history and civilization; each contributor counts Yuri as a colleague, friend, or teacher (or all three), and the studies in the present volume affirm our individual and collective esteem not only for Yuri's own contributions to the study of Central Asia, or for the high standards of his scholarship, but for the example of courage, resilience, and forthright acceptance of the scholar's public responsibilities that he has set throughout his life and career. Yuri is without question one of the leading historians of Islamic Central Asia in the world; but his life has been marked by an extraordinary succession of interruptions, shifts, and new directions, occasioned by his direct confrontation of the grimmest forces the 20th century had to offer, and the energy, productivity, and high standards that distinguish his scholarly career are all the more remarkable against the backdrop of a life that took him from Moscow to Central Asia, to the front lines of the war against Nazi Germany, to a Soviet labor camp, to Israel, and finally to America.

Iurii Ènokhovich Bregel' was born in Moscow on November 13, 1925, and grew up in the city; both his mother and father were trained as economists, and his father, who published numerous books in his field, was known as the only professor of political economy in the USSR who was not a Communist Party member. In the fall of 1941, as the German army neared the outskirts of Moscow, Yuri's family was evacuated eastwards to Perm, near the Urals; soon (in January, 1942), following an invitation to Yuri's father from the Moscow Institute of Oriental Studies (which had been moved to Central Asia), the family relocated far to the south, in the town of Fergana, and it was there that Yuri's lifelong fascination with Central Asia was first awakened. It was far from clear at that point that he would master the region's languages and devote his career to its history. In fact, of course, it was far from clear that a young man of his generation would survive to have a career at all, with the war's staggering human toll on the Soviet Union.

After completing his secondary schooling in Fergana in 1943, Yuri moved on not to a university, but to artillery school, in preparation for service in the Soviet army; he went to the front in January 1944, and his anti-tank artillery unit fought in the Crimea, in Belorussia, in Poland, and in Germany. At the front, in the fall of 1944, Yuri was wounded in the leg by a German bullet that might well have done graver damage had it not been deflected, fortuitously, by the revolver strapped to his belt. Twice decorated, Yuri saw the end of the war in Germany, where he occasionally served as an interpreter, and was assigned for some time to the work of dismantling chemical plants in Poland; he left the army in the summer of 1946, and planned to resume his education.

Yuri had excelled in mathematics in high school, but decided that he was already too old to be just starting out in that field; so he enrolled at the history department at Moscow University, gaining admission despite the anti-Semitic atmosphere that pervaded the department at that time. He studied in general courses under historians such as S. V. Bakhrushin and N. M. Druzhinin, in medieval history under S. D. Skazkin and A. I. Neusykhin, in modern history under E. V. Tarle, and in archeology under A. V. Artsikhovskii; he specialized eventually in the history of Central Asia, working under some of the leading figures of Soviet scholarship on the Middle East and the eastern Islamic world from the generation that followed the great Russian orientalist V. V. Bartol'd, including the Iranist B. N. Zakhoder, I. M. Reisner, and A. F. Miller. Yuri's university years—from 1946 to 1949, and from 1954 to 1956, with the five-year interruption discussed below—afforded him not only training as a historian, but language study and broader disciplinary work as well. He studied Persian under P. I. Petrov, and Turkic languages under È. N. Nadzhip, and later worked in the department of ethnography under S. A. Tokarev and M. I. Cheboksarov. A special course on Khwārazm with the noted historian and archeologist S. P. Tolstov sparked Yuri's interest in a region whose history, in the Islamic period, was to become a major focus of his scholarly work; Yuri would later take part in an ethnographic and archeological expedition there,[1]

[1] This was facilitated by Yuri's former fellow-student, G. E. Markov, who had completed his education during Yuri's imprisonment and became Yuri's academic advisor; the Turkmen ethnographic expedition entailed travel to regions close to the Soviet border and was thus a sensitive matter, but Markov, who was the expedition's organizer, allowed Yuri to participate even before his formal rehabilitation.

but his real love was the rich corpus of manuscripts and written documents, mostly unexplored even now, that are the primary sources for Central Asian history.

In the fall of 1949, however, came the second 'interruption' in Yuri's life, when he was arrested and imprisoned on charges of anti-Soviet activity. One of his fellow students, it turned out, was an informer for the secret police who reported on private conversations with Yuri and another student, his friend Vladimir Kabo (who later completed his training as an ethnographer and eventually emigrated, in 1990, to Australia). As was the usual procedure, the informer led the way in making explicit anti-Soviet remarks in order to elicit similar comments from his unsuspecting friends, and then took the material to the secret police 'organs,' turning what were casual jokes and anecdotes into threats against the state,[2] and fabricating other 'evidence' wholesale; the informer's denunciations had begun already in 1948. Kabo was arrested first, and Yuri's arrest came a month later, on November 7; as a result of the informer's denunciations, and without trials, Yuri and Kabo were given ten-year sentences. Yuri was sent to a labor camp in the northern Urals, where he spent nearly five years at hard labor; aside from three months during which he was 'employed' in clerical tasks, he spent his sentence doing rough physical work, mostly chopping wood.

After Stalin's death was announced on March 9, 1953—a date marked every year afterwards by Yuri and his family—it was another year and a half before Yuri was released from the labor camp, in September, 1954, as part of a large-scale amnesty; full exoneration and 'rehabilitation' came only in 1956, after the famous 20th Communist Party congress that launched the 'de-Stalinization' campaign. A decade later, in the spring of 1964, Yuri took what can only be regarded, in the context of Soviet society, as a courageous and principled stand—seemingly quixotic, perhaps, but ultimately prescient—for accountability

[2] Yuri and Kabo were accused of making anti-Soviet statements in their conversations with the informer, and of having listened to BBC and Voice of America broadcasts. One of Yuri's offenses was a joke he reportedly told about Stalin: Stalin had lost his pipe, and had ordered Beria (his chief of the secret police) to find who had taken it; after awhile, Stalin himself had found his pipe, and had told Beria to call off the search, but Beria had explained, "20,000 people have been arrested, and all have confessed." Yuri was also reported to have commented, following a companion's remark that people from the Caucasus are often blessed with long lives, that this was a pity (an allusion to Stalin's Georgian origins).

after the abuses of the Stalinist system. He appeared at the informer's dissertation defense, for which the rules allowed comments on the candidate's public profile, and spoke of the denunciations that had cost two innocent men five years of their lives; this public identification of the informer—a virtually unprecedented act in a society still permeated by the secret police—caused a stir in Moscow, and a recent writer has described Yuri's role in exposing his denouncer in 1964 as "an important step in undermining the system" that relied on government informers and secret denunciations.[3]

The same informer—who met with both Yuri and Kabo not long after the dissertation defense and unapologetically portrayed himself as the victim—had also been involved, in the late 1940s, in efforts to entrap the daughter of the French naval attaché in Moscow, Hélène Peltier, who was studying at Moscow University; yet another student, Andrei Siniavskii, was coerced into this effort as well, but found a way to break off contact with the young woman after first letting her know of the danger. Peltier later aided Siniavskii in sending his writings abroad to be published outside the USSR; for this Siniavskii was brought to trial in 1965, along with fellow dissident writer Iulii Daniel', and the man who had denounced Yuri and Kabo turned up as a prosecution witness. Siniavskii (who died in 1997) later included a lightly fictionalized account of these events—including the arrest of Yuri and Kabo, the informer's feigned concern, in the midst of his denunciations, during a visit with one of Yuri's close relatives in Tashkent, and the informer's meeting with his former friends after the dissertation defense, all recounted in a passage presented as Siniavskii's dialogue with his accuser—in his novel *Spokoinoi nochi*, published from exile, in Paris, in 1984.[4] The events have also been

[3] Kevin Windle, "The Belly of the Whale Revisited: The History and Literature Surrounding a Character in Terts's *Spokoinoi nochi*," *The Slavonic and East European Review*, 76/1 (1998), pp. 1-27 (see especially pp. 2, 5-8, 15, 19-20, 27), with further references.

[4] Abram Terts, *Spokoinoi nochi* (Paris: Syntaxis, 1984), pp. 384-388; and the English translation, Abram Tertz (Andrei Sinyavsky), *Goodnight!*, tr. Richard Lourie [New York: Viking, 1989], pp. 316-319. Yuri's name is rendered in the Russian original as "Breigel'," a spelling that occasioned a note in the 1998 Moscow edition, explaining it as based on the pronunciation of "people not closely acquainted with him" (Abram Terts, *Spokoinoi nochi* [Moscow: Zakharov, 1998], pp. 318-321); in Lourie's English translation, the name has become "Breughel," ironically echoing the Dutch name that may underlie, as Yuri once explained, the Russian *familiia* "Bregel'."

recounted in Kabo's memoirs,[5] and Yuri himself has written a brief account as well.[6]

Following his release from the camp in 1954, Yuri began to rebuild a normal life, and in 1955 he was married, to Liliya (Liusia) Davydovna Rozenberg. They had a son who was born in 1956, but died when he was only eight years old; their daughter Natasha was born in 1966.

Yuri also returned to Moscow University after his release, and quickly made up for lost time, completing his degree in history in 1956. He was recruited by Oleg Dreier, director of the newly established 'Oriental Literature' publishing house of the Soviet Academy of Sciences, and began working as a senior editor and department head there (directing the editorial board for 'the publication of monuments and manuscripts'). Yuri earned his doctorate at the Institute of Oriental Studies in 1961; the following year, he took a position at that institute.

While working with Dreier at the publishing house, Yuri was the driving force behind the project that would eventually see the collection and republication of Bartol'd's scholarly writings;[7] Yuri himself edited several of the ten volumes ultimately produced between 1963 and 1973, adding introductions and notes on relevant scholarship since Bartol'd, and translated into Russian many of Bartol'd's works that had been published originally in German or English. Yuri was also instrumental in launching the well-known 'black series' of text editions and translations of important historical and cultural sources in the languages of the Near East, Central Asia, South and Southeast Asia, and East Asia;

[5] Vladimir Kabo, *The Road to Australia: Memoirs*, tr. Rosh Ireland and Kevin Windle (Canberra: Aboriginal Studies Press, 1998), pp. 125-141, on the arrest, and on the confrontation with the accuser in 1964; cf. pp. 59, 118, 148-149, 153. The Russian original (Vladimir Rafailovich Kabo, *Doroga k Avstraliiu: Vospominaniia*) was published in New York in 1995. Another brief summary of these events appears in Ludmilla Alexeyeva and Paul Goldberg, *The Thaw Generation: Coming of Age in the Post-Stalin Era* (Pittsburgh: University of Pittsburgh Press, 1993; 1st publ. Boston, 1990), pp. 114-115, 136-138.

[6] Iurii Bregel', "Ob'iasnenie posle lageria," *Vremia i my: Mezhdunarodnyi demokraticheskii zhurnal literatury i obshchestvennykh problem* (New York/Jerusalem/ Paris), No. 91 (1986), pp. 224-229, published together with a series of other short accounts, prompted by the publication of the informer's self-justification and renewed denunciation of Siniavskii, collectively entitled "Izvinite za donos" (pp. 218-236).

[7] See the recent comments about Yuri's work on the Bartol'd project in Iu. A. Petrosian, "O. K. Dreier i rossiiskoe klassicheskoe vostokovedenie," *Peterburgskoe vostokovedenie*, 9 (1997), p. 549.

originally entitled *Pamiatniki Pis'mennosti Narodov Vostoka* ("Monuments of the Literature of the Peoples of the East") and later renamed *Pamiatniki pis'mennosti Vostoka* ("Monuments of the Literature of the East"), the series has produced well over a hundred volumes, and is still growing. Also from this period dates the foundation of the annual 'orange series,' *Pis'mennye pamiatniki Vostoka* ("Literary Monuments of the East"), for the publication of specialized articles in the same fields, in which Yuri likewise played a major role; he served as joint editor for the first three volumes, and contributed articles and reviews to the series as well.

Yuri's own scholarship during his years in Moscow was focused on the history of the khanate of Khiva in the 19th century; his two monographs from that period presented editions, translations, and analyses of Khivan documents on the Türkmens and Qaraqalpaqs who were dominated by the rulers of Khiva, and his numerous articles explored other aspects of the political, administrative, economic, and ethnic history of the region. He also began preparing a Russian translation of the first parts of Charles A. Storey's *Persian Literature: A Bio-bibliographical Survey*, dealing with Qurʾānic literature and historical sources in Persian. The 'translation' in fact became much more, as Yuri corrected, updated, and expanded the original work, adding material that amounted to twice the original text on the basis of the many manuscript catalogues that had appeared since Storey's survey was issued in the early 1930s. Yuri's three-volume Russian edition of Storey was published in 1972, and was itself translated into Persian in the early 1980s; it remains an indispensable reference work for all students of Persian-language historical literature.

As the seeming promise of liberalization during the early 1960s gave way to what is now termed, with retrospective mildness, the 'era of stagnation' under Brezhnev, the atmosphere in the Soviet Union steadily worsened; a series of events set in motion by the trial, in 1965-66, of Siniavskii and Daniel' led to renewed problems for Yuri and, eventually, to his decision to apply to emigrate from the USSR. As noted, Yuri's accuser from 1949 was a prosecution witness against Siniavskii and Daniel. Transcripts of testimony at the two dissidents' trial, published outside the Soviet Union, in 1967, by another dissident writer, Aleksandr Ginzburg, included a note on the earlier denunciations of Yuri and Kabo;[8] Yuri signed a petition protesting the firing of one of

[8] Aleksandr Ginzburg, *Belaia kniga po delu A. Siniavskogo i Iu. Danièlia* (Frankfurt: Possev-Verlag, 1967), p. 262.

Siniavskii's former professors after he served as a defense witness at the trial, and later signed a letter calling for a fair trial for Ginzburg when he too was prosecuted for his critical account of the Siniavskii-Daniel' affair and its consequences.

After Yuri signed the Ginzburg letter, his telephone was tapped, and neighbors reported visits by investigators asking about Yuri and his family; as the general atmosphere worsened following the 1968 Soviet invasion of Czechoslovakia, Yuri's disgust for the regime led him to resolve to try to leave the USSR. Understanding that an attempt to emigrate would effectively end his career, Yuri saw through the publication of his translation and expansion of Storey's *Persian Literature*, and then in July, 1973 he applied to emigrate. The application itself entailed a double uncertainty: it was unclear what would await Yuri and his family in Israel (there was no guarantee that he could work in his field), and it was far from clear that the application would ever be approved. The application might well have been denied, indeed, with Yuri and his family joining the ranks of Jewish 'refuseniks' of the 1970s and '80s, had it not been for a small uproar, at the 1973 meeting of the International Congress of Orientalists, held in Paris, over another Soviet scholar who had been denied an exit visa; Yuri's case was raised specifically, by Bernard Lewis and J. D. Pearson, in the course of western protests taken up with the Soviet delegation (threatening Soviet hopes to host a subsequent meeting of the Congress), and shortly thereafter, Yuri's application to emigrate was approved (as were those of several other scholars).

Though Yuri was not fired from his position until the formal approval of the application to emigrate, the application itself induced some friends to turn away, fearing for their own safety, and some colleagues warned of the dire conditions that awaited Yuri and his family outside the Soviet Union. In the Soviet academic world, Yuri became a 'non-person:' his name was removed from several publications he had edited, his translation of Storey was cited without mention of its translator or its substantial expansion, many friends and colleagues feared to associate or correspond with him, and for many years, until the waning days of the Soviet state, merely mentioning the name "Bregel'" when citing one of Yuri's works could earn a scholar a summons from a Communist Party committee to explain why he or she had made reference to someone who had turned his back on the Soviet homeland, and to face chastisement for such a lapse in judgment. Of his Soviet colleagues, only the late Petr Griaznevich, an Arabist, maintained regular correspondence with Yuri in Israel and the United States; former colleagues feared to associate with him even when traveling abroad (of the Soviet delegation to a conference Yuri attended in Turkey following his emigration, only the late Ziia Buniiatov greeted him as one would an old friend). Near the end of the Soviet regime, in the era of *glasnost'*, however, old colleagues began to reestablish contact,[9] and Yuri hosted Soviet scholars, visiting Bloomington to attend conferences, in his home; recently some of Yuri's scholarship has been published in Moscow.[10]

Yuri and his family departed Moscow early in January, 1974, traveling first to Vienna and then to Israel, where Yuri began teaching at Hebrew University in Jerusalem, in the Department of the History of Islamic Countries; in 1978, after a year away at the Institute for Advanced Studies in Princeton, he assumed an endowed chair at Hebrew University, as the Eliahu Elath Professor of the History of the Muslim Peoples. In 1981, however, he was lured away from this post by Denis Sinor to join what was then the Department of Uralic and Altaic Studies (now Central Eurasian Studies) at Indiana University, an institution at which, Yuri hoped, it would be possible to begin to build a center for serious scholarship in Central Asian studies. His arrival at Indiana meant the addition of the field of Islamic Central Asia to a program that had previously emphasized the pre-Islamic period and other parts of the Inner Asian world.

At Indiana, Yuri taught Central Asian history from the 16th to 20th centuries, guided students through Persian and Chaghatay Turkic manuscripts, and deciphered documents with them; he also taught courses on the ethnic history of Central Asia, and on "Everyday life in Central Asia" in the 19th century, as well as seminars on Central Asian historical sources and on the 19th-century khanates. Yuri inspired his students both with high standards of scholarship, and with the joys of scholarly exploration and meticulous analysis; his students invariably

[9] Yuri's comments on the early signs of renewed contacts are quoted, together with a survey of his career, in Susan Wintsch, "Inner Reaches: Soviet Émigré Studies Remote Central Asia," *Research & Creative Activity* (Office of Research and Graduate Development, Indiana University), 12/1 (November 1988), pp. 19-24.

[10] Neither Yuri's emigration, however, nor his scholarly activity in Israel and the United States, is mentioned in the entry on him in S. D. Miliband, *Biobibliograficheskii slovar' otechestvennykh vostokovedov s 1917 g.* (2nd, revised ed., Moscow: Nauka, 1995), vol. I, p. 193.

sought to do their best for him. Yet he also provided them with an example of a humble, self-effacing scholar with a wry sense of humor and a healthy skepticism toward scholarly puffery; thereby he offered them, in the midst of an environment all too often fraught with self-importance, intellectual arrogance, and self-aggrandizing careerism, an alternative academic 'style.'

In addition to his teaching, Yuri served for twelve years as director of the Research Institute for Inner Asian Studies (RIFIAS), and for nine years headed the Inner Asian and Uralic National Resource Center, supported by federal Title VI funds. He retired from his administrative roles in 1997, and from teaching in the spring of 2000.

Yuri's tenure as RIFIAS director saw the addition of an unparalleled collection of microfilms of manuscript sources on Central Asia to the institute's library resources; Yuri also oversaw the RIFIAS' program as a host institution for the Rockefeller Foundation's Humanities Fellowships, launched the *Papers on Inner Asia* series, organized a joint colloquium on unpublished sources on Inner Asian history with what was then still the Leningrad Branch of the Institute of Oriental Studies of the Soviet Academy of Sciences, and convened an international conference, together with Indiana University's School of Public and Environmental Affairs, on the ecological crisis of the Aral Sea.

Yuri's stewardship of the Center maintained and strengthened a tradition of using its resources to foster serious scholarship and to support the in-depth, historically grounded study of Inner Asia. Yuri had had direct acquaintance, in the Soviet environment, with the potential impact of shifting political winds on the direction and integrity of scholarly work, through governmental involvement in the academic world, and he came to understand also the frequent tendency, in American academic life, for the faddish and the superficial to take precedence over the substantive and the profound; for both reasons, undoubtedly—and for the more basic reason that he is no more tolerant of nonsense in administrative matters than he is in matters of scholarship—Yuri sought to ensure that the Center served the original goals of the Title VI program—to ensure a supply of specialists with a deep knowledge of particular areas, as opposed to the quick and superficial 'expertise' increasingly called upon by government and the media—and his efforts as Center director often involved actively challenging short-sighted initiatives, developed by bureaucrats, that favored 'outreach' activities over support for serious scholarship, and reflected the political concerns of the moment rather than long-term understanding. His role as Center director also enabled him to play a decisive role in significantly expanding the faculty of the Department of Central Eurasian Studies; indeed, the net result of his administrative efforts was to strengthen all the components of Indiana's program.

Yuri's years at Indiana proved among his most productive in scholarly terms, despite the administrative duties to which he devoted over a decade. In 1988 he completed his critical text edition of the *Firdaws al-iqbāl*, a major 19th-century Chaghatay Turkic history from the khanate of Khiva; his English translation of the work, with extensive notes, appeared in 1999, opening up a major primary source on a region all too often 'known' through secondary literature of uneven quality. The text and translation mark the culmination of over a quarter-century of painstaking work on three continents; they also stand as perhaps the most apt testimonial to Yuri's central devotion to the study, publication, and analysis of written sources. His work in this direction began already in the 1950s, when Yuri worked in archives and manuscript collections in Central Asia and Leningrad. At that time, the serious study of the primary sources for Central Asian history had hardly begun; yet Yuri's work in identifying and analyzing documentary sources was not only pioneering, but of enduring value as well.

Yuri's publications, whether in Russian or English, are marked by precision, accuracy, penetrating analysis, and impeccable scholarship rooted in the sources; the same high standards are evidenced in his often lengthy, and often trenchant, reviews of scholarly works, most recently his analysis of the historiography of Central Asia in the west and in post-Soviet Central Asia itself. Yuri has also been committed, however, to doing the kind of work that opened doors to other scholars and facilitated a much broader body of scholarly production; whether in the publication of Bartol'd's works, in the translation into Russian of an important reference work on the metric equivalents of weights and measures employed in the Islamic world, in the Russian edition of Storey, or in his monumental three-volume bibliography of Islamic Central Asia, published in 1995, Yuri has produced indispensable aids to serious research in Central Asian history, and scholars in many fields far from Yuri's own are indebted to him.

* * *

A bibliography of Yuri's scholarly publications follows; it was prepared largely on the basis of Yuri's own *curriculum vitae*.

Yuri Bregel: Bibliography

I. Books:

1. *Khorezmskie turkmeny v XIX veke.* Moscow: Izd-vo Vostochnoi literatury, 1961; 442 pp.

2. *Dokumenty arkhiva khivinskikh khanov po istorii i ètnografii karakalpakov.* Moscow: Nauka, 1967; 539 pp.

3. Ch. A. Stori, *Persidskaia literatura: Bio-bibliograficheskii obzor*, Parts I-III (translation into Russian, with revision and expansion, of C. A. Storey, *Persian Literature: A Bio-bibliographical Survey*, vol. I, Sections 1 and 2 [London, 1927-1936]). Moscow: Nauka, 1972; 1884 pp.

Reviews:

I. Afshār, *Rāhnamā-yi kitāb*, 16/4-6 (1973), pp. 212-213.

J. Aubin, *Studia Iranica*, 2/2 (1973), pp. 284-285.

J. D. Pearson, *Journal of the Royal Asiatic Society*, 1975, pp. 68-69.

J. W. Clinton, *Journal of the American Oriental Society*, 97/2 (1977), pp. 212-214.

Persian translation: *Adabiyāt-i fārsī bar mabnā-yi ta'līf-i Isturī*, ed. Aḥmad Munzavī, vols. 1-2 (Tehran, 1362/1983-84).

- Review: N. Anṣārī, *Nashr-i Dānish*, 4/4 (1984), pp. 38-43.

4. Shīr Muḥammad Mīrāb Munis and Muḥammad Rizā Mīrāb Āgahī. *Firdaws al-iqbāl: History of Khorezm*, ed. Yu. Bregel. Leiden: E. J. Brill, 1988 (critical text edition: introduction [60 pp.], Chaghatay text [1284 pp.]).

Review: J. P. Laut, *Zeitschrift der Deutschen Morgenländischen Gesellschaft*, 143/2 (1993), pp. 420-421.

5. *Bibliography of Islamic Central Asia*, Parts I-III. Bloomington: Research Institute for Inner Asian Studies, 1995; lix, xxxv, xxix, 2276 pp.

Reviews:

N. Di Cosmo, *Central Asiatic Journal*, 41/2 (1997), pp. 271-275.
B. A. Litvinskii, *Oriens/Vostok* (Moscow), 1997, No. 4, pp. 176-180.
B. F. Manz, *Journal of Asian History*, 31/2 (1997), pp. 181-183.
D. Sinor, *Journal of the American Oriental Society*, 118/1 (1998), pp. 119-120.
J.-A. Gross, *Religious Studies Review*, 24/4 (1998), pp. 351-352.
S. Akiner, *Bulletin of the School of Oriental and African Studies*, 61/3 (1998), pp. 581-582.

6. Shir Muhammad Mirab Munis and Muhammad Riza Mirab Agahi. *Firdaws al-iqbāl: History of Khorezm*, translated from Chaghatay and annotated by Yu. Bregel. Leiden: E. J. Brill, 1999 (Islamic History and Civilization: Studies and Texts, ed. U. Haarmann and W. Kadi, vol. 28); lxxvii, 718 pp.

Review: C. E. Bosworth, *Journal of the Royal Asiatic Society*, 3rd ser., 10/3 (2000), pp. 402-405.

II. Edited works:

7. Muḥammad ibn Nadzhīb Bakrān. *Dzhakhān-nāme (Kniga o mire)*. Ed. Iu. E. Borshchevskii. Moscow: Izd-vo Vostochnoi literatury, 1960; 22, 142 pp.

8. *Poslovitsy i pogovorki narodov Vostoka*. Moscow: Izd-vo Vostochnoi literatury, 1961; 736 pp.

9. Akademik V. V. Bartol'd. *Sochineniia*:

I, *Turkestan v èpokhu mongol'skogo nashestviia*. Moscow: Izd-vo Vostochnoi literatury, 1963; 760 pp.

II/1, *Obshchie raboty po istorii Srednei Azii*; *Raboty po istorii Kavkaza i Vostochnoi Evropy*. Moscow: Nauka, 1963; 1020 pp.

II/2, *Raboty po otdel'nym problemam istorii Srednei Azii*. Moscow: Nauka, 1964; 657 pp.

III, *Raboty po istoricheskoi geografii*. Moscow: Nauka, 1965; 711 pp.

V, *Raboty po istorii i filologii tiurkskikh i mongol'skikh narodov.* Moscow: Nauka, 1968; 757 pp.

VII, *Raboty po istoricheskoi geografii i istorii Irana.* Moscow: Nauka, 1971; 663 pp.

VIII, *Raboty po istochnikovedeniiu.* Moscow: Nauka, 1973; 723 pp.

10. *Pis'mennye pamiatniki Vostoka: Istoriko-filologicheskie issledovaniia, Ezhegodnik.* Ed. jointly with V. M. Konstantinov and A. S. Tveritinova. Moscow: Izd-vo Vostochnoi literatury —
    Ezhegodnik 1968 (1970); 312 pp.
    Ezhegodnik 1969 (1972); 422 pp.
    Ezhegodnik 1970 (1974); 504 pp. (the name of Bregel' among the editors for this volume was suppressed because of his emigration to Israel).

11. *Annotirovannaia bibliografiia trudov akademika V. V. Bartol'da*, ed. I. I. Umniakov; *Opisanie arkhiva akademika V. V. Bartol'da*, ed. N. N. Tumanovich. Moscow: Nauka, 1976; 467 pp. (the name of Bregel' as an editor is omitted because of his emigration to Israel).

12. *Papers on Inner Asia*, Nos. 1-33. Bloomington, Indiana: Research Institute for Inner Asian Studies, 1987-2000.

III. Articles:

13. "Zemlevladenie u turkmen v khivinskom khanstve v XIX v." *Sovetskoe vostokovedenie*, 1957, No. 3, pp. 123-136.

14. "Rasselenie turkmen v khivinskom khanstve v XIX v. (Po materialam arkhiva khivinskikh khanov)." *Strany i narody Vostoka*, 1 (Moscow, 1959), pp. 242-256.

15. "Ètnicheskaia karta Iuzhnoi Turkmenii i Khorasana v XVII-XVIII vv." *Kratkie soobshcheniia Instituta ètnografii*, 31 (Moscow, 1959), pp. 14-26 (with 2 maps).

- abridged English translation: "The Peoples of Southern Turkmenistan and Khorasan in the 17th and 18th Centuries." *Central Asian Review*, 8/3 (1960), pp. 264-272 (with 2 maps).

16. "Plemia sakar v khivinskom khanstve." *Kratkie soobshcheniia Instituta vostokovedeniia*, 38 (Moscow, 1960), pp. 59-68.

17. "Dokument po istorii turkmen iz arkhiva khivinskikh khanov." *Problemy vostokovedeniia*, 1960, No. 1, pp. 168-172.

18. "Sochinenie Baiani 'Shadzhara-ii khorezmshahi' kak istochnik po istorii turkmen." *Kratkie soobshcheniia Instituta narodov Azii*, 44 (Moscow, 1961), pp. 125-167.

19. "Arkhiv khivinskikh khanov: Predvaritel'nyi obzor novykh dokumentov." *Narody Azii i Afriki*, 1966, No. 1, pp. 67-76.

20. "Novaia rukopis' sochinenia Mu'in ad-Dina Natanzi." *Narody Azii i Afriki*, 1968, No. 4, pp. 164-165.

21. "Termin 'vilayet' v khivinskikh dokumentakh." *Pis'mennye pamiatniki Vostoka, Ezhegodnik 1968* (Moscow, 1970), pp. 32-39.

22. "O sozdanii bio-bibliograficheskogo svoda istorii persidsko-tadzhikskoĭ literatury" (with Iu. E. Borshchevskii). *Narody Azii i Afriki*, 1970, No. 3, pp. 104-119.

23. "K izucheniiu zemel'nykh otnoshenii v khivinskom khanstve (Istochniki i ikh ispol'zovanie)." *Pis'mennye pamiatniki Vostoka, Ezhegodnik 1969* (Moscow, 1972), pp. 28-103.

24. "Vostochnye rukopisi v Kazani." *Pis'mennye pamiatniki Vostoka, Ezhegodnik 1969* (Moscow, 1972), pp. 355-373.

25. "The Preparation of a Bio-bibliographical Survey of Persian Literature" (with Yu. E. Borshchevskii). *International Journal of Middle East Studies*, 3 (1972), pp. 169-186 (expanded version of No. 23).

26. "The Tawārīkh-i Khōrazmshāhīya by Thanā'ī, the Historiography of Khiva, and the Uzbek Literary Language." *Aspects of Altaic Civilization II: Proceedings of the XVIII PIAC, Bloomington, June 29-July 5, 1975*, ed. Larry V. Clark and Paul Alexander Draghi (Bloomington: Research Institute for Inner Asian Studies, 1978; Uralic and Altaic Series, Vol. 134), pp. 17-32.

27. "The Sarts in the Khanate of Khiva." *Journal of Asian History*, 12/2 (1978), pp. 120-151.

28. "The Bibliography of Barthold's Works and the Soviet Censorship." *Survey* (London), 24/3 (1979), pp. 91-107.

29. "The Role of Central Asia in the History of the Muslim East." The Asia Society, Afghanistan Council, *Occasional Papers*, No. 20 (New York, 1980), 20 pp.

30. "Barthold and Modern Oriental Studies." *International Journal of Middle East Studies*, 12 (1980), pp. 385-403.

31. "Nomadic and Sedentary Elements among the Turkmens." *Central Asiatic Journal*, vol. 25/1-2 (1981), pp. 5-37 (with map).

   - German translation: "Nomadische und sesshafte Elemente unter den Turkmenen." *Turkmenenforschung*, 12 (1987), pp. 129-164 (with map).

32. "Tribal Tradition and Dynastic History: The Early Rulers of the Qongrats According to Munis." *Asian and African Studies (Journal of the Israel Oriental Society)*, 16/3 (1982), pp. 357-398.

33. "Turko-Mongol Influences in Central Asia." *Turko-Persia in Historical Perspective*, ed. Robert Canfield (Cambridge: Cambridge University Press, 1991), pp. 53-77.

34. "Notes on the Study of Central Asia." *Papers on Inner Asia*, No. 28 (Bloomington, Indiana: Research Institute for Inner Asian Studies, 1996), 61 pp.

   - repr. in *Oriens/Vostok* (Moscow), 1997, Nos. 4-5.

IV. Encyclopedia articles:

A) *Encyclopaedia of Islam*, 2nd ed. (Leiden: E. J. Brill) [years indicated are those in which the relevant fascicle was published]

35. "Āgahī, Muḥammad Riḍā Mīrāb." *EI*², Supplement, vol. I (1980), p. 46.

36. "Atalïḳ." *EI*², Supplement, vol. I (1980), pp. 96-98.

37. "Ḳosh-begi." *EI*², V (1980), pp. 273-274.

38. "Čawdor, or Čawdïr." *EI*², Supplement, vol. I (1981), pp. 168-169.

39. "Dīwān-begi." *EI*², Supplement, vol. I (1981), pp. 227-228.

40. "Ersarï." *EI*², Supplement, vol. I (1982), pp. 280-281.

41. "Ḥāfiẓ Tanïsh." *EI*², Supplement, vol. I (1982), p. 340.

42. "Ïnaḳ." *EI*², Supplement, vol. I (1982), pp. 419-420.

43. "Labāb." *EI*², V (1982), pp. 581-582.

44. "Mangïshlaḳ." *EI*², VI (1988), pp. 415-417.

45. "Manghït." *EI*², VI (1988), pp. 417-418.

46. "Manghïts." *EI*², VI (1988), pp. 418-419.

47. "Mangu-Timur." *EI*², VI (1988), pp. 419-420.

B) *Encyclopaedia Iranica* (Costa Mesa, California: Mazda Press) [years indicated are those in which the relevant fascicle was published]

48. "ʿAbd-al-ʿAzīz Solṭān b. ʿObaydallāh Khan." *EIr*, I (1982), pp. 101-102.

49. "ᶜAbd-al-Raḥmān b. Moḥammad Laṭīf Mostaǰerr Samarqandī." *EIr*, I (1982), p. 147.

50. "ᶜAbdallāh Khān b. Eskandar." *EIr*, I (1982), pp. 198-199.

51. "Abu'l-Ḵayr Khan b. Dawlat Shaikh Oḡlān." *EIr*, I (1983), pp. 331-332.

52. "Abū Saᶜīd Khan b. Kučkunči." *EIr*, I (1983), pp. 381-382.

53. "ᶜArabšāhī." *EIr*, II (1986), pp. 243-245.

54. "Barthold V. V." *EIr*, III (1989), pp. 830-832.

55. "Bātman." *EIr*, III (1989), pp. 869-870.

56. "Behbūdī." *EIr*, IV (1989), pp. 99-100.

57. "Bigār." *EIr*, IV (1989), pp. 249-251.

58. "Bukhara. III (After the Mongol invasion)." *EIr*, IV (1989), pp. 515-521.

59. "Bukhara. IV (The Khanate of Bukhara and Khorasan)." *EIr*, IV (1989), pp. 521-524.

60. "Būstānī," *EIr*, IV (1990), pp. 574-575.

61. "Central Asia: 12th-13th/18th-19th centuries." *EIr*, V (1990), pp. 193-205.

62. "Ḥeṣār." *EIr* (forthcoming).

63. "[Persian] Historiography: Central Asia." *EIr* (forthcoming).

C) Others

64. "Bukhara." *Dictionary of the Middle Ages*, II (New York: Charles Scribner's Sons, 1983), pp. 396-397.

65. "Bukhara, Khanate of." *Encyclopaedia of Asian History*, I (New York: Charles Scribner's Sons/London: Collier Macmillan, 1988), pp. 194-195.

66. "Khiva, Khanate of." *Encyclopaedia of Asian History*, II (New York: Charles Scribner's Sons/London: Collier Macmillan, 1988), pp. 298-300.

67. "Khokand, Khanate of." *Encyclopaedia of Asian History*, II (New York: Charles Scribner's Sons/London: Collier Macmillan, 1988), pp. 301-303.

68. "Timurids." *Dictionary of the Middle Ages*, XII (New York: Charles Scribner's Sons, 1989), pp. 56-59.

69. "Ulugh Beg." *Dictionary of the Middle Ages*, XII (New York: Charles Scribner's Sons, 1989), pp. 56-257.

V. Reviews, Translations, and Miscellaneous Contributions:

70. "Novoe izdanie vazhnogo istochnika po istorii turkmen" (review of A. N. Kononov, *Rodoslovnaia turkmen: Sochinenie Abu-l-Gazi khana khivinskogo* [Moscow/Leningrad, 1958], with È. N. Nadzhip). *Problemy vostokovedeniia*, 1959, No. 1, pp. 169-173.

71. "Turetskie poslovitsy i pogovorki" (translated from Turkish into Russian). In *Poslovitsy i pogovorki narodov Vostoka* (Moscow, 1961), pp. 521-550 (see No. 8 above).

72. "Ot redaktsionnoi kollegii po izdaniiu 'Sochinenii' Akademika V. V. Bartol'da." In V. V. Bartol'd, *Sochineniia*, I (Moscow, 1963), pp. 5-13.

73. "Predislovie." In V. V. Barthold, *Sochineniia* II/2 (Moscow, 1964), pp. 5-21.

74. Translations into Russian of 31 of Bartol'd's articles from the first edition of the *Encyclopaedia of Islam*. In V. V. Barthold, *Sochineniia* II/2 (Moscow, 1964), pp. 485-548.

75. Review of *Vostokovednye fondy krupneishikh bibliotek Sovetskogo Soiuza* (with B. L. Riftin). *Narody Azii i Afriki*, 1964, No. 1, pp. 202-206.

76. Translation into Russian of several articles by V. V. Bartol'd. In V. V. Bartol'd, *Sochineniia*, VI, *Raboty po istorii Islama i arabskogo khalifata* (Moscow, 1966):
   - pp. 613-614, "al-Abza'i;"
   - pp. 615-616, "K voprosu o prizvanii Mukhammeda;"
   - pp. 659-665, "Islam na chernom more;"
   - pp. 669-675 (two of Bartol'd's articles for the first edition of the *Encyclopaedia of Islam*).

77. *Pravila izdaniia serii 'Pamiatniki pis'mennosti Vostoka.'* Moscow, 1966; 83 pp.

78. Review of B. V. Lunin, *Sredniaia Aziia v dorevoliutsionnom i sovetskom vostokovedenii* (Tashkent, 1965). *Pis'mennye pamiatniki Vostoka, Ezhegodnik 1968* (Moscow, 1970), pp. 260-284.

79. *Musul'manskie mery i vesa s perevodom v metricheskuiu sistemu* (translation from German, with numerous corrections, of W. Hinz, *Islamische Masse und Gewichte umgerechnet ins metrische System* [Leiden: E. J. Brill, 1955]). Moscow: Nauka, 1970; pp. 5-74 (published together with E. A. Davidovich, *Materialy po metrologii srednevekovoi Srednei Azii*).

80. Translation into Russian of several articles by V. V. Bartol'd. In V. V. Bartol'd, *Sochineniia*, VII, *Raboty po istoricheskoi geografii i istorii Irana* (Moscow, 1969):
   - pp. 337-353, "K istorii Saffaridov;"
   - pp. 359-370, "Persidskaia shu'ubiia i sovremennaia nauka;"
   - pp. 469-472, "Iranskii buddizm i ego otnoshenie k islamu;"
   - pp. 475-513 (26 of Bartol'd's articles for the first edition of the *Encyclopaedia of Islam*).

81. Translation into Russian of several articles by V. V. Barthold. In V. V. Barthold, *Sochineniia*, VIII, *Raboty po istochnikovedeniiu* (Moscow, 1972):
    - pp. 441-444, "Pamiatnik vremeni rasprostraneniia islama v Srednei Azii;"
    - pp. 465-468, "Rukopis' Zamakhshari so staro-tiurkskimi glossami;"
    - pp. 483-485, Review of *Mirabilia descripta. Les Merveilles de l'Asie. Par le Père Jourdain Catalani de Sévérac*, ed. and tr. Henri Cordier (Paris, 1925);
    - pp. 581-601 (11 of Bartol'd's articles for the first edition of the *Encyclopaedia of Islam*).

82. Review of John E. Woods, *The Aqquyunlu: Clan, Confederation, Empire. A Study in 15th/9th Century Turko-Iranian Politics* (Minneapolis-Chicago, 1977). *Journal of Asian History*, 14/1 (1980), pp. 72-77.

83. Review of Michael Khodarkovsky, *Where Two Worlds Met: The Russian State and the Kalmyk Nomads, 1600-1771* (Ithaca, New York: Cornell University Press, 1992). *Slavic Review*, 52/4 (1993), pp. 901-902.

84. Review of Audrey Burton, *The Bukharans: A Dynastic, Diplomatic and Commercial History 1550-1702*, *Journal of Asian Studies*, 57/3 (1998), pp. 849-851.

85. "Historical Maps of Central Asia, 9th-19th Centuries A.D.," ed. Yuri Bregel. *Papers on Inner Asia*, Special Supplement (Bloomington, Indiana: Research Institute for Inner Asian Studies, 2000); 11 maps.

BUKHARA FINALE

Richard N. Frye

Harvard University

This paper is probably my last word about ancient Bukhara, unless some new sources appear which would change the remarks below. It was on my way to Bukhara that I first met Yuri in Moscow, and I am happy to dedicate this 'leg of a locust' to our many years of friendship.

1. *The name.* The earliest occurrence of the name Bukhara is on the debased silver coins formerly called the "Bukhār Khudāt" coins, but the earliest specimens of which are simply copies of the dirhams of the Sasanian ruler Bahrām V with Pahlavi legends. Later we have the legend *bwx'r xwb k'w'*, "Bukhara king emperor," according to Henning. Or the last word may also be read as *k'n'*, since in the Bukharan form of the Sogdian alphabet the letters *w*- and *n*- are virtually indistinguishable from one another.[1] I favor the interpretation of the reading "Kānā" as a personal name of a ruler of Bukhara for the following reasons.

At the outset, to repeat, everyone agrees that the Bukharan coins are copied from the coins of the Sasanian ruler Bahrām V (421-439). Since 'barbarian' copies of his coins with Pahlavi legends have been found, one may postulate a date some time later than his rule, perhaps ca. 500, or even later, depending on the length of time the copies circulated. It should be noted that the coins of Bahrām V do not have legends with the Middle Persian title *kay*, written *kdy*, but it appears later, especially in the reign of Peroz where the legends on his coins do have *kdy pylwç MLK'*, "Kay Peroz king." Nowhere, as far as I have been able to determine, does the epithet *kdy* appear after the name and title of the Sasanian ruler. It is claimed that the reading *k'w'* is a Sogdian form of the Middle Persian word, and it is possible that this is a Sogdian calque on the Middle Persian *kdy*.[2] I suggest, however, that if a kingly epithet

[1] Richard N. Frye, *Notes on the Early Coinage of Transoxiana* (New York: American Numismatic Society, 1949; Numismatic Notes and Monographs, No. 113), pp. 41-49.

[2] W. B. Henning, "Mitteliranisch," *Handbuch der Orientalistik*, Erste Abteilung, Vierter Band, *Iranistik*, ed. B. Spuler, Erster Abschnitt, *Linguistik* (Leiden: E. J. Brill,

is desired, the word should mean not "emperor," but rather "heroic" or "regal." If the ruler of Bukhara copied the coinage of Bahrām V, then one should conclude that he added the word *k'w'* in imitation of a later Sasanian potentate. One should emphasize that the title appears *after* *xwb*, the Sogdian word for king, while on the Sasanian coins the title *kdy* comes *before* the title. I see no compelling reason to suppose that the Bukharan ruler faithfully copied and then translated into Sogdian the legend from Sasanian coins. If one accepts the reading *k'w'*, then the meaning, in my opinion, would be the "heroic" or "regal king of Bukhara."

Second, and more important in my view, the usual titulary on coins, silver vessels, and inscriptions follows the formula "country—title or ruler—personal name."[3] Why should a ruler of Bukhara depart from this model and use a general appellative or epithet instead of his name, which would make the reading of the legend "Bukharan king-regal"? It is more reasonable to assume that the standard model was followed in the coinage, thus Bukhara-king-personal name.

Third, the name K'n'k, to be read Kānā, appears as a Sogdian name, so this would not be out of the ordinary.[4] Furthermore, in Narshakhī's history of Bukhara, a ruler who first issued coinage in Bukhara in the time of the Caliph Abū Bakr is called Kānā.[5] Since the date of the first issue of these coins is earlier than the seventh century, everyone has rejected the notice in Narshakhī as false, even claiming that Narshakhī, or his source, misread the legend on the coins, and falsely interpreted the word as *k'n'* rather than *k'w'*.[6] This implies that the author admittedly could read Bukharan Sogdian, but a modern scholar knew better to correct him, which premise I doubt. Therefore I propose that we should not abandon Kānā as the personal name of a ruler of Bukhara, and not reject it for a reading of *kāwā*, unless it is interpreted as another proper name, Kāwā, as noted below. It is also possible, as

1958), p. 53.

[3] R. N. Frye, "Additional Notes on the Early Coinage of Transoxiana," *American Numismatic Society, Museum Notes IV* (New York, 1950), p. 110.

[4] H. Reichelt, *Die soghdischen Handschriftenreste des Britisch Museums* (2 vols., Heidelberg, 1930), II, p. 49.

[5] Richard N. Frye, tr., *The History of Bukhara, translated from a Persian Abridgment of the Arabic Original by Narshakhī* (Cambridge, Massachusetts: The Mediaeval Academy of America, 1954), p. 35.

[6] Henning *apud* Frye, *Notes on the Early Coinage of Transoxiana*, p. 29.

some have suggested, that the original Bukharan legend had *k'w* as the last word, and that the addition of an *-a* was the result of a breaking of the final *-w* into two parts. It is difficult to determine which coins are the earliest, but the discovery of more coins or other sources may resolve this problem. Let us instead turn to the other possibility as a name.

The proper name Kāwā or Kāw existed in eastern Iran, as we learn from the Tochi Inscriptions in the Northeast Frontier Province of Pakistan.[7] We also find this as a personal name in the Bactrian documents from the Samangan area of present Afghanistan.[8] Whether we are dealing with *kānā* or *kāwā* is uncertain, but in any case I propose that the last word in the coin legends is a proper name rather than a title.

The next appearance of the name Bukhara is in the Old Turkic runic inscription telling of the delegations that came to Mongolia about 732, for the funeral of Prince Kül Tegin, a prominent figure in the Orkhon Turkic kingdom. There the form is *bwk'r'k ulus*, which I suggest means that the persons who came represented the oasis of Bukhara, not solely the town, just as *Sogd (ulus)* meant the "Sogdian people," not just those from Samarkand. The ending *-āk* (ancient *-āka*) is a Sogdian ending attached to nominal and adjectival stems. For example, we have *''z't'k*, "freed or noble," from *''z't*, "clear, perfect, free," or *xwyc'k* from *xwyc*, "pain," etc.

I always had considered the remark in Narshakhī's history of Bukhara about the name "Bukhārā" meaning *fākhira*, "splendid" or "glorious" in Arabic, to be *Volksetymologie*, and not to be taken seriously. Since the historian Juvaynī in his history of the Mongols claimed that the name "Bukhārā" was derived from *vihārā*, a Buddhist monastery, and the province of India called Bihar was also said to come from the same word, I accepted that Bukhara was named after an ancient *vihārā* that existed on the site.[9] Now I believe I was mistaken in not taking Narshakhī more seriously. For he, and other local historians of

[7] H. Humbach, "The Tochi Inscriptions," *Festschrift Georg Buddruss* (Reinbek: Verlag für Orientalische Fachpublikationen, 1994; = *Studien zur Indologie und Iranistik*, 19), pp. 137-156.

[8] Nicholas Sims-Williams, *New Light on Ancient Afghanistan* (London: School of Oriental and African Studies, University of London, 1997), p. 18.

[9] ʿAlāʾ al-Dīn ʿAṭā Malik Juvaynī, *Tārīkh-i Jahān-gushā*, ed. Muḥammad Qazvīnī, vol. I (London: Luzac, 1912; Gibb Memorial Series, vol. XVI, 1), p. 76.

Bukhara, surely knew the Sogdian language, since Narshakhī came from the village of Narshakh, present-day Vabkent, and not from the city of Bukhara, where Persian probably was widely spoken in his time. Furthermore, two Sogdian phrases appear in his text as it has come down to us, offering evidence that he knew whereof he spoke. We now know that a word *fwx'r* existed in Christian Sogdian, with a meaning similar to the Arabic word, which coincidentally happens to be close to the Sogdian word in form and meaning, though of course not related to it. If Henning is correct in deriving the Sogdian form from a Middle Persian *farrūkh*, then we may suppose that the name of the oasis, afterwards applied to its principal town, did not come into existence before the sixth century of our era.[10] The original form of the word might be reconstructed as **pwk'r'k*, an area which was lovely or exceptional, with the *-āk* suffix added to the adjective. The pronunciation would have been **bukhāre*, which the Arabs wrote with a long final *alif*. The Sogdian would have been written *pwx'r*, and we should abandon the etymology that posits "Bukhārā" as a form of *vihārā*.

This does not mean that there was no settlement at all on the site of the future city of Bukhara, for it seems from Arabic, Persian, and Chinese sources that a village called Numijkath or Namijkath existed there. This town's name was probably derived from the name of the Zarafshan River in pre-Islamic times (Namik or Nami),[11] or, less likely, means "ninth town," on the model of Panjikant and other such names. The name Numijkath/Namijkath was transferred to another village near the city of Bukhara, when the latter became the center of the oasis and took the name of the oasis. This may be compared to an earlier time regarding the name of the province of Fārs in Iran in the time of the Achaemenids, when the tribal and then provincial name Parsa was also given to the royal site Parsa (Persepolis for the Greeks). The same was the case of Bactria and its principal city, Bactra or Balkh.

2. *Pre-Islamic history*. There were many settlements in the oasis of Bukhara and the town of Pāykand was one of the most important. Vardāna also had a local ruler as we learn from Arabic sources. There

[10] W. B. Henning, *Ein manichäisches Bet- und Beichtbuch* (Abhandlungen der Preussischen Akademie der Wissenschaften [Berlin], Jahrgang 1936, Philosophisch-historische Klasse, No. 10 [Berlin, 1937]), p. 89.

[11] Josef Markwart, *Wehrot und Arang: Untersuchungen zur mythischen und geschichtlichen Landeskunde von Ostiran*, ed. H. H. Schaeder (Leiden: E. J. Brill, 1938), p. 378.

were geographical reasons for the prominence of Pāykand as a trading center, since it was built on elevated land where the deltas of the Zarafshan and Kashka rivers almost joined before both were dissipated just short of reaching the Amu Darya. Pāykand remained an important town in the oasis after the creation of many canals and the rise of Bukhara.

We may suppose that the town of Bukhara owed its growth and preeminence to at least two factors: its geographical location, where the Zarafshan divided into several branches, and second the ability of its rulers both to control the water for irrigation of a large and fertile oasis, and to exercise successful rule over other towns in the oasis. Thus the ruler of Numijkath became the ruler of the oasis of Bukhara. In all probability this happened not long before the coming of the Islamic armies to the oasis. The Arab commanders saw the advisability of selecting a center for their further activities in Central Asia to the east of the Amu Darya, and the town now called Bukhara was an obvious choice.

There were several rulers of Bukhara before the invasion of the Muslims, as we know from a silver bowl with a Sogdian inscription, and from coins. Ol'ga Ivanovna Smirnova has provided a list of those rulers, especially after the coming of the Arabs, which need not be repeated here, and to which the reader is directed.[12]

There is more to say about the later history of the oasis which, however, cannot occupy us here. As the Arabic chronicles say, "but this is in part and not all," and scholarship is ever changing with new discoveries and new insights.

[12] O. I. Smirnova, *Ocherki iz istorii Sogda* (Moscow: Nauka, 1970), pp. 278-281.

THE TERMINOLOGY OF SLAVERY AND SERVITUDE
IN MEDIEVAL TURKIC

Peter B. Golden

Rutgers University

The vocabulary of slavery in many early societies derived from military terms. When one considers that military force, employed either in large-scale campaigns or in smaller-scale raids and kidnapping, has, historically, been the principal means of slave-acquisition, this is hardly surprising.[1] The Hsiung-nu or Inner Asian Huns, a nomadic tribal confederation of still undetermined ethno-linguistic affiliations (2nd century B.C.–2nd century A.D.), according to Ssŭ-ma Ch'ien had the custom that "after a battle those who have cut off the heads of the enemy or taken prisoners are presented with a cup of wine and allowed to keep the spoils they have captured. Any prisoners that are taken are made slaves."[2] Hsiung-nu precedents are of some importance as they shaped the early forms of the steppe imperial political culture of which the Türks were among the ultimate heirs. Other methods of slave acquisition enumerated by Orlando Patterson in his comparative study of this institution include "tribute and tax payment, debt, punishment for crimes, abandonment and sale of children, self-enslavement, birth."[3] The status of slave, however achieved, invariably involved a wrenching separation from one's family and home environment (the 'loss of natality') and marginalization in a foreign (even if ethnically and linguistically related) milieu resulting in 'social death.'[4] The military slaves or slave-soldiers (Arabic *ghulām* or *mamlūk*) of the ʿAbbāsid

[1] O. Patterson, *Slavery and Social Death* (Cambridge, Massachusetts, 1982), pp. 39-41; R. L. O'Connell, *Ride of the Second Horseman. The Birth and Death of War* (Oxford/New York, 1995), p. 95.

[2] Sima Qian, *Records of the Grand Historian*, II, tr. B. Watson (Hong Kong/New York; revised ed., 1993), p. 137.

[3] Patterson, *Slavery and Social Death*, pp. 105-131.

[4] Patterson, *Slavery and Social Death*, pp. 5, 7, 38-39, 45-51.

Caliphate provide an interesting example of this phenomenon. As Patricia Crone notes, "the combination of cultural disassociation and personal dependence was a very forceful one in that it obliterated the soldiers public personality." Although usually manumitted and (at least nominally) converted, they were largely segregated from society. They were, as Crone writes, "designed to be not a military elite, but military automata."[5] This proved to be a serious miscalculation.

In some of the earliest Turkic texts, the Orkhon inscriptions stemming from the early 8th century, power and powerlessness are often expressed in the terminology of slavery. Thus, in noting the extent and might of the Türk domain, the Kül Tegin Inscription (KT, E21) comments: *ol ödke qul qulluġ bolmïš erti küng künglüg bolmïš erti*, "at that time, the slave became a slave-holder, the handmaiden became a handmaiden-holder."[6] These remarkable inscriptions, part history, part biography, part propaganda, alternately boastful, cajoling, cautioning and threatening in tone, sought to impress on the audience the necessity of Türk/A-shih-na[7] rule. The necessity for this rule, mandated by Heaven and assured by the possession of heavenly good fortune (*qut*), is a constant theme of the Orkhon inscriptions. A sign of this *qut* was independence and the wealth and affluence signified by the possession of

[5] P. Crone, *Slaves on Horseback: The Evolution of the Islamic Polity* (Cambridge, 1980), pp. 78-79.

[6] Citations from the Old Türk inscriptions are noted in the following abbreviations: KT = Kül Tegin, BQ = Bilge Qaghan; E = East, N = North, etc. The texts may be found in Talât Tekin, *A Grammar of Orkhon Turkic* (Bloomington, Indiana, 1968; Indiana University Uralic and Altaic Series, vol. 69) or his more recent *Orhon Yazıtları* (Ankara, 1988); G. Aidarov, *Iazyk orkhonskikh pamiatnikov drevnetiurkskoi pis'mennosti* (Alma-Ata, 1971); H. N. Orkun, *Eski Türk Yazıtları* (Ankara, 1936-41; repr. Ankara, 1987).

[7] The Chinese rendering of the name of the Türk ruling clan, A-shih-na, has been plausibly connected by C. Beckwith, *The Tibetan Empire in Central Asia* (Princeton, 1987), pp.206-208, with the Tokharian title *Ārśilānci* and with the name of "Ἀρσίλας [*Aršila], the more senior monarch of the Turks" (ὃ δὲ τῷ παλαιτέρῳ μονάρχῳ Τούρκων) noted by the late 6th–early 7th-century Byzantine historian Menander (see R. C. Blockley, ed. and tr., *The History of Menander the Guardsman* [Liverpool, 1985], pp. 172-173; Blockley renders this as "The senior ruler of the Turks was named Arsilas"). More recently, Sergei Kliashtornyi has suggested an etymology deriving from Khotanese Saka *aššeina/aššena*, "blue" = Kök Türk (see S. G. Kliashtornyi and D. G. Savinov, *Stepnye imperii Evrazii* [St. Petersburg, 1994], pp. 13-14).

personal slaves or dependents by even the lowliest members of the dominant tribal grouping.

Conversely, frequent allusions to the causes of the decline and fall of the First Türk Qaghanate (Eastern Qaghanate 552-630; the Western Qaghanate fell in 659) are also an important theme of the inscriptions. Here, too, images associated with slavery are adduced: (KT, E7, E24) *tabġač budunqa beglik urï oġïl'in qul boltï ešilik qïz oġïl'in küng boltï*, "Their male children [i.e., those of the Türks, pbg] who were fit to be lords (*beglik*[8]) became slaves (and) their daughters who were fit to be lordly ladies (*ešilik*[9]) became handmaidens." The theme is repeated elsewhere (BQ, E7, E20[10]). Disloyal vassals would also suffer similar fates. Thus, of the Az, whose ruler had been elevated to the qaghanal status by the Türks and who had been given an A-shih-na princess as a bride, it is noted (KT, E20; BQ, E17) that the Az Qaghan *öz yangïltï qaġan ölti bodunï küng qul boltï*, "himself erred. The Qaghan died. His people became handmaidens and slaves." Similarly, Bilge Qaghan informs us (BQ, E36) of the sometimes obstreperous Toquz Oghuz, who having gone towards China *atï küsi yoq boltï bu yerde manga qul boltï*, "their name and fame became nothing. In this land, they became my slaves." From these and other references, it is clear that slavery or some sort of dependent status denoted by the terms *qul* ("male slave") and *küng* ("female slave, handmaiden") was a not unanticipated consequence of military defeat. Political dependence was expressed in the vocabulary of slavery.[11]

[8] See G. Clauson, *An Etymological Dictionary of Pre-Thirteenth Century Turkish* (Oxford, 1972) [henceforth *ED*], p. 326.

[9] Clauson, *ED*, p. 256.

[10] Cf. BQ, E7: *tabġač bodunqa beglik türk urï oġïl'in qul qïltï ešilik qïz oġïl'in küng qïltï türk atïn ïttï tabġačġï begler tabġač atïn tutupan tabġač qaġanqa körmiš*, "(the Türks) made their sons who were fit to be lords slaves and their daughters who were fit to be ladies, handmaidens of the Chinese people. The Türk lords cast aside (*ïttï*) their Türk titles, the Türk lords who were in China took Chinese titles and obeyed the Chinese Emperor." BQ,E 20: *qanïng ügüzče yügürti süngüküg taġča yatdï beglik urï oġlungïn qul qïltïġ ešilik qïz oġlungïn küng qïltïġ*, "your blood ran like a river, your bones lay (piled) like a mountain, you made your sons who were fit to be lords slaves and your daughters who were fit to be ladies handmaidens."

[11] S. G. Kliashtornyi, "Formy sotsial'noi zavisimosti v gosudarstvakh kochevnikov Tsentral'noi Azii (konets I tysiacheletiia do n. è.–I tysiacheletiia n. è.)," in O. G. Bol'shakov and E. I. Kychanov, ed., *Rabstvo v stranakh Vostoka v srednie veka* (Moscow, 1986), pp. 335-336.

Warfare, as with so many other societies, was the primary source of slave-acquisition in the medieval Turkic world. The *Chiu T'ang-shu* graphically notes this s.a. 698 when the newly reviving Türk state staged a dramatic raid that netted some 80,000-90,000 Chinese captives.[12] Paradoxically, the ability of the nomads to provide for the slave market helped to increase the demand for slave labor in neighboring sedentary societies.[13] This, in turn, could further stimulate slave-raiding by the nomads to met this need. As R. Brian Ferguson has noted, "slave capture is a major goal in many indigenous raiding and war patterns of chiefdoms and states."[14]

There were also groups of population that may have moved into Türk lands and become a dependent element there. The *T'ang-shu* mentions, s.a. 630, that the Chinese Emperor bought with gold and silk some 80,000 men and women who had "fled to the barbarians during a period of disorders under the Sui dynasty."[15]

Servile status, once imposed, was not easily removed. The 10th century Arab author, Ibn al-Faqīh, in the *Kitāb Akhbār al-buldān* (Mashhad MS, ff. 173a-b)[16] reports, on the authority of a certain Saᶜīd b. al-Ḥasan as-Samarqandī, that the nomadic Turks "recognize no royal authority and submit to no one, attacking one another and seizing women and children. From time to time, some grouping (of these nomads) leaves their tribe and joins another. Together with them, those women who earlier had stemmed from that tribe [which they have now joined (*pbg*)] also join, as do the children of these women who were made

[12] Liu Mau-tsai, ed. and tr., *Die chinesischen Nachrichten zur Geschichte der Ost-Türken (T'u-küe)* (Wiesbaden, 1958; Göttinger Asiatische Forschungen, Bd. 10), I, p. 163.

[13] A. M. Khazanov, *Sotsial'naia istoriia skifov* (Moscow, 1975), p. 282, n. 4.

[14] R. B. Ferguson, "Explaining War," in J. Haas, ed., *The Anthropology of War* (Cambridge, 1990), p. 48. Subsequently, contact with the markets for the European slave trade provided even greater incentives; see R. B. Ferguson and N. L. Whitehead, "The Violent Edge of Empire," in R. B. Ferguson and N. L. Whitehead, ed., *War in the Tribal Zone* (Santa Fe, New Mexico, 1992), pp. 23-24.

[15] Liu, ed. and tr., *Die chinesischen Nachrichten zur Geschichte der Ost-Türken*, I, p.196.

[16] Cited by Kliashtornyi, "Formy sotsial'noi zavisimosti v gosudarstvakh kochevnikov," p. 328.

slaves. The tribe taking in the newcomers does not punish them for their kinsmen who became slaves, but considers the latter slaves, just like their own slaves, according to their custom and what they have agreed on."

This is, perhaps, in some respects, remarkable given the circumstance that the nomadic economy does not make wide use of slaves. As Anatoly Khazanov has pointed out, among the Kalmyks of the 19th century, two shepherds were sufficient to manage a herd of 1000-1500 sheep and 300 horses. Similar patterns have been observed among other Eurasian nomads. Increases in productivity were dependent on ecological factors, not additional human power. The need for additional manpower could usually be met from within the kinship groups (poor relatives, certainly viewed as more reliable than outsiders) or through cooperative labor.[17]

A somewhat different approach with respect to Türk society has been suggested by Sergei Kliashtornyi. He also sees warfare (whether inter-tribal or directed against sedentary society in the form of raids) as the primary source of slaves, but argues that the main emphasis was on capturing women and children. This underscores the domestic character of slavery among the Türks. It is further understandable in light of the fact that women performed most of the household tasks and chores that transformed the produce of the nomadic economy into useful goods. The larger the nomadic economy, the more women were needed. Moreover, as Kliashtornyi argues, polygamy, the levirate, and the high cost of the bride-price were all incentives to seek wives through raiding other tribes and peoples. For many poor nomads this was the only means to begin a family.[18] The British military man, Captain F. Burnaby, during his travels to Khiva in the 1870s, reported that among the Qazaqs the average price for a young bride was 100 sheep.[19] Although the question of minimal herd size necessary for a nomadic family unit to survive can vary considerably according to the local ecology, recent studies, among

[17] Khazanov, *Sotsial'naia istoriia skifov*, pp. 140-141. On the near enslavement of relatives in early modern Qazaq society, see S. E. Tolybekov, *Kochevoe obshchestvo kazakhov v XVIII-nachale XX veka* (Alma-Ata, 1971), pp. 525 ff.

[18] S. G. Kliashtornyi, "Raby i rabyni v drevnetjurkskoi obshchine," in R. S. Vasil'evskii, ed., *Drevnie kultury Mongolii* (Novosibirsk, 1985), p. 164.

[19] Capt. F. Burnaby, *A Ride to Khiva* (London, 1876; repr., Oxford, 1997), p. 179.

the Qazaqs, cite 15-20 camels, 4-5 horses and 100-150 sheep and goats.[20] The high bride-price, then, was a considerable obstacle which the less affluent overcame by raids and kidnapping.

Male slaves could be and were used as shepherds (of sheep and cattle, not horses), but were always a security risk. This tallies with observations made of other early societies. Male captives were either immediately killed, returned home or adopted. Enslaved female captives, however, were viewed as an economic benefit and posed fewer security problems. Their chores were generally performed in or near the home and they were more easily kept under surveillance. In some societies (e.g., the Iroqois of Northeastern America or the reindeer nomads of Siberia), captured and enslaved males were dressed in women's clothing and often terrorized by beatings.[21] In the early modern nomadic confederations of the Eurasian steppe, such as the Qazaqs and Kalmyks, there were a number of lineages that were descended from slaves.[22]

Of the early medieval Turkic peoples, it was only the Qïrghïz, who, having a more developed agricultural component requiring irrigation in their Yenisei home territory, had a greater need for and made use of male slaves. In general, captured males were sent to the slave markets which supplied the sedentary world. Kliashtornyi's conclusion is that notwithstanding its largely but not exclusively domestic character, slavery was an important institution of Türk society.[23]

In time, the Türks, like the Hsiung-nu before them, created colonies in Eastern Turkistan of skilled slaves or dependents who were artisans or

[20] See the discussion in A. M. Khazanov, *Nomads and the Outside World*, tr. J. Crookenden (Cambridge, 1984), pp. 28-29.

[21] H. H. Turney-High, *Primitive War. Its Practices and Concepts*, ed. A. Roland, 2nd ed. (Columbia, South Carolina, 1991), pp. 178, 181-182. The Iroquois, faced with population losses brought on by European contact, adopted the captives. Indeed, this became an important goal of their military and diplomatic policies; see T. Abler, "Beavers and Muskets: Iroquois Military Fortunes in the Face of European Colonization," in Ferguson and Whitehead, ed., *War in the Tribal Zone*, p. 159.

[22] L. Krader, *Social Organization of the Mongol-Turkic Pastoral Nomads* (The Hague, 1963; Indiana University Uralic and Altaic Series, vol. 20), pp. 279-280.

[23] Kliashtornyi, "Formy sotsial'noi zavisimosti v gosudarstvakh kochevnikov," pp. 328-334; S. G. Kliashtornyi and T. I. Sultanov, *Kazakhstan: Letopis' trekh tysiacheletii* (Alma-Ata, 1992), pp. 147-149; and Kliashtornyi's "Raby i rabyni," pp. 162-167.

agriculturalists.[24] The Chinggisid Mongols did this on a much greater scale.[25] Given the nature of the skills required for the nomadic economy, it is more than likely that there were always a certain number of such individuals in the steppe. Obviously, empires had greater needs. In juridical documents stemming from the Uyghur diasporan states that formed in Eastern Turkistan after the fall of the Uyghur Qaghanate (744-840), we also find mention of slave-artisans. One such document tells of the marriage of a male slave-blacksmith (*temirči qarabaš*) and a "female weaver or seller of cotton cloth" (*epči qarabaš bözči*) done without the permission of their owners.[26] The matter was settled by the agreement that each of the slave-artisans would pay his/her owner the *bert*. This term, a general word for tax, had according to Maḥmūd al-Kāshgharī the specific meaning of "the tax which a master receives from his slave each year."[27]

Although it is not our intention to discuss the history of slavery in the Turkic steppe, some background information is nonetheless useful for our theme. On the whole, we are poorly informed regarding slavery in the Uyghur Qaghanate, but, as noted above, there are scattered references to this institution in the juridical documents of the later Uyghur polities. In one such document, we learn of the unfortunate plight of Qoludï Bintung who sought to leave his servile status to become a priest. Having acquired a letter of manumission (*boš bitig* [on *boš*, see below]), he entrusted it to his master (*beg*) who, he then claimed, misplaced it (perhaps deliberately) and was trying to make him a slave

24 Khazanov, *Sotsial'naia istoriia skifov*, p. 144; T. Nagrodzka-Majchrzyk, *Geneza miast u dawnych ludów tureckich (VII-VXII w.)* (Wroclaw/Warsaw/Krakow, 1978), p. 29.

25 T. Allsen, *Mongol Imperialism. The Policies of the Grand Qan Möngke in China, Russia, and the Islamic Lands, 1251-1259* (Berkeley, 1987), pp. 110 ff., and his "Ever Closer Encounters: The Appropriation of Culture and the Apportionment of Peoples in the Mongol Empire," *Journal of Early Modern History*, 1 (1997), pp. 2-23.

26 W. Radloff, *Uigurische Sprachdenkmäler*, ed. S. Malov (1928; repr. Osnabrück, 1972), pp. 125-126 (doc. 73); cf. the discussion in D. I. Tikhonov, *Khoziaistvo i obshchestvennyi stroi uigurskogo gosudarstva X-XIV vv.* (Moscow-Leningrad, 1966), p. 176. For *bözči*, see Clauson, *ED*, p. 390.

27 See Clauson, *ED*, p. 358; Maḥmūd al-Kāšγarī, *Compendium of the Turkic Dialects. Dīwān Luγāt at-Turk*, ed. and tr. R. Dankoff and J. Kelly (Cambridge, Massachusetts, 1982-1985) [henceforth Kāshgharī/Dankoff], I, p. 269.

again (*yana bir qul alqalï*) in order to sell him.[28] Another document tells of the sale by a father, in concert with his older sons in need of money, of his youngest son, Mubārak Qoč.[29] Male slaves seem to have fetched higher prices than female slaves.[30] Documents from the era of Chinggisid rule indicate the continuance of similar patterns of domestic slavery in Uyghur Eastern Turkistan.[31]

We possess only scattered references to slavery in the Eurasian steppe. The earliest of these comes from the account of Herodotus regarding the ancient Iranian nomads, the Scythians. The 'Father of History' makes the rather startling statement that "the Scythians blind all (their) slaves because of the milk which they drink." After discussing their milking process and how blind slaves are used in this, he concludes "because of all this, the Scythians blind whomever they capture. For they are not agriculturalists, but nomads" (*οὐ γαρ ἀρόται εἰσὶ ἀλλὰ νομάδες*). Some male slaves (one out of every hundred that were captured) were sacrificed to the God of War.[32] Khazanov has doubts about the accuracy of this account. It is clear, however, that slaves were acquired through warfare and were used largely for domestic purposes.[33]

As for the successors of the Scythians, the Iranian Sarmatians and the Hephthalites (of probable Altaic, War-Hun origins; their state was centered in Afghanistan, encroaching on parts of North India and Central Asia[34]), they were primarily interested in the acquisition of slaves for sale in the lucrative slave-markets. The Hsiung-nu, noted above, who also took slaves from subject or tributary peoples (such as the Wu-huan) in lieu of the payment of tribute (livestock and hides from nomadic

[28] S. E. Malov, *Pamiatniki drevnetiurkskoi pis'mennosti* (Moscow-Leningrad, 1951), pp. 201-204; Tikhonov, *Khoziaistvo*, pp. 175-176.

[29] Radloff, *Uigurische Sprachdenkmäler*, pp. 100-101 (doc. 57); Tikhonov, *Khoziaistvo*, p. 179.

[30] Tikhonov, *Khoziaistvo*, pp. 179-181.

[31] A. Sh. Kadyrbaev, *Ocherki istorii srednevekovykh uigurov, dzhalairov, naimanov i kireitov* (Almaty, 1993), p. 78.

[32] Herodotus, *Historiae*, ed. C. Hurde, 3rd ed. (Oxford, 1927; repr., 1988), I, iv, 1-4, 62.

[33] Khazanov, *Sotsial'naia istoriia skifov*, pp. 133-134.

[34] See the discussion in P. B. Golden, *An Introduction to the History of the Turkic Peoples* (Wiesbaden, 1992), pp. 79-83.

groups),[35] subsequently appear to have developed an agricultural and crafts sector in which slave labor may have been employed. Slaves were also used in livestock herding. There is some debate, however, as to whether the Hsiung-nu polity should be considered a 'slave-holding society;' a recent study, nevertheless, suggests that the Hsiung-nu had a slave population of about 180,000-190,000 out of a total population of 1.5-2 million.[36] In any event, the Hsiung-nu, as was typical of nomadic polities, were involved in the slave trade. Their onetime subjects, the Wu-huan, offered male and female slaves to the Chinese court as part of their tribute to the Han.[37]

The *Hou Han Shu* ("History of the Later Han") reports that in 110, the Southern Hsiung-nu, fearful of a Chinese advance, returned some 10,000 captives to China, a number that included both those captured by the Hsiung-nu and those purchased from others.[38] Mention is also made in the Chinese sources of a 'tribe' called the *tzi-!u* (*tzi* being the Chinese transcription of the Hsiung-nu word for "slave") that was "not of one race" but had been formed from fragments of "Tung-hu, Tingling and many Chien who live together with them. And this is because, originally, they were slaves of the Hsiung-nu."[39] Since "warfare is their business,"[40] as Ssŭ-ma Ch'ien informs us, the acquisition of slaves for the market or for domestic use must have been an integral part of their economy.

Slavery was also known to the European Huns (whose relationship to the Hsiung-nu remains the subject of debate), warfare being the major source of acquisition. Some were brought into the Hunnic military forces. Thus, Priscus tells the story of a well-to-do Greek merchant who had fallen captive to the Huns. Allotted to a high ranking Hun, he

[35] V. S. Taskin, ed. and tr., *Materialy po istorii drevnikh kochevykh narodov gruppy dunkhu* (Moscow, 1984), p. 65.

[36] E. I. Kychanov, *Kochevye gosudarstva ot gunnov do man'chzhurov* (Moscow, 1997), p. 35.

[37] Taskin, *Materialy*, p. 66; S. cf. S. Jagchid and V. J. Symons, *Peace, War, and Trade Along the Great Wall* (Bloomington/Indianapolis, 1989), pp. 34-35.

[38] Khazanov, *Sotsial'naia istoriia skifov*, p. 143; Kychanov, *Kochevye gosudarstva*, pp. 34-35; Taskin, *Materialy*, p. 89.

[39] É. Chavannes, "Les pays d'Occident d'après le Weilio," *T'oung-Pao*, ser. 2, 6 (1905), pp. 525-526.

[40] Sima Qian/Watson, II, p. 143.

proved his mettle in battle and with his spoils was able to purchase his freedom. Having by that time acquired a 'barbarian' wife and family, he elected to remain in the service of his lord and "now enjoyed a better life than he had previously."[41] Priscus also mentions other high-born captives, in this instance the wife and children of a Roman, whom the Huns were unwilling to free at his request, wishing, instead, "to sell them at a high price." Eventually, Attila relented and "dismissed the wife for five hundred *solidi* and sent the children to the Emperor as a gift." The ransoming of relatives from Hunnic captivity was part of the normal diplomatic activity between the Huns and Byzantium. The freeing of prisoners without ransom was a special sign of amity. There is ample evidence of domestic slavery. Although integrated into Hunnic society, not all were resigned to their lot. Slaves who revolted were put to a grisly death.[42] Maenchen-Helfen suggests that the majority of captives were sold at the Roman slave markets because the Hunnic economy had little use for them.[43]

Although we have very few notices on the subject, it would appear that similar patterns of limited domestic slavery and the sale of captives were to be found in the stateless nomadic polities of Western Eurasia, such as the Pechenegs and Cuman-Qïpchaqs. Al-Bakrī reports that former captives of the Byzantines or others who came to the Pecheneg territory were given the right to remain among them and intermarry.[44] The Rus' Chronicle mentions that the Polovtsi (Modern Russian *Polovtsy*, i.e., the Cuman-Qïpchaqs) held captives from other nomadic groups that were in service with the Rus' princes and hence in potential opposition to them.[45] Cuman depredations in which parts of the

[41] R. C. Blockley, ed. and tr., *The Fragmentary Classicising Historians of the Later Roman Empire. Eunapius, Olympiodorus, Priscus and Malchus* (Liverpool, 1981, 1983), II, pp. 268/269. The founder of the Jou-jan royal line, Mu-ku-lü, was of servile origin. According to the *Wei-shu* when he reached adulthood he was manumitted and became a mounted warrior (see Taskin, *Materialy*, p. 267).

[42] Blockley, *The Fragmentary Classicising Historians*, pp. 290-299.

[43] O. Maenchen-Helfen, *The World of the Huns*, ed. M. Knight (Berkeley, 1973), pp. 199-200.

[44] Khazanov, *Sotsial'naia istoriia skifov*, p. 145; al-Bakrī, *Kitāb al-masālik wa'l-mamālik*, ed. A. van Leeuwen and A. Ferre (Dār al-Gharb al-Islāmī, 1992), I, pp. 445-446.

[45] *Polnoe sobranie russkikh letopisei* [henceforth *PSRL*] (Moscow-St. Petersburg/Petrograd/Leningrad, 1843-1995), II, cols. 506-507.

sedentary population were driven off into slavery form a constant theme of the Rus' annals. Only a few notices, however, give numbers. Thus, in 1152, a Rus' force "drove off the Cumans, captured their tents, seized their horses and livestock and released from bondage a multitude of Christians." In 1160, we are told that "more than a myriad of souls" were taken "and others slaughtered" when a Cuman force allied to one of the warring Rus' princes raided the Smolensk region.[46] On the other hand, there are also notices in which large numbers of Cuman captives, "beyond counting," were brought back to Rus'.[47]

We have little information on slavery among the various Turkic tribal confederations of Central Asia such as the Oghuz, Qarluqs, Yaghma (both of whom would later coalesce into the Qarakhanid state, 992-1212) and Kimeks (from whom the Qïpchaqs derived).[48] Ibn Faḍlān mentions the presence of slaves among the Oghuz. They are noted here in a domestic capacity.[49] All of these nomadic polities had commercial and sometimes military relations with the Islamic world, the Turkic steppe peoples being one of the most important sources of military slaves for the ʿAbbāsid Caliphate which imported them through Khazaria and Irano-Islamic Transoxiana. For example, Ibn Khurdādbih (mid-9th century), in noting the *kharāj* paid by the Kabul region, records some 2000 Oghuz prisoners valued at 600,000 dirhams.[50] Maḥmūd al-Kāshgharī's *Dīwān lughāt al-turk* provides us, as we shall see, with some interesting information about slaves and the terminology for them in these tribal societies and in the Qara-khanid state.

Of other Turkic states in this region, we know that the Khazar Qaghanate (ca. 650-ca. 965) was extensively involved in the slave trade, functioning as one of the primary providers of slaves entering the Islamic

[46] *PSRL*, I, col. 339; II, col. 508.

[47] A. I. Popov, "Kipchaki i Rus'," *Uchenye zapiski Leningradskogo Gosudarstvennogo Universiteta*, seriia istoricheskikh nauk, 14 (1949), p. 101.

[48] On them, see Golden, *Introduction to the History of the Turkic Peoples*, pp. 189 ff.

[49] A. Z. V. Togan, ed. and tr., *Ibn Faḍlān's Reisebericht* (Leipzig, 1939; *Abhandlungen für die Kunde des Morgenlandes*, 24/3), Arabic text, p. 14, German tr., pp. 26-27. They are noted here as caring for their sick masters, a task that, given their presence, is normally avoided by the ailing person's kinfolk.

[50] Ibn Khurdādbih, *al-Masālik wa'l-mamālik*, ed. M. J. De Goeje (Leiden, 1889), p. 37.

world.[51] Some of these slaves, as was also true subsequently of other nomadic peoples in Western Eurasia, sold their own children into slavery in times of hardship (see below). Thus, al-Iṣṭakhrī (with Ibn Ḥawqal following him) reports that "those of the Khazars who happen to be slaves (*raqīq*) are the idolators (*ahl al-awthān*) who allow the sale of their children and the enslavement of one another. As for the Jews and Christians among them, they deem it forbidden to enslave one another."[52] Chinggis Qan gave whole groupings of enslaved clans (defeated in warfare) to various individuals as a reward for service.[53] Others were permanently attached to the Chinggisids themselves. Rashīd al-Dīn writes that "from that date until now, that tribe of the Jalayir have become the *ötegü boġol*,[54] hereditarily, of Chīnggīz Khān and his clan (*uruġ*)."[55] In this instance, the vocabulary of slavery is being used to denote a kind of vassal relationship.[56] The Mongol Chinggisid states were similarly engaged, but also settled numbers of the captured as taxpayers in their towns and cities. The Crimea in particular became a major center of the 'Tatar' slave trade.[57] The defeated Qïpchaqs of the Chinggisid realm, until their Islamization in the 14th century and afterwards, were a major source of recruitment for the military-slave regime

[51] D. Ludwig, *Struktur und Gesellschaft des Chazaren-Reiches im Licht der schriftlichen Quellen* (Münster, 1982), pp. 209-210.

[52] Al-Iṣṭakhrī, *Kitāb Masālik al-mamālik*, ed. M. J. De Goeje, 2nd ed. (Leiden, 1927), p. 223; Ibn Ḥawqal, *Kitāb Ṣūrat al-arḍ* (Beirut, 1992), p. 334.

[53] Cf. the granting of the "hundred Jirgin" to the wife, son, and further progeny of Quyildar noted in *The Secret History of the Mongols*, trans. F. W. Cleaves (Cambridge, Massachusetts/London, 1986), I, p. 113 (§185); see the discussion in B. Ia. Vladimirtsov, *Obshchestvennyi stroi mongolov* (Leningrad, 1934), p. 97.

[54] Literary Mongol *ötegü*, "old man, senior;" *boġol*, "slave."

[55] Rashīd al-Dīn, *Jāmiᶜ al-tawārīkh*, ed. M. Rawshan and M. Mūsavī (Tehran, 1373/1994), I, p. 231.

[56] See the discussions in Vladimirtsov, *Obshchestvennyi stroi mongolov*, pp. 63-64, and in S. Jagchid and P. Hyer, *Mongolia's Culture and Society* (Boulder, Colorado, 1979), pp. 283-285 (following Vladimirtsov, they have the misreading of *unaġan* for *ötegü*).

[57] L. Tardy, *A Tatárországi rabszolgakereskedelem és a Magyarok a XIII-XV században* (Budapest, 1980), pp. 59 ff.; Khazanov, *Sotsial'naia istoriia skifov*, pp. 145-146.

in Egypt-Syria, the Mamlūks.[58] Al-ʿUmarī reports that Qïpchaq children were often stolen or were sold off into slavery by their impoverished parents in times of drought, to meet tax needs or simply for survival.[59]

In the Uzbek Bukharan khanate, there was an extensive commerce in slaves. The latter were acquired through warfare, raids, indebtedness, the sale of children, etc., and taken from the neighboring Slav (Muscovite), Chinese, Turkic and Mongol populations. Major suppliers of these captives were nomadic peoples such as the Noghays, Bashkirs, Kalmyks and Qazaqs.[60]

Qïrghïz folklore has preserved the memory of slave raids and the fate of those taken captive: *bizdin qatïn, qïzdï oljolop, kül čïġarġan küng qïldï*, "(the enemy) took our wives and daughters from us and made them into slaves (*küng*, "female slave;" see below) who take out the soot." In Modern Qïrghïz, a "tasty morsel" is termed *qul jebes* or *küng jebes* (lit., "[that which] a male slave/female slave does not eat").[61]

The Türkmens were justly feared for their slave-raiding which focused largely on children. Those who were not sold off into the slave-markets became 'second class' children of their masters. Nonetheless, they had some standing in society. Females were married off with a bride-price and were treated, after marriage, as other brides. Sons of servile origins, despite often being given smaller shares and having a less well-defined status than the biological sons of their master/father, were, nonetheless, helped to establish an independent household. They comprised, however, a distinct social category.[62]

58 See the numerous studies of D. Ayalon, most recently his "The Mamlūks of the Seljuks: Islam's Military Might at the Crossroads," *Journal of the Royal Asiatic Society*, 6/3 (November, 1996), pp. 305-333.

59 K. Lech, ed. and tr., *Das mongolische Weltreich. Al-ʿUmarī's Darstellung der mongolischen Reiche in seinem Werk Masālik al-Abṣār fī Mamālik al-Amṣār* (Wiesbaden, 1968), Arabic text, pp. 70, 72, 73, 80-81, German tr., pp. 138, 140, 141, 145. One of his sources reports that they sold their sons only in instances of the most dire need.

60 A. Burton, *The Bukharans. A Dynastic, Diplomatic and Commercial History 1550-1702* (New York, 1997), pp. 379-380, 427-428, 431, 432.

61 K. K. Iudakhin, *Kirgizsko-russkii slovar'* (Moscow, 1965), pp. 242, 467.

62 W. Irons, *The Yomut Turkmen: A Study of Social Organization Among a Central Asian Turkic Speaking Population* (Ann Arbor, 1975; University of Michigan Museum of Anthropology, Anthropological Paper No. 58), p. 121.

An important, but nonetheless relatively meager source of information about the lives of slaves in the medieval Turkic world is provided by Maḥmūd al-Kāshgharī. We have already noted his definition of the term *bert*. This tells us that slaves (most probably artisans in this instance) were required to pay their masters an annual tax. Regrettably, we have no information as to the size of the tax, whether it was paid in coin or in produce, and what role the income from one's slave(s) played in the master's economy. On the internecine warfare among the Turkic tribes that led to captivity, Kāshgharī cites this poem: *iši anig artašïp / oġraq bile örtešip / boynïn alïp qaḏrïšïp / tutġun alïp qul satar*, "his affair has deteriorated. They have burned each other's tribes [lit., "he and Oghraq have burned each other"]; after their necks are twisted he was taken captive (and ransom was taken from him as through he were) a slave that is sold."[63] Slaves resisted their unfree status, going against their lord (*qul begke tetti*, "the slave opposed the emir [or other]") or running away (*qul küredi*, "the slave ran away").[64]

The disloyalty of slaves was proverbial: *qul yaġï, it böri* (lit., "the slave is an enemy, the dog is a wolf"), which Kāshgharī explains as, "a slave (if he has power over his master's property will take part of it, seizing the opportunity, and carry it away, like) an enemy; a dog is a wolf (in his own household since he never guards anything edible once he has gotten hold of it." Kāshgharī further comments that "this is coined about the lack of a slave's loyalty to his master."[65] The mistreatment of slaves is noted in a variety of expressions: *ol qulïn uruġ urdu* ("he gave his slave a real beating"), *ol qulïn tepig tepdi* ("he gave his slave a strong kick"), *er qulïnï urġan ol* ("that man is one who constantly beats his slave"), *ol qulïn urdï* ("he struck his slave"), *er qulïn bösdi* ("the man beat his slave severely"), *er qulïn urġalï sešindi* ("the man was about to beat his slave"), *er qulïn suwda čapturdï* ("the man made his slave swim in the water"), *qul boynï kertildi* ("the slave was humbled—although this derives from 'notching' [the neck] it is used to express humiliation"), *ol qulïn tasġattï* ("he had his slave slapped") *er qulïn kišedi* ("the man bound his slave"), *ol qulïn qasïġladï* ("he punched his slave"), *ol qulïn tulungladï* ("he struck his slave on the jaw

[63] Kāshgharī/Dankoff, II, p. 71.

[64] Kāshgharī/Dankoff, II, pp. 109, 286.

[65] Kāshgharī/Dankoff, I, p. 266.

or under the ear"[66]), *ol qulïn boynï kertti* ("he notched his slave's neck").[67]

Slaves were property and could be given or sent at will: *ol qulïn id̲sadï*, "he wanted to send his slave to me."[68] Of slave apparel, we have only the sentence *qul čekreklendi*, "the slave put on a woolen garment."[69]

The term *qul* could be used for "worshipper" ("slave" of God), and Kāshgharī gives a number of examples: *qul tengrike tapdï* ("the slave [worshipper] worshipped God Most High"); *qul tengrike bütti* ("the slave [worshipper] confessed the unity of God Most High"); *qul tengrike yükündi* ("the slave [worshipper] bowed down to God Most High"); *qul tengriden qorqdï* ("the slave [worshipper] feared God"); *qul tengrike yinčgelendi* ("the slave [worshipper] humbled himself, mortified himself, worshipped, fasted, prayed and submitted to God"); *qut qïwïġ berse id̲im qulïnga / künde iši yükseben yoqar aġar* ("if God gives fortune to his slave his status rises daily").[70]

Manumission could come in a variety of ways: *ol qul boš qïldï* ("he freed the slave"); *ol anig qulïn küretti* ("he urged his slave to run away"); *qul yulundï* ("the slave was freed when he paid his own value to his owner"); *ol qulïn yulturdï* ("he had his slave buy himself from his owner").[71] A "free man" was termed *boš kiši*.[72] The Old Turkic *Irq Bitig* notes the following reading: *qul sabï. begingerü ötünür, quzġun sabï tengrigerü yalbarïn, üze tengri ešitdi asra kiši bilti tir. anča biling edgü ol* ("The slave's words are a request to his master; the raven's words are a prayer to heaven. Heaven above heard it, men below understood it, it says. Know thus: (The omen) is good."[73]

[66] Literally, "he struck the slave on the temple," < *tulung*, "temple" (see Clauson, *ED*, p. 501).

[67] Kāshgharī/Dankoff, I, pp. 81, 86, 176, 246, 295, 388, 392; II, pp. 52, 80, 132, 288, 321, 360, 369.

[68] Kāshgharī/Dankoff, I, p. 233.

[69] Kāshgharī/Dankoff, II, p. 100.

[70] Kāshgharī/Dankoff, I, pp. 257, 388; II, pp. 110, 190, 366, 381.

[71] Kāshgharī/Dankoff, I, p. 262; II, pp. 116, 191, 196.

[72] Kāshgharī/Dankoff, II, p. 211; see also Clauson, *ED*, p. 376.

[73] T. Tekin, ed. and tr., *Irk Bitig. The Book of Omens* (Wiesbaden, 1993), pp. 22/23 (§54).

TERMINOLOGY

We do not find traces of Chinese, Iranian or Arabic loanwords in the terminology for slavery in Medieval Turkic. With regard to the slave trade, the Turkic peoples were in particularly close contact with Iranian Central Asia and the ᶜAbbāsid Caliphate in which many Turks served as slave-soldiers. The social structure of the Iranian states (Sogdia and Khwārazm) with which the nomadic Turkic world had political and commercial ties is still not fully elucidated. On the basis of the Sogdian documentation, several forms of slaves can be distinguished: *βntk*, "slave, male slave" (cf. Persian *banda*, from the root *band-*, "to bind"); *δʾyh*, "female slave;" *npʾk* (or *npʾq*), "hostage" (cf. Khwārazmian *nibāk*, "pledge," Middle Persian *nipāk*, "debt-slave"); *wmʾʾk*, "conquered, captive;" *ġyrδ*, "bondsman" (lit. "oneself, own"), "one remaining under the protection of someone, personally belonging to someone." Some distinction was made between slaves who could be bought or sold and those who were being held as hostages or prisoners. The latter category may have also included those who sold themselves into bondage in payment of debts. Those in the latter category, however, could be transformed into full slaves, as it were, by being sold.[74] Middle Persian/Pahlavi has *bandak*, "slave," *anšahrīk*, "outlander, slave" (an indication of the slave's origin), *rahīk*, "bound," *tan*, "body," *vēšak*, "belonging to a *vis*, i.e., a *gens*," "household slave" (cf. Khotanese *bisa*, "slaves"), as well as the special category of temple-slaves (*ātaḫš bandak*, *āturān bandak*). There is also an important vocabulary of dependency, often expressed in terms for "youth, young man," e.g., *rēdak*, *rētag* (NPers. *rīdak*, "a servant boy, a beardless youth"); *rasēk*/*rahēk* (NPers. *rahī*, "slave"), "famulus, servus, ghulām, banda, čākir" (the latter, denoting "servant, apprentice," often used in connection with the personal military retinue of the ruler).[75]

Medieval Arabic has a very extensive terminology for slavery. As Goitein points out, aside from the military, which was "largely

[74] V. A. Livshits, *Sogdiiskie dokumenty iz gory Mug*, *Iuridicheskie dokumenty i pis'ma*, vyp. II (Moscow, 1962), pp. 34-36; O. I. Smirnova, *Ocherki iz istorii Sogda* (Moscow, 1970), pp. 77-82; H. W. Bailey, *The Culture of the Sakas in Ancient Iranian Khotan* (Delmar, New York, 1982), p. 39.

[75] *The Cambridge History of Iran*, III/2, *The Seleucid, Parthian and Sasanian Periods*, ed. E. Yarshater (Cambridge, 1983), pp. 635, 640; M. Zakeri, *Sāsānid Soldiers in Early Muslim Society* (Wiesbaden, 1995), pp. 71, 72, 79-80, 180-182; R. N. Frye, *The History of Ancient Iran*, p. 221.

composed of mercenaries who were legally slaves," slavery in the Middle East was for the most part "not collective, but individual. It was personal service in the widest sense . . ."[76] There were, however, latifundial estates employing large numbers of slaves (stemming largely from sub-Saharan Africa) that exploded in revolt in 9th-century Iraq.[77] We cannot enter into all the details of this terminology but may take note of the following: *ʿabd*, "slave:" in the late Middle Ages this increasingly came to denote "black slave," while *mamlūk* (lit. "possessed, owned"), the common term for a military slave, also came to mean "white slave."[78] Other terms are: *ābiq*, "runaway (slave);"[79] *ama*, "bondmaid, slavegirl;" *asīr*, "captive;" *buqʿān*, "slave from Ethiopia;" *ġulām*, "boy, youth, lad, slave, servant;" *jālib*, "imported, foreign slave;" *jāriya*, "girl, female slave;" *khādim*, "domestic servant, eunuch;" *maʾdhūn*, "slave who has received permission to conduct business or trade, slave with limited legal rights;" *mawlā*, "a slave who was subsequently freed and who contracted a *walāʾ* relationship with his old master;" *qinn*, "slave, serf;" *raqīq*, "slave;" *waṣīf*, "slave" (this was also the name of a powerful *ġulām* officer in the mid-9th century ʿAbbāsid caliphate).[80]

China, arguably the most developed society of pre-modern times, presents a rather different pattern. Many scholars argue that in China there were basically two sources of slaves: impoverished debtors who sold themselves or family members into slavery, and penal slaves, i.e., those enslaved by the state in payment for their crimes. Chinese law (e.g., the T'ang law code) tried to retard or prevent the sale of impoverished commoners into the slavery and made the sale of slaves more carefully monitored than that of animals. Even when a commoner

[76] S. D. Goitein, *A Mediterranean Society* (Berkeley, 1967-1984), I, pp. 130-131.

[77] See A. Popovic, *La révolte des esclaves en Iraq au IIIe/IXe siècle* (Paris, 1976).

[78] B. Lewis, *Race and Slavery in the Middle East* (Oxford, 1990), p. 56.

[79] Definitions, unless otherwise indicated, may be found in *The Hans Wehr Dictionary of Modern Written Arabic*, ed. J. M. Cowan, 4th ed. (Ithaca, 1994), and D. Pipes, *Slave Soldiers and Islam* (New Haven, 1981), pp. 195, 197.

[80] On the Turkic guard corps, see H. Töllner, *Die Türkischen Garden am Kalifenhof von Samarra* (Walldorf-Hessen, 1971), and H. D. Yıldız, *İslâmiyet ve Türkler* (Istanbul, 1976).

became a slave because of debt, the law sought to prevent his sale to a third party.[81]

Scholarly opinion, however, is divided over the sources and extent of slavery in Ancient and Medieval China. Some recent Chinese scholars maintain that large-scale slavery existed in Early China, largely drawing on prisoners of war. Others have countered that China did not take in large numbers of war prisoners. Military activity in the North, the area of greatest interest to us, was primarily aimed at opening and maintaining the trade routes to Central Asia. Its goals were trade/tribute, not conquest and prisoners. Western scholars note that the fate of those who were captured is by no means clear. Some may have been enslaved, while others were, most probably, sent off as colonists. In periods of greater military activity, it seems likely that some were brought into the military. In short, as Orlando Patterson concludes, China treated prisoners of war "differently during different periods of their vast history."[82] During the T'ang era, when China was very active in Central Asia and Central Asians in China, Schafer concludes that war prisoners and slaves were brought into China in "large numbers."[83] The only region in which there may have been something of a slave-trade was the South, aimed largely at the indigenous Tai-related peoples.[84] This does not seem to be relevant to possible Chinese influences on the Turkic notions of slavery. Moreover, although there are important loan-words in Turkic from Chinese, we do not find any linguistic traces indicating Chinese influences in this area. Chinese terms for slave derive from the root term *nu*, e.g., *nu-li*, "slaves," *nu-shou*, "a bondsman, a slave," *nu-p'u*, "male slave," *nu-pei*, "female slave."

Byzantium, another sedentary neighbor with whom the Türks had come into direct contact ca. 568, had a rich array of terms for slaves.[85]

[81] J. Gernet, *A History of Chinese Culture*, tr. J. R. Foster (Cambridge, 1982), p. 77; V. Hansen, *Negotiating Daily Life in Traditional China. How Ordinary People Used Contracts 600-1400* (New Haven, 1995), pp. 41, 42, 51-52.

[82] Patterson, *Slavery*, pp. 108-110, and the literature cited there.

[83] E. H. Schafer, *The Golden Peaches of Samarkand. A Study of T'ang Exotics* (Berkeley, 1963; repr., 1985), pp. 40 ff.

[84] E. G. Pulleyblank, "The Chinese and Their Neighbors in Prehistoric and Early Historical Times." in D. N. Keightley, ed., *The Origins of Chinese Civilization* (Berkeley, 1983), pp. 434-435.

[85] See H. Köpstein, *Zur Sklaverei im ausgehenden Byzanz* (Berlin, 1966).

Individuals from various Turkic groups served in Byzantium (e.g., the Khazars in the imperial bodyguard),[86] but there is nothing to indicate that Byzantine terminology had any influence on the Turkic.

In Medieval Turkic[87] the two fundamental terms for "slave" are *qul*, "male slave" (in the Mamlūk Qïpchaq dictionaries often translated *mamlūk*, but also rendered by *ʿabd* and *ġulām*) and *küng*, "female slave" (cf. also *qulsïġ er*, "a slavish man," and the verbs *qulad-*, *küngad-*, "to become a slave").[88] The *Codex Cumanicus* also cites the forms *küni*, "Konkubine, 'amica'," and *küniden toġa(n)*, "Kebskind, 'bastardus'."[89] The term *qul* could denote all forms of subordination, political and otherwise.[90] It is in some sources combined with *qarabaš* (see below): *qul qarabaš* (in the *ʿAtabat al-ḥaqāʾiq*).[91] In the Mamlūk Qïpchaq glossary *al-Tuḥfat al-zakīya fī'l-lughat al-turkīya* we encounter the pair *qul qutan*, defined as "servants and servitors/retinue" (*al-khadam wa'l-ḥasham*). It is compared with other collective terms such as *qum quš*, "a flock of birds."[92]

abïnču/avïnču [*Irq Bitig*, Qarakhanid, Khwārazmian], "concubine" < *avïn-*, "to enjoy oneself" < *avï-*, "to enjoy, be happy." The *Irq Bitig* has the omen: *qamïš ara qalmïš. tengri unamaduq. abïnču qatun bolzun tir. anča bilingler edgü ol*, "(a slave girl) remained (alone)

86 W. Treadgold, *Byzantium and its Army 284-1081* (Stanford, 1995), pp. 110, 115; M. Whittow, *The Making of Byzantium 600-1025* (Berkeley, 1996), pp. 169-170.

87 It is impractical to cite all the sources. These have for the most part been outlined in V. M. Nadeliaev, *et al.*, *Drevnetiurkskii slovar'* (Leningrad, 1969), pp. xxi-xxxvii; Clauson, *ED*, pp. xiii-xxx. For the Qïpchaq texts, see R. Toparlı, *Kıpçak Türkçesi Sözlüğü* (Erzurum, 1993), pp. 1-8. Citations are largely limited to Clauson, who offers a wide range of sources, including works going beyond the chronological framework (13th century) of his study.

88 See Clauson, *ED*, pp. 615, 726.

89 K. Grønbech, *Komanisches Wörterbuch* [henceforth, Grønbech/CC] (Copenhagen, 1942), p. 159.

90 A. N. Bernshstam, *Sotsial'no-èkonomicheskii stroi orkhono-eniseiskikh tiurok VI-VII vekov* (Moscow-Leningrad, 1946), p. 126.

91 Edib Ahmed b. Mahmud Yükneki, *Atebetü'l-Hakayık*, ed. R. R. Arat (Istanbul, 1951), p. 64.

92 *Ettuhfet-üz-Zekiyye fil-Lûgat-it-Türkiyye*, ed. B. Atalay (Istanbul, 1945), f. 86a (recte 85b). *Quṭan* is elsewhere (f. 7b/recte 7a) noted as "pelican." Kāshgharī/Dankoff, I, p. 315, knows it as a "man's name."

among the reeds. Heaven was not pleased with it. 'May (this) slave girl be a queen,' it says. Know thus: (the omen) is good."[93]

bulun [Orkhon,[94] Qarakhanid, Old Osm.], "captive, prisoner."[95] Kāshgharī quotes the victory poem: *apang qolsa uḏu barïp / tutar erdim süsin tarïp / bulun qïlïp bašï yarïp / yaluġ barča manga yïġdï*, "Had I wished, I would have followed him, taken him, dispersed his troops, made him captive, and split open his head; (but) he gathered for me much ransom (so I granted him freedom)."[96] Elsewhere, he records the sentence, *ol bulunuġ bošattï*, "he released the prisoner."[97] The term *bulun* is still found in Old Ottoman, in this sense.[98] In some Medieval Qïpchaq dialects it simply denoted "a predatory raid" or "booty, gain," i.e., *bulunladï*, "he gained booty" (*ghanima*).[99] This term is probably to be connected to the Chaghatay *bulġun*, "captive, servant," but it is more than a stretch to connect it with Mongol *boġul* and Kalmyk *mokhlä* as Sevortian suggests.[100] The Mongol *boġul*, *boʿol*, "slave," probably stems from **boġā-*, "binden" (cf. semantic parallels with Iranian *banda*), Middle Mongol *boʿo-*, "versperren."[101] Closely related to *bulun* is the verb *bulna-*, "to capture" (e.g., Kāshgharī, *er yaġïnï bulnadï*, "the man captured the enemy").[102]

[93] Clauson, *ED*, p. 13; *Irq Bitig*, ed. Tekin, pp. 18/19 (§38).

[94] Designating here both the Türk and Uyghur inscriptions. The Uyghur juridical documents published by Radloff, *Uigurische Sprachdenkmäler*, are noted as "Uyghur."

[95] Clauson, *ED*, p. 343, from *bul-*, "to find."

[96] Kāshgharī/Dankoff, I, p. 305.

[97] Kāshgharī/Dankoff, II, p. 117.

[98] *Tarama Sözlüğü* (Ankara, 1963-1972), I, p. 692.

[99] Abū Ḥayyān, *Kitāb al-Idrāk li-Lisān al-Atrāk*, ed. and tr. A. Caferoğlu [henceforth *Idrāk*/Caferoğlu] (Istanbul, 1931), Arabic text, p. 36. It also has the meaning there, in Qïpchaq, of "dry land connected to an island."

[100] L. Budagov, *Sravnitel'nyi slovar' turetsko-tatarskikh narechii* (St. Petersburg, 1869-1871), I, p. 290; È. V. Sevortian, *Ètimologicheskii slovar' tiurkskikh iazykov* (Moscow, 1974- ongoing), II, pp. 252-253.

[101] N. Poppe, *Vergleichende Grammatik der altaischen Sprachen* (Wiesbaden 1960), I, p. 21. Poppe relates it to Evenki *bōk*, "zurückhalten, aufhalten," *bokān*, "Sklave," *bōlgīčān*, "Sklaverei," and Old Turkic *boġ-*, "erwürgen."

[102] Clauson, *ED*, p. 344; Kāshgharī/Dankoff, II, p. 304; II, p. 138, *ol anï bulnattï*, "he ordered him to be taken captive."

čaġa [Qïpchaq], in Turkic denotes "a little child, a chicklet,[103] bear cub." It was borrowed into the Rus' tongue in the meaning of "young girl, female slave," and is presumed to have had that meaning as well in Cuman-Qïpchaq.[104]

eget [Qarakhanid], "the maidservant sent with the bride on the night of the nuptial procession to serve her," and *egetlik qarabaš*, "the maid-servant who is to be sent with the bride on the night of the nuptial procession. And the bride is *egetlig* . . . The meaning is that the bride has or is the possessor or companion of the maidservant."[105] The term survives in Siberian Turkic *eget*, "servant retainer, someone who accompanies," Qarachay-Balqar *eget*, "myrmidon, vassal, puppet, hireling," and in the Anatolian dialects, *ekdi/ekti*, "servant."[106]

igdiš qul [Qarakhanid], noted in the *Qutadghu Bilig*: *men igdiš qulung men tapuġči sening*, "I am your slave bred in your household, I am your servant." The term *igdiš* < *igiḏ-*, "to feed (a person or animal)" denotes "an animal bred domestically," later "cross-bred, hybrid."[107] Although in Modern Turkish it means "castrated, a gelding," it earlier denoted "a Turk of mixed ethnicity, i. e. born of a non-Turkic mother;"[108] its earlier meaning appears to have been a "slave born in the household."

ilin- [Orkhon, Qarakhanid, Qïpchaq, Chaghatay, Old Osm.], "to catch oneself or something, to be attached to, to be caught suspended,

[103] In Mamlūk Qïpchaq (*Idrāk*/Caferoğlu, Arabic, p. 43, "a young bird (*farkh*) before its feathers have grown in and any other small new-born."

[104] V. V. Radlov, *Opyt' slovaria tiurkskikh narechii* (St. Petersburg, 1893-1911; repr. Moscow, 1963), III/2, cols. 1842-1843; O. Pritsak, "An Eleventh-Century Turkic Bilingual (Turkic-Slavic) Graffito from the St. Sophia Cathedral in Kiev," *Harvard Ukrainian Studies*, 6/2 (1982), p. 156; N. A. Baskakov, *Tiurkskaia leksika v "Slove o polku Igoreve"* (Moscow, 1985), p. 157.

[105] Kāshgharī/Dankoff, I, pp. 98, 168; see also II, pp. 241, 245, *qïz egetlendi*, "the bride acquired a maidservant who was sent with her," *ol qïzïn egetledi*, "he sent a maidservant with his daughter to her husband's house."

[106] Clauson, *ED*, p. 102; Radloff, I, col. 697; È. R. Tenishev, Kh. I. Suiunchev, *Karachaevo-balkarsko-russkii slovar'* (Moscow, 1989), p. 763 (cf. also there *köt eget*, "groveller" (lit. "one who accompanies an anus," or more directly, "an ass-kisser").

[107] Clauson, *ED*, p. 103; *Kutadgu Bilig*, ed. R. R. Arat, 2nd ed. (Ankara, 1979), I, p. 172.

[108] See Budagov, *Slovar'*, I, p. 71, and C. Cahen, *Pre-Ottoman Turkey*, trans. J. Jones-Williams (New York, 1968), pp. 192-193.

hung on it, to be bound, taken, to be, caught, to be entangled." Kāshghari records this poem: **Yabdu manga ilindi / emgek körü oli̇ndi̇ / qi̇lmi̇šinga ilendi / tutġun bolup ol qatar,*[109] "Yabdu fell prisoner in my hand, and suffered hardships until he was weary with life, then he repented and reproached himself for what he had done; now (as a captive) he has become hardened after being soft."

inčü/yinčü [Qarakhanid, Chaghatay, Osm.]: This is a very complicated term. In Chinggisid times, it may have become conflated with Mongol *inji/ingji*, "dowry, trousseau; serfs as part of the dowry,"[110] which may itself go back to Turkic. Kāshgharī, our earliest source, notes this term in two meanings, which he connects: "pearl" (a borrowing from Chinese[111]) and adds "female servants are sometimes called *yinčü*." In Oghuz and Qi̇pchaq, he notes, it is pronounced *jinčü*.[112] Chaghatay has *inčü*, "vassal who goes voluntarily to a *beg*, enters his service and works for him." Ottoman has *inčü*, "prisoner, slave" (*inčüleri yaʿnī esirleri ve qullari̇*). This term also denoted "family or clan property, in particular the chief's own property," "estates," and "fiefs."[113]

köle [noted only in Osm. and Azeri[114]], "a male slave;" *kölemen*, "a Circassian slave brought up as a warrior in Egypt, a Mameluk, one of a similar corps of slave warriors . . ."[115]

[109] Kāshgharī/Dankoff, I, p. 197.

[110] F. Lessing, *et al.*, ed., *Mongolian-English Dictionary*, 3rd reprinting (Bloomington, 1995), p. 411.

[111] M. Räsänen, *Versuch eines etymologischen Wörterbuchs der Türksprachen* (Helsinki, 1969), p. 203.

[112] Kāshgharī/Dankoff, II, p. 162.

[113] See the discussion in Clauson, *ED*, p. 173; Räsänen, *Versuch*, p. 44; Sevortian, *Ėtimologicheskii slovar'*, I, pp. 361-362. The latter, citing a full range of medieval and modern sources, notes the following meanings: "dowry, inheritance, testament, private property, appanage lands, fief, slave, slave in the private possessions of the son of the king, servitor, a gift (usually livestock) given by the father to his children, reward, prize, ransom given by the defeated to the victors in the form of women, girls and men."

[114] The Türkmen dialect form *köle*, "child born out of wedlock" (see N. A. Baskakov, *et al.*, *Turkmensko-russkii slovar'* [Moscow, 1968], p. 412), is from Persian *kola* (see F. Steingass, *A Comprehensive Persian-English Dictionary* (London, 1892; repr. Beirut, 1970) [henceforth "Steingass"], p. 1063.

[115] J. Redhouse, *A Turkish and English Lexicon* (Constantinople, 1890; repr. Beirut, 1974), p. 1601; O. F. Musaev, *et al.*, ed., *Azerbaijani-English Dictionary*

mamu [Qarakhanid, Qïpchaq]: According to Kāshgharī this is a "name for a woman sent with the bride on the wedding night. Not an original word."[116] Clauson, however, viewed it as "quasi-onomatopoeic." In Mamlūk Qïpchaq it is also noted as "a word to address an older woman or to refer to her."[117]

qara: This is the normal Turkic for "black." In Mamlūk Qïpchaq it is also recorded as denoting "slave, slave girl."[118] In the Mamlūk setting this may have been influenced by the presence of Black slaves. The term *qara*, however, figures in a number of Turkic terms for "slave." In Orkhon Turkic the "common people" were referred to as *qara* as well (cf. the Ongin inscription[119]). In early modern Qazaq society, those who were without family (clanless) and did not enjoy full rights were termed *qara qarïn*, "black belly."[120]

qarabaš/qaravaš [Uyghur, Qarakhanid, Khwārazmian, Qïpchaq, Old Osm.], a general term for "slave" (lit. "black head"). Kāshgharī says it is "a word that refers to 'slave' (*Mamlūk*) used for both male and female. Its meaning is 'black head'" (see also *egetlik qarabaš*, noted above).[121] In some Qïpchaq dialects and Ottoman it came to denote

(Baku, 1996), p. 349 (*kölä*, "slave," *kölälik*, "slavery, servitude, servility, slave-holding"). The term, according to the *XIII Yüzyıldan beri Türkiye Türkçesiyle Yazılmış Kitaplardan Toplanan Tanıklarıyle Tarama Sözlüğü* (Ankara, 1969), p. 2691, is recorded in 1634. The 15th-century *Ṣaltuq-nāma*, however, also knows this term, see Fahir İz, ed., *Ṣaltuḳ-nâme. The Legend of Sarı Ṣaltuḳ collected from Oral Tradition by Ebü'l-Ḫayr Rûmî*, in *Sources of Oriental Languages and Literatures*, 4, Turkish Sources, IV, ed. Ş. Tekin (Cambridge, Massachusetts, 1974-1984), I, f. 29b. I am indebted to Robert Dankoff (University of Chicago) for this reference. The Turkic glosses of Sulxan Saba Orbeliani's famous Georgian dictionary (compiled 1685-1716) translate Georgian *mona*, "slave, servant," with Turkic *köle* (*k'ola*); see C'. Abuladze, *Sulxan-Saba Orbelianis lek'sikonis sitqvanis t'urk'uli t'argmanebi* (Tbilisi, 1968), p. 110. The etymology of this term, which seems limited to Oghuz, is unclear; perhaps it derives from Persian *kola*, "foolish, stupid, dull, ignorant, short, dwarfish" (see Steingass, p. 1063).

116 Kāshgharī/Dankoff, II, p. 272.

117 Clauson, *ED*, p. 766; *Idrāk*/Caferoğlu, Arabic text, p. 88.

118 Clauson, *ED*, pp. 643-644.

119 *qarasïn yïġdïm begi qačdï*, "I gathered up its [their] people, their begs fled" (see Orkun, *Eski Türk Yazıtları*, I, p. 130, who translates *yïġdïm* as *yendim* [= *yïqdïm*]; see also R. Giraud, *L'empire des Turcs célestes* [Paris, 1960], pp. 87-88).

120 Tolybekov, *Kochevoe obshchestvo*, p. 531.

121 Kāshgharī/Dankoff, II, p. 265.

"female slave."[122] In Chaghatay, however, the term is often equated with *nöker*, "servitor, servant."[123]

qara qul [Qarakhanid-Khwārazmian], "slave" (lit. "black slave").[124]

qara yüz [Qarakhanid]: This form appears in one of the manuscripts of the *Qutadghu Bilig* instead of *qarabaš*, "slave" (lit. "black face").[125]

qïrnaq [Qarakhanid, Qïpchaq, Oghuz, Chaghatay], "slave girl." Kāshgharī writes: "(slave) girl. District of Yabaqu, Qay, Chömül, Basmïl, Oghuz, Yimek, Qifchaq." In Mamlūk Qïpchaq (*al-Tuḥfa*) it appears to have replaced *küng* (cf. the usage, ***bir qïrnaq saṭïn al yoqsa bir qul***, "buy a female slave or a male slave"). It is also found in the Oghuz and Oghuz-Qïpchaq Turkic sections of the Rasūlid Hexaglot (ca. 1376).[126] It survives only in Modern Oghuz (Osm. *ḳïrnaḳ*, Türkmen *ġïrnaq*).[127]

qïrqïn [Uyghur, Qarakhanid, Khwārazmian], "originally maiden, young woman, later perhaps more specifically 'slave girl'." Uyghur Buddhist texts refer to the *küydeki yinčge qïrqïnlar*, "the delicate ladies of the harem."[128] Kāshgharī notes the collective term *qïz qïrqïn*,

[122] Clauson, *ED*, p. 644; cf. the Uyghur usages, *er qarabaš*, "male slave," *epči qarabaš*, (Radloff, *Uigurische Sprachdenkmäler*, pp. 125-126).

[123] O. F. Sertkaya, "Mongolian Words and Forms in Chagatay Turkish and Turkey Turkish (Western Turkic)," *Türk Dili Araştırmaları Yıllığı Belleten* (1987), p. 269.

[124] A. K. Borovkov, *Leksika sredneaziatskogo tefsira XII-XIII vv.* (Moscow, 1963), p. 200.

[125] *Kutadgu Bilig*, ed. Arat, p. 179.

[126] See *The King's Dictionary. The Rasūlid Hexaglot: Fourteenth Century Vocabularies in Arabic, Persian, Turkic, Greek, Armenian and Mongol*, ed. with notes and commentary by Peter B. Golden, translated by T. Halasi-Kun, P. B. Golden, L. Ligeti and E. Schütz, with introductory essays by P. B. Golden and Th. T. Allsen (Leiden: Brill, 2000), pp. 190B28, 202C17, where it corresponds to the Arabic *jāriya*, Persian *kanīzak*, Greek *sklava*, Armenian *aġaxin*, and Mongol *šibekčin*. See the facsimile edition of the ms. by D. M. Varisco, G. R. Smith, eds., *The Manuscript of al-Malik al-Afḍal al-ʿAbbās b. ʿAlī b. Dāʾūd b. Yūsuf b. ʿUmar b. ʿAlī Ibn Rasūl. A Medieval Anthology from the Yemen* (Wiltshire, England, 1998), pp. 190, 202.

[127] Clauson, *ED*, p. 661; Toparlı, *Kıpçak Türkçesi Sözlüğü*, p. 119; Kāshgharī/Dankoff, I, p. 353; *Ettuhfet*, ed. Atalay, f. 87a (recte 86b). Clauson notes its possible connection with Arabic *ġurnūq*, "a good-looking boy or girl." Cf. also Arabo-Persian *ġurnayq*, *ġirnīq*, "a tender, comely youth" (Steingass, p. 885).

[128] Clauson, *ED*, p. 654.

"girls"[129] (*jawārī*, which can also mean "handmaidens"). In the Khwārazmian Turkic of Chinggisid times it regularly designates "female slaves" and is used to make clear that *qaravaš* refers to "female slaves," e.g., *buyurdï qul qaravaš oš qïz qïrqïn*, "he ordered the male and the female slaves, that is girl slaves."[130] This collective term survives in Qïrghïz *qïz qïrqïn*, "girls, young girls, daughters."[131]

qïz [Orkhon, Qarakhanid, all Turkic] has the basic meaning of "'girl, unmarried woman' but often used with a more restricted meaning 'daughter, slave girl' and the like." Kāshgharī refers to a *yinčge qïz*, "concubine," and notes further: "this word can refer either to a free girl or to a slave (*mamlūka*). Its root-meaning is 'virgin;' the others are by extension from that."[132] In the *Codex Cumanicus* we find *evdegi qïz*, "Dienstmädchen, domicella."[133]

**qoščï*, "slave, captive." In Medieval Rus' (the Igor' Tale), we find the term *koshchei* denoting "plebeian, captive, slave." Its origins are unclear, but it has been suggested that it stems from Qïpchaq **qoščï*, unattested in this meaning. In Modern Qazaq we find *qoššï* (< *qoščï*), "worker who takes care of the packhorses."[134] Baskakov surmised that since the **qoščï*s who served in the wagon train or were drivers of pack animals were taken prisoner in Rus' attacks, the term, in Rus', came to denote "prisoner, slave."[135] It would appear that any servile connotations would have been acquired on Rus' soil and hence were not native to Turkic. But, the account of the journey of the Caucasian Albanian Catholicos to the camp of the *Shad*, son of "Jebu Xak'an" (the Yabghu Qaghan of the West Türks), after the plundering of Tbilisi in 626, reports that he asked for the "release of all those taken prisoner by your soldiers and detained in your tents, men and women, girls and youths."

129 Kāshgharī/Dankoff, I, p. 260.

130 A. Zajączkowski, *Najstarsza wersja turecka Ḫusrav u Šīrīn Quṭba* (Warsaw, 1958, 1961), I, p. 139.

131 Iudakhin, *Kirgizsko-russkii slovar'*, p. 476.

132 Clauson, *ED*, pp. 679-680, 945; Kāshgharī/Dankoff, I, p. 260. *Yinčge* literally means "thin, slim, delicate."

133 *CC*/Grønbech, p. 96.

134 B. N. Shnitnikov, *Kazakh-English Dictionary* (The Hague/London/Paris, 1966; Indiana University Uralic and Altaic Series, 28), p. 269.

135 Baskakov, *Leksika*, pp. 157-158.

When this was granted, he was able to retrieve the "young boys who had been hidden among the baggage or the harness of the pack-horses."[136] In other words, the association of young male captives with the care of the baggage and pack-horses might well have given a servile connotation to *qoščï* within Turkic.

oġlan [Common Turkic]: This is a collective plural from *oġul*, "offspring, child," later more commonly denoting "son." In time, the form *oġlan* came to denote "servant" or "bodyguard." In Mamlūk Qïpchaq, *owul* (with Qïpchaq *ġ* > *w* shift) is translated by Arabic *ġulām*, "boy, page," etc.[137]

tapïġčï, tapuġčï, tapučï [Uyghur, Qarakhanid, Khwārazmian, Qïpchaq], "servant" < *tapïġ*, "service" < *tap-*, "to serve" (both humans and God).[138]

tayaq [Qarakhanid], literally "prop, support, walking stick," but developing the meaning "personal slave of a bride;" cf. Kāshgharī: *küḏegü tayaq berdi*, "the groom gave a slavegirl or slaveboy for the bride to lean upon when dismounting. This is a custom of the well to do, and he becomes her personal property."[139]

tegin [Orkhon, Qarakhanid]: Originally an ancient Inner Asian title inherited by the Türks. In Türk usage it denoted "prince, son or grandson of the ruling qaghan." By Kāshgharī's time, this had to some extent been forgotten. He cites "slave" (*ʿabd*) as "the root-meaning. Thus, *Kümüš tegin*, 'a slave clear-colored as silver.' *Alp tegin*, 'strong slave.' *Qutlugh tegin*, 'blessed slave.' Then this word became a title pure and simple for the sons of the Khāqānīya . . . The reason why this name was transferred from the slaves (*mawālī*) to the sons of Afrāsiyāb is simply that the latter used to pay their respects to their fathers by addressing them in the following way, both orally and in letters, 'Your slave did such-and-such and performed such-and-such.' This showed modesty on their part and respect for their fathers. Afterwards this name was reserved for them (when uttered alone), while as a name for slaves

[136] Movsēs Dasxuranc̣i, *The History of the Caucasian Albanians*, tr. C. J. F. Dowsett (London, 1962), pp. 101, 102.

[137] See the discussion in Clauson, *ED*, pp. 83-84; *Idrāk*/Caferoğlu, Arabic text, p. 16.

[138] Clauson, *ED*, pp. 435, 437, 438.

[139] Clauson, *ED*, p. 568; Kāshgharī/Dankoff, II, p. 235.

it remained joined to some other element, so as clearly to distinguish the two."[140] Another explanation, however, might be the fairly widespread use of this former title in the names of the Turkic slaves serving at the Caliphal court, e.g., Erte Tegin or Ertegin, a Turkic *ġulām* commander of the 870s, his contemporaries Asā Tegin, Kelbe Tegin, Kü Tegin, and many others.[141] Similarly, there were many Turkic *ġulāms* of that same period who had the Old Inner Asian title *čur/čor*[142] in their names (e.g., Belge čur, Arnāt čur, Ṭolma čur, and others[143]). One suspects that the use of titles in names became distinguishing marks of the Turkic slave-soldiers. These titles also figured in Old Turkic names.[144]

til [Common Turkic], "tongue."[145] This was used figuratively to describe "an enemy captive . . . Thus, *til tuttïm*, "I have taken one of the enemy."[146]

tutġun [Qarakhanid, Qïpchaq, Osm. *dutġun*], "prisoner, captured" < *tut-*, "to take."[147]

**tüge/*tünge* [Qïpchaq], "female slave, servant." In the *Kitāb-i Majmūᶜ-i tarjumān-i turkī wa ᶜajamī wa muġalī*, this term is equated with *qïrnaq*, *qaravaš*.[148] It is an obscure term, perhaps related to

140 Kāshgharī/Dankoff, I, p. 314.

141 Al-Ṭabarī, *Taʾrīkh al-Ṭabarī. Taʾrīkh al-rusul wa'l-mulūk*, ed. M. Ibrāhīm (Cairo, 1967-1969), IX, pp. 270-271, 459-461.

142 Clauson, *ED*, pp. 427-428.

143 Al-Ṭabarī, ed. Ibrāhīm, IX, pp. 219, 283, 284.

144 Nadeliaev, *et al.*, eds., *Drevnetiurkskii slovar'*, p. 157; Gy. Németh, *A honfoglaló magyarság kialakulása*, 2nd rev. ed. (Budapest, 1991), pp. 246, 259-260.

145 Clauson, *ED*, pp. 489-490.

146 Kāshgharī/Dankoff, I, p. 266. The word, in this sense, was loan-translated into Medieval Russian, Polish, Hungarian, Mongol and Manchu; see P. B. Golden, "Turkic Calques in Medieval Eastern Slavic," *Journal of Turkic Studies*, 8 (1984), pp. 107-108.

147 Clauson, *ED*, p. 453.

148 See M. Th. Houtsma, *Ein Türkisch-Arabisches Glossar* (Leiden, 1994), Arabic text, p. 32; Toparlı, *Kıpçak Türkçesi Sözlüğü*, p. 216. A. K. Kuryshchanov, *Issledovanie po leksike "Tiurksko-Arabskogo Slovaria"* (Alma-Ata, 1970), p. 206, compares it with the Modern Noghay *tövke* and Qazaq *tüge*, a form of dismissive and impolite address to people.

(Qarakhanid) *tükün*, "barren, sterile," and hence "a woman who can no longer bear children" < *tüke-*, "to come to an end, finish" (?).[149]

uḏmaq [Qarakhanid], "follower, servant" < *uḏ-*, "to follow."[150]

yalnguq [Uyghur, Qarakhanid, Oghuz, Qïpchaq], "human being" (its primary meaning in Uyghur and Qarakhanid, lit. "stripped naked"). In Medieval Qïpchaq, Oghuz and the Turkic Suwar dialect [in Volga Bulgharia], according to Kāshgharī, it acquired the meaning "slave girl."[151]

yuluġluġ kiši [Qarakhanid], "a man who is ransomed" < *yul-*, "to pull out, pluck, to take back, recover;" [Qarakhanid] *er bulunuġ yuldï*, "the man redeemed the captive;" *ol bulunuġ yulturdï*, "he had someone ransom the captive;" *ol qulïn yulturdï*, "he had his slave buy himself from his owner;" *qul yulundï*, "the slave was freed when he paid his own value to his owner;" *bulun yulundï*, "the captive was ransomed and freed."[152]

* * *

As can be seen from this list, the majority of the terms deal with female servitude. The ransoming back of male prisoners (the sources do not quote usages denoting the ransoming back of females) was, clearly, the more common practice. This underscores the domestic nature of slavery in the nomadic Turkic world of the Middle Ages.

According to Morton Fried, societies have a niche for slave labor making use of war captives to do 'drudge labor' only "after a prior differentiation has taken place within the social fabric of the community that would hold slaves." In short, only a stratified society can develop a genuine slave caste. "Slavery," he argues, "can also play an important role in speeding up the precipitation of state institutions." This is because slaves are not part of the normal kinship system on which

149 J. Eckmann, *Middle Turkic Glosses of the Rylands Interlinear Koran Translation* (Budapest, 1976), p. 298; M. Erdal, *Old Turkic Word Formation* (Wiesbaden, 1991), I, p. 303.

150 Kāshgharī/Dankoff, I, p. 130; Clauson, *ED*, pp. 38, 60.

151 Kāshgharī/Dankoff, II, p. 347; Clauson, *ED*, p. 930.

152 Kāshgharī/Dankoff, II, pp. 181, 191, 196; Clauson, *ED*, pp. 918, 925 (*yuluġ*, "ransom," in Qïpchaq *yuluv*), 927 (*yuluġla-*, "to offer, or pay (something) as a ransom").

political relations are (nominally) built. These slaves or "alien clients" are "completely dependent on their masters" and "can be used as a violent force against restive expropriated locals." They are also convenient scapegoats.[153]

We find no evidence for such a niche in Medieval Turkic steppe society in the pre-Chinggisid period. Turkic states that were grafted onto the structures of already existing sedentary societies (e.g., the Seljuks in the Middle East) readily adopted the pre-existing military-slave institution, the traditional political strategy by which rulers in the lands of the ʿAbbāsid Caliphate acquired an alien force to rule the local population. The Chinggisid Mongols, while drafting thousands of captive artisans and others with skills (including cultural and scientific workers, bureaucrats, etc.) needed by the dynasty, used the ancient Eurasian comitatus, in Mongol terminology the *nökür* institution, to achieve this goal, taking those who had broken with or left their clan to take service with a charismatic warlord. These *nöküd* were the functional equivalents of the *ġilmān* of the Islamic world. Given this available source, prisoners of war (especially steppe peoples) were simply incorporated into the Mongol armies, rallied to the pan-nomadic Steppe Imperial Tradition and given a stake in the enterprise.[154] To some degree, the Chinggisids made certain Mongol tribes the *ötegü boġul*, that is, "senior [= of long standing] slaves," i.e., "hereditary vassals" of the dynasty and used them to run the empire.[155] Thus, even in the Mongol Empire, the greatest of the steppe empires, alien slaves (non-steppe peoples) do not play a crucial role as military props for the state.

In the medieval Turkic nomadic, steppe polities, we find an even less well-articulated system with regard to 'vassals' and slaves. Subject peoples (such as the Soghdians in the Türk and Uyghur empires) played

[153] M. H. Fried, "Tribe to State or State to Tribe in Ancient China," in Keightley, ed., *The Origins of Chinese Civilization*, p. 480.

[154] V. V. Trepavlov, *Gosudarstvennyi stroi Mongol'skoi imperii XIII v.* (Moscow, 1993), pp. 57-58.

[155] Vladimirtsov, *Obshchestvennyi stroi*, pp. 68, 98-99; I. Togan, *Flexibility and Limitation in Steppe Formations. The Kerait Khanate and Chinggis Khan* (Leiden, 1998), pp. 112 ff.; and P. B. Golden, "'I Will Give the People unto Thee:' The Čінggisid Conquests and Their Aftermath in the Turkic World," *Journal of the Royal Asiatic Society*, Series 3, 10/1 (2000), pp. 21-41.

important roles within the bureaucracy, as diplomats and culture-bearers.[156] These were, however, subjects, not slaves. For stateless Turkic steppe polities, there were even fewer pressures to develop elaborate governmental systems. In such societies, slaves were few and exclusively of the domestic type.

[156] See Golden, *Introduction to the History of the Turkic Peoples*, pp. 144-145, 172-175.

FAMILY AND RULER IN TIMURID HISTORIOGRAPHY

Beatrice Forbes Manz

Tufts University

The story of the Timurid dynasty in its first three generations is a tale of transformation. For recent historians, the central change was that from the great warrior, leading an army of nomads and setting out to recreate the Mongol empire, to an educated dynasty ruling over Iranian cities, and patronizing the culture they found there. For Timurid rulers and historians, the fundamental transformation may have been a somewhat different one: the change from a single ruler whose personal power was sufficient to overcome his second-rate genealogy to a dynasty holding a reduced realm and ruling by right of the deeds and descent of their ancestor, but not through the line he had explicitly chosen to succeed him. Rulers and historians faced the need to explain this change and to legitimize, first, the rule of the dynasty, and then that of each successive ruler within it.

Starting with a dual heritage of Turco-Mongolian and Perso-Islamic populations, Temür had had to cope with the fact that he himself was not a descendant of Chinggis Khān, and thus not personally entitled to the supreme power he actually wielded. While he was modest in his formal legitimation, reserving the highest titles for his Chinggisid puppet *khān*, in his actions and the histories he commissioned, Temür presented a picture of himself as an equal to Chinggis Khān and as the supreme Muslim ruler of his time—restorer of Mongol order and fighter for the Islamic faith.[1] In his court ceremonial he echoed the Mongol rulers, while he recalled the great Ghaznavid Sulṭān Maḥmūd in his profitable wars for the faith and his collection of brilliant scholars.[2] Temür's

[1] B. F. Manz, "Tamerlane and the Symbolism of Sovereignty," *Iranian Studies*, 21/1-2 (1988), pp. 110-114.

[2] For Maḥmūd of Ghazna, see for instance, Niẓām al-Dīn Shāmī, *Histoire des conquêtes de Tamerlan intitulée Ẓafarnāma, par Niẓāmuddīn Šāmī*, ed. F. Tauer, 2 vols. (Prague, 1937, 1956 [vol. II contains additions made by Ḥāfiẓ-i Abrū]), I, p. 283.

successors had more complicated problems. They had to devise a new legitimation based on descent from Temür himself, while still maintaining Mongol and Islamic traditions. An additional difficulty was the fact that Temür had publicly designated an heir apparent, who did not succeed in gaining the throne. As things worked out, no one Timurid line succeeded in holding power and indeed, by the end of the dynasty, the only line that had not produced a major ruler was the one that Temür had chosen: that of his high-born son, Jahāngīr. Timurid historians presented Temür as a dynastic founder, and his successors as descendants worthy of the great man. At the same time, they provided an appropriate moral explanation showing why each line of his descendants had lost its mandate to rule.

TEMÜR AS DYNASTIC FOUNDER

Temür's successors and their historians made full use of the image Temür had created, and elaborated those aspects of his persona which were most useful for their purposes. The importance he held for the claims of his descendants is apparent in the rhetoric of the succession struggle that followed his death in 807/1405. All the princes competing for power in Temür's realms invoked his will to back their claims—whether they were fighting to uphold his testament or to go against it. His grandson Khalīl Sulṭān, seizing power in Samarqand and opposing Temür's designated successor, enthroned as *khān* a different prince of the same line, and claimed to be upholding Temür's testament.[3] Shāhrukh and his historians claimed adherence to Temür's wishes first to keep ambitious princes in their own provinces and later to justify Shāhrukh's own position of supreme rule.[4]

If we look at the timing of historical writing, we can see a close, and not surprising, correlation between the writing of history and claims to power. Temür had taken pains to have his exploits commemorated,

[3] Beatrice F. Manz, "Tamerlane and the Problem of a Conqueror's Legacy," *Journal of the Royal Asiatic Society*, 3d Series, 8/1 (1998), pp. 34-35; Ḥāfiẓ-i Abrū, *Majmūʿa*, MS Istanbul, Damad Ibrāhīm Pasha, No. 919, f. 926a; Ḥāfiẓ-i Abrū, *Zubdat al-tavārīkh*, ed. Sayyid Kamāl Ḥājj Sayyid Javādī (Tehran, 1372/1993-94), p. 12; Muḥammad b. Fażlullāh Mūsavī, *Tārīkh-i khayrāt*, MS Istanbul, Turhan Hadica Sulṭān No. 224, ff. 436a-437a.

[4] ʿAbd al-Ḥusayn Navāʾī, ed., *Asnād wa makātibāt-i tārīkhī-i Īrān* (Tehran, 2536/1977), pp. 141-142; Ḥāfiẓ-i Abrū, *Majmūʿa*, f. 929b.

and had had several histories of his reign written, of which only one survives, the *Ẓafarnāma* of Niẓām al-Dīn Shāmī, completed in 806/1404. Within a few years of his death, the more ambitious among his descendants began to commission works chronicling the history of Temür's last years, and putting his career into the framework of the Islamic and Mongol worlds. These new histories promoted an image of Temür as dynastic founder which developed in complexity over a number of years. In 813-14/1410-12, when Shāhrukh was establishing his control over Transoxiana, two court historians wrote histories for him completing the story of Temür's life. Shāhrukh's court historian Ḥāfiẓ-i Abrū, who had been in Temür's following and then served Shāhrukh in Khurāsān, produced a continuation of Shāmī's *Ẓafarnāma,* continuing through Temür's death. The vizier Tāj al-Dīn Salmānī, who had been in Transoxiana in the turbulent years after Temür's death and was close to Temür's follower Shāhmalik, present at Temür's death, wrote a history of Temür's last year and the first period of the succession struggle, entitled *Shams al-ḥusn.* Both these histories contain a description of Temür's final days.

In Ḥāfiẓ-i Abrū's continuation of the *Ẓafarnāma* this is a relatively simple account, showing merely Temür's prescience and strength of will. Temür, knowing he was to die, raised first one and then two fingers, asking those around him what he meant, and then explaining that he had only one or two days left to live. The doctors, called in, confirmed his prediction. There is no mention in this account of Temür's deathbed appointment of Pīr Muḥammad b. Jahāngīr as successor; instead verses are given suggesting that Shāhrukh was his chosen successor.[5] The *Shams al-ḥusn* gives a different and more elaborate story, including Temür's religious preparation for death, his deathbed instructions, his appointment of Pīr Muḥammad b. Jahāngīr, and his call for unity among his sons.[6]

[5] Ḥāfiẓ-i Abrū, "Continuation du Ẓafarnāma de Niẓāmuddīn Šāmī par Ḥāfiẓ-i Abrū," ed. F. Tauer, *Archiv Orientální,* 6 (1934), pp. 453-456, 459. The verses mentioning Shāhrukh appear to have been in the first rescension of this work, written in 814/1412, at least in the one manuscript still extant, which dates from 1428, and also in the final version, the *Zubdat al-tavārīkh,* finished in 830/1427, but not in the manuscripts of the *Majmūʿa.*

[6] This story is most fully given in Tāj al-Salmānī, *Šams al-ḥusn: Eine Chronik vom Tode Timurs bis zum Jahre 1409 von Tāğ al-Salmānī,* ed. and tr. Hans Robert Roemer (Wiesbaden, 1956), pp. 26-31, ff. 31b-42a). The historian Mūsavī, writing after 830/1427, took his account from here (Mūsavī, ff. 428b-429b, 432a, 433b). Ḥāfiẓ-i Abrū's account, in his continuation of Shāmī's *Ẓafarnāma*, is characteristically

In Fārs, the sons of Shāhrukh's older brother, ʿUmar Shaykh, held power, fighting each other and other lines of the dynasty. One of them, the ambitious and daring prince Iskandar Sulṭān, soon began to claim independence. In 816/1413-14, the local historian Muʿin al-Dīn Naṭanzī wrote a world history for him, the *Muntakhab al-tavārīkh,* which included an account of Temür's career. Iskandar failed to hold his position against Shāhrukh, and in 817/1414 Naṭanzī offered a slightly revised version of the same work to Shāhrukh. This composition, which was independent of the Herat histories, was written in very simple style, and had only a short description of Temür's death, with no account of a testament. The version presented to Shāhrukh stated baldly that he was the chosen successor.[7] A synopsis of Temür's life and family written for Iskandar at about the same time as Naṭanzī's first rescension had an equally brief account of Temür's death with the statement that Iskandar was the successor.[8]

In 820/1417-18, after Shāhrukh had inflicted a final defeat of the troublesome princes of Fārs, he was able to claim power over the whole of Temür's realm. At this time there was another upsurge of historical writing. In the same year Ḥāfiẓ-i Abrū completed his compilation of histories, the *Majmūʿa*, commissioned by Shāhrukh, and the historian Jaʿfar b. Muḥammad al-Ḥusaynī Jaʿfarī of Yazd presented to Shāhrukh a short world history entitled the *Tārīkh-i Wāsiṭ*. Two years later, the historian Sharaf al-Dīn ʿAlī Yazdī began his reworking of the *Ẓafarnāma* of Niẓām al-Dīn Shāmī for Shāhrukh's son, Ibrāhīm Sulṭān, whom Shāhrukh had installed in Shīrāz as governor of Fārs. In about 828/1424-25, Yazdī completed his work, which included a long and elaborate description of Temür's deathbed instructions, apparently based on the *Shams al-ḥusn*, but adding new material, notably about the *ʿulamā* who read the Qurʾān for Temür as he died and the prayers after his death, and the *amīr* who washed his corpse.[9] This account of Temür's

---

simple, omitting the testament, but including a description of Temür's ability to foresee his death (Ḥāfiẓ-i Abrū, "Continuation," pp. 452-459).

[7] Muʿīn al-Dīn Naṭanzī, *Extraits du Muntakhab al-tavārīkh-i Muʿīnī (Anonym d'Iskandar)*, ed. Jean Aubin (Tehran, 1336/1957), p. 406.

[8] "Synopsis of the House of Timur," in Wheeler Thackston, ed. and tr., *A Century of Princes: Sources on Timurid History and Art* (Cambridge, Massachusetts: The Aga Khan Program for Islamic Architecture, 1989), p. 239.

[9] Sharaf al-Dīn ʿAlī Yazdī, *Ẓafarnāma*, ed. Muḥammad ʿAbbāsī (Tehran, 1336/1957), II, pp. 463-472.

death became the standard one; we find it repeated by the historian Mūsavī, writing in Herat at the end of Shāhrukh's reign, and later by ᶜAbd al-Razzāq Samarqandī in the *Maṭlaᶜ al-saᶜdayn* and by Khwāndamīr in the *Ḥabīb al-siyar.*[10] In Jaᶜfarī's second rescension of his world history, the *Tārīkh-i kabīr*, which he wrote shortly after Shāhrukh's death, there is a short account of Temür's death and testament, an abridged version of the one given by Sharaf al-Dīn ᶜAlī Yazdī, but with one or two differences. In this version Temür on his deathbed appointed Pīr Muḥammad b. Jahāngīr as successor and also enjoined obedience to his wife, Saray Malik, who is not mentioned in Yazdī.[11]

What we see here then is a common tendency to elaborate the death and testament of Temür, for which various historians presented slightly different stories. Separate courts and historians apparently influenced each other first by bringing up a new subject and thus giving the impulse to present a story to match, equal or supplant those presented elsewhere. The actual borrowing of text came at a slightly later date. The simplest versions of Temür's death, those of Naṭanzī, Iskandar's 'unknown historian,' and Ḥāfiẓ-i Abrū, were written by historians who had not been close to the events of Temür's death and simply presented one or another prince as chosen successor, without supporting narrative. These accounts proved less popular than the more elaborate ones, begun by Tāj al-Salmānī and continued, with somewhat different details, by Sharaf al-Dīn ᶜAlī Yazdī and Jaᶜfarī, in which Pīr Muḥammad was presented as the chosen successor, through Temür's own words to specific amīrs.

We see in other aspects of Timurid historiography as well a tendency towards common concerns at different courts. The major new historical initiative which Sharaf al-Dīn ᶜAlī Yazdī undertook for Ibrāhīm Sulṭān in Shīrāz soon found a response in Herat. In 830/1427,

[10] Mūsavī, ff. 428b-430b; ᶜAbd al-Razzāq Samarqandī, *Maṭlaᶜ al-saᶜdayn wa majmaᶜ al-baḥrayn*, MS St. Petersburg, Sankt-Peterburgskii Filial Instituta vostokovedeniia Rossiiskoi Akademii nauk, No. C443, ff. 250b-251b; Ghiyāth al-Dīn b. Humām al-Dīn Khwāndamīr, *Habibu's-siyar, Tome Three*, trans. Wheeler M. Thackston (Cambridge, Massachusetts, 1994; *Sources of Oriental Languages and Literatures*, 24), Part 1, pp. 295-296.

[11] Jaᶜfar b. Muḥammad al-Ḥusaynī Jaᶜfarī, *Tārīkh-i kabīr*, MS St. Petersburg, Publichnaia Biblioteka im. Saltykova-Shchedrina, PNS 201, ff. 293a-b; trans. Abbas Zaryab, "Das Bericht über die Nachfolger Timurs aus dem Ta'rīḫ-i kabīr des Ǧaᶜfarī ibn Muḥammad al-Ḥusainī," Doctoral Dissertation, Johannes Gutenberg-Universität zu Mainz, 1960, pp. 32-33. Unfortunately I do not have access to Jaᶜfarī's earlier world history, the *Tārīkh-i Wāsiṭ*, presented to Shāhrukh in 820/1417-18.

shortly after the composition of Yazdī's *Ẓafarnāma*, Ḥāfiẓ-i Abrū completed his great work, the *Majmaᶜ al-tavārīkh*, an historical compilation reworking Rashīd al-Din's *Jāmiᶜ al-tavārīkh* , Shāmī's *Ẓafarnāma*, and other histories.[12] The last section of this work, covering the period from the Ilkhan Abū Saᶜīd's death up to the time of writing, called the *Zubdat al-tavārīkh-i Bāysunghurī,* was dedicated to Shāhrukh's son Bāysunghur, who was partially in charge of Shāhrukh's *dīvān*, and also served as governor of Astarābād and the regions of Ṭūs and Abīward.[13] It is significant that this section corresponded approximately to the coverage provided in Yazdī's *Ẓafarnāma*, written for Ibrāhīm.

In both these new histories the personality of Temür was further elaborated to enhance the legitimacy of the dynasty. In the *Majmaᶜ al-tavārīkh,* Ḥāfiẓ-i Abrū discussed Temür's excellence in his youth and provided a portait of Temür as *paterfamilias*. He described in detail Temür's concern for his family, with an account of how he used to summon to his court the pregnant women of the royal family, oversee the raising of their sons, and personally designate tutors, instructing them on the course of education they should follow.[14] Sharaf al-Dīn ᶜAlī Yazdī, in his account of Temür's early years, included verses about his childhood showing him as a precocious leader who played king among his playmates. This was almost certainly a tale which had earlier circulated by word of mouth within court circles, since we find a less flattering version recounted in the history of the hostile biographer Ibn ᶜArabshāh, who left the Timurid realm in 811/1408-09.[15] The story was subsequently elaborated for the Moghul rulers and popularized in Renaissance Europe. By the later Timurid period accounts of Temür's extraordinary powers during his childhood appear to have proliferated; Dawlatshāh Samarqandī, known for his use of anecdotes, reproduced an elaborate tale of Temür's childhood administrative genius.[16]

[12] John E.Woods, "The Rise of Tīmūrid Historiography," *Journal of Near Eastern Studies*, 46/2 (1987), pp. 84-85, 88; Tauer, introduction to Shāmī, *Histoire des conquêtes*, II, p. xv; C. A. Storey, *Persidskaia literatura*, tr. and rev. Iu. È. Bregel' (Moscow, 1972), I, p. 351.

[13] Ḥāfiẓ-i Abrū, *Majmaᶜ al-tavārīkh*, MS Istanbul, Fatih 4371/1, f. 1b.

[14] *Majmaᶜ*, ff. 3a-10b.

[15] Yazdī, *Ẓafarnāma*, ed. ᶜAbbāsī, I, pp. 11-12; Aḥmad Ibn ᶜArabshāh, *Tamerlane or Timur, the Great Amir*, tr. J. H. Sanders (London, 1936), pp. 2-5.

[16] Dawlatshāh Samarqandī, *The Tadhkiratu'sh-Shuᶜara ("Memoirs of the Poets")*, ed. E. G. Browne (London, 1901), p. 333.

During his lifetime Temür had informally circulated claims to a certain level of supernatural power, as I have discussed elsewhere.[17] Like the stories about Temür's childhood, these claims began to appear in the histories after Temür's death, though in indirect and more fully Islamic form. It is clear that the image of Temür as a person of mythic proportions quickly found its way into literary and religious sources. Quite shortly after his death, Temür was used by the poet Sakkākī as a literary figure, talking to an ant and learning from him how to persevere despite his crippled arm.[18] Temür's stature proved useful also to the Sufi shaykhs of the Timurid period, for whom he served as a figure against whom they could measure their spiritual stature. Jürgen Paul has discussed the numerous reports of spiritual duels between Temür and the shaykhs of his time, in some of which Temür triumphed and in more, the shaykh himself.[19] Although Temür was not always favorably portrayed in such stories, these anecdotes, by setting up a competition, implicitly recognized Temür's possession of spiritual power, and made of him a figure to be used for legitimation in the mystical sphere. By the end of the Timurid period, stories of Temür's supernatural insight had found their way into some of the Timurid historical writing. The historian Isfizārī, who completed a history of Herat, the *Rawżāt al-jannāt*, in 899/1493-94, related the story of a hospice built by the Sufi shaykh Ghiyāth al-Dīn Muḥammad, whose administrators requested a tax exemption from Temür. As the dervishes waited before him in the audience, Temür turned his magical gaze on them and asked what they wanted. At first he refused their request, but then, on seeing a vision of a lion attacking him, acceded.[20]

During Temür's life, the image of Temür as a supra-natural figure was created through his actions and through stories circulated orally. In the history written for him while he was alive, we find a more sober picture; he was given the attributes of the model ruler, protector of

[17] Manz, "Symbolism," pp. 117-118.

[18] J. Eckmann, "Die tschaghataische Literatur," *Philologiae Turcicae Fundamenta*, II (Wiesbaden, 1964), p. 318.

[19] Jürgen Paul, "Scheiche und Herrscher im Khanat Čağatay," *Der Islam*, 67 (1990), pp. 297-313.

[20] Muʿīn al-Dīn Zamchī Isfizārī, *Rawżāt al-jannāt fī awṣāf madīnat Harāt*, ed. Sayyid Muḥammad Kāẓim Imām (Tehran, 1338/1959), I, pp. 143-144; see also II, p. 37, for another mention of Temür's spiritual powers.

religion, patron of arts, religion and good works, and great conqueror. In the chronicles written during Shāhrukh's reign Temür came to be portrayed as something more—a man whose exceptional character was manifested in his childhood, who through personal effort set out to found a dynasty molded according to his own desires, and who left an explicit testament behind himself. For the role of dynastic founder, the first episode elaborated was his deathbed testament, most immediately relevant to individual descendants in the succession struggle. After this came accounts of his role as *paterfamilias*, molding the lives of his descendants, and of his exceptional personality, showing in his games as a child and in his display of spiritual powers. Stories which had circulated by word of mouth during Temür's life now found their way into dynastic histories. By the end of the Timurid period, several of the myths which made Temür's figure popular in Renaissance Europe and useful to later Islamic dynasties were already in place.

THE TIMURID DYNASTY AND THE CHINGGISIDS

Under Shāhrukh, Temür, as a dynastic founder, was accorded a more independent place within the Mongol world than he had been in Shāmī's history. Ḥāfiẓ-i Abrū, in his *Majmūʿa* (820/1417-18) stated that Temür had outdone Chinggis Khān—had in fact placed him on the rubbish heap of history.[21] We should however not take this statement as a denigration of the Mongol tradition, to which Ḥāfiẓ-i Abrū took pains to connect Temür and his family. In his *Majmaʿ al-tavārīkh* (830/1427), Ḥāfiẓ-i Abrū gave the date of Temür's birth as 736/1336, mentioning it explicitly in connection with the death of the last Ilkhan, Abū Saʿīd. As I have suggested elsewhere, this was probably an invented date, chosen to place the Timurids as successors to the Mongols in Iran.[22]

Along with the image of Temür as the progenitor of the current dynasty came an increased interest in his family and tribe in relation to the lineage of Chinggis Khān and the power structure of the Mongol Empire. Chinggisid connections thus remained central to Timurid legitimacy, while the emphasis shifted from legal connective devices, such as the puppet *khān*s used by Temür, to historical and genealogical

[21] *Majmūʿa*, f. 924b.

[22] Manz, "Symbolism," p. 113, note 33. This is repeated in Mūsavī's history, f. 4b.

connections. As John Woods has shown, towards the end of his reign Temür had begun to show increased interest in his family's genealogy and its connection to the house of Chinggis Khān. This emphasis was continued and intensified under his successors.[23] We find among Temür's heirs two interrelated concerns. The first was the genealogy of the Barlās tribe to which they belonged, its common ancestry with Chinggis Khān, and the descent of its leading lineages from the Mongol *amīr* Qarāchār of Chinggis' army. The second concern was Chinggis Khān's appointment of Qarāchār Beg Barlās as advisor to Chaghatay and the inheritance of this role within the line of Temür, as Barlās amīrs served successive Chaghatayid *khāns*.

Temür's grandson Khalīl Sulṭān, who seized power in Samarqand shortly after Temür's death, apparently commissioned a genealogy of the Mongol and Barlās houses, partly in Uyghur script.[24] From about 830/1426-27 on, we find a series of genealogical works connecting Temür to the house of Chinggis Khān, each, interestingly, originating from a different Timurid court. The most ambitious of these was written for Shāhrukh; this was the *Muʿizz al-ansāb*, presented to the ruler in 830/1426-27. The *Muʿizz al-ansāb* was an updated version of the *Shuʿab-i panjgāna* of Rashīd al-Dīn, bringing the genealogy of the four branches of the Chinggisid house into the ninth century, and adding a genealogy of the Barlās tribe, with the descendants of Qarāchār listed in detail.[25] In 831/1427-28, the historian Sharaf al-Dīn ʿAlī Yazdī included a shorter but similar genealogy of the Barlās in the prologue of his

[23] John E. Woods, "Timur's Genealogy," in Michel M. Mazzaoui and Vera B. Moreen, ed., *Intellectual Studies on Islam, Essays written in honor of Martin B. Dickson* (Salt Lake City, 1990), pp. 99-101, 115-16; cf. Woods, "Rise," p. 104. John Woods suggests that the genealogy and Qarāchār myth were fully in place by Temür's death, and were continued under his descendants because of their presence in the texts from which later historians took their material, and that Shāhrukh largely abandoned the Chinggisid legacy. I have argued elsewhere that the great increase in textual evidence of these myths in the Shāhrukh period argues against an abandonment of the Mongol heritage (Manz, "Legacy," pp. 35-38).

[24] Woods, "Genealogy," pp. 85, 99-100, 112.

[25] *Muʿizz al-ansāb,* MS Paris, Bibliothèque Nationale, A.F. Pers. 67. On this work see the discussion of Shiro Ando in his *Timuridische Emire nach dem Muʿizz al-ansāb: Untersuchungen zur Stammesaristokratie Zentralasiens im 14. und 15. Jahrhundert* (Berlin, 1992), pp. 13-50; cf. Sholeh A. Quinn, "The *Muʿizz al-Ansāb* and *Shuʿab-i Panjgānah* as Sources for the Chaghatayid Period of History: A Comparative Analysis," *Central Asiatic Journal*, 33 (1989), pp. 229-253.

Ẓafarnāma. At about this time or later in Transoxiana, an elaborate genealogy was inscribed on Temür's new tombstone, taking his ancestry back to the mythical ancestress of the Mongols, Alan Goa, impregnated by a shaft of light which was the spirit of ʿAlī b. Abī Ṭālib.[26]

These genealogies indicated an increased emphasis on the Mongol Barlās identity of the Timurid dynasty. We see this tendency reflected in the histories written for the Timurids and in the poetry dedicated to them. The prince Bāysunghur in particular was referred to as a Barlās and a member of the Chinggisid family, and later ʿAbd al-Razzāq Samarqandī, writing about Temür's birth, called this the rising of the triumphant sun of Barlās Sultanate.[27] Along with interest in the Barlās came a strong emphasis on the role of the Barlās *amīr* Qarāchār within the Mongol empire, especially in the Chaghatayid Khanate. In the course of Shāhrukh's reign almost every princely court produced a history including the career of Chinggis Khān and the major lineages descended from him, to which a glorified history of Qarāchār and his descendants had been added. According to this story, an ancient Mongol covenant originating with the joint ancestors of Chinggis Khān and the Barlās specified that the line to which Chinggis belonged was to hold sovereignty, while that of the Barlās was to wield military and administrative authority. Later, Chinggis Khān had appointed his Barlās commander Qarāchār to advise his second son Chaghatay, and in subsequent generations the historical covenant had been renewed by successive Chaghatayid *khān*s and Barlās amīrs, up to the period of Temür.[28]

The earliest of these histories was Naṭanzī's *Muntakhab al-tavārīkh,* written in 816/1413-14 for the Prince Iskandar. In 830/1427, the same year that the *Muʿizz al-ansāb* was presented to Shāhrukh, Ḥāfiẓ-i Abrū completed the *Majmaʿ al-tavārīkh,* his universal history, in which he

[26] Woods, "Genealogy," p. 86. Dawlatshāh Samarqandī repeated the genealogy of Temür's tombstone, while emphasizing Temür's common ancestry with Chinggis Khān who thus, perhaps inadvertently, was also identified as a spiritual descendant of ʿAlī (Dawlatshāh, p. 332).

[27] ʿAbd al-Razzāq Samarqandī, *Maṭlaʿ al-saʿdayn wa majmaʿ al-baḥrayn, qismat-i awwal,* ed. ʿAbd al-Ḥusayn Navāʾī (Tehran, 1353/1974-75), p. 102; Samarqandī, *Maṭlaʿ al-saʿdayn wa majmaʿ al-baḥrayn*, ed. Muḥammad Shafīʿ (Lahore, 1360-68/1941-49) (hereafter *Maṭlaʿ*), II, pp. 660-662; Ḥāfiẓ-i Abrū, *Zubdat*, I, p. 511; *idem, Majmaʿ*, f. 499b.

[28] Woods, "Genealogy," pp. 91-94.

included the myth of the Barlās and Qarāchār Noyan and listed his descendants.[29] Like Naṭanzī's world history, the Prologue (*Muqaddima*) to Yazdī's *Ẓafarnāma*, written for Ibrāhīm Sulṭān in 831-32/1427-29, included a history of the four Chinggisid houses into the ninth century, and an elaboration of the Qarāchār myth within the section on Chaghatayid history.[30] Ulūgh Beg, often credited with particular loyalty to the Chinggisid tradition, commissioned a history entitled the *Tārīkh-i ulūs-i arbaʿa*, composed probably while Ulūgh Beg was ruling as Sulṭān after Shāhrukh's death.[31] The original work is lost, but Khwāndamīr in the *Ḥabīb al-siyar* gives several exerpts from it and a later abridgement and adaptation remains, known both as *Ulūs-i arbaʿa* and as *Shajarat al-atrāk*. The evidence in these sources suggests a history very similar to the accounts of the Mongol world included in Naṭanzī and in the prologue of Yazdī's *Ẓafarnāma*. As in other Timurid histories, the story of Qarāchār Barlās and his descendants is inserted into the account of Chinggis' career, his testament and the house of Chaghatay.[32]

The stories of Qarāchār Barlās and his descendants are told somewhat differently in the various sources; as John Woods has shown, Yazdī's Prologue and the *Ulūs-i arbaʿa* are related and different from Naṭanzī and Ḥāfiẓ-i Abrū.[33] Textual evidence strongly suggests that

[29] *Majmaʿ*, ff. 11a-14b.

[30] Sharaf al-Dīn ʿAlī Yazdī, *Ẓafarnāma*, facs. ed. A. Urunbaev (Tashkent, 1972), ff. 61a-82b. For Yazdī's historical works see also Shiro Ando, "Die timuridische Historiographie II: Šaraf al-Dīn ʿAlī Yazdī," *Studia Iranica*, 24/2 (1995), pp. 219-246.

[31] We know of little historical writing commissioned by Ulūgh Beg, perhaps because Transoxiana did not have a strong historiographical tradition. He commissioned a Persian translation of ʿUtbī's history written for the Ghaznavids (MS Istanbul, Topkapı, Hazine, No. 1414). There is also a manuscript of a world history to about 700/1300-01, copied in 853/1449-50, which seems to be similar to Rashīd al-Dīn in coverage (MS Istanbul, Topkapı, III Ahmet Kitaplığı, No. 2935). For further, internal evidence on the date of the *Tārīkh-i ulūs-i arbaʿa*, see the following note.

[32] *Shajarat al-atrāk*, tr. Colonel William Miles, *The Shajrat ul Atrak or Genealogical Tree of the Turks and Tatars, translated and abridged by Col. Miles* (London, 1838), pp. 195-197, 202-382; MS Harvard, Persian 6, ff. 25a-27a, 67b-116a. See also *Ḥabīb*, tr. Thackston, pt. 1, pp. 27, 42. The *Ulūs-i arbaʿa* lists more *khāns* than the *Muqaddima*, but from Khwāndamīr's text citing this work for the *khāns* of the main line, it is clear that the work offered no information for later *khāns* beyond the names that Khwāndamīr reproduced.

[33] Woods, "Genealogy," p. 86; "Rise," pp. 86, 89-93.

Yazdī's Prologue served as a source for the *Ulūs-i arbaʿa.*[34] The variations in the details of the story make the common program of these histories the more striking—all contain the same basic elements, the same concern with the whole of the Mongol Empire, and the same legitimizing story. This was not a matter of several historians copying one text, but of a need felt equally in different centers of power. The commissioning of such histories appears to have been an accepted part of rulership in the early Timurid period.

THE IMAGE AND LEGITIMATION OF SHĀHRUKH

It was Shāhrukh who first succeeded the great conqueror, restored his realm, and faced the task of portraying himself as successor. Shāhrukh presented himself as an exceptionally pious and observant ruler, as indeed he probably was. This image is firmly in place in the works of Ḥāfiẓ-i Abrū. Early in his reign, about 813/1411, Shāhrukh apparently announced that he was abrogating the Mongol *yasa* and restoring the *sharīʿa*. We do not find this act chronicled in the histories, but echoes of it appear in several places—in a mirror for princes presented to Shāhrukh early in his career, in a decree of Ulūgh Beg written in 814/1411, and in the letter that Shāhrukh wrote to the Chinese emperor in 815/1412-13.[35]

The question we must ask here is whether Shāhrukh's Islamizing policies were designed to distance him from the figure of his father. In terms of outward expression at least, the answer here is no. This need not surprise us. There is in fact no reason for us to discount Temür's identity as a Muslim and a patron of religious institutions, or to assume

[34] In the *Muqaddima*, the account of Jöchi's descendants in the Dasht-i Qipchaq ended with mention of the Muḥammad Khān who succeeded Darvīsh Khān, and stated that the period of Jöchid rule from its beginning in 621/1224-25 to the present year of 831/1427-28 was two hundred and ten years. In the *Shajarat al-atrāk*, based on the *Ulūs-i arbaʿa*, we find this statement preserved intact, after which the line of Jöchid *khāns* continues to Muḥammad Khān b. Temür Khān (r. ca. 1435-65) (*Shajarat al-atrāk*, tr. Miles, pp. 240-241; MS Harvard, Persian 6, ff. 80b-81a). Khwāndamīr, stating that he took his information from the *Ulūs-i arbaʿa*, presented the same list, and ended with the same *khān* (*Ḥabīb*, tr. Thackston, pt. 1, p. 44).

[35] Maria Eva Subtelny, "The Cult of ʿAbdullāh Anṣārī under the Timurids," in Alma Giese and J. Christoph Bürgel, ed., *God is Beautiful and He loves Beauty: Festschrift in Honor of Annemarie Schimmel* (Bern/Berlin/New York, 1994), p. 380; *Majmaʿ*, ff. 486a-487b; *Zubdat*, I, pp. 466-468.

insincerity in his successors when they presented him in that light. Temür built some of the largest religious buildings of his time and brought back to his court several religious stars; Saᶜd al-Dīn Maḥmūd Taftazānī, Sayyid ᶜAlī Jurjānī, and Shams al-Dīn Muḥammad al-Jazarī were names to conjure with, then and for centuries to come. Shāhrukh's religious establishment was in part trained by these men, and their luster added to the prestige of the dynasty.

In his letter to the Chinese emperor as Ḥāfiẓ-i Abrū has preserved it, Shāhrukh began with a discussion of the prophets and Muḥammad's cancellation of former laws. He went on to describe the conquests of Chinggis Khān, omitting mention of Chinggis's religion, but stating that many of Chinggis's progeny and their regions were now Muslim. When Temür's turn to rule came, he applied the *sharīᶜa* throughout his domains, and promoted men of religion. Now that the throne had come to Shāhrukh, Islamic law was honored, and the court (*yarghu*) and laws of Chinggis Khān had been removed. What followed after this was an oblique suggestion that Islam be spread to the lands of the Emperor.[36]

Shāhrukh, despite his apparently conservative piety, may have followed his father in his claims to supra-normal spiritual powers; at least his historians did so for him. Faṣīḥ Khwāfī, writing during Shāhrukh's lifetime, suggested that Shāhrukh's departure on his third Azerbaijan campaign shortly before the outbreak of plague in Herat in 838/1434 was the result of God-given perception.[37] This was a relatively modest statement, but as with Temür, we find that after Shāhrukh's death stronger claims entered the written record from oral reports. Both ᶜAbd al-Razzāq Samarqandī, author of the *Maṭlaᶜ al-saᶜdayn*, and Dawlatshāh Samarqandī, writing after Shāhrukh's reign, reported incidences of Shāhrukh's supernatural powers, shown in ᶜAbd al-Razzāq's case to himself, and in Dawlatshāh's to his father. Shāhrukh had known miraculously of Qarā Yūsuf Qaraqoyunlu's death, he had appeared in dreams to his subordinates, and he had known about the dreams and thoughts of his servitors.[38]

Shāhrukh's death in 850/1447 unleashed a destructive war of succession among his sons, which opened the door to a new ruler, Abū

[36] *Majmaᶜ*, ff. 486a-487a; *Zubdat*, I, pp. 466-468.

[37] Aḥmad b. Jalāl al-Dīn Faṣīḥ Khwāfī, *Mujmal-i faṣīḥī*, ed. Muḥammad Farrukh (Mashhad, 1339/1960-61), III, p. 278.

[38] *Maṭlaᶜ*, ed. Shafīᶜ, II, pp. 722-723, 785-786; Dawlatshāh, *Tadhkirat al-shuᶜarā*, ed. Browne, p. 327.

Sa^c^īd, who was descended from the lineage of Shāhrukh's older brother, Amīrānshāh. Abū Sa^c^īd displaced Shāhrukh's line to take power in Samarqand in 855/1451, and in Herat in 862/1458. The major tradition of dynastic history descends through the *Maṭla^c^ al-sa^c^dayn*, written by ^c^Abd al-Razzāq Samarqandī, strongly favorable towards Abū Sa^c^īd, whom ^c^Abd al-Razzāq served for many years. The history begins significantly with the Ilkhanid Sulṭān Abū Sa^c^īd, and continues through the reign of the Timurid Abū Sa^c^īd. It became the basic text for coverage of this period in the later histories by Mīrkhwānd (836-37/1436-38 to 903/1497-98) and his grandson Khwāndamīr (889/1484-85 to after 942/1535-36). Despite the fact that he wrote his history in part to legitimize the ruler who had taken power from Shāhrukh's line and had executed Shāhrukh's widow, ^c^Abd al-Razzāq presented a consistently favorable portrait of Shāhrukh, beginning the history of his rule with a passage on Shāhrukh's virtues and the extent of his power, and following the account of Shāhrukh's death with an obituary describing Shāhrukh's piety and observance, his study of religious texts, and the presence of religious men in his *majlis*.[39]

In this obituary, ^c^Abd al-Razzāq devoted much less attention to Shāhrukh's military activities than to his religious and administrative ones; this may be due partly to the fact that Shāhrukh undertook fewer campaigns in the second half of his reign, when Samarqandī was in his service, and also in part to Samarqandī's personal lack of interest in military activities.[40] Shāhrukh's most questionable act, and the one which might call into question his role as promoter of religion, was the summary execution of the *^c^ulamā* of Isfahan who encouraged his grandson Sulṭān Muḥammad b. Bāysunghur to rebel, shortly before Shāhrukh's death in 850/1447. In his account, Samarqandī passed over this act without comment, as did the later *Ḥabīb al-siyar* of Khwāndamīr, taken largely from Samarqandī's narrative.[41] The image of Shāhrukh that was fixed and passed on therefore was primarily that of the pious ruler, rather than that of active campaigner.

39 *Maṭla^c^*, ed. Shafī^c^, II, pp. 5-7, 876-877.

40 Samarqandī reproduced Ḥāfiẓ-i Abrū's account of Shāhrukh's early campaigns, but barely described the third Azerbaijan campaign of 838/1435. The fullest Timurid account of that campaign was that of Ja^c^farī in his *Tārīkh-i kabīr* (Ja^c^farī, tr. Zaryab, pp. 80-100; MS St. Petersburg, ff. 312a-324a).

41 *Maṭla^c^*, ed. Shafī^c^, II, pp. 866-867; Khwāndamīr, *Ḥabīb*, tr. Thackston, Part 2, p. 349.

JUSTIFICATION FOR THE CHANGE IN THE RULING LINEAGE

Although he presented a favorable account of Shāhrukh, ʿAbd al-Razzāq also provided the classic explanation for the fall of Shāhrukh's line and the moral reasons that lay behind their loss of *dawlat*, or divine favor. This was a family drama—the failure of Temür's descendants to maintain the unity which he had enjoined on them. Although Temür's progeny had fought among themselves after his death, those killed in the struggle had died at the hands of others. The fight after Shāhrukh's death was more intense and more murderous. Shāhrukh's one surviving son, Ulūgh Beg, was a major contender for power, who controlled Transoxiana and for a while part of Khurāsān, and issued coins in his own name. After only a couple of years however, Ulūgh Beg was defeated and executed by his rebellious son, ʿAbd al-Laṭīf, who himself only ruled six months before he was murdered by his amīrs. The next ruler in Samarqand, ʿAbdullāh, was the son of Shāhrukh's other son, Ibrāhīm Sulṭān, who had lost Shīrāz to the Türkmens. It was ʿAbdullāh from whom Abū Saʿīd took power in Transoxiana in 855/1451.

Just as the succession struggle after Temür's death did not betoken indifference to Temür's testament, so the assumption of power by a new line after Shāhrukh's death should not be understood as a switch that could be made without good reason. In ʿAbd al-Razzāq's eyes, what justified the loss of power by Shāhrukh's family was the behavior of both Ulūgh Beg and his son ʿAbd al-Laṭīf. There is a distinctly critical tone to Samarqandī's account of Ulūgh Beg's campaign in Khurāsān after Shāhrukh's death and of the devastation it caused in the region of Herat. ʿAbd al-Razzāq recounts that at the end of Ramażān in 852/late November, 1448, when Ulūgh Beg had taken Herat, he allowed his troops to pillage its dependencies. During the obligatory paeans of praise for the ruler, a man, who had had his clothes plundered, jumped out in front of Ulūgh Beg's horse, quaking like a willow, and said, "Oh, just king, you give a good *ʿĪd* to the dervishes; may your life and fortune be long!"[42] During the course of this same campaign, Ulūgh Beg's troops plundered the lands of the influential shaykh Bahāʾ al-Dīn ʿUmar Jaghāragī outside Herat. Although Ulūgh Beg returned Bahāʾ al-Dīn's goods, his apology was not appropriately abject. ʿAbd al-Razzāq, who

[42] *Matlaʿ*, ed. Shafīʿ, II, p. 959.

was close to Bahāʾ al-Dīn, reported the shaykh's prediction that Ulūgh Beg would perish.[43]

While in the *Maṭlaʿ al-saʿdayn* Ulūgh Beg's misbehavior seems to initiate the decline of Shāhrukh's line, it was ʿAbd al-Laṭīf's murder of his father that definitively robbed the lineage of its good name and good fortune. The history of Ulūgh Beg's death became a central moral drama in Timurid historiography. It is introduced as an inevitable tragedy, foreseen in the horoscopes of both father and son, which predicted strife between them. Both men knew of the astrological predictions but did nothing to avert them; Ulūgh Beg saw the decline of his fortune in his son, while ʿAbd al-Laṭīf saw the same, and pushed for it. Ulūgh Beg had furthermore slighted ʿAbd al-Laṭīf on several occasions, and persisted in favoring his less competent son ʿAbd al-ʿAzīz.[44] After recounting ʿAbd al-Laṭīf's cynical use of a Chinggisid *khān* to pronounce judgment against Ulūgh Beg according to the *sharīʿa*, and ʿAbd al-Laṭīf's subsequent execution of both his father and his brother, ʿAbd al-Razzāq wrote that through this shameful deed ʿAbd al-Laṭīf made his name famous to posterity.[45] At this point in the history, despite his critical discussion of Ulūgh Beg's years as ruler, Samarqandī provided a classic laudatory obituary, citing Ulūgh Beg's scientific achievements and his justice and good rule. This man, he wrote, was the father whom ʿAbd al-Laṭīf killed.[46] In the account of ʿAbd al-Laṭīf's death at the hands of his own amīrs, ʿAbd al-Razzāq made it clear that ʿAbd al-Laṭīf's hard and suspicious nature was partly to blame for his death, but still ascribed his misfortune primarily to his murder of his father.[47]

It was during this drama that Sulṭān Abū Saʿīd began his successful bid for power. The historian's account of events following ʿAbd al-Laṭīf's death was carefully organized to justify Abū Saʿīd's takeover. While ʿAbd al-Razzāq did note that ʿAbd al-Laṭīf's amīrs raised Shāhrukh's grandson, ʿAbdullāh b. Ibrāhīm Sulṭān, to the throne in Samarqand, he described much more fully how on the same day in

[43] *Maṭlaʿ*, ed. Shafīʿ, II, pp. 941-942.

[44] *Maṭlaʿ*, ed. Shafīʿ, II, pp. 941, 971-973.

[45] *Maṭlaʿ*, ed. Shafīʿ, II, pp. 991-992.

[46] *Maṭlaʿ*, ed. Shafīʿ, II, p. 993.

[47] *Maṭlaʿ*, ed. Shafīʿ, II, pp. 1005-1006.

Bukhara, Abū Saʿīd gathered people around him to claim power. He was imprisoned by the local authorities—just like the prophet Joseph—but very soon, on hearing of ʿAbd al-Laṭīf's death, the officials released him.[48] The chapter on ʿAbd al-Laṭīf's murder of Ulūgh Beg is entitled, "The Rise of the sun of Raʿyat-i Sulṭāni and his seeking promotion to the throne of sultanate and rule," and the chapter on ʿAbd al-Laṭīf's death bears the title, "The events in Transoxiana, the death of Mīrzā ʿAbd al-Laṭīf, and the sultanate of Mīrzā Sulṭān Abū Saʿīd."[49]

Dissension among Shāhrukh's progeny was also used to provide a justification for Abū Saʿīd's conquest of eastern Iran. In his discussion of Shāhrukh's grandson Abū'l-Qāsim Bābur b. Bāysunghur, who now controlled Khurāsān, ʿAbd al-Razzāq prepared the ground for Abū Saʿīd's later claims on the region. When Abū'l-Qāsim defeated his brother Sulṭān Muḥammad in 855/1451, he did not forgive him as he should have done, but instead had him executed; thus Abū'l-Qāsim showed that fortune had turned against him. Furthermore, no sooner had Abū'l-Qāsim killed one of his brothers than he turned his attention to another, ʿAlāʾ al-Dawla, whom he already held captive, and now ordered blinded. The relation of these deeds was followed by a disquisition on the consequences of such acts.[50]

We have in Samarqandī then a moral explanation of why the line of Shāhrukh lost both worldly power and God's favor, and this account was one that later historians picked up. In Mīrkhwānd's *Rawżat al-ṣafāʾ* and Khwāndamīr's *Ḥabīb al-siyar*, the tale was repeated and elaborated with personal accounts of the last moments of both Ulūgh Beg and Sulṭān Muḥammad. Both were taken away from the court and sent off with orders to kill them, of which they themselves were not informed. Ulūgh Beg guessed the truth and when, at a way-station, a spark from the fire touched his robe, he said to it in Turkish, "So you know too?" Sulṭān Muḥammad, led away from his brother's presence under the impression he was to be forgiven, asked for a handkerchief to bind the wound on his hand, and from his guards' refusal, understood what his brother's orders were.[51] These acts then were too shameful to perform in public, or even to admit openly to the victim himself.

[48] *Maṭlaʿ*, ed. Shafīʿ, II, p. 1006.

[49] *Maṭlaʿ*, ed. Shafīʿ, II, pp. 987, 1003.

[50] *Maṭlaʿ*, ed. Shafīʿ, II, p. 1032.

[51] Khwāndamīr, *Ḥabīb*, tr. Thackston, Part 2, pp. 367-369, 375; Muḥammad b. Khwāndshāh b. Maḥmūd Mīrkhwānd, *Rawżat al-ṣafā fī sīrat al-awliyā va'l-mulūk*

In other Timurid histories we find further justifications for the change in the ruling line. Dawlatshāh Samarqandī wrote his collection of poets' biographies, the *Tadhkirat al-shuʿarāʾ*, in 892/1487, under Ḥusayn Bāyqarā (r. 875/1470-911/1506), a descendant of Temür's eldest son, ʿUmar Shaykh, and his history frequently promotes this line. In his relatively informal composition, he allowed himself open dynastic partisanship, and began the delegitimization of Shāhrukh's line at an earlier moment than ʿAbd al-Razzāq, namely at Shāhrukh's execution of the Isfahan *ʿulamā* who had encouraged his grandson Sulṭān Muḥammad's rebellion of 850/1446-47. Even though Dawlatshāh ascribed the act to the instigation of Shāhrukh's wife Gawharshād, he suggested that the action cost Shāhrukh his royal fortune and that of his descendants. Some say, he wrote, that as these men of religion despaired of life, they cursed Shāhrukh and Gawharshād, asking God to make their offpring suffer. The door of heaven was opened, and the prayer accepted.[52] This interpretation had been offered somewhat earlier—about 875/1470-71—by the historian Abū Bakr Ṭihrānī, who served first Shāhrukh, then the Qara Qoyunlu and the Aq Qoyunlu. He stated that the rebellion of sons against fathers usually came from a turn in the fortune of the ruler himself, and recounted dreams and visions connected to Shāhrukh's punishment for his execution of guiltless men.[53]

Like ʿAbd al-Razzāq, Dawlatshāh used the execution of family members by Shāhrukh's line to descredit their rule, but he took the story back to an earlier time. He blamed the death of Sulṭān Ḥusayn's grandfather, the prince Bāyqarā b. ʿUmar Shaykh, in about 826/1422-23, on the trickery of Shāhrukh and Ulūgh Beg.[54] Ulūgh Beg's destruction of Khurāsān also came up in this history, as did his perfidy toward his nephew Abū Bakr.[55] Finally, Dawlatshāh recounted ʿAbd al-Laṭīf's murder of his father, and his bad end, the usual fate of parricides.[56]

---

va'l-khulafāʾ (Tehran, 1338-39/1960), VI, pp. 761-762, 781. Mīrkhwānd includes the story about Ulūgh Beg, but does not recount the incident of Sulṭān Muḥammad's hand, which Khwāndamīr must have taken from another source.

52 Dawlatshāh, *Tadhkirat al-shuʿarā*, ed. Browne, pp. 339-340.

53 Abū Bakr Ṭihrānī Iṣfahānī, *Kitāb-i Diyārbakrīya*, ed. N. Lugal and F. Sümer (Ankara, 1962-64), pp. 288-289.

54 Dawlatshāh, *Tadhkirat al-shuʿarā*, ed. Browne, pp. 374-375.

55 Dawlatshāh, *Tadhkirat al-shuʿarā*, ed. Browne, pp. 374-375.

56 Dawlatshāh, *Tadhkirat al-shuʿarā*, ed. Browne, pp. 364-365.

The historians' concern to justify the change in the line of rule reflects an acceptance of Shāhrukh's legitimacy, and the previous expectation that rulership would continue within his line. We see numerous signs that Shāhrukh continued to be important to the legitimacy of Timurid rule. When he took the throne Abū Saʿīd married into Shāhrukh's line, taking as wives daughters of Ulūgh Beg and ʿAlāʾ al-Dawla, each of whom had held power in a different section of Shāhrukh's realm. Furthermore, Abū Saʿīd named the children of these unions after people in Shāhrukh's family: Shāhrukh, Bāysunghur, Gawharshād.[57] When the Aq Qoyunlu defeated Abū Saʿīd and took Iran in 873/1469, they justified their rule in Khurāsān by enthroning Shāhrukh's great-grandson Yādgār Muḥammad, and portrayed their execution of Abū Saʿīd as vengeance for his killing of Shāhrukh's widow, Gawharshād.[58] At the base of continuing Timurid dynastic legitimacy then lay a family drama. The family nurtured, educated and brought to rule by Temür had failed to keep the unity enjoined on it in Temür's dying words. In the eyes of later Timurid rulers and historians Shāhrukh's line had justly held power but then had lost it because of its wrong actions—primarily because its members killed each other.

THE ISSUE OF CRITICISM

The next question to address is how much the political programs of historians—the need to praise the current ruler and to show the faults of other lines of the dynasty—actually distorted the information presented in their histories. I will suggest here that dynastic partisanship may pose less of a problem to the modern historian than we might expect. In the eyes of the historians, the wrongful deeds of Shāhrukh's line did not make Shāhrukh or even Ulūgh Beg bad rulers; their reigns were an integral part of Timurid glory and a fitting prelude to those of later rulers. This attitude is not too surprising, since the historians, as well as the amīrs, viziers, and *ʿulamā* of the later Timurids were largely descended from those who had served Shāhrukh. Besides this, of course, historians incorporated into their own works those of earlier historians, whose political programs were not always fully expunged.

[57] John E. Woods, "The Timurid Dynasty," *Papers on Inner Asia*, No. 14 (Bloomington, Indiana, 1990), pp. 35-38; *Muʿizz*, ff. 151b, 153a.

[58] Khwāndamīr, *Ḥabīb al-siyar*, tr. Thackston, Part 2, p. 400; H. R. Roemer, "Tīmūr in Iran," *Cambridge History of Iran*, vol. VI (Cambridge, 1986), p. 117.

It was not at all rare for historians to give both positive and negative portraits of members of the dynasty. Although ʿAbd al-Razzāq Samarqandī criticized Ulūgh Beg's actions towards the population of Khurāsān and towards his own sons, he praised him as a patron of religion and science, and as a ruler just towards the poor. ʿAbd al-Razzāq was concerned to show why Shāhrukh's line justly lost its power, but he was consistently laudatory towards Shāhrukh himself; I have mentioned above ʿAbd al-Razzāq's stories about Shāhrukh's supernatural spiritual powers. Dawlatshāh, since his anecdotal history required no pretense of impartiality, included sharp criticism of both Shāhrukh and Ulūgh Beg. In his description of Shāh Niʿmatullāh Walī, he recounted how Shāhrukh tried and failed to trick him into eating unlawful food.[59] Nonetheless, he too included strong praise of both rulers. Shāhrukh was a sultan acceptable to God, just and exceptionally good to the poor—and due to his good morals and religion, he had reached the state of *vilāyat*.[60] Dawlatshāh praised Ulūgh Beg for his accomplishments in asronomy and mathematics, his good rule and low taxation, and his memory, which was famous.[61]

What we see here then is that the accustomed praises of the ruler could coexist in a narrative with quite severe criticism of specific actions. What is interesting is that we seem to find this pattern even in the discussion of people—rulers and others—who had been close to the historian himself. This is most interestingly illustrated in the work of ʿAbd al-Razzāq Samarqandī, whose history was carefully designed to legitimate Sulṭān Abū Saʿīd. We have seen how the historian organized the events of Abū Saʿīd's accession in a way clearly designed to present Abū Saʿīd as replacing the discredited ʿAbd al-Laṭīf rather than his guiltless cousin ʿAbdullāh, who was actually on the throne when Abū Saʿīd took it. On the other hand, when ʿAbd al-Razzāq chronicles Abū Saʿīd's execution of Gawharshād, he strongly suggests that this act was wrong and follows the account of Gawharshād's execution with a description of her good character and pious endowments.[62]

In his discussion of Shāhrukh's powerful *amīr* Fīrūzshāh, ʿAbd al-Razzāq showed a similar tendency. Fīrūzshāh appears to have been

[59] Dawlatshāh, *Tadhkirat al-shuʿarā*, ed. Browne, p. 335.

[60] Dawlatshāh, *Tadhkirat al-shuʿarā*, ed. Browne, pp. 336-338.

[61] Dawlatshāh, *Tadhkirat al-shuʿarā*, ed. Browne, pp. 361-362.

[62] *Maṭlaʿ*, ed. Shafīʿ, III, pp. 1142-1144.

connected to the same circles as the historian himself, and in several places in his history, ʿAbd al-Razzāq gave him prominent and favorable coverage, changing the text of Ḥāfiẓ-i Abrū to highlight Fīrūzshāh.[63] On the other hand, it is to the *Maṭlaʿ al-saʿdayn* that we owe the critical account of Fīrūzshāh's abuse of power during his last years, which eventually brough about his disgrace and death.[64]

It appears then that the historians chronicling successive sovereigns of the Timurid house neither felt the need to blacken the character of former rulers to please those who had taken the throne, nor felt obliged to refrain from all criticism of those whom they had served. It was not unusual, as we have seen, to condemn the actions of a prince or ruler while painting a highly favorable portrait of his general character. What was necessary was a moral framework within which to fit new rulers, showing how and why power had passed to them. Power changed hands because God willed it, and He chose those who were fit to have it. Former members of the dynasty had forfeited their right to rule not because their character was unworthy, but because specific unworthy actions—notably the killing of family members or *ʿulamā*—made them lose the favor of God and the right to rule. Within this ideology, there need be no contradiction in giving both praise and blame to the same person.

CONCLUSION

Much of Timurid historical writing contained a clear program of political legitimation, which was common to its major courts and rulers,

63 Fīrūzshāh, like ʿAbd al-Razzāq's brother, was an adherent of Shaykh Bahāʾ al-Dīn ʿUmar, and seems, among the *ʿulamā* as well, to have had similar connections (*Maṭlaʿ*, ed. Shafīʿ, II, pp. 671, 742, 772, 832; Terry Allen, *A Catalogue of the Toponyms and Monuments of Timurid Herat* [Cambrdige, Massachusetts: Agha Khan Program for Islamic Architecture, Harvard University and Massachusetts Institute of Technology, 1981], p. 178; Khwāndamīr, *Ḥabīb*, tr. Thackston, Part 2, p. 354; Ghiyāth al-Dīn b. Humām al-Dīn Khwāndamīr, *Ḥabīb al-siyar fī akhbār afrād al-bashar*, ed. Jalāl al-Dīn Humāʾī [Tehran, 1333/1954], IV, pp. 7-8). For ʿAbd al-Razzāq's coverage of Fīrūzshāh, one can compare the account of the 830 assassination attempt on Shāhrukh in Ḥāfiẓ-i Abrū, in which the two great amīrs ʿAlīka and Fīrūzshāh played equal parts, to the rewritten account by ʿAbd al-Razzāq, in which Fīrūzshāh played the starring role. (*Maṭlaʿ*, ed. Shafīʿ, II, pp. 314-315; Ḥāfiẓ-i Abrū, *Zubdat*, II, pp. 911-915; *idem, Majmaʿ*, ff. 603a-b).

64 *Maṭlaʿ*, ed. Shafīʿ, II, pp. 793-795, 837-840.

even those who were in conflict with each other. Whether or not different historians used common sources for their work, it is clear that historians and rulers in various parts of the Timurid realm influenced each other in their discussion of the origins and history of the dynasty. In particular, the courts of Fārs and of Herat, both seats of ambitious rulers and heirs to a rich local historographical tradition, show a pattern of mutual imitation, which in the course of Shāhrukh's reign produced a cohesive dynastic myth, beginning with the origins of the Barlās tribe, connected to the line of Chinggis Khān, and continuing through Temür's direct ancestors, to the extraordinary figure of the dynastic founder himself, and the story of his progeny's failure to maintain unity and peace in the family.

Many elements of this story had their origin during the reign of Temür himself, when they were manifested less in dynastic histories than in patterns of family names or in stories circulated by word of mouth. Separate parts of the collective story found their first written form in a variety of places. The genealogy of the Barlās appears first in Transoxiana, for Khalīl Sulṭān, then in Fārs and Herat. The history of the branches of the Chinggisid house incorporating the story of Temür's ancestor Qarāchār Barlās is included in the world history of Naṭanzī originally written for Shāhrukh's opponent Iskandar Sulṭān in Fārs, and then appeared, based on slightly different sources, in histories written for Shāhrukh and for his sons Ibrāhīm Sulṭān and Ulūgh Beg. The account of Temür's personality and his testament likewise traveled in different variations from one court and one historian to another. The variety in the details in the stories given, pointing to the use of independent sources by different historians, underlines the common appeal and usefulness of the family myth that connected the destinies of Temür's and Chinggis' lines, and made the story of the Barlās into a coherent and continuing drama lasting through the Timurid period. By the end of Sulṭān Abū Saʿīd's reign, when ʿAbd al-Razzāq wrote his history, the story was complete and continuous, serving to explain not only the rise of the Timurid dynasty, but also its many shifts in power over the course of its history. In this form, the drama entered the great universal histories of the late Timurid period, which defined for later generations the history of the Middle East in the Mongol and Timurid periods.

THE MAKING OF *BUKHĀRĀ-YI SHARĪF*:

SCHOLARS AND LIBRARIES IN MEDIEVAL BUKHARA

(THE LIBRARY OF KHWĀJA MUḤAMMAD PĀRSĀ)[1]

Maria Eva Subtelny

University of Toronto

In keeping with the medieval Islamic tradition that accorded every city of importance an epithet or honorific title, Bukhara became known as *Bukhārā-yi sharīf*—Bukhara the Noble—with all the connotations carried by the word *sharīf* in Islam, where nobility stemmed from descent from the Prophet Muḥammad.[2] Only, in the case of Bukhara, its "nobility" derived from its impressive contributions to the study of the religious sciences, in particular the science of the Prophetic traditions, Qurʾānic exegesis, and jurisprudence. Bukhara thus became associated above all with religious scholarship and noted for the prominent scholars (*ʿulamā*) and jurisprudents (*fuqahāʾ*) it produced. This had in fact been true from the earliest Islamic period of the rule of the Sāmānids (9th-10th centuries), who have been identified with Bukhara more closely than any other Islamic dynasty.[3]

The traditionist, Ismāʿīl al-Bukhārī (d. 256/870), was from Bukhara, as were many of the theologians and jurisprudents who were instrumental in the development of the Ḥanafite school of law, such as members of the Burhān and Maḥbūbī families. The Burhān family,

[1] Acknowledgements: This paper has profited greatly from the comments and suggestions of my colleagues, Prof. Robert McChesney (New York University), Prof. Dr. Jürgen Paul (Martin-Luther-Universität, Halle), Prof. Devin DeWeese (Indiana University) and Prof. Michael Wickens (University of Toronto).

[2] It is not known exactly when Bukhara was given the epithet, but it was firmly established by the 19th century. In medieval times Bukhara had also been known as "*fākhira*," "the proud" or "the outstanding" (see Aḥmad b. Maḥmūd Muʿīn al-fuqarāʾ, *Tārīkh-i Mullāzāda*, ed. Aḥmad Gulchīn Maʿānī [Tehran, 1339/1960], p. 1).

[3] See Richard N. Frye, *Bukhara: The Medieval Achievement* (Norman: University of Oklahoma Press, 1965), esp. p. 59.

founded by the famous Ḥanafite scholar, ᶜAbd al-ᶜAzīz Ibn Māza, who was known as "the second Abū Ḥanīfa," spanned roughly the 12th and early 13th centuries and its members authored such definitive works of Ḥanafite jurisprudence as *al-Muḥīṭ*, *al-Mughnī*, *al-Dhakhīra*, and *al-Tatimma*, while members of the Maḥbūbī 'theological dynasty,' which succeeded it into the middle of the 14th century and which included scholars who bore the prestigious epithets, "Ṣadr al-Sharīᶜa" (Vanguard of Islamic Law) and "Tāj al-Sharīᶜa" (Crown of Islamic Law), produced, among other juridical works, *al-Wiqāya* and *al-Tawḍīḥ*, as well as various commentaries on them.[4] Bukhara was arguably also the most important center of Sufism in Central Asia in the post-Mongol period, and the names of Sayf al-Dīn Bākharzī and Bahāʾ al-Dīn Naqshband immediately come to mind.

The *Tārīkh-i Mullāzāda*, which was written in the first half of the 15th century, contains biographies of all the prominent religious scholars and saints who were buried in Bukhara and its immediate vicinity.[5] Citing the *Tārīkh-i Jahāngushā*, the author, Aḥmad b. Muḥammad "Muᶜīn al-fuqarāʾ" ("Helper of Dervishes"), has the following to say about Bukhara in the introduction to his book:[6]

[4] For these families, see Omeljan Pritsak, "Āl-i Burhān," *Der Islam*, 30/1 (1952), esp. pp. 85 and 91-93. For the works mentioned, see Maria Eva Subtelny and Anas B. Khalidov, "The Curriculum of Islamic Higher Learning in Timurid Iran in the Light of the Sunni Revival under Shāh-Rukh," *Journal of the American Oriental Society*, 115/2 (1995), pp. 228-234.

[5] The exact date of composition of the *Tārīkh-i Mullāzāda* is unknown, but it must have been after 822/1420, the date of the death of Khwāja Muḥammad Pārsā, who is mentioned in it as already deceased (*Tārīkh-i Mullāzāda*, p. 17). This contradicts the date of 814/1411-12 proposed by Pritsak, "Āl-i Burhān," p. 96, and, following him, Richard N. Frye, "City Chronicles of Central Asia and Khurasan: The *Kitāb-e Mullāzāde*," in *Avicenna Commemoration Volume* (Calcutta: Iran Society, 1956), p. 89. Other important biographical sources for Bukhara are: *Rawżat al-riżvān* by Badr al-Dīn al-Kashmīrī (end 16th c.); *Tārīkh-i Rāqimī* by Sharaf al-Dīn Aᶜlam (17th century); *Mudhakkir-i aḥbāb* by Ḥasan Nithārī Bukhārī (16th century); and *ᶜUbaydullāh-nāma* by Mīr Muḥammad-Amīn Bukhārī (17th-18th centuries).

[6] *Tārīkh-i Mullāzāda*, pp. 3-4. For the original of the citation from Juvaynī's *Tārīkh-i Jahāngushā*, which dates from the 13th century, see the edition by Mirza Muhammad Qazwini, 3 vols. (London: Luzac & Co., 1912-16), I, pp. 75-76, and the translation by John Andrew Boyle, *The History of the World-Conqueror*, 2 vols. (Manchester: Manchester University Press, 1958), I, pp. 97-98.

Among the countries of the East, Bukhara is the Dome of Islam (*qubbat al-Islām*),[7] and in those parts it [holds a position] similar to the City of Peace (i.e., Baghdad). Its land is adorned with the brightness of the light of jurisprudents (*fuqahā*) and religious scholars (*ʿulamā*), and its parts are embellished with [their] precious attainments.[8] Since ancient times, Bukhara has always been the place where scholars of the prevailing religion of the time have gathered.

The etymology of Bukhara is from [the word] *bukhār*, which in the language of the Magians (i.e., Zoroastrians) means 'center of learning.' This word closely resembles the language of the Uyghur and Eastern Turkestānī (lit. 'Khiṭāy') idolaters (i.e., Buddhists), who call their places of worship, which are idol-temples, '*bukhār*' [i.e., *vihāra* or Buddhist monastery].[9]

Irrespective of whether this etymology was factually correct or not, the popular perception of Bukhara as a former center of idolatry, which appears to have persisted through the 13th century and even into the 15th, may actually have served to strengthen its association with the Islamic religious sciences and to connect it with such Biblical and Islamic figures as Job, who was believed to have visited Bukhara (where the well-known pilgrimage site, *Chashma-i Ayyūb* [Job's Spring], was named after him).

But scholars cannot exist without books and libraries, and this was as true of medieval Islam as it is today, the Islamic bias for oral transmission of knowledge notwithstanding. Like Baghdad, its counterpart in the west, Bukhara became renowned early on for its libraries. The famous library of the Sāmānid, Nūḥ b. Manṣūr (d. 387/997), was described thus by the great philosopher, Ibn Sīnā (Avicenna), who worked in it:

[7] The editor incorrectly explains that by "*qubbat al-Islām*" the town of Balkh was intended.

[8] Read *maʿālī* for *maʿānī*.

[9] The etymology of Bukhara is still being debated in scholarship; see Richard N. Frye, "Bukhara," *EIr*, IV, p. 512, and his contribution in the present volume. For other popular etymological derivations of the word Bukhara, see Narshakhī, *Tārīkh-i Bukhārā*, ed. Mudarris Rażavī (Tehran, 1351/1972), pp. 30-31, and *Tārīkh-i Mullāzāda*, pp. 2-3.

> I was admitted to a building which had many rooms; in each room there were chests of books piled one on top of the other. In one of the rooms were books on Arabic language and poetry, in another, on jurisprudence, and likewise in each room [were books on] a single science. So I looked through the catalogue of books written by the ancients and asked for whichever one I needed. I saw books whose names had not reached very many people and which I had not seen before that time, nor have seen since.[10]

This library soon afterwards burned, and there were rumors that Ibn Sīnā had set fire to it himself so that he could become the sole possessor of the knowledge it contained.[11]

KHWĀJA MUḤAMMAD PĀRSĀ AND THE ḤĀFIẒĪ FAMILY OF BUKHARA

Probably the finest and longest-lived medieval library associated with Bukhara was that connected with the name of Khwāja Muḥammad Pārsā, the scion of another illustrious Bukharan family of Ḥanafite religious scholars and jurisprudents, which deserves more scholarly attention: the Ḥāfiẓī family.

The family's most prominent member and possibly its eponymous founder was Mawlānā Ḥāfiẓ al-Dīn Muḥammad b. Muḥammad b. Naṣr "al-Kabīr" ("the Great") al-Bukhārī (d. 693/1294), who had been an important religious scholar (*ʿālim*) in 13th-century Bukhara,[12] as had his father, ʿAlāʾ al-Dīn Muḥammad b. Naṣr b. Muḥammad b. Abī Bakr al-Qalānisī al-Bukhārī (d. 631/1233).[13] Ḥāfiẓ al-Dīn al-Kabīr was a towering figure in the religious and social history of Bukhara. Born in 615/1218-19, and titled shaykh, jurisprudent (*faqīh*), professor of law

[10] He referred to the library as a *dār al-kutub*. See William E. Gohlman, ed. and tr., *The Life of Ibn Sina* (Albany: State University of New York Press, 1974), p. 37.

[11] W. Barthold, *Turkestan down to the Mongol Invasion*, tr. V. and T. Minorsky, ed. C. E. Bosworth, 4th ed. (London, 1977), p. 9, n. 4.

[12] Fakhr al-Dīn ʿAlī [Ṣafī] b. Ḥusayn Vāʿiẓ Kāshifī, *Rashaḥāt-i ʿayn al-ḥayāt*, ed. ʿAlī Asghar Muʿīniyān, 2 vols. (Tehran, 2536/1977), I, p. 59.

[13] *Tārīkh-i Mullāzāda*, p. 55.

(*mudarris*), traditionist (*muḥaddith*), and exegete (*mufassir*),[14] he had studied the religious sciences with Shams al-Aʾimma Muḥammad b. ʿAbd al-Sattār al-Kardarī (d. 642/1244),[15] and he had related the Prophetic traditions from him and from Abū al-Fażl ʿUbaydullāh al-Maḥbūbī, the father of the famous Aḥmad b. ʿUbaydullāh, known as Ṣadr al-Sharīʿa I (d. 630/1232).[16] His chain of transmission (*sanad*) from Maḥbūbī was regarded as highly prestigious, going all the way back to another famous Bukharan theologian, Abū Ḥafṣ al-Kabīr (d. 217/813), a student of Muḥammad al-Shaybānī, one of the chief disciples and interpreters of Abū Ḥanīfa himself.[17] Later generations regarded Ḥāfiẓ al-Dīn al-Kabīr as the last *mujtahid* (i.e., jurist capable of exercising independent judgement on questions concerning the *sharīʿa* without recourse to authorities),[18] and a descendant of his brother was credited with having converted the pagan Turko-Mongolian population of Eastern Turkistan to Islam.[19]

[14] Muḥammad ʿAbd al-Ḥayy al-Laknawī al-Hindī, *al-Fawāʾid al-bahīya fī tarājim al-Ḥanafīya* (Benares, 1967), p. 160; Ibn Abī al-Wafāʾ, *al-Jawāhir al-muḍīya fī ṭabaqāt al-Ḥanafīya* (Hyderabad, 1332/1914), II, pp. 121-122.

[15] For him see *Tārīkh-i Mullāzāda*, pp. 31-32, 36-37.

[16] *al-Jawāhir al-muḍīya*, II, p. 121.

[17] At time of his death, Ḥāfiẓ al-Dīn al-Kabīr was apparently 15 years old. He studied *al-Jāmiʿ al-ṣaghīr* with him, which he transmitted from him on the authority of ʿUmar b. Bakr al-Zaranjarī, who transmitted it on the authority of his father, who transmitted it on the authority of al-Ḥalvāʾī, who transmitted it on the authority of Abū ʿAlī al-Nasafī, who transmitted it on the authority of Muḥammad b. al-Fażl, who transmitted it on the authority of al-Sabadhmūnī, who transmitted it on the authority of Abū ʿAbdullāh b. Abū Ḥafṣ al-Kabīr, who transmitted it on the authority of his father, Abū Ḥafṣ al-Kabīr, who transmitted it on the authority of Muḥammad [al-Shaybānī] (see *al-Fawāʾid al-bahīya*, p. 160). Among the people who studied and transmitted *ḥadīth* from him were: Ḥusām al-Dīn Ḥusayn al-Sighnāqī, Aḥmad b. Asʿad al-Khayrfaghnavī, ʿAbd al-ʿAzīz b. Aḥmad al-Bukhārī, Maḥmūd b. Muḥammad al-Bukhārī, Shams al-Dīn Maḥmūd al-Kalābādhī al-Farżī, and Abū al-ʿAlāʾ al-Bukhārī (see *al-Fawāʾid al-bahīya*, p. 160; also *Tārīkh-i Mullāzāda*, p. 56).

[18] Thus, in the 16th-century *Tārīkh-i Rashīdī*, he is referred to as "*ākhirīn-i mujtahidīn*" ("the last of the *mujtahids*"); see Mirza Haydar Dughlat, *Tarikh-i-Rashidi: A History of the Khans of Moghulistan*, ed. and tr. W. M. Thackston, 2 vols. (Cambridge, Massachusetts, 1996; Sources of Oriental Languages and Literatures), I, p. 308 (Persian ed.) and II, p. 232 (English tr.).

[19] According to an account in the *Tārīkh-i Rashīdī* (which is not corroborated by other sources), Ḥāfiẓ al-Dīn al-Kabīr was murdered by the Mongols in Bukhara, while his brother, whose name was Shujāʿ al-Dīn Maḥmūd, was exiled to Qaraqorum with his

Khwāja Muḥammad Pārsā was a descendant of Ḥāfiẓ al-Dīn al-Kabīr's, but it is not clear in which generation.[20] His full name was Shams al-Dīn Muḥammad b. Muḥammad b. Maḥmūd (also: Muḥammad b. Maḥmūd) al-Ḥāfiẓī al-Bukhārī, but he was better known as Khwāja-i Pārsā.[21] Although he traced his descent back to ʿAbdullāh

---

entire family, and died there. Shujāʿ al-Dīn's son left Qaraqorum for Katak (in Eastern Turkestan), where he and his descendants were greatly revered by the local population. It was one of the latter's descendants, who is depicted as possessing extraordinary spiritual powers, who is credited by Muḥammad Ḥaydar with the conversion of Tughluq Temür Khān (d. 1362), the ruler of Aqsu, to Islam, and hence as being the Islamizer of the Moghuls of Eastern Turkestan (see *Tarikh-i-Rashidi*, II, pp. 232 and 9-11 [English tr.]).

[20] According to the *Rashaḥāt-i ʿayn al-ḥayāt* (I, p. 59), Ḥāfiẓ al-Dīn al-Kabīr was Khwāja Muḥammad Pārsā's *jadd*, an ambiguous term, which means ancestor, but which could also more specifically mean grandfather. The latter would have been an impossibility, however, given the length of time that separated the two individuals. According to the later Ḥanafite compilation, *al-Fawāʾid al-bahīya* (p. 159), Khwāja Muḥammad Pārsā was simply "descended from" (*min nasl*) Ḥāfiẓ al-Dīn al-Kabīr.

[21] Most contemporary or near contemporary authors give his full name in this form. Thus, the author of *Tārīkh-i Mullāzāda*, a member of the prominent Bukharan family of the Shāristānīs, who was his disciple and who therefore possessed firsthand knowledge, calls him Muḥammad b. Muḥammad al-Ḥāfiẓī al-Bukhārī (see *Tārīkh-i Mullāzāda*, pp. 16-17, 66). So too do Khwāndamīr, who calls him "the son of Muḥammad b. Maḥmūd al-Ḥāfiẓī al-Bukhārī" (Ghiyāth al-Dīn b. Humām al-Dīn Khwāndamīr, *Tārīkh-i Ḥabīb al-siyar fī akhbār afrād al-bashar*, ed. Jalāl al-Dīn Humāʾī, 4 vols. [Tehran, repr. ed., 1362/1984], IV, p. 4), and also ʿAbd al-Raḥmān Jāmī (*Nafaḥāt al-uns min ḥaẓarāt al-quds*, ed. Mahdī Tawḥīdīpūr [Tehran, 1336/1958], p. 392; ed. Maḥmūd ʿĀbidī [Tehran, 1370/1991], p. 397), and following them, the secondary bio-bibliographical sources, such as Carl Brockelmann, *Geschichte der arabischen Litteratur*, 2 vols. (2nd ed., Leiden: E. J. Brill, 1943-49), II, p. 264, and *Supplement*, 3 vols. (Leiden: E. J. Brill, 1937-42), II, p. 282; and Ch. A. Stori [C. A. Storey], *Persidskaia literatura: Bio-bibliograficheskii obzor*, tr. and rev. Iu. È. Bregel', 3 vols. (Moscow, 1972), I, p. 118. Al-Sakhāwī (d. 902/1497), the famous Egyptian polymath, provides the longest form of his name: Muḥammad b. Muḥammad b. Maḥmūd b. Muḥammad b. Muḥammad b. Mawdūd al-Shams al-Jaʿfarī al-Bukhārī al-Ḥanafī (see Shams al-Dīn Muḥammad al-Sakhāwī, *al-Ḍawʾ al-lāmiʿ li-ahl al-qarn al-tāsiʿ*, 12 vols. (Cairo, 1353-55/1934-36), X, p. 20. However, his name is sometimes also given as Muḥammad b. Maḥmūd, as in ʿAbd al-Vāsiʿ Niẓāmī Bākharzī, *Maqāmāt-i Jāmī*, ed. Najīb Māyil Haravī (Tehran, 1371/1993), p. 50 (which actually gives both variants); in an *ijāza* (authorization to transmit) which he granted to one of his disciples in 819/1416, he calls himself Muḥammad b. Maḥmūd al-Ḥāfiẓī (*Rashaḥāt*, II, pp. 647-648); in many manuscript copies of works which are known to have been authored by him, his name appears as Muḥammad b. Maḥmūd al-Ḥāfiẓī (see A. A. Semenov, *et al.*, *Sobranie vostochnykh rukopisei Akademii nauk Uzbekskoi SSR*,

b. Jaʿfar al-Ṭayyār, a nephew of ʿAlī, the fourth caliph and cousin of the Prophet Muḥammad, his name never occurs in contemporary sources with the title *sayyid*, which indicated descent from the Prophet; rather, he is simply styled "*khwāja*."[22] Several different dates are given for his birth in Bukhara,[23] where he appears to have lived his entire life.[24] The sources are in agreement about the date of his death, however, which occurred in Medina on 24 Dhū'l-ḥijja 822/11 January 1420, while he was performing the pilgrimage.[25] He was buried in Medina near the

---

11 vols. [Tashkent, 1952-87; hereafter "*SVR*"], III, p. 256, and Storey-Bregel', *Persidskaia literatura*, I, pp. 118-119); and finally, some of the seals imprinted in books belonging to his library (on which see below) read "*Khwāja-i Pārsā Ibn Maḥmūd al-Bukhārī.*" To complicate matters further, al-Sakhāwī states that a third Muḥammad was sometimes added to the first part of his name (*al-Ḍawʾ al-lāmiʿ*, X, p. 20). There is no doubt, however, that Muḥammad b. Muḥammad b. Maḥmūd and Muḥammad b. Maḥmūd refer to one and the same Khwāja Muḥammad Pārsā. It was not uncommon during this period for individuals to emphasize their relationship to a more famous grandfather or great-grandfather by means of the Persian construct, which was otherwise used to indicate direct filiation. It should also be borne in mind, that the substitution of Muḥammad for Maḥmūd (and vice versa) was one of the most common copyist's errors in medieval Persian manuscripts, and this may have contributed to the confusion.

22 *Ḥabīb al-siyar*, IV, p. 4; *al-Ḍawʾ al-lāmiʿ*, X, p. 20. For ʿAbdullāh b. Jaʿfar al-Ṭayyār, see *EI²*, I, p. 44. The major tomb-shrine of ʿAbdullāh b. Muʿāwiya b. ʿAbdullāh b. Jaʿfar Ṭayyār was located in Herat on the mound of Quhandiz-i Maṣrakh (see Fikrī Saljūqī, ed., *Risāla-i mazārāt-i Harāt* [Kabul, 1967], pp. 8 ff.). Muḥammad Pārsā's descendants, however, evidently adopted the title "*sayyid.*" Thus, the late copies of the *vaqfīyas* of his library, *madrasa*, *khānqāh*, etc., all style him "*sayyid al-sādāt*," "*khulāṣa-i awlād-i ḥażrat-i sayyid al-mursalīn*," etc.

23 746/1345-46, according to al-Sakhāwī (who was reporting from his teacher, Ibn Ḥajar al-ʿAsqalānī), who also states that he died at the age of 76 (*al-Ḍawʾ al-lāmiʿ*, X, p. 20); 756/1355, according to *al-Fawāʾid al-bahīya*, p. 160; and 749/1348-49, according to the editor of *Maqāmāt-i Jāmī*, pp. 278-280 (although he does not name his source).

24 He was still living in Bukhara shortly before his death, as is indicated by the colophon of a manuscript of his *Tafsīr*, dated 820/1417-18 (see Storey-Bregel', *Persidskaia literatura*, I, p. 118); and it was from Bukhara that he set out to perform the pilgrimage (see *Nafaḥāt al-uns*, ed. Tawḥīdīpūr, p. 393; ed. ʿĀbidī, p. 397). Although there is no evidence that he ever lived in Balkh, that impression may have been created by later authors who assumed that his tomb must also have been located at the site of his son's magnificent mausoleum, a notion that may have been reinforced by the fact that his own tomb was far away in Medina.

25 The only source that differs with regard to the place of his death is *al-Ḍawʾ al-lāmiʿ* (X, p. 20), which states that he died in Mecca. For biographical entries on

tomb of ʿAbbās,[26] and his grave was marked by a white headstone, which had been commissioned from Egypt by his contemporary, the influential Sufi shaykh of Herat, Zayn al-Dīn al-Khwāfī, founder of the Zaynī order.[27]

Several members of the Ḥāfiẓī family, including Ḥāfiẓ al-Dīn al-Kabīr and the latter's father, were buried in Bukhara on a funerary mound called Tall-i Bughrā Beg, which was also known in the first half of the 15th century as Tall-i Mawlānā Ḥāfiẓ al-Dīn.[28] Located in the Kalābād district of the city,[29] it represented one of the most important

---

him in contemporary and near-contemporary sources, see: *Ḥabīb al-siyar*, IV, pp. 4-5; Ibn ʿArabshāh, *ʿAjāʾib al-maqdūr fī nawāʾib Taymūr*, ed. Aḥmad Fāʾiz al-Ḥimṣī (Beirut, 1407/1986), p. 468; Faṣīḥ Aḥmad b. Jalāl al-Dīn Muḥammad Khwāfī, *Mujmal-i faṣīḥī*, ed. Maḥmūd Farrukh, 3 vols. (Ṭūs/Mashhad, 1339-41/1961-63), III, p. 244 (although he placed the notice on him under the year 823, he also states that he was believed to have died in 822); *Nafaḥāt al-uns*, ed. Tawḥīdīpūr, pp. 392-396, ed. ʿĀbidī, pp. 397-400; *Rashaḥāt*, I, pp. 101-113; *Maqāmāt-i Jāmī*, p. 50; *al-Ḍawʾ al-lāmiʿ*, X, p. 20; and Sharaf al-Dīn Aʿlam, *Tārīkh-i Rāqimī*, MS St. Petersburg, Sankt-Peterburgskii Filial Instituta vostokovedeniia Rossiiskoi Akademii nauk, No. C813, ff. 49b-50b (for the chronogram on the date of his death). See also H. Algar, "Bahāʾ-al-Dīn Naqšband," *EIr*, III, p. 434.

[26] I.e., ʿAbbās b. ʿAbd al-Muṭṭalib (d. ca. 32/653), half-brother of the father of the Prophet Muḥammad, from whom the ʿAbbāsid dynasty took its name.

[27] *Nafaḥāt al-uns*, ed. Tawḥīdīpūr, p. 395; ed. ʿĀbidī, p. 399.

[28] *Tārīkh-i Mullāzāda*, pp. 55-56. Other relations of Mawlānā Ḥāfiẓ al-Dīn who were buried here were: his son-in-law, the Qurʾānic scholar, Mawlānā Tāj al-Dīn al-Muṣaddir (d. 710/1311); the latter's son, Mawlānā Ḥusām al-Dīn (d. 727/1327); and another relation by the name of Khwāja Yūsuf (d. 768/1367). It was also known as *Tall-i Khwāja Abū Bakr Ṭarkhān*, although in ancient times it had been known as *Tall-i Miyāna*. The graves of many important religious scholars dating from as early as the 4th/10th century were also located here, such as that of Abū Bakr ʿAbdullāh b. Muḥammad b. ʿAlī b. Ṭarkhān al-Balkhī (d. 333/944), after whom, as already indicated, the mound was named at one time (see *Tārīkh-i Mullāzāda*, pp. 54-55).

[29] Sometimes also "Kalābādh." It is No. XII on the schematic map in O. A. Sukhareva, *Kvartal'naia obshchina pozdnefeodal'nogo goroda Bukhary (V sviazi s istoriei kvartalov)* (Moscow, 1976), p. 68, and inside the front cover. Abū'l-ʿAlāʾ al-Bukhārī, who had transmitted *ḥadīth* from Ḥāfiẓ al-Dīn al-Kabīr and who mentioned him in his *Muʿjam al-shuyūkh*, stated that he had been buried at Kalābādh (see *al-Jawāhir al-muḍīʾa*, II, p. 122. In the first half of the 15th century, Kalābād was evidently still outside the city, since Ḥāfiẓ al-Dīn's tomb is described in that part of the *Tārīkh-i Mullāzāda* that treats sites located at least one-half *farsakh* outside Bukhara (see *Tārīkh-i Mullāzāda*, p. 17). By the late 19th and early 20th centuries, however, Kalābād had become completely built up, and Ḥāfiẓ al-Dīn's tomb was now situated in the middle of a public thoroughfare (Sukhareva, *Kvartal'naia obshchina*, p. 246).

concentrations of local pilgrimage sites in Bukhara, and it included the tomb of a mythical personage named Dihqān-i Sughdī ("The Soghdian lord"), which reputedly contained a relic revered throughout the Islamic world—a hair of the Prophet Muḥammad.[30] The Ḥāfiẓī family line continued for many centuries in Bukhara, although Khwāja Muḥammad Pārsā's son and spiritual successor, Khwāja Abū Naṣr Pārsā (d. 865/1460-61), was more closely identified with Balkh, where he was buried and where his tomb became the object of pilgrimage and patronage.[31]

Like other members of the Ḥāfiẓī family, Khwāja Muḥammad Pārsā was also a Qur'ānic exegete (*mufassir*), traditionist (*muḥaddith*), and Ḥanafite jurisprudent (*faqīh*).[32] He studied legal theory (*al-uṣūl*) and substantive law (*al-furūʿ*) with the great scholars of his time, and his

[30] This was one of several to be found at various Bukharan burial sites according to the *Tārīkh-i Mullāzāda*, pp. 12, 60.

[31] For Abū Naṣr Pārsā, see *Ḥabīb al-siyar*, IV, p. 5; and *Nafaḥāt al-uns*, ed. Tawḥīdīpūr, pp. 396-397, ed. ʿĀbidī, p. 401 (according to which his full name was Ḥāfiẓ al-Dīn [also: Burhān al-Dīn] Abū Naṣr Muḥammad b. Muḥammad b. Muḥammad al-Ḥāfiẓī al-Bukhārī). According to *al-Fawā'id al-bahīya* (p. 160), his full name was Abū Naṣr Pārsā Maḥmūd b. Muḥammad al-Ḥāfiẓī al-Bukhārī—again the confusion between Muḥammad and Maḥmūd. For Abū Naṣr Pārsā's descendants, see R. D. McChesney, "Pārsā'iyya," *EI*[2], VIII, pp. 272-273, and McChesney's forthcoming article, "A Fractured Tradition: The Khwājah Abū Naṣr Pārsā Shrine in Western Writing and Image," which should put to rest the controversy surrounding the patrons and construction of his mausoleum in Balkh; see also Ḥasan Nithārī Bukhārī, *Mudhakkir-i aḥbāb*, ed. Sayyid Muhammad Fazlullah (Hyderabad, 1389/1969), pp. 319-321. For a Sayyid Pārsā al-Ḥusaynī, who was an inhabitant of Bukhara some time before 975/1568, and who may have been a descendant of Khwāja Muḥammad Pārsā, see E. È. Bertel's, ed., *Iz arkhiva sheikhov Dzhuibari: Materialy po zemel'nym i torgovym otnosheniiam Sr. Azii XVI veka* (Moscow-Leningrad, 1938), p. 199, doc. 157; Russian translation, P. P. Ivanov, *Khoziaistvo dzhuibarskikh sheikhov: K istorii feodal'nogo zemlevladeniia v Srednei Azii v XVI-XVII vv.* (Moscow-Leningrad, 1954), p. 188. Another possible descendant may have been Muḥammad Pārsā Khwāja Ṣudūr Muftī b. Qāżī al-qużāt Mīrzā Nāṣir Khwāja ʿInāyatullāh, whose round seal is imprinted in a compendium of manuscripts (*majmūʿa*), bearing the date 1273/1856-57 (see *SVR*, XI, p. 88). Could he be the same Muḥammad Pārsā who in 1868 was sent as an emissary by the Amīr of Bukhara to Calcutta and Istanbul to seek aid against Russia? For him, see A. B. Khalidov, "Rukopisi iz biblioteki Mukhammada Pārsā," *Peterburgskoe vostokovedenie*, 6 (1994), p. 516 (citing V. V. Bartol'd, *Sochineniia*, II/1 [Moscow,1963], p. 403).

[32] Ibn ʿArabshāh calls him "*al-khwāja al-kabīr al-mufassir al-ḥāfiẓ al-muḥaddith Muḥammad al-zāhid al-Bukhārī*" (*ʿAjā'ib al-maqdūr*, p. 468).

chain of transmission in the science of jurisprudence (*fiqh*) went back to the Maḥbūbīs, as had that of Ḥāfiẓ al-Dīn al-Kabīr. Through Abū al-Ṭāhir Muḥammad b. Muḥammad b. al-Ḥasan al-Ṭāhirī,[33] he transmitted from Ṣadr al-Sharīʿa II ʿUbaydullāh b. Masʿūd al-Maḥbūbī (d. 747/1346), who had studied with his grandfather, Tāj al-Sharīʿa Shams al-Dīn Maḥmūd b. Ṣadr al-Sharīʿa I Aḥmad b. ʿUbaydullāh (d. 636/1238), who had studied with his father, Ṣadr al-Sharīʿa I Aḥmad b. ʿUbaydullāh (d. 630/1232), who had studied with his father, Jamāl al-Dīn ʿUbaydullāh, who had studied with Imāmzāda,[34] who had studied with ʿImād al-Dīn al-Zaranjarī, who had studied with his father, Bakr al-Zaranjarī, who had studied with al-Ḥalvāʾī, who had studied with Abū ʿAlī al-Nasafī, who had studied with Muḥammad b. al-Fażl.[35] The importance that Khwāja Muḥammad Pārsā accorded to his connection with the Maḥbūbī tradition is underscored by the fact that he devoted a separate work to the genealogy of Ṣadr al-Sharīʿa II.[36]

Many important religious figures studied with or transmitted from Khwāja Muḥammad Pārsā. Ibn Ḥajar al-ʿAsqalānī (d. 852/1449) apparently met with him in Mecca, and Yaḥyā al-Aqṣarāʾī received authorization to transmit from him at Minā just before his death.[37] His well documented trip to Mecca involved meetings along the way with leading religious scholars such as the father of the Persian poet, ʿAbd al-Raḥmān Jāmī.[38] He is also mentioned as one of the authorities in the chains of transmission of the Herati shaykh, Jalāl al-Dīn al-Qāyinī, an important Ḥanafite teacher and traditionist active during the reign of the Timurid ruler, Shāhrukh.[39]

[33] In *al-Ḍawʾ al-lāmiʿ* (X, p. 20) he is called Abū Ṭāhir Muḥammad b. Abū al-Maʿālī Muḥammad b. Muḥammad b. al-Ḥusayn b. ʿAlī al-Ṭāhirī al-Khālidī al-Ūshī.

[34] I.e., Rukn al-Dīn Muḥammad b. Abū Bakr al-Muftī al-Bukhārī, for whom see *Tārīkh-i Mullāzāda*, pp. 68, 91.

[35] *al-Fawāʾid al-bahīya*, p. 160.

[36] Entitled *Nasab al-Shaykh al-Imām Mawlānā Ṣadr al-Sharīʿa* (see *SVR*, I, p. 123).

[37] *al-Ḍawʾ al-lāmiʿ*, X, p. 20.

[38] For a description of this trip, taken just before his death, see *Nafaḥāt al-uns*, ed. Tawḥīdīpūr, pp. 392-393, ed. ʿĀbidī, pp. 397-398. Jāmī was five years old at the time of the meeting.

[39] For him, see Subtelny and Khalidov, "Curriculum of Islamic Higher Learning," p. 220. He was the author of a book of advice on Islamic government, which he dedicated to the Timurid ruler, Shāhrukh (see my forthcoming article, "An Early

Khwāja Muḥammad Pārsā was a disciple and successor (*khalīfa*) of the eponymous founder of the Naqshbandī Sufi order, Bahā᾽ al-Dīn Naqshband (d. 791/1389), and it was from Bahā᾽ al-Dīn that he reputedly received his nickname, "Pārsā," meaning "chaste" or "devout."[40] Like so many members of the religious intelligentsia of his time, who were also Sufis (a point that cannot be overstressed for the period under discussion), he became embroiled in politics. Apparently, as the sole adherent of Bahā᾽ al-Dīn among the Bukharan *ʿulamā*, and as a proponent of the ideas of the Spanish-born mystic, Ibn ʿArabī, he received a cool reception from members of his own professional circle in Bukhara and was even forced to leave the city for a while.[41] According to an account in the Naqshbandī hagiographical work, *Rashaḥāt-i ʿayn al-ḥayāt*, Shāhrukh, whom he had supported in his succession struggles after the death of Temür, helped him to reestablish himself in Bukhara, and the growth of the political influence of the Naqshbandī order may be dated from this time.[42]

Khwāja Muḥammad Pārsā was the author of many important works on the Islamic religious sciences and Sufism, in both Arabic and Persian.[43] His works on Sufism and on early Naqshbandī figures, including Bahā᾽ al-Dīn, defined his role as the intellectual formulator of

---

Timurid Manual of Advice on Islamic Governance: The *Naṣā᾽iḥ-i Shāhrukhī* and its Author").

[40] *Rashaḥāt*, I, pp. 101-103. In later Timurid sources, such as the *Rashaḥāt-i ʿayn al-ḥayāt*, Khwāja Muḥammad Pārsā was viewed as the second successor of Bahā᾽ al-Dīn after ʿAlā᾽ al-Dīn ʿAṭṭār, but this is by no means certain, since the succession appears to have been left open, and both individuals subsequently founded their own respective Naqshbandī lines.

[41] See *Nafaḥāt al-uns*, ed. Tawḥīdīpūr, p. 396, ed. ʿĀbidī, p. 401; cf. *Rashaḥāt*, I, pp. 108-109.

[42] *Rashaḥāt*, I, p. 109; cf. Hamid Algar, "Naḳshbandiyya," *EI²*, VII, pp. 934-935, and Yuri Bregel, "Bukhara," *EIr*, IV, p. 516.

[43] For descriptions of his works, see Brockelmann, *Geschichte der arabischen Litteratur*, II, p. 264, No. 3c, and *Supplement*, II, p. 282, No. 3c; Storey-Bregel', *Persidskaia literatura*, I, pp. 118-119; *SVR*, III, Nos. 2394, 2420, 2421, 2426, 2427 and 2428; O. F. Akimushkin, *et al.*, *Persidskie i tadzhikskie rukopisi Instituta narodov Azii AN SSSR: Kratkii alfavitnyi katalog*, 2 pts. (Moscow, 1964), I, Nos. 666, 786, 4193, etc.; Khwāja Muḥammad b. Muḥammad Pārsā-yi Bukharā᾽ī, *Qudsīya*, ed. Aḥmad Ṭāhirī ʿIrāqī (Tehran, 1354/1975), esp. pp. 70-76; and Khalidov, "Rukopisi," p. 515. A complete bibliography of his works is clearly needed.

the nascent Naqshbandī movement.[44] His works include *Faṣl al-khiṭāb li-vaṣl al-aḥbāb*, an encyclopaedic compendium in Persian on Sufism and orthodox Muslim beliefs and practices, which became the definitive work on the subject in Central Asia; an extensive treatise on Sufi thought, entitled *Tuḥfat al-sālikīn* (also known as *Taḥqīqāt-i Khwāja Muḥammad Pārsā*);[45] *Risāla-i qudsīya*, a collection of the sayings of Bahāʾ al-Dīn Naqshband;[46] *Maqāmāt-i Khwāja* ʿAlāʾ al-Dīn ʿAṭṭār, the sayings of the first spiritual successor of Bahāʾ al-Dīn Naqshband; a Persian commentary on the Qurʾān, which was supposed to have comprised 100 volumes, only a few of which have survived;[47] several commentaries on individual chapters of the Qurʾān; a commentary and marginal notes to Ibn ʿArabī's *Fuṣūṣ al-ḥikam*;[48] a work entitled *al-Fuṣūl al-sitta*;[49] and others.[50] He was possibly also the author of a commentary on *al-Fiqh al-akbar* of Abū Ḥanīfa;[51] and of a

[44] For the best study of the role of Khwāja Muḥammad Pārsā in the Naqshbandī Sufi order, see Jürgen Paul, "Doctrine and Organization: The Khwājagān/ Naqshbandīya in the First Generation after Bahā'uddīn," *Anor*, 1 (Berlin: Das Arabische Buch, 1998), pp. 5 ff.

[45] See the lithograph edition: Muḥammad b. Muḥammad b. Maḥmūd al-Ḥāfiẓī al-Bukhārī, Pārsā, *Tuḥfat al-sālikīn* (Delhi, 1970).

[46] For reference to one published version, see note 43 above. This work would later be required reading for the disciples of Khwāja ʿUbaydullāh Aḥrār (see Jürgen Paul, *Die politische und soziale Bedeutung der Naqšbandiyya im Mittelasien im 15. Jahrhundert* [Berlin/New York: Walter de Gruyter, 1991], p. 65).

[47] For a contemporary reference to his *tafsīr*, see *ʿAjāʾib al-maqdūr*, p. 468. For one of the volumes of the supercommentary he wrote on this *tafsīr*, which also bears the seal of his library and is now in the Bibliothèque Nationale in Paris, see E. Blochet, *Catalogue des manuscrits arabes des nouvelles acquisitions (1884-1924)* (Paris, 1925), p. 242, No. 6349.

[48] See Khwāja Muḥammad Pārsā, *Qudsīya*, p. 73; and the edition, Khwāja Muḥammad Pārsā, *Sharḥ-i Fuṣūṣ al-ḥikam*, ed. Jalīl Misgar-nizhād (Tehran, 1366/ 1987).

[49] Mentioned in *al-Fawāʾid al-bahīya*, p. 160; see also Khwāja Muḥammad Pārsā, *Qudsīya*, p. 73.

[50] For other minor works by him, see *SVR*, I, No. 290, and IV, Nos. 3353 and 3418.

[51] For which see Subtelny and Khalidov, "Curriculum of Islamic Higher Learning," p. 226. It is not entirely certain whether he was the author of this work. In the *ijāza* discussed in this article, which dates from early 15th-century Herat, his name is given as Shams al-Dīn Muḥammad al-Ḥāfiẓī al-Bukhārī.

hagiographical work on the life of Bahāʾ al-Dīn Naqshband, entitled *Anīs al-ṭālibīn va ʿuddat al-sālikin*.[52]

There is an interesting anecdote in the *Rashaḥāt-i ʿayn al-ḥayāt*, which relates to Khwāja Muḥammad Pārsā's interest in and knowledge about books and libraries. When the senior traditionist and theologian of the early Timurid period, Shaykh Shams al-Dīn al-Jazarī, came to Samarqand to verify the chains of transmission of the traditionists of Transoxiana, some of Khwāja Muḥammad Pārsā's political opponents among the Bukharan *ʿulamā* asked al-Jazarī to verify his chains of transmission as well. Khwāja Muḥammad Pārsā was summoned to Samarqand to appear before an august assembly of religious scholars, which had been organized by al-Jazarī and the Shaykh al-Islām. Al-Jazarī asked Khwāja Muḥammad Pārsā to relate a certain tradition and to state his chains of transmission for it. After he had done so, al-Jazarī stated that he was unable to confirm the soundness of his chains of transmission. Khwāja Muḥammad Pārsā then related the tradition again, but with different chains of transmission, and these too were rejected by al-Jazarī. Khwāja Muḥammad Pārsā then asked al-Jazarī whether he considered a certain book on the traditions as authoritative. When the latter replied in the affirmative, he stated that the tradition in question had been recorded with those very same chains of transmission in that book, and that the book was in the Shaykh al-Islām's own library. He even provided the volume and page number, and described its location in the library. The book was brought before the assembly and the soundness of Khwāja Muḥammad Pārsā's chains of transmission was confirmed. This demonstration of clairvoyance was all the more astounding since the Shaykh al-Islām had apparently not even been aware that he possessed the book.[53]

[52] Also referred to as *Maqāmāt-i Khwāja Bahāʾ al-Dīn Naqshband* (see Khwāja Muḥammad Pārsā, *Qudsīya*, pp. 74-75, and Paul, *Die politische und soziale Bedeutung*, p. 9, n. 22 [citing A. T. Tagirdzhanov, *Opisanie tadzhikskikh i persidskikh rukopisei Vostochnogo otdela Biblioteki LGU*, I (Leningrad, 1962), pp. 286 ff.]).

[53] *Rashaḥāt*, I, pp. 106-108. For a discussion of this in the context of the early part of Ulūgh Beg's reign, see Bartol'd, *Sochineniia*, II/2, p. 122.

THE LIBRARY OF KHWĀJA MUḤAMMAD PĀRSĀ

Curiously enough, there are no references to the library of Khwāja Muḥammad Pārsā in the contemporary sources of the Timurid period. Our only sources of information about it are a late copy of a deed of endowment; the seal of the library, which was imprinted on books belonging to it; and inscriptions on the fly-leaves of books that had been donated to it.

The distinctive features of the library were that it was housed in a separate building and privately endowed. The independent library was by no means a widespread phenomenon in medieval Islam, although some scholars see the precedent for it in the *dār al-ʿilm* (or *dār al-kutub*) first founded in the 10th century, a good example of which was the library of the Buyid *vazīr*, Ṣābūr b. Ardashīr, in Baghdad.[54] Royal or private libraries had always been the norm,[55] and from the 11th century onward, libraries attached to *madrasa*s, which were intended primarily for the use of students and professors, predominated.[56] Contemporary or near-contemporary examples of annexed libraries are the *madrasa*-library (*kitābkhāna*) complex of Ulūgh Beg in

[54] See Youssef Eche, *Les bibliothèques arabes publiques et semi-publiques en Mésopotamie, en Syrie et en Égypte au moyen âge* (Damascus, 1967), pp. 67 ff., 102 ff., and 138 ff.; Johannes Pedersen, *The Arabic Book*, tr. Geoffrey French, ed. Robert Hillenbrand (Princeton: Princeton University Press, 1984), p. 123; and George Makdisi, *The Rise of Colleges: Institutions of Learning in Islam and the West* (Edinburgh: Edinburgh University Press, 1981), pp. 24-25 (for various other terms used for libraries), and esp. pp. 305 ff., where he questions Eche's conclusion that the *madrasa* took over the functions of the *dār al-ʿilm*.

[55] See, for example, Ulrich Haarmann, "The Library of a Fourteenth Century Jerusalem Scholar," *Der Islam*, 61/2 (1984), pp. 327-333; and Max Weisweiler, "Avicenna und die iranischen Fürstenbibliotheken seiner Zeit," in *Avicenna Commemoration Volume* (Calcutta, 1956), pp. 47-63.

[56] See Pedersen, *Arabic Book*, pp. 113 ff.; and Eche, *Les bibliothèques arabes*, pp. 265. In the opinion of Eche, the first Sunnī *madrasas* (the Niẓāmīya and the *madrasa* of Abū Ḥanīfa, both founded in 459/1066) were the direct successors of the Shīʿite *dār al-ʿilm*, which had been destroyed by the Saljuqs (Eche, *Les bibliothèques arabes*, p. 154). Libraries were frequently also attached to mosques, *khānqāhs*, caravanserais, and hospitals (see Yaḥyā Maḥmūd Saʿātī, *Vaqf va sākhtār-i kitābkhānahā-yi islāmī*, tr. Aḥmad Amīrī Shādmihrī [Mashhad: Āstān-i Quds-i Rażavī, 1374/1995], pp. 109 ff.).

Bukhara;[57] the *khānqāh*-library (*bayt al-kutub*) complex established by the Sufi shaykh, Zayn al-Dīn Khwāfī, in Herat;[58] the library of Gawharshād located in the *masjid-i jāmiᶜ* she built at the shrine of Imām Riżā in Mashhad;[59] and later, the library in the *madrasa* of Muḥammad Shībānī Khān in Samarqand (beginning of the 16th century).[60] An indication of how widespread the practice was of incorporating libraries into *madrasa*s is the fact that formulary manuals used by lawyers to draw up deeds of endowment usually contained a separate section on the document for a library (*kitābkhāna*) connected to a *madrasa*.[61]

The only other example of a freestanding library from the Timurid period appears to have been the one founded by Sulṭān Aḥmad Mīrzā in Herat.[62] An example from Bukhara from a much later period was the library founded in the second half of the 17th century, during the reign of the Ashtarkhanid ruler, Subḥān Qulī Khān.[63]

[57] Based on an inscription over the entrance, the building itself has been dated to 823/1420, or to 820/1417; see Lisa Golombek and Donald Wilber, *The Timurid Architecture of Iran and Turan*, 2 vols. (Princeton: Princeton University Press, 1988), II, p. 228.

[58] See Maḥmūd "Fāżil" Yazdī Muṭlaq, "Vaqfnāma-i Zayn al-Dīn Abū Bakr Khwāfī," *Mishkāt* (Mashhad), 22 (spring 1368/1989), pp. 196-198.

[59] For which see ᶜAzīzullāh ᶜUtāridī, *Tārīkh-i Āstān-i Quds-i Rażavī*, 2 vols. (Tehran, 1371/1993), II, p. 758.

[60] See R. G. Mukminova, *K istorii agrarnykh otnoshenii v Uzbekistane XVI v.: Po materialam "Vakf-name"* (Tashkent, 1966), p. 23.

[61] See for example the early 16th-century Persian legal formulary, *al-Javāmiᶜ al-ᶜalīya fī'l-vathā'iq al-sharᶜīya va'l-sijillāt al-marᶜīya*, compiled by the Ḥanafite jurist, ᶜAlī b. Muḥammad ᶜAlī al-Mukhtārī al-Khwārazmī al-Kubravī, MS Tashkent, Institut vostokovedeniia Akademii nauk Respubliki Uzbekistan, Inv. No. 9138, ff. 62b ff. For a description of the work, see *SVR*, VIII, pp. 313-317, No. 5872.

[62] He was the brother-in-law of the Timurid ruler of Herat, Sulṭān Ḥusayn-i Bāyqarā Mīrzā (see Ghiyāth al-Dīn b. Humām al-Dīn Khwāndamīr, *Khātima-i Khulāṣat al-akhbār fī aḥvāl al-akhyār*, in *Ma'āthir al-mulūk/Khātima-i Khulāṣat al-akhbār/Qānūn-i Humāyūnī*, ed. Mīr Hāshim Muḥaddith (Tehran, 1372/1994), p. 193; also Khwāndamīr, *Ma'āthir al-mulūk*, in *Ma'āthir al-mulūk*/etc., p. 177 (where it is stated that Sulṭān Aḥmad made many rare books *vaqf* for the library). See also *Mazārāt-i Harāt*, p. 181.

[63] See A. A. Semenov, "Sredneaziatskie rukopisnye fondy i vazhnost' ikh izucheniia," in *Materialy Pervoi vsesoiuznoi nauchnoi konferentsii vostokovedov v Tashkente 4-11 iiunia 1957 g.* (Tashkent, 1958), p. 913.

THE DEED OF ENDOWMENT

Like other religious, charitable, and educational institutions in medieval Islam, the library was dependent for its financial support on the pious endowment (*vaqf*).[64] Once the legal objections to the endowment of books, which were considered moveable and therefore impermanent property, had been overcome in the Ḥanafite legal school, the endowment of books became a regular feature.[65] Although the donor (*vāqif*) relinquished ownership of the properties he conveyed to *vaqf*, he still retained a considerable degree of control over their management and maintenance through the trusteeship (*tawliyat*) and through the conditions (*sharāʾiṭ*) he set in the deed of endowment (*vaqfīya*), which had to be notarized, witnessed, and registered with the appropriate judicial authorities.

The deed of endowment of Khwāja Muḥammad Pārsā's library has survived in a late 18th-century copy (see fig. 1).[66] It is unpublished, although it has been referred to by several scholars, most notably Ol'ga Sukhareva, who used it in her study on the urban history of Bukhara.[67] The document, which dates from 810/1407-08, is actually a

[64] For the first endowed libraries in Islam, see Eche, *Les bibliothèques arabes*, p. 101.

[65] For a discussion of Islamic legal opinions on the endowment of books, see Eche, *Les bibliothèques arabes*, pp. 68-74 and 301 ff.

[66] It is currently held in the Central State Archive of Uzbekistan; see *Vaqfīya-i kitābkhāna-i mutabarraka-i Ḥażrat-i Khwāja-i Pārsā*, MS Tashkent, Tsentral'nyi gosudarstvennyi arkhiv Respubliki Uzbekistan/Uzbekiston Respublikasi Markazii davlat arkhivi (= TsGA), Fond I-323, No. 55/14 (hereafter *Vaqfīya*). The document is described, although not entirely accurately, in [I. Miradylov], *Tsentral'nyi gosudarstvennyi arkhiv Uzbekskoi SSR, Fond I-323, Kollektsiia vakufnykh dokumentov* (typescript, Tashkent, 1983), opis' 1, kniga 1 (za 1535-1927gg.), No. 55/14.

[67] Sukhareva, *Kvartal'naia obshchina*, p. 220. It has also been referred to recently by Ashirbek Muminov and Shavasil Ziyadov, "L'horizon intellectuel d'un érudit du XVe siècle: Nouvelles découvertes sur la bibliothèque de Muḥammad Pârsâ," in *Patrimoine manuscrit et vie intellectuelle de l'Asie centrale islamique* (= *Cahiers d'Asie Centrale*, 7 [Tashkent/Aix-en-Provence, 1999]), ed. Ashirbek Muminov, Francis Richard, and Maria Szuppe, p. 80 and n. 15, although it does not appear that they actually consulted the document, since they cite as the reference for it also the document numbers of the endowment deeds for the *madrasa* (55/13) and the *khānqāh* (1291/16).

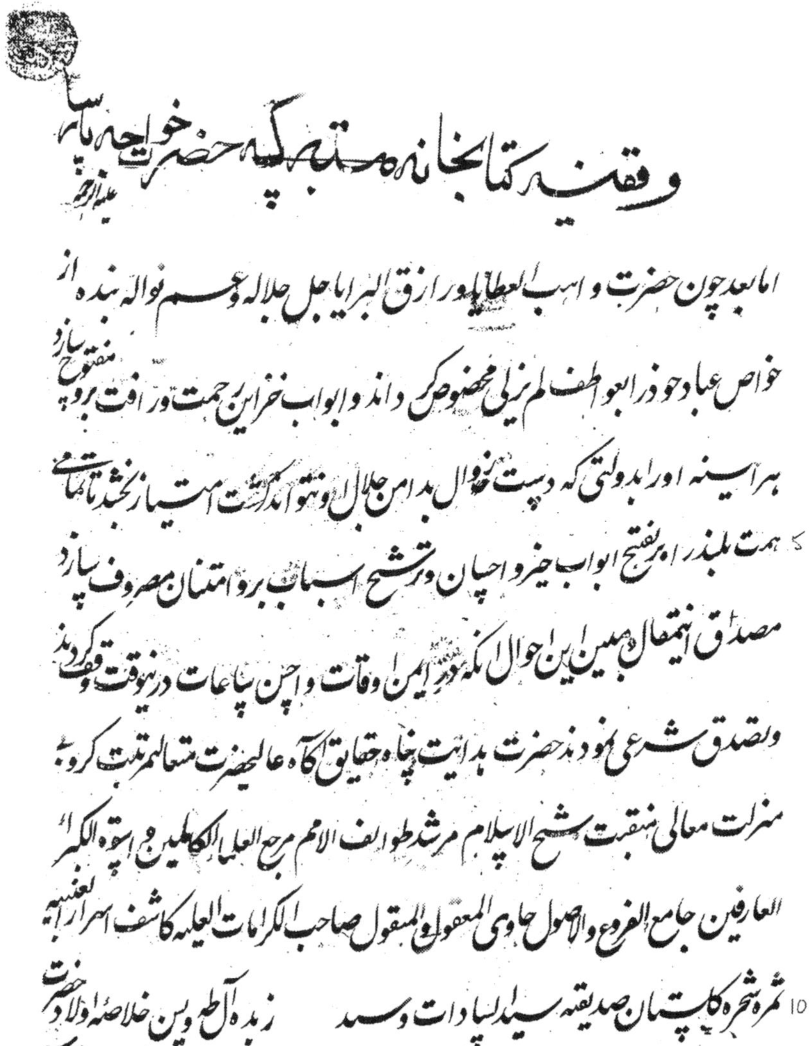

وقفیه کتابخانهٔ متبرکهٔ حضرت خواجه پارسا علیه الرحمه

اما بعد چون حضرت واهب العطایا و رازق البرایا جل جلاله و عم نواله بنده از
خواص عباد خود را بعواطف لم یزلی مخصوص کرداند و ابواب خزاین رحمت و رافت بروی مفتوح سازد
هر آینه او را بدولتی که دست زوال بدامن جلال او نتواند گذشت امتیاز بخشد تا تمامی
همت بلند را بر تفتیح ابواب خیر و احسان و ترشیح اسباب بر و امتنان مصروف سازد
مصداق این مقال مبین این احوال آنکه درین اوقات و احسن ساعات در نهوقت وقف کردند
و تصدق شرعی نمودند حضرت هدایت پناه حقایق آگاه عالیحضرت متعالی مرتبت گروهٔ
منزلت معالی منقبت شیخ الاسلام مرشد طوایف الامم مرجع العلماء الکاملین و اسوة الکبراء
العارفین جامع الفروع و الاصول حاوی المعقول و المنقول صاحب الکرامات العلیه کاشف اسرار الغیبیه
ثمرهٔ شجرهٔ کاپستان صدیقه سید السادات و سند زبدهٔ آل طه و یس خلاصهٔ اولاد حضرت
سید المرسلین ناصح زمرهٔ ملوک مرشد ارباب سلوک قطب الاولیاء غوث الاصفیاء ولدا قدس

Fig. 1: Deed of endowment of the library of Khwāja Muḥammad Pārsā in Bukhara (beginning)
Tashkent, Central State Archive of Uzbekistan, *Vaqf* Collection I-323, No. 55/14
(late 18th-century copy)

summary, or maybe even the summary of a summary, of a charter deed of endowment.[68]

Since the copy was made almost four hundred years after the date of the document, some inaccuracies have inevitably crept in. For example, several of the blank spaces that had been left in the text for the later insertion of names of villages and individuals were not filled in.[69] Most importantly, Khwāja Muḥammad Pārsā's name and the names of Maḥmūd al-Ḥāfiẓī and Ḥāfiẓ al-Dīn al-Kabīr, which in accordance with medieval Persian chancery practice appear only in the right margin of the document, with the corresponding space in the text being left blank,[70] were listed in reverse order from that in which they should actually occur in the text. To rectify this, the names in the margin and the blank spaces in the text were assigned corresponding numbers by the copyist.[71] When these are matched up, Khwāja Muḥammad Pārsā's filiation reads as follows: Khwāja Muḥammad Pārsā, the son of Khwāja Maḥmūd al-Ḥāfiẓī, the son of Imām Ḥāfiẓ al-Dīn al-Kabīr al-Mujtahid al-Bukhārī.[72]

According to the contents of the *vaqfīya*, the endowment was not just for a library (*kitābkhāna*), but also for a tomb (*mazār*), both of

[68] The date is not contained in the *vaqfīya* itself, but in the confirmatory document that immediately follows it and begins, "in the aforementioned year 810" (*Vaqfīya*, line 63). The copy too is undated, but it bears the seals of the Manghit ruler, Shāh Murād b. Dāniyāl (Amīr Maʿṣūm), who had many endowment deeds transcribed during his rule in Bukhara (1199-1215/1785-1800), so it can be dated to the late 18th century.

[69] Thus, *Vaqfīya*, lines 31 and 37.

[70] For this practice, which was probably intended to emphasize the names of key individuals that would otherwise have been difficult to discern on account of the long titles that usually preceded them, see L. Fekete, *Einführung in die persische Paläographie*, ed. G. Hazai (Budapest: Akadémiai Kiadó, 1977), doc. 84, pl. 200, and doc. 93, pl. 219 (where the name of the addressee appears in the top margin).

[71] *Vaqfīya*, opposite lines 11-14 and 37. Thus, the numbers 2, 3 and 4 beside the names in the right margin correspond to the similarly numbered blank spaces in the text.

[72] The latter is referred to as deceased at the time, while the formula following Khwāja Muḥammad Pārsā's name indicates that he was still alive. Even though the *vaqfīya* appears to provide another argument in support of the "Muḥammad b. Maḥmūd" variant of Khwāja Muḥammad Pārsā's full name, this should be viewed with extreme caution, as he was most certainly more than two generations removed from Ḥāfiẓ al-Dīn al-Kabīr (see p. 84 and notes 20 and 21 above).

which were in the same location.[73] While the name of the person buried in the tomb is not provided, judging from his honorific titles, he may very well have been Khwāja Muḥammad Pārsā's father, who is not mentioned in the *Tārīkh-i Mullāzāda* as having been buried in the Ḥāfiẓī family's burial place at Tall-i Bughrā Beg.[74] As for the library, the name of the individual to whom it belonged appears only in the right margin of the document. When the numbered blank space in the text is matched with its corresponding number in the margin, however, the name that appears is that of Imām Ḥāfiẓ al-Dīn al-Kabīr al-Mujtahid al-Bukhārī![75]

This means that the library associated with the name of Khwāja Muḥammad Pārsa had originally belonged to his illustrious Bukharan ancestor, Ḥāfiẓ al-Dīn al-Kabīr. The existence of a library connected with Ḥāfiẓ al-Dīn al-Kabīr is corroborated by recent findings by two researchers in Uzbekistan, Ashirbek Muminov and Shavasil Ziyadov, who discovered a *vaqf* inscription on the fly-leaf of a 13th/early 14th-century manuscript bearing the seal of Khwāja Muḥammad Pārsā's library, which states that the book had been donated by a private individual to the library (*khizānat al-kutub*) of Ḥāfiẓ al-Dīn al-Kabīr.[76] Furthermore, they found another such inscription on the fly-leaf of a manuscript, which records that in 672/1274 Ḥāfiẓ al-Dīn al-Kabīr himself donated a book to a library (*khizānat al-kutub*) that was connected with the Maḥbūbī family and that was intended for the use of the local *ʿulamā*.[77] While a direct link between these two libraries cannot be demonstrated, it may be assumed that Ḥāfiẓ al-Dīn al-Kabīr's library, which was in existence in the second half of the 13th century,

[73] *Vaqfīya*, lines 1-62, esp. 34-37.

[74] Compare the titles given to the unnamed individual with those applied to Muḥammad Pārsā's father in the first part of the *Vaqfīya*, lines 12-14.

[75] It may also be noted that the honorific titles he is given in the *vaqfīya* are very similar to those applied to him in *Tārīkh-i Mullāzāda*, p. 55.

[76] See Muminov and Ziyadov, "L'horizon intellectuel d'un érudit du XVe siècle," p. 80; for a description of the manuscript (Inv. No. 3256), see *SVR*, IV, pp. 321-322.

[77] For the *vaqf* inscription to this effect, which is in an uncatalogued manuscript in the Institute of Oriental Studies in Tashkent, see Muminov and Ziyadov, "L'horizon intellectuel d'un érudit du XVe siècle," p. 79 (although the epithets applied to the library, which are explained as referring to the Ṣadr family, actually belong to the Maḥbūbī and Burhān families).

had built upon an earlier one belonging to his Mahbūbī intellectual predecessors, and that Khwāja Muḥammad Pārsā's endowment was either an addition to or the renewal of an existing endowment that had been made for the library by his Ḥāfiẓī ancestor. There is nothing in the endowment deed that suggests it was Khwāja Muḥammad Pārsā who built the library.

The summary of the deed of endowment is followed by two documents, also in late 18th-century copies in the same hand: the first, dated 810/1407-1408, is a ruling confirming the validity of the endowment after a pro forma claim was made against it;[78] and the second, dated 12 Shaʿbān 992/19 August 1584, is a ruling on what appears to have been a real claim against the endowment, which confirmed the endowed status of the disputed properties.[79] This second document contains corroboration of the fact that the library had originally belonged to Ḥāfiẓ al-Dīn al-Kabīr, who although not named, is referred to by his well-known honorific title, "*khātim al-mujtahidīn*," that is, "the last *mujtahid*."[80]

LOCATION OF THE LIBRARY

The library is described in the endowment deed as being located in the old citadel (*ḥiṣār*) of Bukhara, in Dihqān Street or Quarter (Kūy-i Dihqān).[81] It was bounded on the east, west, and north by land belonging to the donor, and on the south by a public thoroughfare, most probably Dihqān Street.[82]

Dihqān (or Dihqānān) is mentioned as early as the 10th century in Narshakhī's *Tārīkh-i Bukhārā*,[83] and as late as the end of the 19th and

[78] *Vaqfīya*, lines 63-74.

[79] *Vaqfīya*, lines 75-89. The properties in question must have been donated either much earlier or after 810/1407-1408, since they are not mentioned in the *vaqfīya*.

[80] *Vaqfīya*, line 85. For Ḥāfiẓ al-Dīn al-Kabīr as the last *mujtahid*, see p. 83 above.

[81] *Vaqfīya*, line 37.

[82] *Vaqfīya*, lines 39-41.

[83] *Tārīkh-i Bukhārā*, p. 79; in his English translation of this work, R. N. Frye did not treat it as a toponym, but translated it simply as "the section of the *dihqāns*" (*The History of Bukhara* [Cambridge, Massachusetts: The Mediaeval Academy of America, 1954], p. 57). See also A. M. Belenitskii, *et al.*, *Srednevekovyi gorod Srednei Azii*

beginning of the 20th centuries in a register of the names of the quarters (*guzar*) of Bukhara from the chancery archive of the Qoshbegī (chief minister) of Bukhara.[84] According to the researches of Ol'ga Sukhareva on the historical topography of 19th-century Bukhara, the name of the quarter was changed to Mullā Payravī some time in the first half of the 20th century.[85]

The library was thus located in the eastern part of the city, in the Shahristān section (*jarīb*), northeast of the Goldsmiths' Bazar (Ṭāq-i Zargarān), one of the city's traditional orientation points.[86]

As a result of the misinterpretation of an inscription on the fly-leaf of a book donated to the library by Khwāja Muḥammad Pārsā himself, which refers to it as the "library of the abode of dervishes" (*kitābkhāna-i dār al-fuqarā'*), researchers have almost unanimously concluded that Khwāja Muḥammad Pārsā's library must have been housed in the *khānqāh* or dervish lodge that he also established in Bukhara.[87] But the *khānqāh*, which was adjacent to his *madrasa*, was situated in an altogether different part of the city—in the Khwāja Pārsā quarter, which had obviously been named after him and which was in the Kalābād section (*jarīb*) of the city, where Ḥāfiẓ al-Dīn al-Kabīr's tomb-shrine

(Leningrad, 1973), p. 250, and the map on p. 243; and Sukhareva, *Kvartal'naia obshchina*, p. 294.

[84] See *Upravlenie Kush-begi Èmira Bukharskogo*, MS, Tashkent, TsGA, Fond 126, opis' 1, No. 73. For a description of the register, and a reproduction of a page from it, see Sukhareva, *Kvartal'naia obshchina*, pp. 59-61 (Kūy-i Dihqānān is No. 101).

[85] Sukhareva, *Kvartal'naia obshchina*, pp. 220, 295.

[86] No. X on the schematic map in Sukhareva, *Kvartal'naia obshchina*, p. 206, and inside the front cover.

[87] For the text of this inscription, see *SVR*, IV, p. 141; also Muminov and Ziyadov, "L'horizon intellectuel d'un érudit du XVe siècle," p. 79. In this inscription, the library's location is given correctly as Kūy-i Dihqān. This misinterpretation was repeated in a recent article on the library, which was based on earlier articles by Ch. Baiburdi (1970) and O. F. Akimushkin (1990), who must have used the same reference in *SVR*; see Lola Dodkhudoeva, "La bibliothèque de Khwâja Mohammad Pârsâ," in *Boukhara-la-Noble* (= *Cahiers d'Asie Centrale*, 5-6 [1998]), pp. 127 ff., and notes 13 and 37. Muminov and Ziyadov also suggest in their recent article that "*Dār al-fuqarā'*" must have referred to "un foyer ou . . . un refuge pour les étudiants, les soufis itinérants et les voyageurs" (see their "L'horizon intellectuel d'un érudit du XVe siècle," n. 14).

was located.[88] Moreover, *dār al-fuqarāʾ* is not a term that is customarily used for a *khānqāh*, and in fact Khwāja Muḥammad Pārsā's *khānqāh* is not referred to as such in its deed of endowment. What is more likely is either that the library was formally called "*Dār al-fuqarā*ʾ" ("Abode of Dervishes library"),[89] or, if such a bold assumption might be made, that the reading should actually be "*Dār al-fuqahā*ʾ" (i.e., the library of "The College of Jurisprudents"), which would accord perfectly with the fact that the library had originally been intended for the use of the Bukharan *ʿulamā*.[90]

In interviews conducted with the older inhabitants of the Mullā Payravī (formerly Dihqān) quarter, Sukhareva recorded that they associated the remains of an ancient domed building in their neighborhood with Khwāja Muḥammad Pārsā, although they were not sure whether it had functioned as a place of retreat (*chillakhāna*), a primary school (*maktab*), or a library (*kitābkhāna*). At the turn of the 19th century, the building was still believed to house a tomb (*mazār*), a belief that would have been grounded in fact, as it will be recalled that the deed of endowment states that the endowment was for both a tomb and a library.[91] For this reason, the ruins of the library, like so many other

[88] The Kalābād section of the city is section (*jarīb*) No. XII on Sukhareva's schematic map (see Sukhareva, *Kvartal'naia obshchina*, p. 250 and inside front cover), while Muḥammad Pārsā's library was located in the Shahristān section (*jarīb*) no. X (see note 86 above). Copies of the endowment deeds of the *madrasa* and *khānqāh*, which clearly describe their location, are held in the Central State Archive of Uzbekistan in Tashkent (TsGA), Fond I-323, Nos. 55/13 and 1291/16, respectively. The *madrasa* was mentioned by Khanikoff in his list of the principal *madrasa*s of the city, ca. 1840 (see N. Khanikoff, *Bokhara: Its Amir and its People*, tr. Clement A. de Bode [London: James Madden, 1845], p. 109). Khwāja Muḥammad Pārsā also appears to have endowed a mosque in Bukhara; for its endowment deed, see TsGA, Fond I-323, No. 1291/17.

[89] The name would have been in keeping with Khwāja Muḥammad Pārsā's Sufi inclinations.

[90] On which see n. 77 above. The scribal error of *fuqarā*ʾ for *fuqahā*ʾ would have been all too easy to make. Unfortunately, I have not had the opportunity to verify the reading myself in the *vaqf* inscription in question in manuscripts in the Institute of Oriental Studies in Tashkent.

[91] Sukhareva, *Kvartal'naia obshchina*, p. 221. Local inhabitants also believed that Khwāja Muḥammad Pārsā's *madrasa* housed his tomb. It too became a cultic center and women would bring specially fried cakes here on feast days and take part in dancing sessions; see Sukhareva, *Kvartal'naia obshchina*, pp. 250-251.

ancient monuments in Central Asia, became a cultic center over which was hoisted the customary yak's tail standard.[92] When asked to identify the Mullā Payravī (lit., "The mullā with a following") after whom the quarter was renamed, the older inhabitants told Sukhareva that he had been a contemporary of Bahāʾ al-Dīn Naqshband's—an unmistakable allusion to Khwāja Muḥammad Pārsā.[93] By 1947, the building had become almost completely covered by wind-blown earth, with the result that only the top of the dome remained visible.[94]

CONDITIONS OF THE ENDOWMENT AND DESCRIPTION OF THE ENDOWED PROPERTIES

Among the conditions set by Khwāja Muḥammad Pārsā in the deed of endowment for the library was that he was to act as the trustee (*mutavallī*) of the endowment during his lifetime, after which his male descendants were to inherit the position; in the absence of male descendants, his female descendants were to assume the position; and in the absence of these, the chief *qāżī* of Bukhara was to become the trustee.[95] The trustee was to receive 20% of the revenues of the endowment; 40% was to be used to provide food for the poor during the two major Islamic feast days; and 40% was to be spent on the maintenance of the building and repair of the books.[96] Any surplus left over after the provision of food rations was to be used for the purchase of books on Qurʾānic exegesis (*tafsīr*), the Prophetic traditions (*ḥadīth*), and jurisprudence (*fiqh*).[97] The trustee was not to loan books out without a pledge of some sort (*giraw*), and he was not to allow books to be taken out of the city without a legally justifiable reason (*bī vajh-i sharʿī*).[98]

[92] Sukhareva, *Kvartal'naia obshchina*, p. 221.

[93] Sukhareva, *Kvartal'naia obshchina*, p. 221.

[94] Sukhareva, *Kvartal'naia obshchina*, pp. 220-221, 295.

[95] *Vaqfīya*, lines 41-45.

[96] *Vaqfīya*, lines 46-48.

[97] *Vaqfīya*, lines 49-50.

[98] For the practice of lending out books from libraries in the medieval western Islamic world, see Eche, *Les bibliothèques arabes*, pp. 221, 383 ff. The geographer Yāqūt boasted that he had been able to take out more than 200 volumes from a library in Marv without leaving a pledge (see Pedersen, *Arabic Book*, p. 128). The library probably also functioned as a scriptorium where manuscripts in its collection could be

Moreover, he was to make absolutely certain that books that had been loaned out were deposited back into the library.[99]

The properties endowed by Khwāja Muḥammad Pārsā consisted of six plots of land (*qiṭʿa zamīn*), which had previously been his private property, and which were located in various administrative districts of the Bukhara region (*vilāyat*): four plots in the villages of Hārūn, Kūl-i Jaʿfar, and Danīkak (?) in the district (*tūmān*) of Mīrābād; one in the village of Khārkash in the district of Shāfurkām; and one in the village of Sābān-i Ūrūs in the district of Khutfar; as well as a mill (*ṭāḥūna*) in the above-mentioned village of Hārūn.[100] Also belonging to the endowment was the village of Kījak (?), which was located in the Kām-i Abū Muslim district.[101]

THE SEAL AND CONTENTS OF THE LIBRARY

The imprint of a distinctive, almond-shaped seal in books belonging to the *vaqf* confirms the existence of the library, and also makes it possible to determine the kinds of books it contained, particularly at a later date (see fig. 2).[102] This seal, which bears the inscription, "Endowment *ex libris* Khwāja Muḥammad Pārsā" (*vaqf az kutub-i Khwāja Muḥammad Pārsā*),[103] or "Belonging to the endowment of Khwāja Pārsā Ibn Maḥmūd al-Bukhārī" (*vaqf-i Khwāja-i Pārsā Ibn Maḥmūd al-Bukhārī*),[104] was in some cases imprinted on every single page of a book.[105] The use of seals in books belonging to an endowed library was a common practice in the Islamic world.[106] Another

---

copied by patrons on the premises; for this function of the 'public' library, see Eche, *Les bibliothèques arabes*, p. 378.

[99] *Vaqfīya*, lines 50-52.

[100] *Vaqfīya*, lines 14-34.

[101] *Vaqfīya*, line 78.

[102] Some of the Russian references have described this seal as "diamond-shaped" (*rombovidnaia*) and even "oval;" see *SVR*, I, p. 188; II, p. 18; III, p. 153; IV, p. 196; cf. also Khalidov, "Rukopisi," p. 507.

[103] See, for example, *SVR*, IV, p. 188, No. 3047.

[104] See, for example, *SVR*, II, p. 18, and IV, p. 188, No. 3048.

[105] For examples, see *SVR*, IV, p. 228, No. 3102, and p. 323, No. 3258.

[106] See Sāʿātī, *Vaqf*, pp. 148-50. Another example from Bukhara is contained in a late 16th-century deed of endowment for the library of a *madrasa*, which states as one

Fig. 2: Seal of the library of Khwāja Muḥammad Pārsā, containing the date 1255/1839-40

common practice was to include an inscription on the fly-leaf of a book, which stated that it had been conveyed to *vaqf*, as in the case of a book that had been donated to the library by Khwāja Muḥammad Pārsā himself.[107]

Some of the seals of the library contain dates, which in all known cases are from the first half of the 13th/19th century: 1224/1809-10,

---

of the conditions that the librarian was to imprint new books with the seal of the *vaqf*, which contained the name of the donor; see B. Kazakov, "Kollektsiia istoricheskikh dokumentov Bukharskogo gosudarstvennogo arkhitekturno-khudozhestvennogo muzeia-zapovednika," in *Iz istorii kul'turnogo naslediia Bukhary*, ed. È. V. Rtveladze (Tashkent, 1990), p. 68. For the practice in the Ottoman empire, see Günay Kut and Nimet Bayraktar, *Yazma eserlerde vakıf mühürleri* (Ankara, 1984). Unfortunately, there is no information about the seal of Khwāja Muḥammad Pārsā's library in the otherwise valuable study by G. N. Kurbanov on Bukharan seals, *Bukharskie pechati XVII-nachala XX vekov* (Tashkent, 1987).

[107] See, for example, *SVR*, IV, p. 141. Such inscriptions sometimes even outlined the conditions of the endowment; see Eche, *Les bibliothèques arabes*, pp. 310 ff.

1238/1822-23, 1239/1823-24, 1250/1834-35, 1255/1839-40, and 1259/1843.[108] These late dates pose a problem. Do they represent the dates on which books (many of which are much earlier copies) were acquired for the library? Or were books that already belonged to the library simply imprinted with the library's seal on those dates? Both explanations are possible. Supporting the former is the fact that two books, which are imprinted with seals containing the date 1239/1823-24 (one of which is a 14th-century copy), also have inscriptions on their fly-leaves that state that they had been purchased at that time out of the revenues of the village of Khutfar, a property which is known to have belonged to the endowment.[109] Supporting the latter is a fly-leaf inscription on a book copied in the 13th century by a member of the Ḥāfiẓī family, which was donated to the library by Khwāja Muḥammad Pārsā, and later imprinted with the seal of the library, containing the date 1255.[110]

It is unfortunate that the library's charter deed of endowment has not been preserved, because it would no doubt have contained a complete catalogue of books.[111] Given the problems discussed above, it is extremely difficult to reconstruct the contents of the library during Khwāja Muḥammad Pārsā's time; however, it is possible to do so for the 19th century, on the basis of books that had been imprinted with the seal of the library. A comprehensive survey of such manuscripts was first conducted by Anas B. Khalidov, who was able to identify at least 57 manuscripts dating from all periods, the oldest being a copy of a work on *fiqh* by al-Dabūsī, entitled *Taqwīm al-adilla fī'l-uṣūl*, dated

[108] See, for example, *SVR*, II, p. 18; IV, pp. 59, 140, 188, 196, 201, 229, 230, 281; XI, pp. 89, 122, etc.; cf. Khalidov, "Rukopisi," p. 507, and Muminov and Ziyadov, "L'horizon intellectuel d'un érudit du XVe siècle," pp. 85-92.

[109] See *SVR*, IV, p. 229, No. 3102, and p. 230, No. 3103. For Khutfar, see p. 102 above (although in the 15th century it was a district [*tūmān*], and not a village). In both cases, the books were purchased for a quantity of grain from Amīr Ḥaydar, who could only have been the reigning Manghit Amīr of Bukhara, Ḥaydar Tūra (1800-1826).

[110] *SVR*, IV, pp. 140-141, No. 3123 (the description of the seal is incomplete); see also Muminov and Ziyadov, "L'horizon intellectuel d'un érudit du XVe siècle," p. 87.

[111] See Eche, *Les bibliothèques arabes*, pp. 104, 315 ff. Such a catalogue is contained in the deed of endowment of the library of Ulūgh Beg's *madrasa* in Bukhara (for the reference to which see n. 132 below).

487/1094;[112] a copy of a Qur'ānic commentary, dated 491/1098;[113] and a copy of al-Ghazālī's *Tahāfut al-falāsifa*, dated 555/1160.[114] It is reasonably safe to assume that many others remain to be identified, as a recent update on the contents of the library, which has brought the total number of manuscripts to 121, has demonstrated.[115] None of these manuscripts are currently in Bukhara. The majority are in the Biruni Institute of Oriental Studies in Tashkent; others are in the Institute of Oriental Studies in St. Petersburg; the Bibliothèque Nationale in Paris;[116] Kazan University Library; the Russian State Library in Moscow; and other locations.

Khalidov determined that the subject matter covered by the manuscripts belonged primarily to the religious sciences of *fiqh*, *tafsīr*, and *ḥadīth*, which would have been in conformity with the conditions set by the donor.[117] It would also have reflected the Ḥāfiẓī family's professional interests in jurisprudence and the Prophetic traditions. In fact, inasmuch as the books that have been identified as belonging to the library can be said to be truly representative of its contents, books on *fiqh* predominated in the collection. Included among the titles are many of the canonical texts of Ḥanafite jurisprudence, some of which were authored by members of the Burhān and Maḥbūbī families, such as *Tatimma al-fatāwā*,[118] *Sharḥ al-sunna*,[119] *Taysīr*

[112] See Khalidov, "Rukopisi," p. 510; and *SVR*, IV, p. 184.

[113] Khalidov, "Rukopisi," p. 508.

[114] Khalidov, "Rukopisi," p. 512. This is an extremely early copy, being dated only about fifty years after Ghazālī's death.

[115] See Muminov and Ziyadov, "L'horizon intellectuel d'un érudit du XVe siècle," pp. 79, 85 ff. (for the list of manuscripts held only in the Institute of Oriental Studies in Tashkent, some of which have not yet been described in the catalogue of the collection). Khalidov's original 57 manuscripts had earlier already been increased to 62; see Val. V. Polosin and Efim A. Rezvan, "The Asiatic Museum Project: 1. Data-Base on Muslim Seals," *Manuscripta Orientalia* (St. Petersburg/Helsinki) 1/1 (1995), p. 55.

[116] All are from the Decourdemanche collection, and all bear seals of the *vaqf* with the date 1255 A.H.

[117] See pp. 101-102 above.

[118] See *SVR*, IV, p. 196.

[119] *SVR*, IV, p. 139.

fī'l-tafsīr,[120] *Kitāb al-uṣūl,*[121] *Minhāj al-wuṣūl ilā ʿilm al-uṣūl,*[122] and *al-Hidāya.*[123]

But there were also books on other subjects, such as history (including a unique and anonymous work on the history of the caliphs, written at the beginning of the 5th/11th century);[124] Arabic literature (including the *Maqāmāt* of Ḥarīrī);[125] Arabic grammar (including a work by al-Thaʿālibī copied by Khwāja Muḥammad Pārsā himself);[126] Sufism, with a focus on the works of the 11th-century Hanbalite traditionist of Herat, ʿAbdullāh Anṣārī, particularly his *Manāzil al-sāʾirīn;*[127] Greek, particularly Aristotelian, philosophy;[128] and even mathematics and astronomy.[129] Since the subject matter usually determined the choice of language in medieval Islamic scholarship, most of the books were in Arabic, with only a few in Persian.[130]

It would appear that the subjects covered by the contents of such an 'independent' library were broader than those of a *madrasa* library, especially in the sensitive area of the "foreign sciences," such as Greek

[120] *SVR*, IV, p. 56.

[121] *SVR*, IV, p. 177.

[122] *SVR*, IV, p. 281.

[123] *SVR*, IV, p. 217. For references to some of the preceding works, see Subtelny and Khalidov, "Curriculum of Islamic Higher Learning," esp. pp. 227 ff.

[124] Khalidov, "Rukopisi," p. 513.

[125] Khalidov, "Rukopisi," p. 514.

[126] See Khalidov, "Rukopisi," p. 514.

[127] Khalidov, "Rukopisi," p. 512 (although his comment that works on Sufism are poorly represented is not entirely justified); also *SVR*, III, p. 153, No. 2128 (a page from this, containing the seal of the library, is reproduced on p. 155), and No. 2129. For the surge in interest in Anṣārī's works during the early Timurid period, see Maria Eva Subtelny, "The Cult of ʿAbdullāh Anṣārī under the Timurids," *Gott ist schön und Er liebt die Schönheit / God is Beautiful and He Loves Beauty: Festschrift in Honour of Annemarie Schimmel*, ed. Alma Giese and J. Christoph Bürgel (Bern: Peter Lang, 1994), esp. pp. 400-403.

[128] Khalidov, "Rukopisi," pp. 512-513.

[129] See Moscow, Russian State Library, Collection 726, No. 1, 203 ff. (on which see Khalidov, "Arabic Manuscripts" [forthcoming]). See also *SVR*, VI, No. 4289.

[130] Khwāja Muḥammad Pārsā wrote mainly in Persian himself, but he strongly favored the Arabic language. See his untitled treatise which deals with this subject in *SVR*, IV, p. 381, No. 3353; also Khalidov, "Rukopisi," p. 515.

philosophy.[131] By way of contrast, a 17th-century deed of endowment for the library of Ulūgh Beg, which was attached to his *madrasa* in Bukhara, clearly stipulated that under no circumstances were books on the "sciences of the philosophers" (*ʿulūm-i falāsifa*) to be added to the collection,[132] thus affirming the madrasa's traditional bias in favor of the religious sciences, and its hostility toward speculative thought, including philosophy and astronomy.[133]

As already concluded, the books that constituted the core of the collection must have belonged to Khwāja Muḥammad Pārsā's ancestor, Ḥāfiẓ al-Dīn al-Kabīr. Khwāja Muḥammad Pārsā undoubtedly added many books to the library during his lifetime,[134] and others were purchased after his death out of the income of the endowment.[135] Khalidov speculated that some of the early manuscripts must have belonged to a library collection from an important pre-Mongol center, such as Marv.[136] This is entirely possible, and the agents of the transfer of these books could have been members of the Burhān family of Bukhara, who were known to have had a close connection to Marv and who were the predecessors of the Maḥbūbīs in the Ḥāfiẓī family's chains of transmission.[137]

[131] This had also been true of the Arabic *dār al-ʿilm*; see Eche, *Les bibliothèques arabes*, pp. 98-99, 106, and Makdisi, *Rise of Colleges*, pp. 24 ff.

[132] MS Tashkent, TsGA, Fond I-323, No. 1195/3 (the deed is dated 1054/1644-45, and it also contains the later date of 1199/1784-85).

[133] On this view see Eche, *Les bibliothèques arabes*, pp. 267, 298; and Pedersen, *Arabic Book*, p. 125. This was also true of private libraries donated to such religious institutions as mosques; see Doris Behrens-Abouseif, "The Waqf of a Cairene Notable in Early Ottoman Cairo: Muḥibb al-Dīn Abū al-Ṭayyib, Son of a Physician," in *Le Waqf dans l'espace islamique: Outil de pouvoir socio-politique*, ed. Randi Deguilhem (Damascus: Institut Français de Damas, 1995), p. 131.

[134] For example, a copy of *Sharḥ al-sunna* by al-Baghawī, which contains an inscription to this effect, possibly in Muḥammad Pārsā's own handwriting; see *SVR*, IV, p. 141, No. 2985.

[135] For example, two copies of *Ghāyat al-bayān wa nādirat al-zamān fī ākhir al-awān* were purchased in this way; see p. 104 and n. 109 above.

[136] See Khalidov, "Rukopisi," p. 516 (where he cites as proof a book belonging to Muḥammad Pārsā's library, which contained annotations made in Marv in the early 13th century). See also A. B. Khalidov, *Arabskie rukopisi i arabskaia rukopisnaia traditsiia* (Moscow, 1985), pp. 245-247 (based on an account in Yāqūt's *Muʿjam al-buldān*).

[137] See Pritsak, "Āl-i Burhān," p. 86.

THE FATE OF THE LIBRARY

Possibly founded as early as the 13th century, the library associated with Khwāja Muḥammad Pārsā during the 15th century was still very much a going concern in the 16th.[138] It appears that during this time the library also served as a kind of central archive for important legal documents. By way of illustration, the deed of endowment of the congregational mosque of Balkh, which is dated 947/1540, stipulated that one of seven copies that were to be made of it was to be deposited in "the library of His Excellency Khwāja Muḥammad Pārsā" in Bukhara.[139] This underscores the important function of such independent "public" libraries in the medieval Islamic world, which served not only as repositories for manuscripts and even scientific instruments, but also as archives for legal documents.[140]

The library must still have been in existence in the late 18th century, since the summary of the endowment deed under discussion dates from that period.[141] That it was still functioning in the first half of the 19th century—at least until the 1840s—is attested by the latest known date to be inscribed in its seal: 1259/1843.[142]

During the reign of Amīr Muẓaffar (1860-68), however, an attempt was made to liquidate privately endowed libraries and to deposit their contents in the state treasury. The motives for this are unclear. Some sources state that the Amīr was acting under pressure from the chief *qāżī* (*Qāżī kalān*), Ṣadr al-Dīn; others that it was the Amīr himself who was responsible, since he wanted to do away with books that contained potentially subversive ideas. Whatever the reason, books from some privately endowed libraries ended up in the chancery of the chief *qāżī*

[138] This is attested by the abovementioned confirmatory ruling of 992/1584 which follows the endowment deed.

[139] MS Tashkent, TsGA, Fond I-323, No. 1216, line 174. The library is referred to as a *katībkhāna* [*sic*]. I am indebted to Robert McChesney for this reference (see now the contribution of McChesney in the present volume, pp. 187-243 [DD]). It will be recalled that the Ilkhanid ruler, Ghāzān Khān, also had stipulated that seven copies were to be made of his famous *vaqfīya* and deposited at sites in various cities, including the Kaʿba in Mecca, the Dār al-Quḍāt in Tabriz and Medina, etc.

[140] On this see also Eche, *Les bibliothèques arabes*, p. 299.

[141] See p. 94 above.

[142] See p. 104 above.

or in the library of the Amīr.[143] This was a difficult period in the history of *Bukhārā-yi sharīf.* At a time when other centers of Islamic learning in the east, such as Kazan and Baku, were undergoing a cultural revival in the new climate of Islamic educational reform, Bukhara became a closed city, and the learning with which it had been synonymous became ossified in a scholastic preoccupation with commentary and super-commentary, and jealously guarded by a powerful religious elite.

At the same time, it is also possible that, by the end of the 19th century, the trusteeship of the library, like that of many ancient endowments, had, in the absence of eligible descendants of the donor, devolved upon the chief *qāżī* of Bukhara in accordance with a standard condition found in endowment deeds.[144] Moreover, if the endowment had, through mismanagement or for other reasons, dwindled to the point where it could no longer sustain the library, the chief *qāżī*, as its trustee, would have had the legal right to liquidate it. If this was the fate of Khwāja Muḥammad Pārsā's library, the building must already have fallen into ruin by the late 19th century, and in fact, as already mentioned, only vestiges of it remained by the 1940's.

But what became of the books? No doubt a good many must simply have been dispersed. In his survey of the situation of *vaqf* holdings in the Turkestan region in the 19th century, V. P. Nalivkin, a well-informed Russian government official, stated that there were very few libraries still in existence at the beginning of the 1890's that had been attached to famous *madrasa*s, and that judging from their deeds of endowment, the contents of the surviving ones had already been plundered long ago.[145] This may have been the case with the library of Khwāja Muḥammad Pārsā, as certain precious manuscripts bearing

[143] See Semenov, "Sredneaziatskie rukopisnye fondy," p. 913 (the reason given is that the chief *qāżī*, who was not characterized by great learning, apparently wanted to do away with the books on which fellow members of the *ʿulamā* based their superiority over him in disputations); see also A. I. Kormilitsyn, *Rukopisnye kollektsii i biblioteki na territorii Uzbekistana èpokhi Srednevekov'ia* (Tashkent, 1993), pp. 29, 37-38.

[144] For this condition in the endowment deed of Khwāja Muḥammad Pārsā's library, see p. 101 above.

[145] V. P. Nalivkin, "Polozhenie vakufnogo dela v Turkestanskom krae do i posle ego zavoevaniia," *Ezhegodnik Ferganskoi oblasti* (Skobelev), 3 (1904), p. 7. The region, which came under Russian occupation after 1886, did not, however, include Bukhara.

its seal were recorded as having been purchased on the Bukharan market.[146]

After the abolition of the Bukharan khanate in 1920, the subsequent liquidation of its successor state, the Bukharan People's Soviet Republic, and the creation of the Uzbek S.S.R. in 1924, a concerted effort was made by the Soviet authorities to centralize all library and manuscript holdings. What remained of Khwāja Muḥammad Pārsā's library would already have been transferred earlier to the Bukharan Central Library, and then in the 1930's to Tashkent, the new capital of the Uzbek S.S.R. (possibly via Samarqand, the first capital). It must have been in this way that most of the books that can be identified as having belonged to Khwāja Muḥammad Pārsā's library ended up in the Tashkent State Public Library, all the Islamic manuscript holdings of which were transferred in 1943 to the new Institute for the Study of Oriental Manuscripts (since 1950 the Biruni Institute of Oriental Studies of the Academy of Sciences of Uzbekistan), which became the chief repository of Persian and Arabic manuscripts in Central Asia, the largest collection of Islamic manuscripts in the former Soviet Union, and one of the finest collections in the world. Needless to say, manuscripts imprinted with the seal of Khwāja Muḥammad Pārsā's library are among its most valuable holdings.[147]

[146] See Dodkhudoeva, "La bibliothèque de Khwâja Mohammad Pârsâ," p. 128; and Khalidov, "Arabic Manuscripts" (forthcoming). Compare the dismemberment of the famous Ḍiyāʾīya library in Damascus in the 15th century (Eche, *Les bibliothèques arabes*, pp. 234-235).

[147] See *SVR*, I, pp. 5-6; Semenov, "Sredneaziatskie rukopisnye fondy," p. 915; "Arkhivy Uzbekistana za 40 let," in *Arkhivnyi Otdel MVD UzSSR, Nauchno-metodicheskii biulleten'*, 2-3 (Tashkent, 1958), p. 4; M. A. Akhunova and B. V. Lunin, *Istoriia istoricheskoi nauki v Uzbekistane: Kratkii ocherk* (Tashkent, 1970), p. 57 (where it is stated that, after 1933, many other private libraries were consolidated in the Tashkent State Public Library); Anas b. Khalidov, "Collections of Islamic Manuscripts in the Former Soviet Union and their Cataloguing," in *The Significance of Islamic Manuscripts: Proceedings of the Inaugural Conference of al-Furqān Islamic Heritage Foundation*, ed. John Cooper (London: Al-Furqān Islamic Heritage Foundation, 1992), esp. pp. 32-34; Kormilitsyn, *Rukopisnye kollektsii*, esp. pp. 28 ff.; and most recently, Ashirbek Muminov, "Fonds nationaux et collections privées de manuscrits en écriture arabe de l'Ouzbékistan," in *Patrimoine manuscrit et vie intellectuelle*, ed. Muminov, *et al.*, p. 18.

CONCLUSION

This episode in library history is instructive in that it demonstrates that medieval libraries, such as the library of Khwāja Muḥammad Pārsā and the Ḥāfiẓī family of Bukhara, which functioned for at least half a millennium, preserved books and even documents from much earlier periods, that would otherwise have been lost to posterity. Thus, the preservation of ancient Islamic manuscripts cannot be said to have been the achievement exclusively of European scholarship, as is sometimes claimed (although not entirely without justification), but credit is also due to scholars and bibliophiles like Khwāja Muḥammad Pārsā and his ancestors and intellectual predecessors, who flourished in the climate of learning and scholarship that characterized medieval Bukhara and who contributed so much to the important role it played in the formation of Islamic civilization.

NAQSHBANDĪ APPEALS TO THE HERAT COURT:

A PRELIMINARY STUDY OF TRADE AND PROPERTY ISSUES

Jo-Ann Gross

The College of New Jersey

Scholarship on the Naqshbandī *ṭarīqa* in Timurid Central Asia has demonstrated the existence of close ties between Sufi shaykhs and the state. The factors concerning the basis of these ties include the authority of Naqshbandī shaykhs that fostered a closeness based on prestige, charisma, and spiritual efficacy; the political and economic influence enjoyed by Naqshbandī shaykhs, which was related to the proliferation of *vaqf* endowments and the prominent role played by shaykhs in the local economy; and the worldly thrust of the Naqshbandīya, which encouraged active participation of Sufis in the economy and body politic.[1] One aspect of Naqshbandī-state relations that has not been explored is the active role of prominent shaykhs in directing petitions to rulers and court officials on behalf of individuals, beliefs, and modes of conduct. The *Majmūʿa-i murāsalāt* (also known, from its Russian name, as the "Navāʾī Album"), a corpus of letters in Persian compiled by ʿAlī Shīr Navāʾī (d. 1501), is a valuable source for the study of the appeals process in the late Timurid period, particularly since all of the letters

[1] See Jo-Ann Gross, "Authority and Miraculous Behavior: Reflections on *Karāmāt* Stories of Khwāja ʿUbaydullāh Aḥrār," in *The Legacy of Mediaeval Persian Sufism*, ed. Leonard Lewisohn (London: Khaniqahi Nimatullahi Publications/School of Oriental and African Studies, 1992), pp. 159-172; *idem*, "Multiple Roles and Perceptions of a Sufi Shaikh: Symbolic Statements of Political and Religious Authority," in *Naqshbandis: Cheminements et situation actuelle d'un ordre mystique musulman* (Actes de la Table Ronde de Sèvres, 2-4 mai 1985), ed. Marc Gaborieau, Alexandre Popovic, and Thierry Zarcone (Istanbul/Paris: Éditions Isis, 1990; Varia Turcica XVIII), pp. 109-121; *idem*, "The Economic Status of a Timurid Sufi Shaykh: A Matter of Conflict or Perception?" *Iranian Studies*, 21/1-2 (1988), pp. 84-104; *idem*, "Khoja Ahrar: A Study of the Perceptions of Religious Power and Prestige in the Late Timurid Period," Ph.D. dissertation (New York University, 1982); Jürgen Paul, *Die politische und soziale Bedeutung der Naqšbandiyya in Mittelasien im 15. Jahrhundert* (Berlin: Walter de Gruyter, 1991); *idem*, "Forming a Faction: The *Ḥimāyat* System of Khwaja Ahrar," *International Journal of Middle East Studies*, 23 (1991), pp. 533-548.

were directed to the Herat court.[2] The *Majmūʿa* includes 594 letters, 337 of which belong to ʿAbd al-Raḥmān Jāmī and were published in partial Russian translation and Persian facsimile by Asam Urunbaev in 1982.[3] Of the remaining 257 letters, 128 are those of Khwāja ʿUbaydullāh Aḥrār, and 129 letters are those of Aḥrār's associates, including several of his disciples.[4]

[2] This study is based on MS No. 2178 at the Institute of Oriental Studies of the Academy of Sciences of the Republic of Uzbekistan (Institut vostokovedeniia Akademii nauk Respubliki Uzbekistan, hereafter "IVANRUz"). Two copies of the manuscript were made by I. Adilov in 1939 (MSS Nos. 4145 and 5136). Asam Urunbaev, of the Institute of Oriental Studies, has worked closely with this collection for over thirty years; the enumeration system for the letters used in the present article lists the number assigned by him first, followed by the original number in the manuscript. Although some of the letters do not include a named addressee, it is often possible to discern the addressee from the content of the letter or from the titles used. Many letters are addressed to ʿAlī Shīr Navāʾī; others are addressed to ʿAbd al-Raḥmān Jāmī or to Sulṭān Ḥusayn Bāyqarā. The corpus of letters was compiled between 1490 and 1495 at the Timurid court of Herat; see A. Urunbaev, ed., *Pis'ma-avtografi Abdarrakhmana Dzhami iz 'Alboma Navoi'* (Tashkent: Fan, 1982), pp. 3-37.

[3] Urunbaev, ed., *Pis'ma-avtografi*. A Dārī edition was published in Kabul in 1986 (*Abdur-Rahman Jami's Autograph Letters from the Murraqqa of Mir Ali Sher Nawayi*, ed. A. Urunbaev; collaboration and introduction by Mayel Herawi [Kabul, 1986]); a Tajik edition has also appeared (*ʿAbd al-Raḥmān, Nāmahā /Abdarrakhman Dzhami, Pis'ma*, ed. Asomiddin Urunbaev and Asror Rakhmonov [Dushanbe: Donish, 1989]), and a Persian edition has recently been issued (*Nāmahā va munshaʾāt-i Jāmī*, ed. ʿIṣām al-Dīn Ūrūnbāyif and Asrār Raḥmānūf [Tehran: Mīrāth-i Maktūb, 1378/2000]). The letters of Jāmī are a rich source for late Timurid social and economic history. Many of the letters addressed to ʿAlī Shīr Navāʾī or Ḥusayn Bāyqarā are petitions written by Jāmī on behalf of other individuals concerning taxes, endowments, and other financial concerns.

[4] The coauthored publication of an annotated English translation, with original Persian text, of the 257 letters of Aḥrār, prepared by Asam Urunbaev and myself, is forthcoming; I wish to acknowledge the National Endowment for the Humanities for a grant that supported the research for this project. The *Majmūʿa-i murāsalāt* is distinctive from other collections of Sufi correspondence, such as those of the Indian Sufi, Shaykh Aḥmad Sirhindī, published by Muhammad Abdul Haq Ansari (see his *Sufism and Sharīʿah: A Study of Shaykh Aḥmad Sirhindī's Effort to Reform Sufism* [Leicester: The Islamic Foundation, 1986]), those of the Bihārī saint, Sharaf al-Dīn Manīrī, published by Paul Jackson (*Sharafuddin Maneri: The Hundred Letters*, tr. Paul Jackson [New York, 1980]), or those of Nur al-Dīn Isfarāyinī and ʿAlāʾ al-Dawla Simnānī, published by Hermann Landolt (*Correspondance spirituelle échangée entre Nuroddin Esfarayeni (ob. 717/1317) et son disciple 'Alaoddawleh Semnani (ob. 736/1336)* [Tehran/Paris, 1972]). This is not to deny that many of the letters in the *Majmūʿa* display a profound attachment to Islamic law and the goodness of the spiritual path; however, the preoccupation with the profane world of the court, the land, the

One of the critical questions for the social historian of premodern Sufism in Mavarannahr and Khurāsān concerns the growth and development of the Naqshbandīya in late Timurid Central Asia under the leadership of Khwāja ʿUbaydullāh Aḥrār, and the degree to which the Naqshbandī community appears to have provided a structure for specific socioeconomic and political relationships on a regional and interregional level. The *silsila*-based, institutionalized Naqshbandīya is not representative of all Sufi organizations or communities within or outside of Central Asia.[5] However, based upon the record provided by historical chronicles, *vaqf* documents, correspondence, and hagiographies, it is indicative of the way in which Sufi communities and Sufi leaders could and did provide an organizational structure within their local communities as well as an impetus for interregional contacts and expansionist activities that reached beyond their centers of origin.[6]

The extent to which Khwāja Aḥrār exerted political influence and established an agrarian base in the regions of Samarqand, Tashkent and Bukhara is well known, and has been discussed elsewhere. The purpose of this study is to expand the question of Khwāja Aḥrār's regional base of power and influence to include networks of social alignments between

---

rulers, and the economy makes this collection of letters unique and reflects the worldly thrust of the Naqshbandī community. For two important collections of Persian letters, see Jalāl al-Dīn Yūsuf-i Ahl, *Farāʾid-i Ghiyāthī*, ed. Ḥishmat Muʾayyad (Tehran, 2536/1977 [vol. I], 1358/1979 [vol. II]), and Pīr Jamāl al-Dīn Ardistānī, *Mirʾāt al-afrād*, ed. Ḥusayn Anīsī-pūr (Tehran, 1361/1982).

[5] The work of Devin DeWeese has brought to light the important and largely ignored history of less institutionalized, non-*silsila* based forms of Sufi communities. See, for example, his "An 'Uvaysī' Sufi in Timurid Mawarannahr: Notes on Hagiography and the Taxonomy of Sanctity in the Religious History of Central Asia," *Papers on Inner Asia*, No. 22 (Bloomington: Indiana University, Research Institute for Inner Asian Studies, 1993); *Islamization and Native Religion in the Golden Horde: Baba Tükles and Conversion to Islam in Historical and Epic Tradition* (University Park: Pennsylvania State University Press, 1994); "The *Mashāʾikh-i Turk* and the *Khojagān*: Rethinking the Links between the Yasavī and Naqshbandī Sufi Traditions," *Journal of Islamic Studies*, 7 (1996), pp. 180-207; "Yasavī Šayḫs in the Timurid Era: Notes on the Social and Political Role of Communal Sufi Affiliations in the 14th and 15th Centuries," *Oriente Moderno*, N.S., 15 (76), No. 2 (1996), pp. 173-188; and others.

[6] For the purchase deeds and *vaqfīyas* of Khwāja ʿUbaydullāh Aḥrār, see O. D. Chekhovich, *Samarkandskie dokumenty XV-XVI vv. (O vladeniiakh Khodzhi Ahrara v Srednei Azii i Afganistane)* (Moscow: Nauka, 1974); see also Stephen F. Dale and Alam Payind, "The Ahrārī *Waqf* in Kābul in the Year 1546 and the Mughūl Naqshbandiyyah," *Journal of the American Oriental Society*, 119 (1999), pp. 218-233.

prominent Naqshbandī shaykhs and members of the Herat court. The letters of petition (*ʿarż*) contained in the *Majmūʿa-i murāsalāt* provide clues to a more subtle pattern of reciprocity and exchange that embodies notions of etiquette (*adab*) and concepts of status and prestige. On the basis of a series of letters from the *Majmūʿa-i murāsalāt*, written by Khwāja ʿUbaydullāh Aḥrār and his associates, and dealing with property and trade issues (with reference to hagiographical sources as well), we will examine two issues: first, the role of the Naqshbandī shaykh as agent or broker, and the symbolic implications that role has for understanding patterns of authority and patronage;[7] and second, the factual definition of the involvement of Naqshbandī shaykhs in property and trade transactions and the implications it has for the socioeconomic history of the late Timurid period.

By the late 15th century, a network of Naqshbandī economic, social, and political relations was strongly entrenched in the regions of Bukhara, Samarqand and Tashkent in Central Asia, and in the capital city of Herat in Khurāsān.[8] Although much of Aḥrār's prestige rested on his spirituality as well as his place in the Naqshbandī *silsila* as the successor to Mawlānā Yaʿqūb Charkhī, *vaqf* documents, purchase deeds, narrative stories related in his hagiographies, and correspondence all reveal Aḥrār as a major player in the local economy and society. As Khwāndamīr notes in the *Ḥabīb al-siyar*, "The loftiest of all the shaykhs of Turkistān and grandees of Transoxiana in splendor and greatness as well as in the number of followers and property was Naṣīr al-Dīn ʿUbaydullāh."[9]

In addition to the local network of relationships documented in endowments, property deeds, and biographical references, relationships external to the regions of Samarqand demonstrate the existence of a set

[7] For a provocative study of aspects of sainthood as a social phenomenon in Moroccan Sufism, see Vincent Cornell, *Realm of the Saint: Power and Authority in Moroccan Sufism* (Austin: University of Texas Press, 1998). His analysis of empowerment is particularly relevant to this study.

[8] See, for example, Hamid Algar, "Political Aspects of Naqshbandî History," in *Naqshbandîs*, ed. Gaborieau *et al.* (Istanbul/Paris, 1990), pp. 123-152; Chekhovich, *Samarkandskie dokumenty*; Gross, "Multiple Roles;" Paul, "Forming a Faction;" and Paul, *Die politische und soziale Bedeutung*.

[9] Ghiyāth al-Dīn Khwāndamīr, *Ḥabīb al-siyar*, ed. Jalāl al-Dīn Humāʾī (Tehran, 1333/1954; repr. 1362/1984), IV, p. 109. Aḥrār also served in the capacity of mediator in a number of internecine conflicts among Timurid *sulṭāns* and princes; see Gross, "Multiple Roles."

of strong ties between Aḥrār and the Herat Naqshbandīya as well as the Timurid court. Given the fact that the main urban centers of the Naqshbandīya during the Timurid period were in Samarqand and Herat, and that Aḥrār was much favored and admired by Sulṭān Abū Saʿīd (1452-1468) and his successor, Sulṭān Ḥusayn Bāyqarā (1469-1506), it is not surprising to find the existence of such ties. It should be noted that Abū Saʿīd's success in defeating his enemy, ʿAbd al-Laṭīf, in 1451—a victory that led to Abū Saʿīd's subsequent accession to the sultanate of Samarqand—was attributed to Aḥrār's spiritual support. According to ʿAbd al-Razzāq Samarqandī,

> At that time when he [Abū Saʿīd] had not yet ascended the throne of kingship and was wandering around the countryside asking for the help and guidance of the rightly guided ones, one day he received the honor of an audience with the blessed Khwāja Naṣīr al-Dīn ʿUbaydullāh. His holiness made sweet predictions and planted the thought of ruling the world in the mind of Mīrzā Sulṭān Abū Saʿīd. Mīrzā Sulṭān Abū Saʿīd always considered himself to be his holiness' agent, and if it were ever possible to do anything against his wishes, he still would not do it.[10]

Aḥrār's involvement in trade has been long recognized by scholars familiar with the work of the Soviet orientalist Nabiev; however, other than the work of Asam Urunbaev, no complete examination of this involvement has been made to date.[11] Furthermore, trade activity is weakly documented in other Timurid sources, despite the conditions for an active network of trade relationships between the communities of Herat and Samarqand established by Temür himself through the development of the central trade route. During the late 15th century, the Herat branch of the Naqshbandīya was thriving amidst a prolific court culture of the Timurid capital, led by ʿAbd al-Raḥmān Jāmī (1444-1492) and

[10] ʿAbd al-Razzāq Samarqandī, *Maṭlaʿ al-saʿdayn va majmaʿ al-baḥrayn*, ed. Muḥammad Shafīʿ, II/2-3 (Lahore, 1368/1949), p. 1062.

[11] This is due to the previous inaccessibility to scholars of the *Majmūʿa-i murāsalāt*, in which this involvement is documented; see R. N. Nabiev, "Iz istorii politiko-èkonomicheskoi zhizni Maverannakhra XV v. (Zametki o Khodzha-Akhrare)," in *Velikii uzbekskii poèt* (Tashkent, 1948), pp. 25-49.

ᶜAlī Shīr Navāʾī.[12] It does not seem improbable that the interests of Aḥrār and his disciples in commerce would have extended to trade across the Amu Darya to Herat.[13] Aḥrār not only maintained close relations with the Naqshbandī elite in Herat, but had close ties with the court as well, and in his own region, he controlled an extensive portion of the local economy through his artisanal and commercial activities.

Five letters in the *Majmūᶜa-i murāsalāt* concern trade transactions: two were written by Aḥrār, two by Khwāja ᶜAlī Tāshkandī, and one by Muḥammad b. Amīn al-Dīn. Khwāja ᶜAlī, who authored twenty-two letters in the *Majmūᶜa*, was a pupil, son-in-law, and close companion of Khwāja Aḥrār, and often traveled on Aḥrār's behalf to Herat, where he

[12] See Maria Eva Subtelny, "Socioeconomic Bases of Cultural Patronage under the Later Timurids," *International Journal of Middle East Studies*, 20 (1988), pp. 479-505; *idem*, "ᶜAlī Shīr Navāʾī: Bakhshī and Beg," *Harvard Ukrainian Studies*, 3-4 (1979-80; = *Eucharisterion: Essays presented to Omeljan Pritsak on his Sixtieth Birthday by his Colleagues and Students*), pp. 797-807; *idem*, "The *Vaqfīya* of Mīr ᶜAlī Šīr Navāʾī as Apologia," *Journal of Turkish Studies*, 15 (1991; = *Fahir İz Armağanı*), pp. 257-286; *idem*, "A Timurid Educational and Charitable Foundation: The Ikhlāṣiyya Complex of ᶜAlī Shīr Navāʾī in 15th-Century Herat and its Endowment," *Journal of the American Oriental Society*, 111 (1991), pp. 38-60. An important and neglected source for the social history of late Timurid Herat is ᶜAbd al-Vāsiᶜ Niẓāmī Bākharzī's biography of Jāmī, *Maqāmāt-i Jāmī*, ed. Najīb Māyil Haravī (Tehran, 1992).

[13] Aḥrār's ownership of shops and his related control of artisans is substantiated in a number of hagiographical references, and is documented in a number of purchase deeds. For example, a purchase deed from 1464 records that Aḥrār bought 12 shops in Samarqand (Chekhovich, ed., *Samarkandskie dokumenty*, pp. 59-61, No. 3). A 1470 *vaqf* document endowing the Samarqand *madrasa* of Khwāja Aḥrār lists two shops in Samarqand located on the Registan (*Samarkandskie dokumenty*, pp. 72-78, No. 5). We also know that Aḥrār worked to abolish the *tamghā* market tax, a Mongol imposition and therefore considered by Aḥrār to be illegal. Given Aḥrār's commercial interests, scholars have questioned the self-serving motives with regard to Aḥrār's work to repeal the *tamghā* tax; for a discussion of this issue, see Gross, "Khoja Ahrar" (diss., 1982), p. 141, Paul, *Die politische und soziale Bedeutung*, pp. 221-226, and Paul, "Forming a Faction," p. 538. It was after the rebellion of Nūr Saᶜīd in Bukhara and Samarqand and Aḥrār's unsuccessful appeals for his surrender that Aḥrār visited Abū Saᶜīd in Herat. At that time he asked Abū Saᶜīd to abolish the *tamghā* of Samarqand and Bukhara, which Abū Saᶜīd agreed to do (Mawlānā Shaykh, *Manāqib-i Aḥrār*, MS IVANRUz No. 9730, f. 103a; Mīrkhwānd, *Rawżat al-ṣafā* (Tehran, 1339/1960), VI, pp. 835-836; ᶜAbd al-Razzāq Samarqandī, *Maṭlaᶜ al-saᶜdayn va majmaᶜ al-baḥrayn*, ed. Shafīᶜ, II/2-3, pp. 1105-1106; Muḥammad Burhān al-Dīn Samarqandī (Mawlānā Muḥammad Qāżī), *Silsilat al-ᶜārifīn va tadhkirat al-ṣiddīqīn*, MS IVANRUz No. 4452/I, ff. 71a-b.

was given audience with Sulṭān Ḥusayn Bāyqarā.[14] According to ᶜAlī b. Ḥusayn Vāᶜiẓ Kāshifī, known as "Ṣāfī," author of the *Rashaḥāt-i ᶜayn al-ḥayāt*, the well-known hagiography devoted to Aḥrār, Khwāja ᶜAlī was "among the grandees of the companions and honorable *vakīl*s of his holiness [Khwāja Aḥrār]."[15] Muḥammad b. Amīn al-Dīn, whose letters are addressed mainly to ᶜAlī Shīr Navāʾī (to whom he refers as "son"), had close relations with the Herat court as well as with Aḥrār. The author of 44 letters, he is believed by Asam Urunbaev to have served as a *mudarris* at the Herat *madrasa*.[16]

In addition to the five letters from the *Majmūᶜa-i murāsalāt*, there are a number of hagiographical references that touch upon trade, although the mention of commerce is usually extraneous to the stories. Most notable is a narrative in which Khwāja Muṣṭafā-yi Rūmī, described in the *Rashaḥāt* as "a merchant (*tājir*) who was one of the employees (*kārgarān*) of his holiness [Khwāja Aḥrār]," set out on a trade mission from Bukhara to Samarqand via Shahr-i Sabz, stopping there to meet with Mīrak Ḥasan, chief of Mīrzā Sulṭān Aḥmad's *dīvān*.[17] Another

[14] Jürgen Paul (*Die politische und soziale Bedeutung*, p. 97) describes a central administrative office in the *khānqāh* of Khwāja Aḥrār, a precursor of the later financial administration (*dīvān*) of the Jūybārī shaykhs, and concludes that Khwāja ᶜAlī and Mawlānā Shaykh were the chief managers of the administration. Although it is unclear whether a truly centralized *dīvān* administration was instituted within the *khānqāh*, it is clear from the sources that Khwāja ᶜAlī was a major player in the supervision of a number of tasks, including correspondence. For a description of Khwāja ᶜAlī's duties, see ᶜAlī b. Ḥusayn Vāᶜiẓ Kāshifī, "Ṣāfī," *Rashaḥāt-i ᶜayn al-ḥayāt*, ed. ᶜAlī Aṣghar Muᶜīnīyān (Tehran, 2536/1977), II, pp. 631-632.

[15] *Rashaḥāt*, II, pp. 631-632. The work further states that when Aḥrār went to Samarqand at Abū Saᶜīd's request, he entrusted Khwāja ᶜAlī with "all the worldly affairs" and "gave [him] the reins of power according to his ability" (*Rashaḥāt*, II, p. 633). Paul (*Die politische und soziale Bedeutung*, p. 97) interprets this text to read that Khwāja ᶜAlī is the only representative of Khwāja Aḥrār (*vakīl-i iṭlāq*); however, based on the earlier text that reads, "*az qudamā-yi aṣḥāb va az ajilla-i vukalāʾ-i ḥaẓrat-i īshān*," we conclude that Khwāja ᶜAlī was one of a number of Aḥrār's *vakīl*s.

[16] *Pis'ma-avtografi Abdarrakhmana Dzhami*, p. 17. Urunbaev bases his assumption that Muḥammad b. Amīn al-Dīn taught at the Herat *madrasa* on the content of his letters, several of which concern questions about the financial support of teachers and students. In one letter he petitions on behalf of his "*shāgird*." Many of the letters of Muḥammad b. Amīn al-Dīn concern issues of taxation and land tenure. To my knowledge, there are no references to Muḥammad b. Amīn al-Dīn in the standard sources of the late Timurid period.

[17] *Rashaḥāt*, II, p. 537.

merchant (*bāzarganī*) named Ḥājjī ʿAlī Rūmī, is the subject of a petition written by Aḥrār in which he requests the "retinue" (*mulāzimān*) of the Sulṭān to give Rūmī permission to go to his own region (presumably Asia Minor, to judge from his *nisba*).[18]

In the *Majālis-i ʿUbaydullāh Aḥrār*, the son of a certain Khwāja Mullā Farkatī relates a story concerning his personal conflict in being both a *murīd* and a merchant. "I told his holiness [Khwāja Aḥrār] that when I was appointed by him to do business (lit. "to buy and sell" [*bayʿ-u-sharā*]) in the lampsellers' bazaar, people were laughing at me for what I was doing. So I quit. His holiness Khwāja ʿUbaydullāh got angry and said to me, 'What you are doing may look foolish to foolish people, but it is very much valued by wise persons.'"[19] The latter advice from Khwāja Aḥrār reiterates the activist doctrine of the Naqshbandīya with regard to participation in the two worlds, the spiritual as well as the material. Clearly, Aḥrār did not find trade activity to be contradictory to the spiritual path.

Another reference in the *Rashaḥāt-i ʿayn al-ḥayāt* further confirms the participation of persons in the household and/or employment of Khwāja Aḥrār in trade transactions. The story concerns a raid that occurred as a certain Najm al-Dīn was en route to Turfan, a city on the frontier of China (*Khiṭāy*). The *Rashaḥāt* refers to him as "the honorable Mawlānā Najm al-Dīn, who was an *ʿazīz* from among the servants (*khādimān*) and employees (*kārgarān*) of his holiness [Khwāja Aḥrār], and often used to attend to trade affairs and handled a lot of money . . ."[20]

Two letters in the *Majmūʿa* refer to the transportation of Khwāja Aḥrār's goods to Herat for sale. Both are petitions to the court to grant favor and protection to guarantee the success of the transactions.

The first, written by Khwāja Aḥrār, states:

> After the statement of needs, it is to be reported that because this land is in turbulence, this *faqīr* sent with the bearers of the letter some sheep and horses that I had, so they may sell them on the other side of the river [Amu Darya]. The petition to the

[18] *Majmūʿa*, f. 7b, #54 (55).

[19] Mīr ʿAbd al-Avval Nīshāpūrī, *Majālis-i ʿUbaydullāh Aḥrār*, MS India Office, D.P. 890, f. 191a.

[20] *Rashaḥāt*, II, p. 536.

retinue of His Majesty [the Sulṭān], may Allāh perpetuate the shadow of His favor, is that they [the retinue] should have them [the bearers] in their protection (*dar ḥimāyat-i khūd*), and the noble attention should be directed so that this group may not come to suffer on that side, and [can] sell what they have and return as soon as [possible]. It is certain that the request will be granted by the true absolute grace [of the retinue]. Peace.[21]

The subject of the second letter, written by Khwāja ʿAlī, concerns Sulṭān Maḥmūd's ensuing conflict with his brothers, and the expressed hope for a peaceful settlement. However, midway through the letter, Khwāja ʿAlī writes,

> The blessed Khwāja wrote a letter and sent [it to you in Khurāsān] along with one of his followers, Mawlānā ʿAbd al-Karīm, and several assloads of paper, sesame, rice, cotton, and other [goods], which are connected with the blessed Khwāja (*taʿalluq ba-ḥażrat-i khwāja*).[22] If, through the grace of [your] being, a royal order (*ishārat-i aʿlā*) was given to the retinue to accomplish the affairs of the blessed Khwāja, may Allāh grant him peace, it shall be the ultimate favor.[23]

Jürgen Paul has discussed at length the concept of *ḥimāyat* in the context of what he has termed Khwāja Aḥrār's *ṭāʾifa* or faction. After reviewing the historical application of the term in the post-Mongol

[21] *Majmūʿa*, f. 23a, #313 (317); cited in A. Urunbaev, "Pis'ma-avtografi Dzhami iz 'Al'boma Navoi' kak istoricheskii istochnik," *doktorskaia* dissertation (Institute of Oriental Studies, Academy of Sciences of the Uzbek SSR, 1984), p. 51. Although it is impossible to know what "turbulence" Aḥrār was referring to, it could have been the terrible drought that took place in the Tashkent region late in Aḥrār's life, or the plague that struck Samarqand when Jāmī went to visit him. The plague forced Aḥrār and his guest to withdraw to Andījān (ʿAbd al-Vāsiʿ Niẓāmī Bākharzī, *Maqāmāt-i Mawlavī Jāmī*, MS IVANRUz No. 756, f. 73a; *Maqāmāt-i Jāmī*, ed. Māyil Haravī, p. 115).

[22] Although the letter is vague in attributing ownership, the phrasing implies that the goods belonged either to Aḥrār personally, or to the Naqshbandī community.

[23] *Majmūʿa*, f. 24a, #386 (392); cited in Urunbaev, "Pis'ma-avtografi Dzhami" (diss.), p. 66. In the *Manāqib-i Aḥrār*, Mawlānā Shaykh notes that Khwāja Aḥrār was involved in paper production in Samarqand and that a certain Imām al-Dīn was in charge (MS IVANRUz No. 9730, f. 51a; cited also in Paul, *Die politische und soziale Bedeutung*, p. 105).

period, he concludes that Khwāja Aḥrār served as a protector for groups of people that preferred to deal with him rather than with the *dīvān* directly.[24] As Paul notes, *ḥimāyat* can also signify a more general kind of protection or patronage on the part of rulers, as is the case with the letter above. Aḥrār's letter provides an interesting twist to Paul's interpretation, since Aḥrār uses the term *ḥimāyat* to describe the protection sought by him for the benefit of his agents, who may have been disciples as well. The form of Aḥrār's request is one that ideally recognizes the political authority as well as the religious obligations of a just sultanate, and symbolically expresses the recognition of the prestige and spiritual authority of Khwāja Aḥrār through the expectation of favor granted by the Sultan on his behalf.

Of the final two letters that concern trade, the first, written by Khwāja ʿAlī to ʿAlī Shīr Navāʾī, refers to Khwāja Muḥammad ʿAlī as "among the close ones and people of his holiness the Khwāja . . ." who has "set out to that side (Herat) for trade business (*ba-rasm-i sawdā*) and will be favored with the honor of serving [you]."[25] The second, written by Muḥammad b. Amīn al-Dīn, requests a travel certificate for a certain "distinguished descendant" of one Abī'l-Qāsim [*sic*], who has financial troubles and resides in Herat. He wishes to leave his household and goods (*kūch*) in their native Samarqand, and to go to Gulbarga in India on trade business. He also requests a recommendation to the *mālik al-tujjār* (chief of merchants) in Gulbarga.[26]

The suggestion of a Naqshbandī trade network in India, although not documented in other sources, may be related to the later endowment interests of the Aḥrārī family in Kābul, the frontier of India. Although by the late 16th and early 17th centuries there was a significant increase in the movement of Naqshbandīs to India from Central Asia, some of whom would serve as soldiers, administrators, religious figures, or

[24] Paul, "Forming a Faction," p. 537; cf. *Die politische und soziale Bedeutung*, pp. 198-207. Paul theorizes that the term *ḥimāyat* generally refers to ". . . the intervention of a third person into the relationship between a powerful and weaker person. This third person, the patron giving shelter or protection, was perceived as a barrier not to be overcome by the powerful one who threatened the weaker one."

[25] *Majmūʿa*, f. 41b, #560 (566).

[26] *Majmūʿa*, f. 31b, #429 (434). Gulbarga (Karnataka), located in the Deccan, was the capital of the Bahmanī Sultanate until the 15th century, when the capital was moved to Bidar.

landowners, the *vaqf* document of 1546 mentioned above suggests that an agrarian base as well as an institutional framework for a Naqshbandī community prior to Timurid-Moghul rule may have already been established in Kābul. Based on this document, the revenues of entire villages, agricultural lands, gardens, shops, mills, baths, and houses in Samarqand and the Samarqand-Qashqā Daryā districts were directed for the use of the shrine complex of Khwāja Aḥrār, outside Samarqand in Khwāja Kafshīr.[27]

Although it is unclear to what extent interregional trade was integrated into the organizational framework of the Samarqand Naqshbandīya, the letters and biographical sources discussed suggest that the Naqshbandī communities in Herat and Samarqand provided a conduit for the exchange of goods that was related to the extensive economic organization in the Samarqand Naqshbandī community, the tacit approval of the Timurid rulers, the efficacy of trade routes, and the impetus of Khwāja Aḥrār, from whose direction such transactions were emanating. These interregional contacts coincide with a period of expansion of the Naqshbandīya, during which time Aḥrār sent *khalīfa*s outside the Timurid realm itself to spread the order. ʿAbdullah Ilāhī, the key person responsible for the diffusion of the Naqshbandīya into the Ottoman realm in the late 15th century, is a case in point.[28] But it was not only the Ottoman lands that were affected by Aḥrār's expansionist attitudes. Aḥrār's *khalīfa*s initiated the spread of the Naqshbandī *ṭarīqa* east to Kāshgar, south to India, and west to Iran (particularly to Tabrīz and Qazvīn), Syria, and even the Ḥijāz.

Unlike the topic of trade, which involves the rather direct exchange of goods, property issues in the letters of the *Majmūʿa-i murāsalāt* cover a broad range of financial and legal concerns. These letters, addressed either to ʿAlī Shīr Navāʾī, the retinue of the Sulṭān (*mulāzimān-i sulṭān*), or the Sulṭān himself, concern issues such as inheritance, payment of

[27] Chekhovich, *Samarkandskie dokumenty*, pp. 316-341; Dale and Payind, "The Ahrārī *Waqf*." Despite the paucity of evidence concerning a Naqshbandī community in late-15th- and/or early-16th-century Kābul, this document reveals the considerable interest of the Aḥrārī family in the Kābul region. There are outstanding questions as to the date and provenance of this document.

[28] See Dina LeGall, "Missionaries, Pilgrims and Refugees: The Early Transmission of the Naqshbandiyya to the Ottoman Lands," in *Modes de transmission de la culture religieuse en Islam*, ed. Hassan Elboudrari (Cairo: Institut Français d'Archéologie Orientale du Caire, 1993), pp. 225-240.

debt, exemption from taxes, property sales, and land rights and use. Although it is not always clear exactly where the properties in question are located, they appear to be mostly in Khurāsān, which provides some explanation as to the direction of the appeals to the Herat court. The fact that members of Aḥrār's household or his associates were selling property, purchasing property, or trying to preserve their rights to property in Khurāsān is suggestive of a certain mobility on the part of individuals from Mavarannahr, particularly Samarqand, as well as the existence of interregional contacts on the part of Aḥrār and his following.

Five letters of Aḥrār concern property issues. One letter, addressed to the "retinue" (*mulāzimān*), is a simple petition written on behalf of the devotees of ʿUbaydullāh Aḥrār, and states that "some of the household and persons (*mutaʿalliqān va kasān*)" [of Aḥrār] want to purchase some property (*milk*) in Khurāsān. He asks for the attention of the retinue in making this possible.[29] In another letter, Aḥrār requests the favor of "your honor" (*khidmat-i shumā*), referring to ʿAlī Shīr Navāʾī, in ensuring that the relatives of one Amīr ʿAbd al-Vahhāb are able to successfully sell his properties and estate (*milkī*, *ḥavīlī*, *amlāk*); Sultan Ḥusayn had sent Amīr ʿAbd al-Wahhāb to Mavarannahr, and he now wished to sell his properties in Khurāsān.[30] In a third letter, Aḥrār asks for the support of the retinue (*mulāzimān*) in settling the property of a certain "person of noble birth" who owns some real estate (*milkī*) on "that side" (Khurāsān).[31]

A fourth letter concerns a letter of favor written by Aḥrār on behalf of an individual living in Samarqand whose family was originally from Herat and now sought to reclaim properties there. He states,

> Amīr Tīmūr brought his forefathers [to Samarqand] and appointed [them] to service in various towns. They had possessions and properties (*asbāb-u-amlāk*) on that side [Khurāsān]. [Now] he is experiencing a little poverty. In order to retrieve something from those possessions, he is setting out to that side. It is certain that if his possessions [are found] in the

[29] *Majmūʿa*, f. 18a, #267 (272); cited in Urunbaev, ed., "Pis'ma-avtografi Dzhami" (diss.), p. 49, and in Urunbaev, ed., *Pis'ma avtografi*, p. 10.

[30] *Majmūʿa*, f. 4b, #22 (23).

[31] *Majmūʿa*, f. 22b, #311 (315).

hands of people in opposition to the *sharīʿa*, with the favor of the noble retinue something will come to him, for he is heading for Mecca. Peace.[32]

Aḥrār also appealed to the Herat court regarding a case of inheritance. A certain Amīr Muḥammad ʿAlī Bakhshī had a residential compound (*ḥavīlī*) and underground canal (*kārīz*) that were connected to (*taʿalluq girifta ast*) his young children (*nārasīdagān*). He asks for a royal decree (*ishārat-i aʿlā*) that will order the *ḥavīlī* to go to Amīr Muḥammad ʿAlī Bakhshī, and the *kārīz* to his young children, closing his letter of petition with the following words: "The cause for all this arrogance (*gustākhī*) [by me] is that His Excellency, may Allāh perpetuate the shadow of His favor, has made it imperative upon himself to act in accordance with the *sharīʿa*. Peace."[33] Thus Aḥrār's appeal is based upon the veracity of his own word in attesting to the high position of the Amīr, and upon the *sharīʿa* by which the Sultan is bound to act.

In serving as an agent for the members of his household, most likely his own disciples, and on behalf of friends and associates in the Samarqand region, Aḥrār's requests are situated in a discourse based on his prestige and the merit that is accorded to the addressee, either the Sultan, the retinue, or ʿAlī Shīr Navāʾī, in fulfilling his request. In supporting Aḥrār's requests, the rulers fulfill their duty to act in accordance with the *sharīʿa*, and in doing so, symbolically perpetuate their rule, support and protect the Muslim populace, and recognize the grace and honor of Aḥrār.

In addition to the letters of Aḥrār, several letters written by his disciples concern property issues. Among them are those of Muḥammad Tabādkānī, Aḥrār's son Muḥammad Yaḥyā, and Muḥammad b. Amīn al-Dīn. Two letters concern property relating to lands set aside for the use of Sufis, one in the village of Gavājā [?] and one in Gavāshān.[34]

[32] *Majmūʿa*, f. 33a, #442 (448).

[33] *Majmūʿa*, f. 41a, #548 (544-545).

[34] In letter #421 (427), written by Muḥammad Tabādkānī, the name of the village is only partially legible, and appears to read "Gavājā." In letter #455 (461), written by Muḥammad b. Amīn al-Dīn (discussed below), the name of the village clearly reads "Gavāshān," a village located in the vicinity of Herat (see Ḥāfiẓ-i Abrū, *Jughrāfiyā, qismat-i rubʿ-i Khurāsān, Harāt*, ed. Najīb Māyil Haravī [Tehran, 1349/1970], p. 17; cf. Dorothea Krawulsky, *Ḫorāsān zur Timuridenzeit nach dem Tārīḫ-e Ḥāfeẓ-e Abrū (verf. 817-823 h.)*, vol. II, Übersetzung und Ortsnamenkommentar [Wiesbaden: Dr.

The subject of Muḥammad Tabādkānī's letter is land that had evidently been regarded as *vaqf* for the use of the Sufis. Tabādkānī writes, ". . . It is to be reported that formerly, the cultivated [land] of the village of Gavājā [?], according to the approval of the great son of a *khwāja*, Khwāja . . . Fażlullāh,[35] and the endeavor of his retinue, had come to belong to[36] the dervishes. In these days that [arrangement] has been suspended. No reason [for this] was made apparent." Tabādkānī continues, "Never [before] has there been negligence by his retinue in carrying out the affairs of this side [Mavarannahr]. On the part of the *faqīrs*, extreme consideration was always taken [by you] and [you] also handled the affairs of the people efficiently."[37]

In another letter, written by Muḥammad b. Amīn al-Dīn, he petitions Sulṭān Ḥusayn Bāyqarā to transfer the state land (*zamīn-i khāliṣa*) on which a mosque is located in the village of Gavāshān into *vaqf* so that a group of dervishes can go there on devotional retreat (*muᶜtakaf*). He requests that the land under the mosque, and some other lands in the environs of that mosque, be endowed as a *vaqf* to that mosque, thus revitalizing the mosque and providing a place for the Sufis to engage in prayers and supplications. Muḥammad b. Amīn al-Dīn concludes his letter of petition by stating that "They will be able to rise up to fragrant prayers in the morning and night for the extension of the dominion (*salṭanat*) of His Majesty, causing the increase in the power of that honorable one (*salṭanat-i ān janāb*). 'Do good as God has done good to you' [*Qurʾān*, 28:77]."[38]

One final letter, written by Muḥammad Yaḥyā, concerns the inheritance of Pahlavān Saᶜd al-Dīn, who died in Mashhad. His son, Khwāja Żiyāʾ al-Dīn Muḥammad, living in Samarqand and possibly a *murīd*, was on his way to Khurāsān to settle his estate. Yaḥyā requests that the retinue "issue a directive (*ishārāt*) that the possessions (*amvāl*) of Pahlavān be given to his son, Khwāja Żiyāʾ al-Dīn Muḥammad."[39]

Ludwig Reichert Verlag, 1984], pp. 24, 88). Although I have thus far not found any reference to a village named "Gavājā," I assume, for now, that Gavāshān and Gavājā are two different villages.

[35] Only part of this name is legible.

[36] *taᶜalluq*, literally, "had come to be connected with" the dervishes.

[37] *Majmūᶜa*, f. 30b, #421 (427).

[38] *Majmūᶜa*, f. 34b, #455 (461).

[39] *Majmūᶜa*, f. 33a, #443 (449).

What can we learn from this group of letters concerning property issues? First, there is evidence that the Naqshbandīya had property interests in Khurāsān. Details are lacking concerning the relationship between the purchase of properties in Khurāsān by members of Aḥrār's followers and the organization of the Naqshbandīya in Samarqand. It is therefore possible only to hypothesize that investments may have been made with revenues acquired through the Naqshbandī *ṭarīqa*. Second, Aḥrār, not surprisingly, used his influence and prestige to make appeals to the Herat court on behalf of individuals seeking to make a variety of property settlements, including sales and inheritance rights. Third, prominent shaykhs such as Aḥrār and Muḥammad b. Amīn al-Dīn sought the support of the rulers in preserving the status of endowed properties or in converting private or state land into *vaqf* for the use of Sufis. In these cases the letters are useful as more personalized sources to supplement the traditional documentary sources upon which we base our assessments of land tenure and property issues in the late Timurid period.

This brief study of trade and property issues in the letters of Khwāja Aḥrār and his associates reflects the historical value of the *ʿarẓ* or letter of petition as an important source for understanding social relations in premodern Islamic society. Such letters symbolically embody notions of etiquette (*adab*), concepts of status and prestige, and patterns of reciprocity and exchange. Khwāja Aḥrār and his disciples and associates address a broad range of economic concerns in their letters, only two of which have been discussed here. The flow of appeals to the Herat court, we would argue, was an expression of mutual recognition and support by Naqshbandī shaykhs, Timurid rulers and elite members of the court that was ideologically rooted in an Islamic world view and a deep respect for Khwāja Aḥrār as a Naqshbandī *pīr*. As such, appeals were not necessarily focused on expanding a political or economic base, but rather on exercising the prerogatives of their writers as members of the notable class on behalf of the Muslim populace, whether it be on behalf of another Naqshbandī, an *amīr*, or a family relation.

Although Khwāja Aḥrār's center of activity with regard to his *khānqāh* as well as his economic activities was in Mavarannahr, it is clear from hagiographical evidence as well as the correspondence discussed above that he maintained close relations in Khurāsān with the Herat court, had disciples and associates with interests in Herat, and carried out trade in Khurāsān, India, and even the frontier of China, under the auspices of his own organization in Samarqand. However, the prestige associated with Aḥrār was not confined to his own person. Those associated with Khwāja Aḥrār, through discipleship, political ties, household or familial relations, or employment, were not only empowered through their own closeness to him, but accrued the benefits of that empowerment.

THE MONETARY REFORM OF MUḤAMMAD SHĪBĀNĪ KHĀN

IN 913-914/1507-08

Elena A. Davidovich

Institute of Oriental Studies, Moscow

On a Friday in the middle of Muḥarram 913/late May 1507, in the cathedral mosque of Herat, the *khuṭba* was first recited in the name of the city's new conqueror, Muḥammad Shībānī Khān, and thereby as well the existence of the Timurid dynasty was formally brought to an end. Many oriental sources gave a thorough and detailed description of the political events of the last days of the Timurids' once-brilliant state, and followed, step-by-step, the history of its conquest by the founder of the new, Shībānid power; all but one of them, however, overlooked, amidst the current of minor and major events, one curious fact whose fundamental meaning and significance very few contemporary observers were able to understand from its external manifestations. The one historian in question was Khwāndamīr, and the fact was the monetary reform of Muḥammad Shībānī Khān.

This reform was promulgated immediately after the recitation of the *khuṭba*. As its further analysis reveals, the reform had not only major economic significance, but great political significance as well, and must have furthered the consolidation of its nominal author's power, authority, and even popularity. The brief description by Khwāndamīr is not distinguished by clarity, however. It was thus not by chance that the historian and orientalist A. N. Boldyrev addressed specialists in numismatics with the appeal that they might "express their views regarding this interesting information."[1]

For numismatists as well, however, Khwāndamīr's text has not been simple or clear.[2] Supplementary sources that allow us to understand

[1] A. N. Boldyrev, "Ocherki iz zhizni geratskogo obshchestva na rubezhe XV-XVI vv.," *Trudy Otdela Vostoka Gosudarstvennogo Èrmitazha*, t. 4 (Leningrad, 1947), p. 364, n. 1.

[2] This is shown clearly by two articles devoted to Khwāndamīr's text and the reform of Shībānī Khān: E. A. Davidovich, "Denezhnaia reforma Sheibani-khana (Iz istorii sredneaziatskoi èkonomiki v XVI v.)," *Materialy po istorii tadzhikov i uzbekov*

and explain Khwāndamīr's testimony, and to uncover new data on the substance and purpose of Shībānī Khān's reforms, on the stages of its realization, on the situation prior to the reforms, and on the reformed monetary circulation, are: the coins themselves (gold, silver, and copper), from the relevant period, and hoards of coins; countermarks of silver and copper coins, done under Shībānī Khān; documents (*vathīqas*) and endowment deeds (*vaqf-nāmas*) of the 15th and 16th centuries; and treatises and guides or manuals on the formulation of juridical documents.

1. THE TERMS *TANGA*, *TANGACHA*, AND *DĪNĀR-I KEPEKĪ*

In order to understand Khwāndamīr's text regarding Shībānī Khān's monetary reform, it is first of all essential to elucidate the specific historical meaning, in Khurāsān and Mavarannahr during the 15th and 16th centuries, of the terms *tanga*, *tangacha*, and *dīnār-i kepekī*.

The term *tanga* could refer both to gold and silver coins. In the regions in question during the 15th and 16th centuries, however, it was used specifically as a designation for silver coins, while gold coins were referred to by the term *ashrafī*. If in narrative written sources the term *tanga* was not accompanied by some supplementary characteristic (for example, "red *tanga*," i.e., gold), contemporaries understood it as a designation for silver coins alone. Nevertheless, in documentary sources (*vathīqas*, *vaqf-nāmas*), the *tanga*'s metal was indicated in the course of its description: *tanga-i nuqra*, "silver *tanga*." The fact that the term *tanga* served as a designation for silver coins under Temür, the Timurids, and the Shībānids was well-known. But as in the case of many coin terms, it was by no means a proper name for a silver coin of a single domination—the basic one. By this same term, rather, were denoted fractions of basic denominations, with value in such cases determined by other marks or characteristics. A few concrete examples follow.

On the small silver coins of Mashhad, struck in the name of the last Timurid in Herat, Sulṭān Ḥusayn, the term *tanga* appears in the

---

Srednei Azii, vyp. 1 (Trudy AN Tadzhikskoi SSR, t. 12 [Stalinabad, 1954]), pp. 85-108; M. E. Masson, "Dinary kopeki," *Izvestiia AN Turkmenskoi SSR, Seriia obshchestvennykh nauk*, 1972, No. 4, pp. 27-36. The new numismatic data and information from written sources that have accumulated over nearly a half century require a new examination of this issue.

inscription of the cartouche, together with the name of the city;[3] by weight (around 1.5 g) and size (15-17 mm), these coins represent not a basic denomination, but a small fraction (most likely a third of a basic denomination). In this case it was precisely the weight and size of the coins that determined their fractional denomination; they were designated, however, not by any special term, but simply by the word *tanga*.

On the small silver coins of Herat minted under Shībānī Khān (we will see below that this was a post-reform issue), the inscription *nīm tanga* ("half *tanga*") appears in the cartouche.[4] In this inscription the term *tanga* is the designation of a silver coin of a *basic* denomi-nation.

In late-Timurid and Shībānid *vathīqa*s and *vaqf-nāma*s of various dates, different fractions or multiples—halves, two-thirds of a basic denomination, twice the denomination—are occasionally mentioned, instead of the basic denomination. But all these are designated by the term *tanga*, while their value is determined by supplementary characteristics (i.e., by an indication of their weight, of their correlation with the basic denomination, or of their equivalence to a designated number of copper coins, or through a combination of these indicators).

For example, in a *vathīqa* of 3 Dhū'l-Qaʿda 915/12 February 1510, on the sale of a garden in the district (*tümen*) of Ura-tepa (in present-day Tajikistan), *tanga*s equivalent to ten copper *dīnār*s are mentioned.[5] This is a fraction of a basic denomination. In the text of a *vaqf-nāma* of the 16th century on behalf of the *madrasa* and *ḥawż* of Ghāzīyān in Bukhara, purchase deeds for those objects (plots of land, gardens) that have been converted to *vaqf* are included.[6] In these deeds the dates of the transactions are indicated (for example, 940/1533-34, 941/1534-35),

[3] V. Tizengauzen, "Novyia numizmaticheskiia priobreteniia N. P. Linevicha," *Zapiski Vostochnago otdeleniia Imperatorskago Russkago arkheologicheskago obshchestva* [hereafter *ZVO*], 9 (1896), p. 240, No. 35; unpublished coin of the Hermitage (St. Petersburg), No. 195 c, 44a/538.

[4] V. Tizengauzen, "Vostochnyia monety N. P. Linevicha," *ZVO*, 4 (1890), pp. 312-313, No. 36, Table II/8. Another specimen is preserved at the Hermitage, No. 31361; see E. A. Davidovich, *Korpus zolotykh i serebrianykh monet Sheibanidov. XVI vek* (Moscow, 1992), p. 292, No. 728, type and variant 4/d (description of the type at p. 182), Table 2/728.

[5] A. A. Egani and O. D. Chekhovich, "Regesty sredneaziatskikh aktov," *Pis'mennye pamiatniki Vostoka*, 1974 (Moscow, 1981), p. 50, No. 3, photograph at Ill. 5.

[6] This *vaqf-nāma* is preserved in the Bukharan Museum-preserve, Inv. No. 150.

and the price is given in silver *tanga*s whose weight is one *mithqāl*. During these years the weight standard for the *tanga* of the basic denomination was equal to precisely one *mithqāl*. Hence there follows in the *vaqf-nāma* a list of monetary expenditures, indicated in other silver *tanga*s described thus: "the *tanga* in circulation, each *tanga* equal in weight to four *dāng*s[7] of one *mithqāl* of fine silver, and equivalent, in commercial transactions, to two-thirds of the *tanga* struck at [a weight of] one *mithqāl* of fine silver" (*tanga-i shahrvān ki har tanga az ān ba-vazn-i chahār dāng-i yak-mithqāl-i nuqra-i sara ast va dar muʿāmalāt ba-thulthān-i tanga-i mażrūba-i yak-mithqālī-i nuqra-i sara jārī'st*). In this case the text deals with fractions at two-thirds of the basic denomination. But these and others are equally designated in this *vaqf-nāma* by the term *tanga*.

Finally, in another *vaqf-nāma*, prepared in Rabīʿ I 942/September 1535 for the same Ghāzīyān *madrasa* in Bukhara,[8] the value of the *tanga* is established in the following way: "the well-known *tanga*, each of which amounts to forty *fals*, of the *fulūs*, [weighing] one *mithqāl* and two *nukhūd*s, that are currently in circulation in Bukhara" (*tanga-i ʿurfī ki har tanga az ān ʿibārat ast az chihīl ʿadad fals az fulūs-i yak-mithqāl va dū nukhūdī rāʾij al-vaqt-i bukhārā*). From other documents it is known that the *tanga* of the basic denomination at this time was equal to 20 copper *dīnār*s; it follows that in this description the term *tanga* designates silver coins of *double* value.

The examples cited here allow us to understand the essential meaning and signification of the term *tanga* in the period and region under consideration. The term was polysemantic; on the whole it held the most general meaning of "coin." Diverse features or supplementary characteristics (inscriptions, the weight and size of the coins themselves, descriptions in documentary sources and occasionally in other written sources) specified the metal and the value of these "coins." However, a definite tradition of perception had already taken shape. If in written (though not documentary) sources the *tanga* was mentioned without any qualifiers, contemporaries understood it to mean a silver coin of the basic denomination.

[7] A *dāng* is equal to one-sixth of a *mithqāl*.

[8] Copies of this *vaqf-nāma* are preserved in the State Archive of the Republic of Uzbekistan, *fond* I-323, No. 12, No. 1186/7, No. 1194.

The term *tangacha* ("little *tanga*"), as far as I know, has not been the subject of special investigation for some time. It appears that M. E. Masson was the first to attempt to explain the specific historical meaning of this term. In his view, the term *tangacha* had an independent and *specific* sense, as the special designation for small silver coins whose weight equaled *one fourth* of the one-*mithqāl tanga*. Masson developed this idea in detail in a special article, and formulated his conclusion thus: "The chief denomination under the Timurids was the high-standard silver tenga or tanga (*tanga*), whose weight, to judge by numismatic specimens, was as much as 6 g under Temür, and later, in the course of the 15th century, and even in times of greatest stability, fluctuated roughly between the limits of 4.5 and 5.5 g. . . . From time to time were minted, in smaller quantities, silver half-tengas (*nīm-tanga*) and small coins of one-fourth tenga, 'tengacha' (*tangacha*), corresponding to the '*dirham.*'"[9] Leaving aside the entirely incorrect notions about the weight, and weight changes, of the silver coinage minted under Temür and the Timurids,[10] we may note that the explanation proposed by Masson for the two terms (and for the equivalence: *tanga* = 4 *tangachas*) for some time seemed close to the truth, insofar as it permitted, at first glance, a satisfying explanation of the part of Khwāndamīr's text devoted to the fixed rate of silver coins.

However, the further accumulation of materials has left no doubt that both terms, *tanga* and *tangacha* (in any case after Temür) were used as *synonyms*. A few examples follow, from sources of the 15th and 16th centuries.

In the course of descriptions of silver coins found in *vathīqas* and *vaqf-nāmas* of the 15th century, their denomination was precisely determined, most often through indication of their weight. For instance, among the documents of various periods pertaining to the *mazār* of Tāj al-Dīn Ḥasan (and its inhabitants) in the village of Niyāk (a settlement of the town of Āmul in Māzandarān), there is an entire group of Timurid *vathīqas* of the 15th century; they include detailed descriptions of silver coins, with indications of their weight, and the weight is that of coins of

[9] Masson, "Dinary kopeki," p. 32.

[10] This issue is the object of special examination; see E. A. Davidovich, "O standartakh chistoty i vesovykh standartakh serebrianykh monet Timura i Timuridov (konets XIV–XV vv.)," *Vostochnoe istoricheskoe istochnikovedenie i spetsial'nye istoricheskie distsipliny*, vyp. 4 (Moscow, 1995), pp. 120-142, 147-153.

the basic denomination. The silver coins of Shāhrukh (807/1405-850/1447), in the basic denomination, are designated, in 12 documents of his and later times (in the range 833-878 A.H.), in two ways: in most cases, *tangacha* is used, and in one instance, *tanga* is used.[11]

Khwāndamīr also used both terms with reference to coins of a single value. Their synonymous character is especially noticeable when comparing identical passages in the *Ḥabīb al-siyar* and in the eighth section of the *Rawżat al-ṣafā*. For example, Shībānī Khān imposed an indemnity on Herat. In passages mentioning the amount of this contribution, and the amount of 'gifts' presented by notable figures of Herat, and so forth, the term *tangacha* appears in the *Ḥabīb al-siyar*, while *tanga* is used in the *Rawżat al-ṣafā* (these passages are discussed in more detail below).

Under the Shībānids as well, the terms *tanga* and *tangacha* were used as synonyms. In hundreds of Central Asian *vathīqa*s and *vaqf-nāma*s, in the course of describing silver coins of the basic denomination (their weight is again stipulated relative to the *mithqāl*), they are called *tanga*; but in a *vaqf-nāma* prepared in Jumādā II 947/October 1540, for a series of beneficiaries in Balkh,[12] silver coins of the same weight are called *tangacha*. In this case the synonymity of the two terms is clear from the identical weight of the silver coins. Another type of evidence is provided by an epigraphical monument—the inscription of 1541 on a marble slab mounted in the wall of the Masjid-i Kalān in Bukhara.[13] The inscription refers to exemption from three taxes levied in cash; the amount of each is indicated using the term *tangacha*, while the sum in whole is given using *tanga*.

We may note the following pattern: both terms were used under the Timurids and Shībānids in both Mavarannahr and Khurāsān, but in Mavarannahr the term *tanga* nevertheless predominated.

[11] *Asnād-i Āstāna-i . . . Darvīsh Tāj al-Dīn Ḥasan Valī dar qarya-i Niyāk az bulūk-i Lārījān az shahristān-i Āmul*, ed. Muḥammad Taqī Dānish-pizhūh (Tehran, 1344/1965), pp. 26-27, doc. 7 (*tanga*), doc. 2, 3, 5, 6, 8-11, 13, 15, 24 (*tangacha*) (the sequential enumeration of documents is mine).

[12] State Archive of the Republic of Uzbekistan, *fond* I-323, No. 1216 [see the translation and study of this document in McChesney, "Reconstructing Balkh," in the present volume].

[13] V. A. Shishkin, "Nadpisi na portale Bol'shoi mecheti v Bukhare," *Biulleten' Akademii nauk Uzbekskoi SSR*, 1947, No. 8, pp. 25-26; *idem*, "Firman 1541 g. na portale Bol'shoi sobornoi mecheti Bukhary," *Istoriia material'noi kul'tury Uzbekistana*, vyp. 5 (1964), pp. 161-162.

Naturally a question arises: when and why did two terms, quite different semantically ("*tanga*" and "little *tanga*"), come to be used to designate coins of a single weight and value?

Studying the question of the weight standards adopted for the minting of the silver coins of Temür and the Timurids, I offered the following proposal regarding the origin of the term *tangacha*. In the coinage of Temür a minimum of two weight standards was used. The precise amount of the earlier and higher one has still not been established (it was, in any case, over 7 g), while the second weight standard was equal to a *mithqāl* and two *dāng*s (6.4 g). Under Shāhrukh three weight standards were used: a *mithqāl* plus one and a half *dāng* (= 6.0 g); a *mithqāl* and a *dāng* (= 5.6 g); a *mithqāl* and one-half *dāng* (= 5.2 g). Under the last Timurids the weight standard was equal to one *mithqāl* (4.8 g). The general tendency was a gradual decrease of the weight standard.[14] The typical norm of the reduction was half a *dāng*. The lower weight standard for Temür's silver (a *mithqāl* and two *dāng*s) and the highest weight standard for Shāhrukh's silver (a *mithqāl* and one-and-a-half *dāng*) differed by all of a half *dāng*. The amount of decrease was not large, but this was a reduction of the weight standard that *Temür himself* had established! It appears that the term *tangacha* came into use after Temür, and that the violation of his norms was perceived as something special, distinct from any ordinary reduction of the weight standard. In other words, the appearance of the 'pejorative' term *tangacha* ("little *tanga*") and its use instead of, and as a synonym of, the term *tanga*, was probably the result of the interweaving of the actual situation with its psychological perception.

Much has been written about the term *dīnār*, but its concrete historical meaning in the 15th-16th centuries and in Khurāsān and Mavarannahr has long remained unexplained, as reference literature and general works about the history of the Muslim east vividly demonstrate. In the meantime, however, the gradual accumulation of materials and of individual observations, and the combined analysis of various types of sources (inscriptions on coins and on their countermarks, descriptions of coins in *vathīqa*s and *vaqf-nāma*s, models for the descriptions of coins in works on *shurūṭ*, isolated data in other sources) have allowed us to understand the meaning of this term. Such analysis leaves no doubt about the polysemantic character of the term *dīnār* during the period in

[14] Davidovich, "O standartakh chistoty i vesovykh standartakh," pp. 120 ff.

question.[15] Taken by itself, this term might be used to designate coins of *any metal.* Its connection with gold coins was already sundered in commerce and daily life, and gold coins in Mavarannahr and Khurāsān had their own designations (primarily, as noted above, *ashrafī*); nevertheless the phrase "gold *dīnār*" might appear in a written source, and such use would not have evoked any surprise. Silver and copper *dīnār*s were the reality, and so only epithets or some sort of supplementary qualifier would offer a clear idea of the metal involved. For copper *dīnār*s, in both Mavarannahr and Khurāsān, the most general and widely used qualifier was the term *fulūs* (the plural of the word *fals*). By itself, in that period, it designated any copper coin (independent of its denomination), and for this reason it served as a sufficient qualifier for the other term. The expression *dīnār-i fulūs* indicated that the *dīnār* in question was copper. There were also other supplementary and independent qualifiers for the *dīnār*, which showed that a copper coin, a copper *dīnār*, was intended. In Iran, in particular, the names of the cities in which these coins were minted were used as epithets for the specification of the copper *dīnār* (for example, the Herātī *dīnār* or "*dīnār* of Herat," the Tabrīzī *dīnār*, etc.).

It is clear that the term *dīnār* did not require any sort of qualifier *in the inscriptions on the copper coins themselves* or their countermarks, and indeed the word *dīnār* is often supplied independently in coin inscriptions (for example, on the *dīnār*s of Ḥiṣār, Tirmidh, and Qundūz from 907/1501-02). But in coin inscriptions as well, the term *dīnār* is quite often qualified by some word emphasizing that this was a real copper coin—a "copper *dīnār*" (for example, on the *dīnār*s of Marv from 912/1506-07 and of Samarqand from 914/1508-09). The specification of the *dīnār*'s metal in circumstances when this is not required reflects the inertia of the polysemantic character of the term itself.

Among all the epithets that qualified the word *dīnār* in the 15th century, the most problematical is the epithet *kepekī* (*kebekī*, *kopekī*; different authors have adopted different vocalizations); this term has received varied and even contradictory interpretations. The *dīnār kepekī* is quite often mentioned in various written sources recounting events of the age of Temür and the Timurids. For a long time it was supposed

[15] E. A. Davidovich, *Istoriia denezhnogo obrashcheniia srednevekovoi Srednei Azii (mednye monety XV–pervoi chetverti XVI v. v Maverannakhre)* (Moscow, 1983), pp. 32-57.

that the *dīnār kepekī* of the 15th and 16th centuries was a large silver coin that received its designation from the name of the Chaghatayid *khān* Kepek (r. ca. 1318-1326), who initiated their minting in Mavarannahr. V. V. Bartol'd thought that the silver *dīnār*s introduced by Kepek Khān weighed two *zolotnik*s (appr. 8.5 g) and subsequently were called by his name (down to the time of Temür and the Timurids). From different comments by Bartol'd it is evident that in his view, the very coins that were struck under Kepek himself survived to the time of the Timurids.[16] While Bartol'd did not mention the origin of the *kepekī dīnār*s, he nonetheless stressed that under the Timurids they were silver and weighed two *mithqāl*s.[17] At the same time, Bartol'd also knew about copper *dīnār*s. He relied on the testimony of Bābur regarding *tūmān*s (i.e., units of 10,000) of copper coins, and on the *vaqf-nāma* of the first quarter of the 16th century for the *madrasa* of Muḥammad Shībānī Khān in Samarqand.[18] It is important to emphasize that Bartol'd did not equate copper *dīnār*s with *kepekī dīnār*s, since he considered the latter to have been *silver* coins weighing two *zolotnik*s, or two *mithqāl*s.

The meaning of the *dīnār kepekī*, as Bartol'd treats it, does not fit with Khwāndamīr's account of the reform of Shībānī Khān (on the reform, see Sections 3-4 of this article). In particular, it is stressed in Khwāndamīr's text that, according to the reform, the former (i.e., Timurid) one-*mithqāl tangacha* would be equal to five *kepekī dīnār*s. If the *kepekī dīnār* weighed two *zolotnik*s or two *mithqāl*s, then five *dīnār*s would have been equal to ten *zolotnik*s or ten *mithqāl*s (with a *zolotnik* of 4.26 g, this would amount to 42.6 g, or, with a *mithqāl* of 4.8 g, to 48 g). The one-*mithqāl* Timurid *tangacha* (with a weight standard of 4.8 g) could not have been equal to five *kepekī dīnār*s of *that* sort (i.e., from 42.6 to 48 g)! Bartol'd, regarding the *kepekī dīnār*s as coins of the Chaghatayid ruler Kepek Khān himself (r. ca. 1318-1326), assumed thereby that they were in circulation for a long time, two centuries and more. In general this is possible, and there are examples of the

[16] V. V. Bartol'd, "Ulugbek i ego vremia," *Sochineniia*, II/2 (Moscow, 1964), p. 33; *idem*, "Istoriia Turkestana," *Sochineniia*, II/1 (Moscow, 1963), p. 152; *idem*, "Istoriia kul'turnoi zhizni Turkestana," *Sochineniia*, II/1 (Moscow, 1963), p. 263.

[17] Bartol'd, "Mir Ali-Shir i politicheskaia zhizn'," *Sochineniia*, II/2 (Moscow, 1964), p. 216.

[18] Bartol'd, "Tuman," *Sochineniia*, V (Moscow, 1968), pp. 570-571.

prolonged circulation of certain coin issues.[19] But in such cases the weight of the coins diminishes substantially and differentially. For example,[20] the *tanga*s of Muḥammad Raḥīm (the first *khān* of the Manghït dynasty in Bukhara, r. 1166/1753-1172/1758), circulated in Central Asia for more than a century and a half. Their weight standard was 4.8 g, and their actual weights were in the range of 1.09–3.90 g (that is, a weight loss in the range of 20–80%); their external features were worn (in most cases the inscriptions and cartouches were entirely invisible, or nearly so). In other words, the *dīnār*s of Kepek Khān would have had, by the beginning of the 16th century, a quite low and *varied* actual weight, and it would thus have been absurd to fix the rate for other coins, or changes in the rate, in terms of them. In addition, the composition of hoards of silver coins from the 15th century and the beginning of the 16th does not at all confirm Bartol'd's assumption regarding such a prolonged circulation of the *dīnār*s of Kepek Khān. In hoards of Timurid and early Shïbānid silver coins there are no silver *dīnār*s of the Chaghatayid Kepek Khān.

M. E. Masson, evidently, was the first to consider *kepekī dīnār*s to have been, rather, *copper* coins. He defined the precise relationship between the terms *tanga*, *tangacha*, and *dīnār kepekī* (and the coins referred to by these three terms) as follows: the basic silver denomination was the *tanga*, the "quarter" (the numerous silver coins weighing one fourth of a *tanga*) was the *tangacha*, and *copper* coins were the *kepekī dīnār*s. This conception was set forth in considerable detail in a special article, "Dinary kopeki."[21]

The conclusion that the *dīnār kepekī* was a *copper* coin did not arouse any doubt for some time, since it found, as it then seemed, more and more confirmation. The most consequential was the discovery of the term *dīnār* in inscriptions on copper coins themselves and in their

[19] E. A. Davidovich, "O sredneaziatskikh srednevekovykh monetakh v sviazi s datirovkoi arkheologicheskikh ob'ektov," *Istoriia, arkheologiia i ètnografiia Srednei Azii* (Moscow, 1968), pp. 247-248.

[20] E. A. Davidovich, "O proiskhozhdenii i znachenii termina *miri* v denezhnom khoziaistve Srednei Azii XV–nachala XX v.," *Istoriia i kul'tura narodov Srednei Azii (Drevnost' i srednie veka)* (Moscow, 1976), p. 125.

[21] M. E. Masson, "Dinary kopeki," pp. 27-36. Masson considered that the very word *kepekī* (which he vocalized "*kopekī*") was not connected with the name of the Chaghatayid ruler Kepek Khān, but was, apparently, a "popular term" for the copper coins that were officially termed "*dīnār*s."

countermarks. In several articles from 1950-1953, I published these remarkable copper coins of the first decade of the 16th century (mints of Marv, Samarqand, Ḥiṣār, Qundūz, and Tirmidh).[22] As it turned out, such coins had been published often in scholarly literature, but this most important, key word, *dīnār*, had not been read by the scholars who published them.

However, further investigation of direct and indirect data from the sources has shown convincingly that the term *dīnār kepekī* was *never* the designation of a copper coin.

In 1965 I published quite interesting evidence from of a source close to the time under consideration, and to the reform of Shībānī Khān. From this evidence it followed that silver coins, not copper, were known as *kepekī dīnār*s, although copper coins were also called *dīnārs*—but *not* "*kepekī*." The metal of the coins called *dīnār*s was specified by an epithet; the epithet "*kepekī*" gave contemporaries the clear impression that a *silver* coin was intended.[23] Nevertheless, Masson disregarded the published reference to that source, and in the article mentioned above, from 1972, he repeated and further developed his old notion about the *kepekī dīnār* as an exclusively *copper* coin under the Timurids.

The source mentioned here, which revealed the meaning of the term *dīnār-i kepekī* (so important for understanding Khwāndamīr's text about the monetary reform of Shībānī Khān), was a guidebook, the *Mukhtār al-ikhtiyār ʿalā madhhab al-mukhtār*, a manual for judges concerning legal procedure and the preparation of documents in judicial processes. The author was Ikhtiyār b. Ghiyāth al-Dīn al-Ḥusaynī (d. 927/1520), a well-known judge of Herat. The work was completed, evidently, in 908/1502.[24] Various sections of this work include detailed

[22] E. A. Davidovich, "K mednym nominalam kontsa XV–nachala XVI v. po dannym chekana Khisara i Kunduza," *Soobshcheniia Tadzhikskogo filiala AN SSSR*, vyp. 24 (Stalinabad, 1950), pp. 39-46; *idem*, "Nekotorye cherty obrashcheniia mednykh monet v Srednei Azii XV-XVI vv. i rol' nadchekanov," *Izvestiia AN TadzhSSR*, Otdelenie obshchestvennykh nauk, 1953, No. 3, pp. 55-61; *idem*, "Shaartuzskii klad dvoinykh dinarov 906/1500-1501 i 907/1501-1502 gg.," *Doklady AN TadzhSSR*, vyp. 9 (1953), pp. 31-42.

[23] E. A. Davidovich, "Materialy dlia kharakteristiki denezhnoi reformy Ulugbeka," *Iz istorii èpokhi Ulugbeka* (Tashkent, 1965), p. 281.

[24] On this work see B. S. Sergeev, *Perechen' vostochnykh rukopisei V. L. Viatkina v Gosudarstvennoi publichnoi biblioteke UzSSR*, t. I (Tashkent, 1935), p. 85, No. 212 (the author considered the date of the work's completion to be 899/1493, and dated the copy to 908/1502); *Sobranie vostochnykh rukopisei Akademii nauk Uzbekskoi SSR* (hereafter "*SVR*"), IV (Tashkent, 1957), pp. 292-293, Nos. 3208-3209 (here the

recommendations regarding the description of money, as well as examples of such descriptions. For our purposes two variants of a description of silver coins whose weight was equal to a third of a *mithqāl* are of special interest, insofar as the term or epithet *kepekī* appears in precisely these variants.

In the section called "*vathīqa* [formalizing] a purchase," the formulary for this type of document is presented, and in the appropriate place appears the following monetary description: "for one thousand *dīnār*s of fine silver struck at the mint of the city [region?] of Herat, three of which *dīnār*s are equal in weight to one *mithqāl* according to the *mithqāl*s accepted in Herat, and go for 18 *dīnār*s of Herat" (*ba-yak hazār dīnār-i nuqra-i sara-i mażrūba be-żarb-i balada-i harāt ki har sa dīnār az ān ba-vazn-i yak-mithqāl ast ba-mathāqīl-i mutadāvil ba-harāt va ba-hizhda dīnār-i haravī jārī ast*).[25]

In another section, various items are first described, and their prices are given in *dīnār*s (without qualification); then the following general description of these *dīnār*s is included: "the *ʿadlī* of excellent quality, in circulation, of *kepekī* type, three of which *dīnār*s [equal] one *mithqāl* of fine silver and in Herat go for 18 *dīnār*s of Herat" (*ʿadlī-i jayyid-i rāʾij-i kepekī ast ki har sa dīnār az ān yak-mithqāl-i nuqra-i sara va dar harāt ba-hizhde dīnār-i haravī jārī ast*).

In both cases identical coins are under discussion: these are not accounting units, but actual coins ("struck" in the first description, "in circulation" in the second); they have one and the same weight standard (three of them equal a *mithqāl* of Herat); they were minted of silver ("silver" in the first description, equated to a *mithqāl* of silver in the second); and each of these minted silver coins weighing a third of a *mithqāl* is equal to six "*dīnār*s of Herat." Consequently, identical coins are at issue in the two descriptions. The guidebook allowed that the description of these identical coins would vary textually, but would necessarily include the following characteristics: designation of the

work is dated 908/1502; the date did not arouse suspicion, and hence the work was included in the index of manuscripts whose date was "precisely determined," see p. 540). I have used the two copies of the work in the Institute of Oriental Studies of the Academy of Sciences of the Republic of Uzbekistan, and I cite the manuscript bearing Inventory No. 2064 [Cat. No. 3209], ff. 105a and 196a; there are no substantive variant readings in the corresponding passages from the second manuscript.

[25] For the Arabic-script versions of this, and of the three subsequent descriptions of the *kepekī dīnār* and the *ʿadlī kepekī*, see Davidovich, *Istoriia denezhnogo obrashcheniia srednevekovoi Srednei Azii*, pp. 48-49.

metal (silver), the weight (a third of a *mithqāl*), and the fixed rate (in terms of "*dīnār*s of Herat"). There are two designations: *dīnār* and *ʿadlī*. Consequently, these designations are synonyms. Their synonymous character can be established even from one of the descriptions (the second), in which the terms *ʿadlī* and *dīnār* substitute for one another. Moreover, in this second description, the term *ʿadlī* is supplied with the epithet *kepekī*. From this it is possible to conclude with certainty that the epithet *kepekī* determined the *metal* of a coin that was 'amorphously' called sometimes *dīnār* and sometimes *ʿadlī*. These designations are 'amorphous' in that they could be used for coins of different metals. The use of the term *dīnār* for *copper* coins of the period in question was already mentioned above; but the term *ʿadlī* as well was used as a designation for *copper* coins, as is clear both from coin inscriptions, and from written sources.[26]

Thus, a comparative analysis of the two examples of monetary description included in a work from the beginning of the 16th century allows us to draw the first important conclusion: small silver coins weighing a third of a *mithqāl* were called, in that period, *dīnār kepekī* or *ʿadlī kepekī*.

This conclusion is further confirmed by another monetary description, discovered by O. D. Chekhovich in a guidebook for the preparation of private documents, written, according to her determination, under the designation *al-Javāmiʿ al-ʿalīya fī'l-vathāʾiq al-sharʿīya va'l-sijillāt al-marʿīya*, by a Bukharan judge of the late 15th and early 16th centuries, ʿAlī b. Muḥammad ʿAlī b. ʿAlī b. Maḥmūd al-Mukhtārī al-Khwārazmī al-Kubravī. Chekhovich published this description (with reference to analogous material in my article from 1965) in paraphrase: "Kepekī *dīnār*s, of silver, by weight one third of a *mithqāl*, exchangeable in Herat for six local *dīnār*s apiece."[27]

Professor Chekhovich was so kind as to copy for me this passage of the text (which I cite below in transcription from the Arabic script and in translation); its value is heightened by the precise date, since the

[26] E. A. Davidovich, *Istoriia denezhnogo obrashcheniia srednevekovoi Srednei Azii*, pp. 35-38, 56-57.

[27] O. D. Chekhovich, "Cherty èkonomicheskoi zhizni Maverannakhra v sochineniiakh po *fikkhu* i *shurutu*," *Blizhnii i Srednii Vostok. Tovarno-denezhnye otnosheniia pri feodalizme* (Moscow, 1980), p. 228 and note 40 at p. 230; see the description of the apparently unique manuscript (MS IVAN RUz 9138) at *SVR*, VIII, pp. 313-317, No. 5872.

monetary description was excerpted from a document (on the sale of land in villages in the region of Balkh) entered into the work under the year 901/1496: "for the sum of 23,000 *kepekī dīnār*s, three of which *dīnār*s [equal] by weight one *mithqāl* of fine silver and are exchangeable in Herat for 18 *dīnār*s" (*ba-mablagh-i bīst-ū-sa hazār dīnār-i kepekī ki har sa dīnār az ān ba-vazn-i yak-mithqāl-i nuqra-i sara ast va dar harāt rā'ij ba-hizhda dīnār*). In this description the terms *dīnār* and *kepekī* are already linked directly.

In the three virtually identical descriptions of *silver dīnār*s, *dīnār*s of another type figure as well, called "*dīnār*s of Herat;" the fixed rate of the silver *dīnār*s is specified through them: the *dīnār kepekī* = *ʿadlī kepekī* is equal to *six dīnār*s of Herat. It is clear that these *dīnār*s of Herat are *copper* coins; that is, the value and rate of *kepekī dīnār*s is specified in terms of weight in silver (three *kepekī dīnār*s equal a *mithqāl* of silver) and in terms of copper coins circulating in Herat. It should be noted that the fixing of the rate for silver coins in terms of copper coins was a widespread practice.[28]

Just one question arises: do the three equivalent descriptions of *kepekī dīnār*s reflect real things from the end of the 15th century and the beginning of the 16th, or are they abstract recommendations about the components needed for a proper characterization (metal, weight, fixed rate)? Evidence of an altogether different type confirms that these were indeed real things. In 910/1504-05, a manuscript was purchased (the manuscript itself contains a note to this effect) for 1000 *dīnār*s, a sum then equal to 55 *tangacha*s.[29] As was established above, the *tangacha* was at that time minted according to a weight standard of one *mithqāl*, and from pure silver. This means that in 910/1504-05 a *mithqāl* of fine, pure silver was equal to 1000 : 55 = 18 *dīnār*s. Precisely the same equivalence (a *mithqāl* of fine silver = 18 copper *dīnār*s of Herat) was stipulated in the three examples of monetary descriptions cited above.

The *dīnār kepekī* was thus not a copper coin, but a silver one. In the sources cited here from the end of the 15th century and the beginning

[28] In hundreds of preserved documents prepared in Mavarannahr beginning from the second half of the 15th century under the Timurids, and in the 16th century and the first half of the 17th under the Shībānids and Jānids, it is precisely *copper dīnār*s that fix the rate of silver *tanga*s.

[29] O. I. Smirnova, "Iz biografii rukopisi 'Ta'rikh-i guzida' sobraniia LO IVAN SSSR," *Srednevekovyi Vostok. Istoriia, kul'tura, istochnikovedenie* (Moscow, 1980), pp. 243-244.

of the 16th, one *mithqāl* of silver (meaning also the one-*mithqāl tangacha*) was equal to three *kepekī dīnār*s, and each silver *dīnār kepekī* (*ʿadlī kepekī*) was equal to six copper Herātī *dīnār*s.

Supplementary data about the real significance of the term *dīnār-i kepekī* appears in a *vaqf-nāma* from 912/1506, drawn up in Herat.[30] This document was discovered and studied by Chekhovich, who kindly sent me the text of the monetary description: "All the cash money that was mentioned is the current *ʿadlī kepekī*, six of which *dīnār*s are equal, by weight, to one *mithqāl* of fine silver and in Herat go for 36 *dīnār*s of Herat" (*majmūʿ-i naqda ki madhkūr shod az ʿadlī-i rāʾij-i kepekī ast ki har shash dīnār az ān ba-vazn-i yak-mithqāl-i nuqra-i sara ast va dar harāt ba-sī va shash dīnār-i haravī rāʾij*).

In this description (unlike the preceding ones), a *mithqāl* of fine silver is equal not to three, but to *six dīnār*s of the *kepekī-ʿadlī* type, and not to 18, but to 36 copper *dīnār*s of Herat.

It turns out that in the various sources cited above, silver coins of *two* values are referred to as *kepekī dīnār*s: there are *kepekī dīnār*s weighing one *third* of a *mithqāl*, and weighing one *sixth* of a *mithqāl*. From this it follows, above all, that the term *dīnār kepekī* was not an individual designation for some absolutely specified silver coins of a single value.[31]

The testimony of Clavijo (the Spanish ambassador to Temür's court in Samarqand) regarding the currency of Samarqand at the very beginning of the 15th century is worth noting here. From his account it appears that the small silver coin amounting to one *fourth* of the basic silver denomination was called *mīrī*. Clavijo's testimony is reliable, since it is confirmed by other data. First of all, silver coins equal by weight to a fourth of the basic denomination were actually minted, and are found in hoards together with silver *tanga*s of the basic denomination. Second, the term *mīrī* entered firmly into monetary affairs and continued to exist in Central Asia down to the beginning of the 20th century, preserving its initial sense: a *mīrī* was one-*fourth* of the basic

[30] State Archive of the Republic of Uzbekistan, *fond* I-323, No. 1427.

[31] Does it not follow from this that *any* silver coin could be called a *kepekī dīnār*, that is, both a basic denomination and any fraction of it? In other words, was not the term *dīnār-i kepekī* in the 15th century and the beginning of the 16th *synonymous* with the terms *tanga* and *tangacha*? Some indirect evidence attests to the usefulness of such a suggestion, but it will not be reviewed in the present article, insofar as the question has no connection with the reform of Shībānī Khān.

denomination.[32] Consequently, under Temür and the Timurids there was a concrete designation for coins of a *single* value. Was the term *mīrī* used as a designation for a silver coin one fourth the value of the basic denomination in Khurāsān as well? Conversely, was the expression *dīnār-i kepekī* used as a synonym for the term *tanga* in order to designate fractions of the basic silver denomination in Mavarannahr? The most reliable answer to these questions would be provided by the discovery of the term *mīrī* in documents prepared in any city of Khurāsān, and of the term *dīnār-i kepekī* in documents originating from any city of Mavarannahr. For now the possibility of local variants of monetary terminology should not be mechanically excluded. But in any case, the use in Mavarannahr of the term *mīrī* as a designation for a silver coin of a single determined value (a quarter of the basic denomination) does not refute the conclusion drawn above: that the expression *dīnār kepekī* (in Khurāsān, in any event) was used to designate two (or any?) *fractions* of the basic silver denomination, with the actual value of these fractions determined by supplementary characteristics (in the instances cited above, their fixed rate, specified in terms of copper *dīnār*s, and their weight).

2. THE PRE-REFORM SITUATION IN MAVARANNAHR AND KHURĀSĀN

The history of Mavarannahr at the time of its conquest by Shībānī Khān is so saturated with military campaigns, sieges, battles, and the plundering and devastation of the population, that these events could not but affect the economic circumstances of the region, and its monetary trade even moreso. Especially difficult during this period was the lot of central Mavarannahr (Samarqand, Bukhara, and other towns), which became the arena for the most bitter internecine struggle among various rulers of the Timurid house; Shībānī Khān as well participated actively in this struggle, and then moved on to the systematic conquest of Mavarannahr. The Timurid Bābur—a participant in all these events—describes the extent to which this brought ruinous and disastrous consequences for the region's inhabitants.[33] Suffice it to say that after

[32] E. A. Davidovich, "O proiskhozhdenii i znachenii termina *miri*," pp. 124-127. The term was polysemantic, and began to be used as a designation for coins of other metals (from copper and gold) as well, but in every case for the designation of precisely a *quarter* of the basic denomination.

[33] *Babur-name. Zapiski Babura*, tr. M. Sal'e (Tashkent, 1958), pp. 93-102. A. A. Semenov examined the struggle during these years between the Timurids and

his second seizure of Bukhara, Shībānī Khān subjected the city to pillage and imposed an enormous indemnity upon it; during his four-month siege of Samarqand a frightful famine set in, as there was no importation of provisions. But even in this difficult period—when the city was changing hands, famine and the devastation of the population were the marks of the age, and prices could not help but soar—various rulers tried to extract revenues through the minting and circulation of money, thereby further worsening the situation.

After the decisive conquest of central Mavarannahr by Shībānī Khān (1501), an attempt was made to normalize monetary trade within cities and among cities, and to provide a certain stability in monetary circulation, without forgoing fiscal revenues in the process. The following numismatic data attest to this effort.

1. *An attempt to return silver coins to the market.* In 907/1501, in Samarqand, the issue of *silver* coins in the name of Shībānī Khān was begun, but silver coins of his from subsequent years are not known. It was, of course, impossible for Shībānī Khān to reestablish a regular and substantial minting (of free silver or of exchequer silver) after prolonged devastation and lack of confidence in the future.

For the normal life of the market, however, silver coins were essential. A simple solution was found: to permit legal commerce using the silver coins of the Timurids. This is confirmed first of all by *anonymous countermarks* on Timurid silver coins, done under Shībānī Khān in the very first years of his rule. These were countermarks of Type 1 (the criterion for the type of countermark is the form of the cartouche; see Figure 1/1), with two dates given, in numerals, with complete reliability, i.e., 907 A.H.[34] and 909 A.H.[35] It is important that this was a sustained action over several years, and it had the aim,

---

Shībānī Khān in detail in his "Sheibani-khan i zavoevanie im imperii Timuridov," *Materialy po istorii tadzhikov i uzbekov Srednei Azii*, vyp. 1 (Trudy AN Tadzhikskoi SSR, t. 12 [Stalinabad, 1954]), pp. 39-83.

[34] Hermitage, Nos. 31263, 31267. Two coins with these countermarks were published by A. K. Markov (see his *Inventarnyi katalog musul'manskikh monet imp. Ėrmitazha* [St. Petersburg, 1896], p. 678, Nos. 249, 252), but he misread the date of the countermark on the first as 917 A.H.: for the numeral in the tens place he adopted a line located somewhat lower and at an angle (it forms the top of the letter "*lām*"), whereas in fact a point, indicating zero, appears in its proper place.

[35] Unpublished coins, State Historical Museum, Moscow, No. 939278; Samarkand Museum (Uzbekistan), No. 428.

accordingly, of saturating the market with a large quantity of Timurid silver coins, of a unitary rate, with countermarks. The prolonged duration of this measure attests to its success: Timurid silver coins (undoubtedly hoarded by their possessors during the time of internecine wars) were returned to the market and found new life with the aid of countermarks of Type 1.

Figure 1

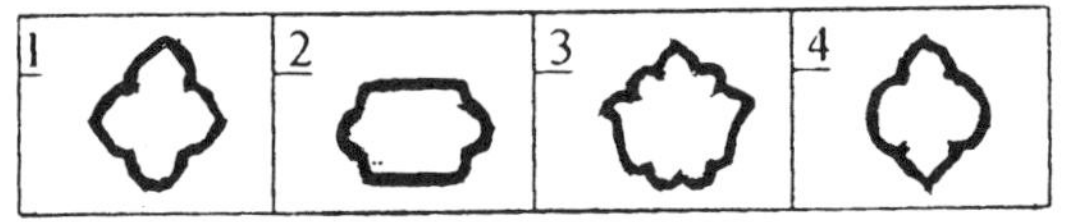

Types 1-3: Anonymous Countermarks of Shïbānī Khān on Timurid Silver Coins
Type 4: Anonymous Countermarks of Köchkünjī Khān

Timurid silver coins without anonymous countermarks were also in circulation. The composition of hoards formed later attests to this. But as indisputable as it is that the rate of Timurid silver coins without countermarks and of those with anonymous counter-marks of type 1 varied, the rate of the latter was higher. This is not only a logical supposition; concrete materials relating to the organization of silver coin circulation in the 16th century under the Shïbānids shows that silver coins minted according to a single weight standard and a single standard of fineness (a decreed standard) were divided into two legal groups of different fixed rates. We do not know the scale of the difference in the fixed rate between the Timurid coins without countermarks and those with anonymous countermarks of type 1 under Shïbānī Khān, but there was a difference, and it was stipulated and communicated to the population. If at some point a document should be discovered from the first years of Shïbānī Khān's rule in central Mavarannahr, formalizing some sort of transaction made for silver coins, and accompanied by a reliable and detailed description of these coins, then this official difference in the rate will perhaps become known. Later on under the Shïbānids it was always equal to ten percent.

2. *An attempt to overcome inflation of copper coins and to organize their state-wide circulation at an equal rate.* In 907/1501-02 a

decentralized minting of uniform single-type copper coins of a basic denomination—copper *dīnār*s—was begun. In the capital, Samarqand, they were issued each year from 907 to 910 A.H. In other words, the 'old' *dīnār*s, which had undergone profound inflation, were prohibited, and the new single-type *dīnār*s, in the course of four years, 'filled the place' thus left open: this issue of coins itself brought in revenue to the treasury, but there were not the usual attempts to increase revenues by a quick replacement of some copper *dīnār*s by others. The Samarqandī *dīnār*s of 907–910 A.H. were freed from fluctuations in rate, which should have facilitated the stabilization of retail trade in the sphere of copper circulation. Copper *dīnār*s of Bukhara, of this very type, are so far known only with one date, 907/1501-02, i.e., the date when the issue of coins was decreed. It is not impossible that the minting of these coins in Bukhara continued into the subsequent years, but without changing the date on the reverse (such *series* in the minting of copper coins in Central Asia are well known). After the seizure of Ḥiṣār, an issue of copper coins on the model of those of Samarqand and Bukhara was carried out there as well. The uniformity of type in the decentralized minting of copper *dīnār*s had a clear goal: to provide for their circulation, with a single fixed rate, among cities in the entire territory of the conquered state of the Mavarannahrid branch of the Timurids.

Figure 2

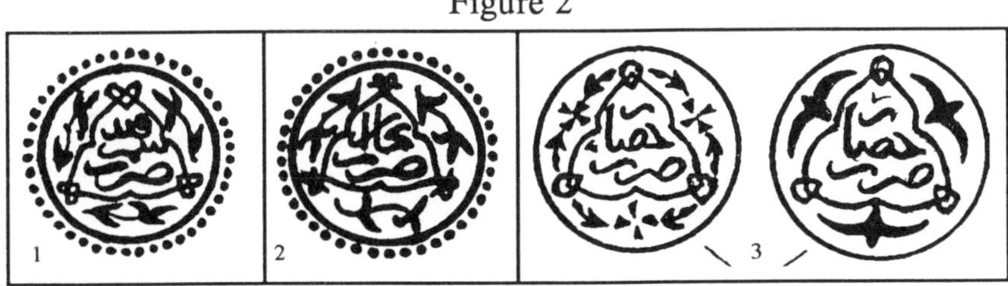

Single-Type Copper *Dīnār*s of Samarqand, Bukhara, and Ḥiṣār, 907-910 A.H.

One further detail is worth noting. Late Timurid silver coins and the silver coins of Shībānī Khān from 907/1501-02 were minted according to a weight standard of one *mithqāl*. The new anonymous copper coins, whose issue began in 907/1501-02, were also minted according to a weight standard of one *mithqāl*. An identical weight standard for silver and copper coins of the basic denomination always attests to a 'systematic approach' to the minting of currency and the organization of its circulation. The common conception in the case at hand was to overcome the inflation of copper coins, to return silver coins (both those in the name of Shībānī Khān and those of the Timurids, with and without anonymous countermarks) to the market, and to unify the weight standard of coins of various metals. The specific rates of silver coins from this period, expressed in terms of the new copper *dīnār*s, remain unknown. But there can be no doubt that these rates were *fixed*, as is confirmed by the experience of preceding and subsequent times, when, following inflation or crises of monetary circulation efforts were made to stabilize monetary trade. A return to an old rate, or the stipulation of a new one, was the most important component in stabilization.

To evaluate the organization of monetary circulation in central Mavarannahr under Shībānī Khān in the years 907-910 A.H., a comparison with Ḥiṣār is relevant. Prior to 907 A.H. both central Mavarannahr and Ḥiṣār belonged to the Timurids, but monetary policy and the forms and intensity of the use of coin *regalia* were completely independent in these two subregions; consequently, at the turn of the 15th-16th centuries, the condition of monetary trade in the two subregions was not identical. In central Mavarannahr a complex of political and economic causes created a near-crisis situation; the situation in Ḥiṣār may be appraised, without exaggeration, as one of acute crisis.

Beginning from 907/1501-02, central Mavarannahr and Ḥiṣār were separated politically, and measures were taken in the two subregions, in the very same year, 907 A.H., to normalize monetary circulation; the measures were not only independent, but also fundamentally different both in substance and in results. The initial conditions in Ḥiṣār were worse, but there, instead of stabilization through old methods, a *fundamental reform* in the minting and circulation of copper coins was carried out.[36] Here it will suffice to mention three elements of the reform. First was the issue of completely new coins of three denominations, with the denominations of two of these indicated, in their inscriptions, in Persian, understandable to the local population: *dū dīnār* ("two *dīnār*s") and *yak dīnār* ("one *dīnār*"). Second was a full restructuring of the scale of prices: the *double dīnār* became the basic denomination, and such coins were issued, beginning in 907 A.H., in

[36] Davidovich, *Istoriia denezhnogo obrashcheniia srednevekovoi Srednei Azii*, pp. 211-222.

Ḥiṣār, Tirmidh, and Qundūz, on a scale appropriate to the issue of a basic denomination. This element of the reform marked an effort to adapt the supplies of money to a stable rise in prices. Third was a prohibition of any further circulation of the old, discredited, pre-reform copper coins. After the successful reform, which took into account the depth of the crisis, stability in the rise of average prices, and social psychology, Ḥiṣār enjoyed a period of unprecedented stability, and for several years there were no changes of any kind.

Beginning in 910/1504-05, the fiscal policy of Shībānī Khān changed radically. In that year, the countermarking of copper *dīnār*s was conducted on a state-wide scale; the measure worked to the disadvantage of the population, but nonetheless preserved the foundation for these coins' state-wide circulation at a single fixed rate. Later on these foundations as well were destroyed, as Shībānid appanage-holders carried out frequent countermarking for their own benefit. This again led to inflation, and copper coins lost the peoples' confidence, as countermarks with the Persian inscription *khūb* ("good [coin]")—an obvious distress signal—attest with particular eloquence.

Less is known about the situation, beginning in 910/1504-05, of the minting and circulation of *silver* coins in Mavarannahr. The countermark of Bukhara, from 911/1505-06 (Type 2, Fig. 1/2), on a silver Timurid *tangacha* suggests that fiscal policy with respect to organizing the circulation of silver Timurid coins had also ceased to be state-wide.

It is not possible to evaluate, with similar thoroughness, the pre-reform situation in monetary trade in Khurāsān, insofar as copper coins from this region have not been studied at all. In hoards found in the territory of Mavarannahr and Ḥiṣār, only isolated examples appear of coin issues from cities of Khurāsān (Marv, Herat, and others). Hoards of copper coins from the territory of Iran are unknown to me; it is precisely coin hoards, meanwhile, that remain the fundamental source for the study of all questions regarding the minting and circulation of copper coins, and the condition of retail trade in goods of wide-scale use.

The written sources cited above (see Section 1 of this article) do give some idea about the pre-reform situation in Khurāsān. They established the rate of silver *kepekī dīnār*s in terms of copper *dīnār*s. These data allow the recalculation of the equivalence between a *mithqāl* of pure silver (including, hence, the one-*mithqāl* Timurid *tangacha*) and copper coins; it turned out that the one-*mithqāl* Timurid *tangacha* made of pure silver was at first equal to 18 copper *dīnārs*, and then to 36. The latest date for which the first rate is established is 910/1504-05; and from the description of money in the *vaqf-nāma* of 912/1506 it is evident that a *mithqāl* of silver was then equal to 36 copper *dīnārs*. Khwāndamīr mentions the same rate, when he writes about the pre-reform Timurid one-*mithqāl tangachas*, which were equal to six *kepekī dīnārs* (i.e., 36 copper *dīnārs*). It thus appears that sometime between 910/1504-05 and 912/1506-07, the monetary market underwent a profound shock. This is understandable under the circumstances, when Shībānī Khān had already conquered central Mavarannahr, Khwārazm, and the subregion of Ḥiṣār. It was clear that his next goal would be the capital of Herat and the other possessions of the Timurids. Inflationary expectations led to substantial changes already before Shībānī Khān crossed the Amū Daryā, crushed the Timurid army, and on 8 Muḥarram 913/20 May 1507 encamped not far from Herat, where the notables soon decided to surrender the city to him without a fight.

Thus, at the moment when Shībānī Khān took possession of Herat, and the monetary reform was announced in his name in the cathedral mosque of Herat in Muḥarram 913/1507, the situation with monetary trade in both Mavarannahr and Khurāsān was in all reality one of crisis. These very circumstances, it seems, were among the most important reasons for the announcement of reform *immediately* after the seizure of Herat. It was evidently foreseen that the reform would change the situation for the better, and would provide stability in monetary trade, thereby drawing trust and sympathy toward Shībānī Khān.

3. KHWĀNDAMĪR'S ACCOUNT OF THE MONETARY REFORM OF 913/1507 IN THE LIGHT OF NUMISMATIC DATA

The substance of the reform of Shībānī Khān, announced in the cathedral mosque of Herat in Muḥarram 913/1507, is set forth in three works. The fullest characterization appears in Khwāndamīr's *Ḥabīb al-siyar*: Shībānī Khān, we are told, "ordered that half a *dāng* be added to the earlier *tangachas*, and that, when adorned by the imperial name, each should be regarded as the equivalent of six *kepekī dīnārs*, while the former one-*mithqāl tangachas* should be taken for five *dīnārs* apiece" (*farmān dād ki nīm-dāng bar tangachāt-i sābiqa iżāfa namāyand va chūn be-sikka-i humāyūn zīb va zīnat yābad har yak-rā shash dīnār-i kapakī jārī dānand va tangachāt-i yak-mithqālī-i sābiqa-rā ba-panj dīnār satānand*).[37]

The text of the eighth section of the *Rawżat al-ṣafā* (also written by Khwāndamīr) contains no new information. In the Lucknow lithograph, which I have used, the description appears shorter at first glance, but in fact this is the result of errors (words have been omitted);[38] the substance of the passage itself is not different, however, so the following reading may be conjectured (with the words supplied in brackets missing from the texts consulted): Shībānī Khān "ordered that the [former] *tangacha*s be augmented [by half a *dāng*], and that, when adorned by the [imperial] name, each should be regarded as the equivalent of six *kepekī dīnār*s, while the former one-*mithqāl tangacha* should be taken for five *dīnār*s apiece" (*farmān dād ki [nīm-dāng] bar tangachāt [-i sābiqa] iżāfa namāyand va chūn be-sikka [-i humāyūn] zīb va zīnat yābad har yak-rā shash dīnār-i kepekī jārī dānand va tangachāt-i yak-mithqāl-i sābiqa-rā ba-panj dīnār satānand*).

In a later work, the *Musakhkhir al-bilād* (written by Muḥammad-Yār b. ʿArab Qattaghān no earlier than 1015/1606-07), Khwāndamīr's account is repeated. In the St. Petersburg manuscript,[39] there is an obvious error (reading "*dirham va dīnār-rā*" instead of "*nīm-dāng*"), but otherwise the text corresponds fully with that of Khwāndamīr (hence there is no need to cite the full text in transcription).

[37] *Ḥabīb al-siyar*, lith. Bombay, p. 359; in the Tehran lithograph utilized by Boldyrev ("Ocherki," p. 364, n. 1), there is only a grammatical difference ("*tangachāt-i sābiqa-rā*" instead of "*bar tangachāt-i sābiqa*"). [Translator's note: The four-volume printed edition of this work corresponds to the Bombay lithograph in reading "*bar tangachāt-i sābiqa,*" and agrees with the text as given by the author except for the minor difference of reading "*har yak-rā ba-shash dīnār-i kapakī*" (*Ḥabīb al-siyar*, ed. Jalāl al-Dīn Humāʾī [Tehran: Khayyām, 1333/1954; repr. 1362/1983], IV, p. 379); see also the translation of Wheeler M. Thackston, Khwandamir, *Habibu's-siyar, Tome Three* (Cambridge, Massachusetts, 1994; *Sources of Oriental Languages and Literatures*, 24), Part 2, p. 540.]

[38] *Rawżat al-ṣafā*, lith. Lucknow, part VII, p. 106. The same errors appear in a manuscript preserved in Tashkent (MS IVANUz No. 2928, f. 139b); it is possible that examination of other manuscripts and lithograph versions may allow the discovery of this text without errors. [Translator's note: the printed edition of this work gives the text just as in the lithograph and manuscript cited by the author, without the added words (Mīrkhwānd, *Rawżat al-ṣafā* [Tehran: Khayyām, 1338-39/1960], VII, p. 328).]

[39] MS St. Petersburg, Sankt-Peterburgskii Filial Instituta vostokovedeniia Rossiiskoi Akademii nauk, No. C465, f. 56a.

Let us return, however, to Khwāndamīr's text. Examined outside the numismatic context, it presents two chief, interrelated questions, and allows, at first glance, two different answers to them.

1. What does it mean "to adorn by the imperial name"—to carry out the countermarking of the "earlier" coins, i.e., the Timurid *tangachas*, with the name of Shībānī Khān, or *to issue new coins* in the name of Shībānī Khān?

2. What does it mean "to add half a *dāng*" (that is, one-twelfth part of something) to the "former," meaning Timurid, *tangachas*—to increase their fixed *rate* (if countermarking was implied) or their *weight* (if an issue of new coins was understood)?

As far as I know, precisely two such *different* interpretations of this part of Khwāndamīr's text have been published in scholarly literature.

The first belongs to Masson; it was formulated in 1943, and repeated and elaborated in an article from 1972.[40] He concluded that the account has to do with the *countermarking* of Timurid silver coins and with changes in their fixed *rate*. Masson's conclusion was as follows: Shībānī Khān

> issued an order whose meaning amounted to the following: the 'former *tengachas*' (that is, those minted under Sulṭān Ḥusayn) were declared to be worth a total of one-half *dāng*—that is, twelve times less. After they were presented to the mint and a countermark with the name of Shībānī Khān was placed upon them there, they would be accepted into normal circulation at six then-current *kopekī dīnārs* (*dīnār-i kepekī-i rāʾij*) each. It was proposed to consider the old Timurid *tengachas*, not of such full weight, as corresponding to five such *dīnārs*.

There is no reference to a source, but the specific elements of the account (e.g., mention of "half a *dāng*," of "former *tangachas*," and of equivalents to five and six *kepekī dīnārs*) clearly show that Khwāndamīr's text was utilized. Masson interpreted the phrase "when they are adorned by the imperial mint," to refer to the countermarking of "former" Timurid *tangachas*; he turned the "augmentation" or "addition" of half a *dāng* to the "former" (i.e., Timurid) one-*mithqāl tangachas* into its very opposite, a "decrease" by half a *dāng*, which was

[40] Masson, "Dinary kopeki," p. 34.

interpreted, moreover, as a reduction in value by a factor of 12. The origin of this calculation is incomprehensible. Equally incomprehensible is the evident contradiction regarding the fixed rate of the "former" *tangacha*s: on the one hand, the Timurid coins without countermarks are equated with five *kepekī dīnār*s (that is, they have 'lost' one *kepekī dīnār*), marking a 'reduction in value' by 1/6; on the other hand, we have the 'reduction in value' by a factor of 12. The difference between the two calculations is so improbable as to immediately warrant caution.

In my article from 1954,[41] Khwāndamīr's account was explained in the following way: Shībānī Khān ordered that silver coins be *minted* in his name; that the *weight* of these coins should be raised by half a *dāng* (i.e., by 1/12) compared with the one-*mithqāl* weight of the Timurid coins (that is, that a new weight standard be established, of one *mithqāl* plus half a *dāng* of a *mithqāl*); that the *rate* of the "former," i.e. Timurid, one-*mithqāl* coins be lowered to five *kepekī dīnār*s; and that the coins minted in the name of Shībānī Khān should be equal to six *kepekī dīnār*s.

Let us examine Khwāndamīr's testimony in the numismatic context. Countermarks from the time of Shībānī Khān on Timurid silver coins are known (see Fig. 1), but they are all *anonymous*—that is, they do not address the straightforward meaning of the phrase, "adorn by the imperial name." On the other hand, *coins* with the name and titles of Shībānī Khān, specially minted beginning from 913 A.H., are numerous. Consequently, the only correct response to our first question is that the reform intended precisely the *minting* of new coins in the name of Shībānī Khān.

But this means also that the "addition" of half a *dāng* to coins that were not yet in existence, but would be minted in the name of Shībānī Khān, meant an *increase in weight* by half a *dāng* relative to the "former," Timurid *tangacha*s, whose weight (one *mithqāl*) is indicated in Khwāndamīr's text.[42] It follows from this that the reform defined a new and higher weight standard for the *tangacha* of Shībānī Khān: a *mithqāl* plus half a *dāng* of a *mithqāl* (13/12 *mithqāl*). This calculation as well can and should be verified by numismatic data.

[41] Davidovich, "Denezhnaia reforma Sheibani-khana," pp. 88-90.

[42] The weight standard (the decreed weight) of silver coins of the basic denomination under Temür and the Timurids changed several times; in the latest period it equaled precisely one *mithqāl* (see Davidovich, "O standartakh chistoty i vesovykh standartakh," pp. 119-154).

Silver coins in the name of Shībānī Khān, the contents and formularies of their inscriptions, the principles of classification, criteria of type (the basic classificatory units), and descriptions of *six* types that have so far been brought to light (Fig. 3) have been published;[43] hence we may deal here with summary data. By all

Figure 3

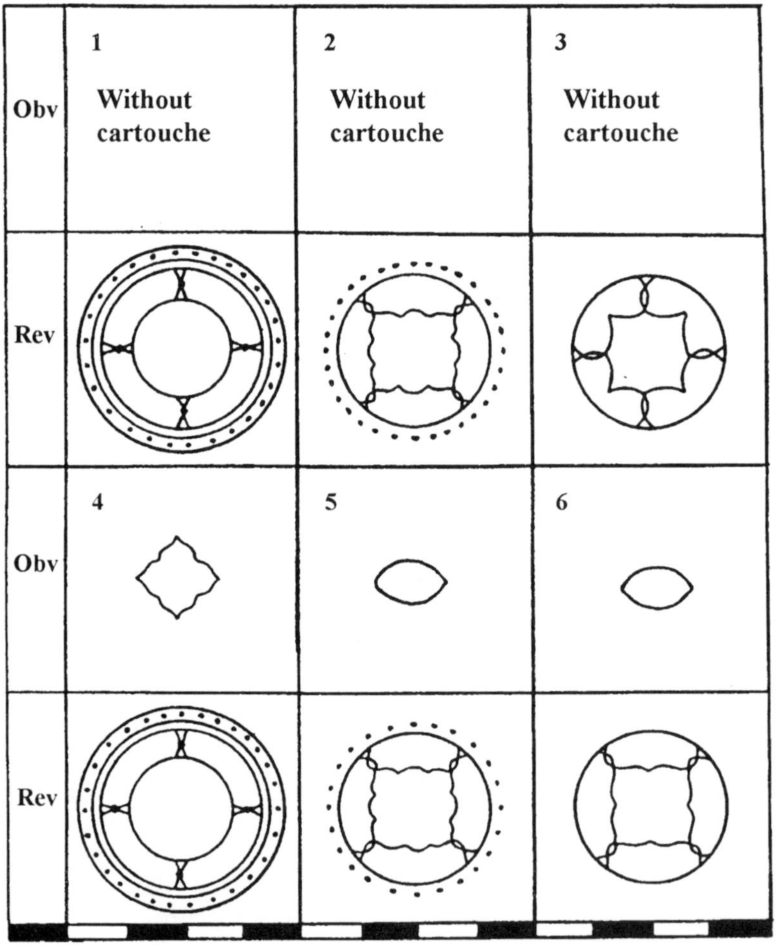

	1	2	3
Obv	**Without cartouche**	**Without cartouche**	**Without cartouche**
Rev			
	4	**5**	**6**
Obv			
Rev			

Silver Coins of Shībānī Khān, Types 1-6

[43] Davidovich, *Korpus*, pp. 77-80, 181-183; Nos. 1-108, 2677-2695 in the catalogue, pp. 268-295, 358-359.

indicators, the fundamental changes occurred precisely in 913 A.H.; this year, in the minting of coins with the name and titles of Shībānī Khān, is like a watershed. The *first* indicator is the radically different design of the types of coins—that is, the absence (Types 1-3) or presence (Types 4-6) of a cartouche on the obverse. The *second* indicator involves the places and dates of minting: coins of Types 1-3 were issued in Mavarannahr (Samarqand and Bukhara in the range 907-913; at present just these two years, 907 and 913 A.H., have been established); coins of Type 4 (Table 1) were minted not only in Mavarannahr, but in many cities and regions conquered by Shībānī Khān (14 mints have already been registered), with the issue of coins of this type beginning in 913 A.H. (the well-known coins of Herat), continuing until 916 A.H., the year of Shībānī Khān's death (the most abundant issue was in 914 A.H.).

Table 1: Post-Reform Silver Coins of Type 4: Mints and Dates

Date, A.H.	Astarābād	Balkh	Bukhara	Herat	Qāyin	Marv	Mashhad	Nīmrūz	Nisā	Nīshāpūr	Samarqand	Sabzavār	Sarakhs	Tūn
913				•										
914	•		•	•		•	•	•	•	•		•		•
915		•	•			•	•			•	•			
916			•								•			
None				•	•	•		•					•	

The *third* indicator involves the titles of Shībānī Khān. At present two titles have been found on his silver coins. In the inscriptions on coins of Types 1-3 is found one title which, it appears, has not been mentioned earlier in the literature (hereafter called the "*first*"): *al-sulṭān al-aʿẓam khalīfat al-raḥmān nāṣir al-dīn* ("the greatest *sulṭān*, vicegerent of [God] the Compassionate, defender of the faith"). In the inscriptions on coins of Types 4-6 appears an entirely different and quite well-known title (hereafter the "*second*"): *imām al-zamān khalīfat al-raḥmān abū'l-fatḥ* ("*imām* of his time, vicegerent of [God] the Compassionate,

Abū'l-Fatḥ"). The titles do not have the same meaning; in the second a theocratic idea is expressed with substantially greater clarity and 'assertiveness,' when it stresses that Shībānī Khān is the "*imām* of his time."

That the appearance of the *second* title on coins of Type 4, and precisely in 913 A.H., is not just coincidental is clear from Khwāndamīr's text. When, in the mosque of the capital city of Herat, the *khuṭba* was first recited in the name of Shībānī Khān, the latter directed that his *laqab*s were "*imām* of his time and vicegerent of [God] the Compassionate." After this phrase follows, in Khwāndamīr's text, the description of the monetary reform cited above. In other words, ambitions grew and the theocratic idea was strengthened after the taking of Herat, a development definitively reinforced and emphasized in such 'documents' as the *khuṭba* and coin inscriptions.

The *fourth* indicator is the *weight* of the coins; this indicator deserves examination in more detail. A sufficient number of specimens has now accumulated in order to obtain convincing results from the study of the actual weight of the coins, which may allow a determination of their average weight and weight standard using a graphic method (a histogram). In order to evaluate the graphs, the following must be kept in mind.

If coins were not in circulation, a graph of their weights would resemble an isosceles triangle, with the *remedium* (i.e., the allowable legal deviation of a coin's actual weight from its weight standard) as its base; the top of the 'triangle' would be both the weight standard and the average weight. But if the coins were in circulation, the 'silhouette' of the triangle changes, and it shifts from isosceles to irregular because of the movement of the actual weight of all or some of the coins toward a lower number. The top of such an irregular triangle would be the average weight, which would be *less* than the weight standard. The difference between the weight.standard and the average weight can vary, depending on the average duration of circulation for the group of coins under consideration. In case of a very prolonged circulation of coins, they become so worn away that a graph of their actual weights no longer resembles a triangle at all, and does not establish an average weight.

For a study of the weight of Shībānī Khān's silver coins, *tangacha*s of Types 2 and 4 offer the most important material. In the present article, because of space considerations (stemming from the large quantity of coins), graphic tables (histograms) of weight have been restructured as statistical tables, showing both the absolute number of coins of each weight and their percentage of the total number of the sample. The weight of the coins has been rounded to tenths of a gram.

Of Type 2, 630 coins have been registered.[44] All the coins were minted in Samarqand in 913 A.H. The value of this selection for studying weights lies not only in the large number of coins, but also in the fact that they left circulation at the same time (629 coins of Type 2 formed a hoard[45]), meaning that their weight loss from circulation is on average identical.

In this case, as is clearly evident from the statistical Table 2, a graphic presentation of the data would still preserve the form of an

Table 2: Weight of Coins of Shībānī Khān of Type 2
(Samarqand, 913 A.H.)

Weight (g)	4.9	4.8	4.7	4.6	4.5
Quantity	12	272	320	26	-
Percentage	1.9	43.2	50.8	4.1	-

isosceles triangle; the movement toward lower numbers is insignificant. The main quantity of coins (592 specimens, or around 94%) weighs 4.7–4.8 g each, giving an average weight of 4.75 g. This high average weight allows a determination of the weight standard in terms of Muslim weight units.

Combined study of the information from written sources and from Central Asian coins of different metals allows us to ascertain that the *mithqāl* of Bukharan origin, which achieved state-wide status, provided the foundation of coin minting under Temür and the Timurids (late 14th–15th centuries), and in the states of the Shībānids (16th century) and Jānids (17th–18th centuries); the weight of this *mithqāl* was 4.8 g. The average weight (4.75 g) of the coins of Type 2 corresponds to a weight standard of one *mithqāl* (4.8 g). Table 2 shows clearly that the coins of Samarqand of Type 2 had already been in circulation, though for a short time. The following particulars of the table support these two

[44] Davidovich, *Korpus*, pp. 268-289, Nos. 2-631.

[45] Davidovich, *Korpus*, pp. 17-18 and Table 1 (hoard No. 1).

conclusions. There are in all 26 coins of lower weight (4.6 g), or 4.1%, with, in fact, actual weights even higher than 4.6 g by several hundredths of a gram (in the range of 4.61–4.64). Coins weighing 4.7 g are somewhat more numerous (320 specimens, or 50.8%) than coins whose weight exactly corresponds with the weight standard of 4.8 g (272 specimens, or 43.2%). In evaluating this fact several points are significant. First of all, there are coins that weigh 4.9 g, allowing us to determine the remedium: 0.1 g on either side of the established weight standard. This means that a weight of 4.7 g comes within the limits of the remedium, as initially set, and only the increase in the number of coins with real weights of 4.7 g attests to losses in the course of circulation. Secondly, among the coins that weigh 4.7 g, those whose actual weight is several hundredths of a gram higher than this rounded figure (in the range of 4.71–4.74 g) predominate. It is clear that the total duration of circulation for coins of Type 2 was insignificant (as is evident also from the homogeneous composition of the hoard, in which no later coins are found). All this allows us to conclude that the weight standard for coins of Type 2 was *one mithqāl* (4.8 g).

There are in all just two specimens of coins of Type 1 (Samarqand, 907 A.H.) and Type 3 (Bukhara, 913 A.H.); their individual weights (4.68 and 4.77 g), taken in isolation, would allow us to *suppose* that their weight standard was equal to one *mithqāl*. Comparison with Type 2 turns this supposition into certitude and allows us to conclude that in Bukhara and Samarqand, silver coins of Types 1-3 were issued on the basis of a weight standard of one *mithqāl*, equal to 4.8 g.

For the study of the weight of silver coins of Type 4 a selection of 157 specimens has been used.[46] Their graphic tabulation gives a quite distinct picture, well-reflected in the statistical Table 3. The great bulk of the coins (127 specimens, or around 81%) weigh 5.1–5.2 g each, with coins of 5.2 g even somewhat more numerous. The average weight is thus equal to 5.15 g. Around 8% of the coins weigh more (5.3 g); hence, the remedium was not less than 0.1 g in each direction (in the range of 5.3–5.1 g). This means that the total number of coins that weigh 5.1 g each was formed in part because of the remedium, and in part because of the coins' wear from circulation (which shaped also the

[46] Davidovich, *Korpus*, pp. 289-295, 358-359; Nos. 633-805, 2677-2695. In Table 3, fragmentary coins, specimens of half and, most likely, 2/3 of the basic denomination, and some coins weighing in the range 4.4–4.7 g have not been taken into account.

Table 3: Weight of Coins of Shībānī Khān of Type 4 (913-916 A.H.)

Weight (g)	5.4	5.3	5.2	5.1	5.0	4.9	4.8
Quantity	1	12	65	62	10	6	1
Percentage		7.6	41.4	39.5	6.4	3.8	

beginning of the movement of the coins' actual weight in the direction of lower numbers, 5.0 and 4.9 g). All these indices allow us to conclude that *the weight standard for coins of Type 4* was equal to 5.2 g, and that the average norm of wear may be estimated at 0.05 g. A weight standard of 5.2 g is easy to express in terms of Muslim Central Asian units of weight: it equals one *mithqāl* (4.8 g) plus half a *dāng* of a *mithqāl* (0.4 g).

The weight standard for silver coins of Types 5-6[47] cannot be ascertained at present. The single coin of Type 5 is fragmentary. On the basis of its size one can conclude only that it was a basic denomination. Of two coins of Type 6, the weight of only one is known: 3.59 g. The small size of this coin (21-22 mm) is noteworthy, and distinguishes it markedly from coins of the basic denomination; it is clear that this is not a basic denomination, but a smaller fraction. The possibility of issuing coins of two-thirds of a basic denomination must be kept in mind (with a weight standard of the basic denomination at 5.2 g, the weight standard of a fraction of two-thirds ought to equal 3.5 g). The minting and circulation of coins of two-thirds of the basic denomination under the Shībānids is attested in the *vaqf-nāma* cited above (in Section 1), from later in the 16th century.[48] The fact that *fractions* of the basic denomination were issued in the name of Shībānī Khān is reliably known; as mentioned above (in Section 1), a coin of *half* the basic denomination was issued, with its value specified in the very inscription on the coin, as *nīm tanga* ("half a *tanga*"). This post-reform coin

[47] Davidovich, *Korpus*, p. 295, Nos. 806-808.

[48] *Vaqf-nāma* for the Ghāzīyān *madrasa* and *ḥawż* in Bukhara, preserved in the Bukharan Museum-Preserve, Inv. No. 150.

(Type 4) was issued in Herat, and weighs 2.43 g, with dimensions of 17-18 mm.[49]

Thus, the fourth indicator is a different weight standard: for coins of Types 1-3, it was equal to one *mithqāl* (4.8 g), continuing the late-Timurid tradition; for coins of the basic denomination of Type 4, the weight standard was equal to one *mithqāl* plus half a *dāng* of a *mithqāl* (5.2 g)—that is, higher by one-half *dāng*! It must be noted that the weight standard of a *mithqāl* plus half a *dāng* also continued a Timurid tradition, but a different one. Under the Timurid Shāhrukh (807/1405-850/1447), precisely this weight standard (a *mithqāl* plus half a *dāng* of a *mithqāl*) formed the foundation of the minting of his coins during the course of a quite extended period, as is clear from the direct evidence of documentary sources of the 15th century,[50] and as is confirmed by the actual weight of some of his coins. Shāhrukh's silver coins were in circulation after his death as well, a fact demonstrated both by the dates of several documentary sources and by the composition of hoards of silver coins.

The silver coins of Shībānī Khān of Types 2-3 were issued in Mavarannahr in 913 A.H.—that is, after the announcement of the reform in Herat—but in these issues the prescriptions of the reform had not yet been implemented. They were minted still according to the old, pre-reform weight standard of one *mithqāl*, and their inscriptions contain the pre-reform (*first*) titles of Shībānī Khān. They dropped out of circulation, moreover, in quite good condition, and apparently quite quickly, in the course of the implementation, in Mavarannahr, of all the prescriptions of the reform, including the weight standard.

The issue of *tangacha*s of Type 4 conforms, in all its indicators, to the reform described by Khwāndamīr. Among all the indicators in this context let us emphasize three: the *new* type of coin (Type 4), identical for all mints; the new, *second* title; and the *new* weight standard. The clarification of the weight standard of silver coins of Type 4 (5.2 g) leaves no doubt that the "addition" of half a *dāng* to the former one-*mithqāl* (4.8 g) Timurid *tangacha*, which Khwāndamīr reported, was in

49 Davidovich, *Korpus*, p. 292, No. 728.

50 Davidovich, "O standartakh chistoty i vesovykh standartakh," pp. 119-154. Under Shāhrukh silver coins were minted with three weight standards; the weight standard of a *mithqāl* plus half a *dāng* (5.2 g) was, with regard to the time of its inception, the latest in the coinage of Shāhrukh.

fact an increase in the weight, by half a *dāng*, for coins that would henceforth be minted in the name of Shībānī Khān.

In Khwāndamīr's text five points in the reform are stipulated: an order regarding the minting of money in the name of Shībānī Khān, the weight standard of his prospective coins, and their fixed rate; and permission for the ongoing circulation of "former" Timurid *tangacha*s of one *mithqāl*, and their rate. The numismatic data brought to bear on the analysis of the text have fully confirmed *three* points. The weight standard for the reformed coins of Shībānī Khān, with his name (Type 4), was indeed equal to a *mithqāl* and half a *dāng* of a *mithqāl* (4.8 + 0.4 = 5.2 g); and the issue of such reformed coins was indeed begun (Type 4), and was carried out throughout the state. The composition of hoards of silver coins further confirms that the "former" one-*mithqāl* silver coins indeed continued to circulate under Shībānī Khān (and even after his death).[51] The general conclusion is that the three enumerated points in Khwāndamīr's account should be accepted as reliable.

The numismatic data, as it turns out, allow us to reveal still other elements of the reform and of the reformed monetary circulation (on this, see below, Section 5), which were not mentioned by Khwāndamīr, but the question about the relative *rate* of the two groups of coins—that is, two of the five points from Khwāndamīr's text—are beyond the capabilities of a numismatic source. Is Khwāndamīr's account of the rate designated for the "former" (i.e., Timurid) *tangacha*s and for the 'future' *tangacha*s, to be "adorned" with the name and titles of Shībānī Khān himself, trustworthy?

4. RATE-RELATED ASPECTS OF THE REFORM OF SHĪBĀNĪ KHĀN (AN EVALUATION OF THE RELIABILITY OF KHWĀNDAMĪR'S ACCOUNT)

In Khwāndamīr's *Ḥabīb al-siyar*, two terms figure in his description of the monetary reform of Shībānī Khān: *tangacha* and *dīnār kepekī*. We know now that *tangacha* in the given context is a designation of a basic silver denomination; the "former," i.e., Timurid, *tangachas* were designated as "one-*mithqāl*" (meaning that their weight standard was equal to a *mithqāl*, 4.8 g), while for the *tangacha*s with the name of

[51] Especially convincing in this respect are the hoards in which silver coins of Shībānī Khān form the chief part, but with Timurid *tangacha*s mixed in among them.

Shībānī Khān, which were then only expected to be minted (and which were later indeed actually minted), a different weight standard was indicated, half a *dāng* higher (that is, a *mithqāl* plus half a *dāng* of a *mithqāl*, or 5.2 g). This part of Khwāndamīr's account was completely confirmed by numismatic data.

The *rate* of the two groups of *tangacha*s is indicated in Khwāndamīr's text in terms of *kepekī dīnār*s—that is, as we now know, in terms of actual small silver coins. The reform established that the one-*mithqāl* Timurid *tangacha* would henceforth be equal to *five kepekī dīnār*s, while those that were to be "adorned by the imperial name" (i.e., with the name of Shībānī Khān) would be equal to *six kepekī dīnār*s. What was the rate of the one-*mithqāl* Timurid *tangacha*s prior to the conquest of Herat by Shībānī Khān and before the promulgation of his monetary reform? Another report, likewise from Khwāndamīr, answers this question clearly; it describes the indemnity that was imposed upon the inhabitants of Herat: "a sum of 100,000 one-*mithqāl tangacha*s, each of which *tangacha*s was in those days worth six *kepekī dīnār*s" (*mablagh-i ṣad hazār tangacha-i yak-mithqālī ki har tangacha az ān dar ān avān ba-shash dīnār-i kepekī jārī būd*).[52] The indemnity was collected still prior to the promulgation of the reform, so that the one-*mithqāl tangacha*s intended here were clearly Timurid coins, whose rate at the beginning of 913 A.H. was equal, accordingly, to precisely six *kepekī dīnār*s. From the sources cited above (Section 1) it is clear, as we have seen, that the term *dīnār-i kepekī* was used to refer to silver coins whose weight standard was equal sometimes to one-third of a *mithqāl* (1.6 g) and sometimes to one-sixth of a *mithqāl* (0.8 g). In Khwāndamīr's text, both in noting the size of the indemnity and in describing the reform, the latter are meant, since six *kepekī dīnār*s of that kind (at 0.8 g each) would have been equal to the one-*mithqāl* Timurid *tangacha* (4.8 g). It works out, according to the reform, that the official rate of the one-*mithqāl* Timurid *tangacha* would be reduced to *five kepekī dīnār*s, while the future *tangacha*s of Shībānī Khān, of a higher weight (5.2 g) would circulate at a rate of *six kepekī dīnār*s of that sort. Only at first glance do the rate changes entailed by the reform appear logical, since the *tangacha*s of higher weight (5.2 g) have also a higher rate, while those of lower weight have a lower rate.

[52] Khwāndamīr, *Ḥabīb al-siyar*, lith. Bombay, p. 358; Tehran edition, IV, p. 378; tr. Thackston, Part 2, p. 539. Khwāndamīr mentions the six-*dīnār* Timurid *tangacha* and *tanga* many times.

In actuality the specific passages dealing with the rate-related aspects of Shībānī Khān's reform, as set forth by Khwāndamīr, are not simple and straightforward, but are in fact contradictory. First and foremost arises this question: why does Khwāndamīr indicate the rate of two groups of *silver tangacha*s in terms of *silver kepekī dīnār*s? In the first section of this article, monetary descriptions in documentary sources, and the recommended formats (formularies) for monetary descriptions (from times near the reform) were cited; there the rate of silver coins was specified in terms of *copper* coins. Khwāndamīr himself, referring to the disproportionately high price of sheep, which he had to buy for silver coins, explains their rate through a conversion into copper coins. In the *vaqf-nāma* from the second half of the 15th century, and in hundreds of Shībānid and Jānid *vathīqa*s and *vaqf-nāma*s from the 16th and 17th centuries, the rate of silver coins is likewise expressed in terms of copper coins. Khwāndamīr, in laying out the substance of the reform, could easily have had recourse to this tried and true method of fixing the rate.

But Khwāndamīr, in order to specify these rate conversions, gave preference to silver *kepekī dīnār*s, disregarding the two-fold in appropriateness of this method from the economic point of view.

First of all, silver *dīnār*s of the *kepekī* type were fractions of the basic silver denomination; their rate would have fluctuated simultaneously with that of the basic denomination, and therefore *kepekī dīnār*s could not have been used to fix the rate of the *tangacha*. Second, the equivalences cited are impossible from the standpoint of weight. In actuality, six *kepekī dīnār*s were equal to a *mithqāl* of silver—that is, the "former" one-*mithqāl* Timurid *tangacha* was equal in weight to precisely six *kepekī dīnār*s; yet Khwāndamīr affirms that the reform made the Timurid *tangacha* equal to five *kepekī dīnār*s, or 5/6 *mithqāl*. The *tangacha* of Shībānī Khān, which weighed a *mithqāl* plus half a *dāng* of a *mithqāl*, was equivalent to 6.5 *kepekī dīnār*s; yet Khwāndamīr affirms that it was made equal to six *kepekī dīnār*s—that is, to a *mithqāl* of silver. The absurdity of the two rate stipulations is even more noticeable if we translate Muslim Central Asian units of weight into grams.

As was noted already, the weight of the *kepekī dīnār* that figures in the description of the reform was equal to 4.8 : 6 = 0.8 g. It turns out, according to Khwāndamīr, that 4.8 g of silver (the one-*mithqāl* Timurid *tangacha*) would be made equal, after the reform, to 4.0 g of silver (five *kepekī dīnārs*), while 5.2 g of silver (the *tangacha* of Shībānī Khān) would be made equal to 4.8 g of silver (6 *kepekī dīnārs*).

In *both* instances there is an undervaluation of the silver in the coin, which would have led to hoarding or to a drain of coins beyond the borders of the state. If we may assume that the reform provided an economic way to 'get rid of' the Timurid *tangachas*, it is surely quite impossible to account for a wish to 'get rid of' the *tangachas* of Shībānī Khān as well, and to doom them in advance to disappear from the market.

In connection with this problem two hypotheses appear: either Khwāndamīr did not report everything about the substance of the reform, or he made a mistake in describing its rate-related aspect.

Khwāndamīr says nothing about the standard of fineness (the decreed standard) of the Timurid *tangachas* or the *tangachas* of Shībānī Khān, although the organization of the minting and circulation of silver coins provided for the *legality* of changes in the standard of fineness: it was not concealed from the people if an alloy was added to silver, the amount of alloy was well-known, and in the course of describing money, in *vathīqas* and *vaqf-nāmas*, the standard of fineness of coins was precisely indicated. Khwāndamīr's silence might mean that the reform did not touch on this aspect of monetary affairs, and that the standard of fineness was the same for the *tangachas* of Shībānī Khān as it was for the Timurid *tangachas*. The standard of fineness of the latter has been known from documentary sources and has been confirmed by chemical quantitative analysis: it was determined that the Timurid *tangachas* were minted from pure silver.[53] It is precisely in these circumstances that the impossible situation arises, with the *tangacha* of Shībānī Khān undervalued in advance by 0.4 g of silver: there were 5.2 g of silver in them, but they were made equal to 4.8 g of silver.

Khwāndamīr's silence regarding the standard of fineness might, however, have other causes: he may have forgotten, or he may not have felt it necessary, to indulge in minutiae and describe all details. He wrote his *Ḥabīb al-siyar* many years after these events (from 927/1520-21 to 930/1524), and details of the reform had already become 'history;' Khwāndamīr 'selected' that part of his information that seemed important to him, after a decade and a half, and gave, from his perspective, a sufficient idea of the content and significance of the

[53] Davidovich, "O standartakh chistoty i vesovykh standartakh," pp. 142-147.

reform. He mentioned that the *weight* of the *tangacha* was increased by half a *dāng* of a *mithqāl* (and this corresponds to the weight of the post-reform *tangacha*s of Shībānī Khān of Type 4), but he forgot or did not think it necessary to record that this increase of the overall weight was accomplished through the addition of an alloy. The first hypothesis: were not the *tangacha*s of Shībānī Khān of Type 4 combinations of 4.8 g of silver plus 0.4 g of an alloy (copper)? Only in this case would Khwāndamīr's account of their equivalence to six *kepekī dīnār*s—that is, 4.8 g of silver—be accurate. Half a *dāng* of a *mithqāl* of alloy would be around 7.7% of the total weight of Shībānī Khān's *tangacha*s of Type 4. Consequently the quantity of pure silver in them should not, in this case, exceed 92%, and should, in fact, be even lower (considering the sometimes insufficiently complete preliminary refining of the silver metal[54]).

The quality of metal in the *tangacha*s of Shībānī Khān was examined using three methods. An assay (with the use of a touchstone) of five of his silver coins in the collection of the State Hermitage (St. Petersburg) revealed an identical assay of 960, the highest possible. The adopted intervals of the assay (the next was 916) are so great that a standard of 960 could mask both pure silver and silver with a certain amount of alloy; but coins in which the amount of silver did not exceed 92% would correspond better with the assay of 916.

In the physical laboratory of the State Hermitage the composition of metal in seven *tangacha*s of Shībānī Khān was examined by two methods.[55] Hydrostatic suspension showed that the contemporary density of the metal in these coins ranged from 10.33–10.43 (with the density of silver equaling 10.5). X-ray fluorescence analysis of the coins revealed a very small admixture of copper (in the range of 1.1–2.0%), gold (in the range of 0.26–0.56%), and lead (in five coins, in the range of 1.0–1.5%), as well as traces of other metals; but these cannot be considered artificial additions. It is significant that one of these seven

[54] The qualitative chemical analysis of the coins of Temür and the Timurids has shown that the standard of silver was very high, but that small and *different* amounts of alloy were nonetheless present (see Davidovich, "O standartakh chistoty i vesovykh standartakh," p. 146, Table 7); this does not reflect an artificial addition, however, since it is clear from descriptions of silver coins in *vathīqa*s of the 15th century that they were, supposedly, minted from *pure* silver.

[55] Conclusion No. 238, from 25 February 1986, by laboratory director A. I. Kosolapov.

coins was minted in 907 A.H., well before the reform, but by all the indicators, the post-reform *tangacha*s do not differ from it.

Thus, the results of studying the metal in Shībānī Khān's *tangacha*s, using three methods, eliminate the hypothesis regarding a decreed addition of half a *dāng* of a *mithqāl* of alloy to his post-reform coins (of Type 4). We may conclude that the standard of fineness in the *tangacha* of Shībānī Khān continued the Timurid tradition. The coins of the Timurids (according to the description in most documents of the 15th century) were minted from "pure" (*pākīza*) silver, and the standard of fineness of the *Shāhrukhī tangacha* was "ten tenths" (*ba-ʿiyār-i dah dah*).

The second hypothesis proposes that there was no change in the standard of fineness—that the weight of Shībānī Khān's *tangacha*s, that is, was increased by the addition of half a *dāng* of a *mithqāl* (0.4 g) of *silver*—but that Khwāndamīr's account of the rate of these reformed *tangacha*s was mistaken, with the number of *kepekī dīnār*s 'rounded,' since the reformed *tangacha* (5.2 g of silver) was equal not to six *kepekī dīnār*s (0.8 X 6 = 4.8 g), as Khwāndamīr says, but to 6.5 *kepekī dīnār*s (5.2 g). In other words, the second hypothesis requires that Khwāndamīr's text be emended in the following way: Shībānī Khān "ordered that half a *dāng* be added to the earlier *tangacha*s, and, when adorned by the imperial name, that each should be regarded as equal to six [and a half] *kepekī dīnār*s." It was already noted that Khwāndamīr did not indicate the rate of the "former" or new *tangacha*s in copper *dīnār*s. If the reform did not alter the relationship between the *kepekī dīnār* and the copper *dīnār*, then (calculating in terms of the conjecture under consideration) the *tangacha* of Shībānī Khān would have been equal to 39 copper *dīnār*s, while the "former" one-*mithqāl* Timurid *tangacha* would have been equal to 30. In support of this hypothesis and this conjecture may be cited two considerations.

According to Khwāndamīr, the reform lowered the rate of the "former" one-*mithqāl tangacha*s, equal to six *kepekī dīnār*s each, to five *kepekī dīnār*s—that is, in terms of copper coins, from 36 to 30 copper *dīnār*s. In this part of the text there is no error. The sources cited above showed that prior to the reform, the one-*mithqāl tangacha* was indeed equivalent to 36 copper *dīnār*s. After the reform their rate should have amounted to precisely 30 copper *dīnār*s; and this is what it indeed became, as one curious fact directly confirms. Already after Shībānī Khān's conquest of Herat (and thus also after the promulgation of his reform, but in practical terms prior to the large-scale issuing of post-reform *tangachas* in the name of Shībānī Khān), Khwāndamīr, in Herat, bought sheep for 20 *khānī tangachas* per head, which then amounted to 600 copper *dīnārs* of Tabrīz.[56] From this it is clear that the *khānī tangacha* was equal to 30 copper *dīnārs* of Tabrīz. The "*khānī tangacha*" referred to here is a Timurid coin,[57] and its rate corresponds to what was calculated above.

Was such a model possible in organizing the circulation of silver coins, wherein the rate of one group of coins (the future *tangachas* of Shībānī Khān) was made equal to six and a half *kepekī dīnārs* (5.2 g)—i.e., corresponding to their weight—while the rate of another group (the "former" Timurid *tangachas*) was made equal to five *kepekī dīnārs*—that is, significantly reduced in comparison with their weight (4.8 g)? The size of the undervaluation of silver in the Timurid *tangachas*, according to the reform, exceeded their weight by 16% (or somewhat less, taking into account weight losses due to circulation).

As it turns out, such a model was possible, and has an analogy. The study of hundreds of *vathīqas* and *vaqf-nāmas* of the 16th century permits a reconstruction of the organization of the circulation of silver coins in the Shībānid state and the means of extracting revenue from this organization. From 1525 down to the end of the 16th century, Shībānid *tangas* that were identical by weight and standard were divided into two rate groups. The *tanga* of the latest issue was called "new" ("*jadīda*" or "*naw*" in documents), while all previous issues were called "old" ("*kuhna*" in documents).[58] The fixed rate of the "new" was stipulated in terms of copper coins. At first, the "new" *tangas* were equal, for the most part, to 20 copper *dīnārs*; toward the end of the century they equaled 30. The "old" *tangas* were designated by one additional phrase: "nine tenths" ("*dah nuhī*" in documents). This allows us to conclude that the fixed rate of the "old" coins was equal to 9/10 of the fixed rate

[56] A. N. Boldyrev, *Zainaddin Vasifi. Tadzhikskii pisatel' XVI v (Opyt tvorcheskoi biografii)* (Stalinabad, 1957), p. 62.

[57] In both documentary and narrative sources, Timurid silver coins are often marked by the epithet "*khānī*."

[58] The practical criterion for distinguishing the "new" from the "old" *tangas* was their type, i.e., the forms of the cartouches on the two sides of the coin disk. The diversity of accumulating types did not create difficulty, since it was sufficient to know the type of the "new" *tangas*; all the rest formed a single rate group of "old" *tangas*.

of the "new" ones. For example, if the fixed rate of the "new" coins equaled 30 copper *dīnār*s, the fixed rate of the "old" ones would equal 27. This conclusion has not evoked doubts, but has indeed received additional confirmation. In two documents from the end of the 16th century, "the old nine-tenths" *tangas* are equated to precisely 27 copper *dīnār*s.[59]

In this way, in the 16th century, the fixed rate of "old" *tanga*s was reduced by 10% in comparison with the fixed rate of *tanga*s that were precisely the same, but "new;" this process was an important source of income for the treasury and a cause of losses for the population. We may assume that, in the market, this compulsory rate difference correlated with prices for goods and products (different in "old" and "new" *tanga*s), but in relations between the treasury and private individuals the official rate difference was observed. At the same time, it was not only urban taxes on crafts and trade, or rent payments for state land and for state structures in a city, that took a monetary form, but even various rural taxes as well (for example, those on clover crops, on gardens, and so forth), and also separate taxes benefiting officials, and extraordinary taxes. Shībānid appanage-holders" and officials would purchase products and goods (for cash or on credit) at the markets, and they too would utilize the rate difference of the two groups of *tanga*s. It is also worth noting that transactions are formalized in "new" *tanga*s in many hundreds of documents from the 16th century, while "old" *tanga*s are used only in isolated instances. In trade, "new" *tanga*s predominate markedly, as people sought to 'unload' them (before they too were declared "old").

Thus, a model for organizing the circulation of silver *tanga*s, based on the coexistence of two groups of coins, of which the fixed rate of the "former" (or "older") ones was reduced, did in fact exist. In light of this conclusion, the second hypothesis and proposed conjecture appear fully convincing: the *tangacha*s of Shībānī Khān were equal not to six *kepekī dīnār*s (as Khwāndamīr has it), but to six and a half; the "former" Timurid *tangacha*s received the reduced rate indicated by Khwāndamīr (they were made equal to five *kepekī dīnār*s). It must be stressed that this reduced rate became a reality at once, as is attested by the concrete example, cited above, of the circulation of silver Timurid *tangacha*s equal to 30 copper *dīnār*s apiece.

[59] Davidovich, "K voprosu o kurse," pp. 143-144.

The construction of such a model for organizing the circulation of two groups of *tangachas* with two different fixed rates also served, probably, an additional goal: to induce, without direct prohibitions, but by a purely economic device, the hoarding of Timurid *tangachas* (and a portion of Timurid silver coins did indeed fall out of circulation, into hoards), and to turn the new *tangas* of Shïbānī Khān into the *basis* for trade.

5. SUPPLEMENTARY NUMISMATIC DATA ON THE REFORM OF SHÏBĀNĪ KHĀN AND THE COMPOSITION OF THE POST-REFORM SUPPLIES OF MONEY

Gold Coins of Shïbānī Khān:

Khwāndamīr said nothing about gold and copper coins, but the numismatic data enables us to conclude that the reform reorganized the minting and circulation not only of silver coins, but of others as well.

I am aware of only two gold coins minted in the name of Shïbānī Khān. They are of the same type (Type 1), meaning that they have identical forms of the cartouches on the two sides of the coin disk (Fig. 4). Neither has preserved the identification of the mint, and

Figure 4

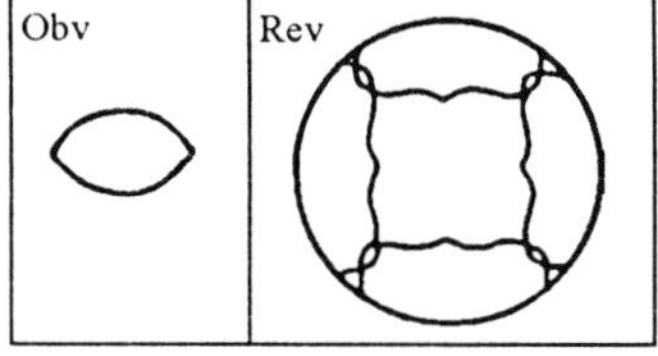

Gold Coins of Shïbānī Khān

both lack a mint date (it was worn away or not included to begin with).[60] The title of the head of the dynasty, however (just as in the *post-reform* silver coins of Type 4) allows us to conclude with certainty that both were minted after the promulgation of the reform, and thus represent a component of the post-reform issue of coins. The weight of the two

[60] Both coins were acquired by the Hermitage in 1946; see Davidovich, *Korpus*, p. 179 (description of the type) and p. 267, No. 1-2 (catalogue).

specimens (4.74 and 4.77 g) corresponds most readily to the weight standard of one *mithqāl* (4.8 g), but two coins are insufficient for a convincing conclusion. If a larger number of Shībānī Khān's *ashrafī*s should become known, and their real weight confirms the suggestion regarding the one-*mithqāl* weight standard in the minting of gold, this would mean that the reform did not envision a unification of the weight standards for the *ashrafī* and the *tangacha*.

One fact is worthy of attention: the complete correspondence of type between these gold coins and silver coins of Type 6 (Fig. 3/6), and their partial correspondence (an identical cartouche on the obverse) with silver coins of Type 5 (Fig. 3/5). Moreover, it is not only the cartouches on the obverse that correspond completely, but the content and disposition of the inscriptions. In the cartouche on the obverse of silver coins of Types 5-6 and gold coins of Type 1 appear two terms (*ʿadl*, *shīrmard*); around the cartouche is the name of the head of the dynasty, his post-reform titles, benedictions upon him, and the designation of the mint (effaced) after the word *żarb*. On the reverse in the cartouche is the *shahāda*, while along the edges, in segments, are the names of the first four Caliphs (ʿUthmān's appears with the name of his father, while the names of the rest appear with their honorary epithets). It was already noted above that silver coins of Type 5 evidently represented the basic denomination, and Type 6 a smaller denomination (whose value was possibly equal to two-thirds). It is reasonable to assume that the *tangacha*s of Types 5-6 and the *ashrafī* of Type 1 reflect simultaneous actions. In any case, there is certainly a connection between them, but their relationship with the *tangacha*s of Type 4—the basic reformed minting of 913-916 A.H.—cannot yet be clarified. Only one thing may be concluded: the post-reform minting of the *tangacha*s of Type 4 (the basic denomination and a fraction in the amount of one-half) was at some point supplemented by an issue of gold coins (Type 1, a basic denomination) and of silver coins (Type 5, a basic denomination, and Type 6, a fraction of, apparently, two-thirds).

Copper Dīnārs of Bukhara and Samarqand from 914/1508-09:

Copper coins are not mentioned at all by Khwāndamīr in his description of the reform of Shībānī Khān. The *dīnār*s of Samarqand and Bukhara, from 914 A.H., are very important for an understanding of the reform's substance and development. On the reverse of these *dīnārs* is the date, given in words; here we give a reconstruction (Fig. 5) and description of the obverse.

Figure 5

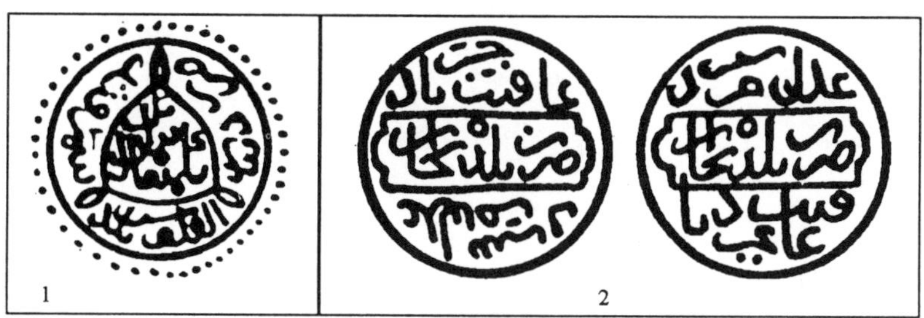

Reconstruction of Copper *Dīnārs* of 914 A.H. (Obv.):
1 - Samarqand; 2 - Bukhara

I discovered coins of this type and year from Bukhara, within a hoard, and reconstructed them and published them for the first time in 1980. Coins from Samarqand of the type described here were known already in the 19th century; the first attempt to read their unusual inscriptions was that of Ch. M. Fraehn [Kh. M. Fren] in 1826. Later, some of the most prominent Russian specialists in numismatics (V. V. Vel'iaminov-Zernov, A. K. Markov, W. G. Tiesenhausen [V. G. Tizengauzen], M. E. Masson) concerned themselves with this inscription, and proposed various readings and understandings of its sections; the date and the city were correctly determined, but the key words in the cartouche were not understood, while the key word around the cartouche was not read. I published a full reading, reconstruction, and interpretation in 1954. The inscription is the key to understanding the policy with respect to the weight of copper coins from the end of the 15th century, and to the elaboration of a method for determining their weight standard, using actual and average weight.[61]

[61] On the development of policy regarding the weight of *copper* coins since the end of the 15th century, and on the weight standards utilized, and the methods for determining them, see Davidovich, *Istoriia denezhnogo obrashcheniia srednevekovoi Srednei Azii*, pp. 129-143.

Samarqand, 914/1508-09		*Bukhara, 914/1508-09*
Obv.: In a figured cartouche, an inscription on the weight of the coin: *yak mithqāl nīmdāng*. In three segments around the cartouche, the designation of the coin and the name of the city: *żarb dīnār / al-fulūs balada / samarqand*		Obv.: In a figured cartouche, the name of the city: *żarb balada bukhārā*. In segments outside the cartouche, the phrases *ʿadl shīrmard* (from the top or from the bottom) and *ʿāqibat khayr bād* (correspondingly, from the bottom or from the top)

The two portions of the inscription most important for present purposes appear on the coins from Samarqand: "*yak mithqāl nīmdāng*" (in the cartouche) and "*dīnār al-fulūs*" (along the edge of the cartouche). The latter phrase means a *dīnār* of the *fulūs* type, or a "copper *dīnār*," the basic denomination in copper coinage of that period. The former phrase refers to the weight standard stipulated for the copper *dīnār* of Samarqand in 914/1508-09: one *mithqāl* and half a *dāng* of a *mithqāl* (5.2 g). One detail is noteworthy: the language of the two parts of the inscription. The inscription along the edges of the cartouche must be recognized as Arabic (judging from its grammatical construction), even though both terms—*dīnār* and *fulūs*—had entered firmly into the Persian/Tajik language of the local population of Central Asia. The inscription inside the cartouche, meanwhile, was made in Persian, as is clear from the words *yak* ("one") and *nīm* ("half"). The language of the inscriptions confirms that the indication of the weight standard was not accidental, but was specifically designed to be read and understood. Even taken in isolation, the mere fact of the designation of a coin's weight in the coin's inscription—quite rare in Muslim coinage—attests to some kind of weight fluctuations. But changes in the weight standard of Central Asian copper coins at the end of the 15th century and the beginning of the 16th occurred frequently without being reflected in any way in coin inscriptions. Nor does the weight standard itself, or its size (a *mithqāl* plus half a *dāng* of a *mithqāl*), considered in isolation, help us to understand the need for an inscription specifying it on the coin itself. A weight standard of that size was used in copper coinage both before and after the issue of the *dīnār*s of Samarqand from 914 A.H. For example, precisely the same weight standard (a *mithqāl* plus half a *dāng* of a *mithqāl*) was prescribed for the copper *dīnārs* of Samarqand from 898/1492-93; it is registered in a *vaqf-nāma*, from Rabīᶜ I 942/1535, for the Ghāzīyān *madrasa* in Bukhara, in which a description of money mentions the weight of copper coins as one *mithqāl* and two *nukhūds*[62] (two *nukhūds* are equal to one-half *dāng*).

The peculiarities of the Samarqandī *dīnārs* from 914 A.H. cease to surprise us upon comparison of three indicators: the weight standard, the fact of its indication in the coin's inscription, and the mint date. Such a comparison reveals that in this case, the weight standard of a *mithqāl* plus half a *dāng* was not an isolated act of raising the weight of copper *dīnārs*, but rather *the unification of the weight standard of silver and copper coins within the framework of the reform of Shībānī Khān.*

We may observe as well that the unification of the weight standard for coins of two metals also rested on tradition. As was mentioned above, following the conquest of Mavarannahr by Shībānī Khān, beginning from 907 A.H. uniform copper coins were issued in Bukhara and Samarqand, and later in Ḥiṣār, at a weight standard of one *mithqāl*—that is, corresponding to the weight standard for Timurid *tangachas* of that period and for the first issue (Samarqand, 907 A.H.) of silver coins of Shībānī Khān himself. In other words, *in 907 A.H., the issue of coins of two metals with a single weight standard was decreed.*

Even with the clear preference for a unified weight standard in circumstances when the rate of silver coins was stipulated in terms of copper coins, such a unification was not always carried out. Policy with regard to the weight of copper coins was more often independent. For example, at the end of the 15th century and the beginning of the 16th, as we have managed to show, the following weight standards were used for copper coins of, for instance, Samarqand: 898/1492-93, a *mithqāl* and half a *dāng* (5.2 g); 900/1494-95, a *mithqāl* and a *nukhūd* (5.0 g); 917/1511-12 and the beginning of 918/1512-13, four *dāng*, i.e., 2/3 *mithqāl* (3.2 g); 918/1512-13 and 919/1513-14, 3.5 *dāng* of a *mithqāl* (2.8 g). The weight standard for *silver* Timurid and Shībānid *tangachas* during these time-frames was different. The situation of a half-century later turns out to have been analogous: the Shībānid silver *tanga* weighed one *mithqāl* (4.8 g), while the copper coins (mentioned under 942 A.H.) weighed a *mithqāl* plus two *nukhūds* (5.2 g).

Under Shībānī Khān the unification of the weight of coins of two metals became a policy, and was carried out twice: one *mithqāl* (4.8 g)

[62] State Archive of the Republic of Uzbekistan, *fond* I-323, No. 12 (and others).

in 907/1501-02 (within the framework of measures intended to stabilize monetary circulation in Mavarannahr); and a *mithqāl* plus half a *dāng* of a *mithqāl* (5.2 g) in 914/1508-09 (within the framework of the state-wide reform begun a year earlier). From the economic point of view this was not really all that essential, since copper coins in any case were in use at a compulsory rate, and their real cost (in terms of metal and labor) was lower than their nominal value. But it was important from the perspective of social psychology, and was a supplementary argument for the rationality and reliability of the policy that was being conducted, and for the solidity and usefulness of the shift.

In evaluating the significance of the unification of the weight standard for copper and silver coins within the framework of Shībānī Khān's reform, we must not lose sight of the fact that, in Mavarannahr between 910 and 914 A.H., the independent monetary policy of Shībānid appanage-holders in some major towns destroyed what had been up to that time the state-wide circulation of copper coins. Against this background, the unification of the weight standard, together with its simultaneous increase, appears as an even more important and decisively positive aspect of the reform of Shībānī Khān; it appealed for confidence and received it.

On the copper *dīnār*s of Bukhara from 914 A.H., their weight standard is not indicated in their inscriptions. But their actual weight corresponds fully to a weight standard of 5.2 g. This means that in Mavarannahr, despite the variety of types of copper coins, their weight was the same, and the weight-related aspect of the reform was conducted consistently.

Post-Reform Countermarks on Silver Coins:

Countermarks of Shībānī Khān identified by his name are unknown, but among the anonymous countermarks, several can be reliably linked with the financial activity of his treasury.

Among the countermarks on silver Timurid and Safavid coins, one group of anonymous countermarks is distinguished by the term "*shīrmard*;"[63] the attribution of these is not a simple matter by far. For

[63] Discussion about the number of letters (five or six) in this term, and its reading and meaning, have continued for more than a century and a half (for a brief survey, see Davidovich, *Istoriia denezhnogo obrashcheniia srednevekovoi Srednei Azii*, pp. 17-18). I have adopted the reading "*shīrmard*" (with six letters), since in a series of inscriptions I discovered diacritical marks above the first letter (*shīn*) and beneath the second (*yā*).

some time it was believed that this term itself appeared in coin inscriptions under the Shībānids; this led to the whole group of countermarks being regarded as Shībānid. However, the term came to be found in inscriptions on *Timurid* copper coins, and the dynastic boundary of its appearance ceased to be rigid.[64] It must be noted, however, that the *regular* use of this term in coin inscriptions and countermarks does indeed begin under the Shībānids.

The second difficulty with the attribution of countermarks of this group lies in the fact that even among Shībānid rulers alone, two are now known under whom anonymous countermarks with the term "*shīrmard*" were produced: not only Shībānī Khān (907-916 A.H.), but Köchkünjī Khān as well, the second head of the dynasty (916-936 A.H.). In order to study the reform of Shībānī Khān and the post-reform circulation, then, the preliminary task is that of distinguishing on a sound basis, within this group, the countermarks produced specifically under Shībānī Khān, and specifically after the reform that was begun in 913/1507.

There are several criteria for attribution: the *type* (the form of the countermark's cartouche), *variant* (the contents of the inscriptions within the cartouche), the geography of *single-type* countermarks, and the time of issue of the countermarked coins.

From the standpoint of the contents of the inscriptions, the countermarks of the group under consideration may be divided into four basic variants:

A: *ʿadl shīrmard* + date in numerals;
B: *ʿadl shīrmard* (without date);
C: *ʿadl shīrmard* + place of minting + date in numerals;[65]
D: *ʿadl shīrmard* + place of minting (without date).

An attempt to study countermarks on silver and copper coins of the 15th and 16th centuries has allowed the discovery of the following pattern: *single-type* countermarks (like single-type coins) were produced in the same time-frame; inscriptions on single-type countermarks can

[64] It appears on coins of 901/1495-96 and 906/1500-01; see Davidovich, *Istoriia denezhnogo obrashcheniia srednevekovoi Srednei Azii*, p. 17, Fig. 1/1-2.

[65] There is in addition a single countermark, known so far, from Bukhara in 911 A.H. (Type 2, Fig. 1/2), in which the word *żarb* is found instead of *ʿadl*.

differ (especially by the presence or absence of the date in numerals, or by different dates). If at least one countermark of the type under investigation has the date in numerals in its inscription, this serves as an orientation point with regard to the time of production for all the other countermarks of the same type that bear no date. Two concrete examples may be offered within the framework of the group under consideration, with the term *shīrmard*. There are countermarks of Type 1 (Fig. 1/1), without identification of the mint, both without any date (variant B) and with dates (variant A). Two dates are known in countermarks of Type 1, 907 and 909 A.H.; it is clear that these reflect the longstanding pre-reform measure of Shībānī Khān in Mavarannahr (see Section 1 of this article). Countermarks of another type are fairly numerous, also without indication of the mint, and variants A and B of the inscription within the figured cartouche (Fig. 1/4)—that is, some have the date, others do not. But these reflect a single act. As additional evidence we may note that there are countermarks without dates on the *tanga*s of Köchkünjī Khān; consequently they were all produced no earlier than the period during which he was head of the dynasty. The time of their production is given precisely by countermarks of the same type that bear the date in numerals: 934 A.H.[66]

The attribution of those types in whose inscriptions no date has yet been discovered in any countermark is decidedly more complicated. In similar cases it is very important to collect a quantitatively significant body of material. For this goal it is essential to work through the entire body of Timurid and early Ṣafavid silver coins, but so far no one (myself included) has carried out such work. I have at my disposal only a selection, which nevertheless allows us to regard one type of countermarks as a post-reform measure of Shībānī Khān.

Unfortunately publications of countermarks with the term *shīrmard* rarely contain data for the determination of type (there are no drawings or photographs of the cartouches). For example, A. K. Markov published countermarks from Bāvard (Abīvard, in southern Turkmenistan) and Herat,[67] but it was possible to determine their type only upon examination of the coins in the State Hermitage (they belong

[66] For countermarks of this time, with and without dates, see Davidovich, *Korpus*, pp. 401-402, Nos. 872, 909, 917, 922.

[67] Markov, *Inventarnyi katalog*, p. 678, Nos. 257, 255.

to Type 3 according to my classification [Fig. 1/3]). Countermarks of Type 3 from Herat are the most numerous, and have been discovered on many, primarily unpublished, Timurid coins, preserved in various museums: in the State Hermitage in St. Petersburg,[68] in the State Historical Museum in Moscow,[69] in the Museum of the History and Culture of Samarkand in Uzbekistan,[70] in a hoard from southern Turkmenistan,[71] and so forth. There are also countermarks of Type 3 from Khwāf and Qarshī.[72]

In 1966, N. M. Lowick devoted a special excursus to countermarks linked in some fashion with the Shībānids[73] (Shībānid countermarks on their own silver coins and on foreign coins, and, conversely, foreign countermarks on Shībānid silver coins); he divided them into four categories, designated by letters. His category "C" consisted of Shībānid countermarks on Persian coins (meaning silver coins of the Timurids and Ṣafavids). He cites *only two* such countermarks. One is the pre-reform countermark of Type 2 (Fig. 1/2), from Bukhara, 911 A.H., mentioned above (cited after the publication of Tizengauzen); the second, produced in Nīshāpūr, was on a Ṣafavid coin from the collection of the British Museum (for which there is no description of the type, and no figure of the cartouche).

Stephen Album, writing in 1987, knew of six coins with countermarks whose inscriptions include the name of the mint.[74] Two of these were already known (Timurid and Ṣafavid), and the information on their countermarks (done in Bukhara in 911 A.H., and in Nīshāpūr) was drawn from Lowick. The four new coins were in the author's own collection. They bear countermarks from Herat, Nīshāpūr, Turbat, and

[68] Nos. 31271-31272 (the first has been published; see Markov, *Inventarnyi katalog*, p. 678, No. 255).

[69] No. 939259, and others.

[70] No. 5668.

[71] Davidovich, *Korpus*, hoard No. 2, note 27 on p. 164.

[72] The countermark from Khwāf is on a Timurid coin in the State Historical Museum in Moscow; the countermark from Qarshī is on a Timurid coin in a private collection.

[73] N. M. Lowick, "Shaybānid Silver Coins," *Numismatic Chronicle*, Seventh Series, 6 (1966), p. 262.

[74] S. Album, "Oubeh: A Hitherto Unrecorded Islamic Mintplace," *Oriental Numismatic Society, Newsletter*, No. 108 (September-October, 1987), pp. 5-6.

Awbah (*a.w.b.h*). The countermark from Awbah was the principal focus of Album's publication; the reading of the town's name and its localization (on the Harīrūd river, east of Herat) were convincingly established, and the inscription, a figure of the cartouche, and a photograph of the coin were included. It belongs to Type 3 according to my classification. The type (or types) of the countermarks from Herat, Nīshāpūr, and Turbat on the coins from his collection were not described, nor were drawings of their cartouches provided. Album considered *all* the countermarks he enumerated to have been done under Shībānī Khān after he conquered Herat in 913 A.H.—i.e., during the years 913-916 A.H. (in this he was forgetting about the date 911 A.H. in the countermark from Bukhara). On the other hand, he offered a useful consideration regarding the countermarks from Turbat and Awbah, which could not have been produced, under Shībānī Khān, earlier than 913 A.H.

Lowick and Album, in short, discuss six countermarks, produced in five places: Bukhara, Herat, Nīshāpūr, Awbah, and Turbat. The type, however, is known for only two of these: for Bukhara (thanks to Tizengauzen's illustration and for Awbah (thanks to Album's illustration). For these two sites, moreover, the countermarks are of different types and different times. Because Album combines *all six* countermarks into one group (even though it thus includes the countermarks from Bukhara and Awbah, of *different* types), it is impossible to determine the *type* of countermarks from Herat, Nīshāpūr, and Turbat on the coins from Album's collection on the basis of his publication.

Thus, it is possible to say with confidence that countermarks of Type 3 were produced after 913 A.H. in Qarshī, Bāvard, Herat, Khwāf, and Awbah. After 913 A.H., countermarks were also produced in Nīshāpūr and Turbat, but their *type* remains unknown to me, and for this reason I cannot include them in characterizing the action formalized by the countermark of Type 3. A thorough examination of museum collections of Timurid and Ṣafavid silver coins would reveal a larger quantity of countermarks of Type 3, including new sites of their production. The material cited here, however, confirms that the countermark of Type 3 was a large-scale post-reform measure.

CONCLUSION (RESULTS AND QUESTIONS)

The determination of the actual meanings of the terms *tanga*, *tangacha*, *dīnār*, and *dīnār-i kepekī* in the 15th-16th centuries in Mavarannahr and Khurāsān; the analysis of the text of Khwāndamīr regarding the reform of Shībānī Khān; and the introduction of other written sources and numismatic data have together allowed us to describe the pre-reform situation, and to understand the substance of Shībānī Khān's reform and the post-reform monetary circulation; nevertheless, unresolved questions remain.

The reform was initiated in conditions of differing, but serious, shocks in the monetary circulation in both Mavarannahr and Khurāsān. Its chief constituents were promulgated immediately after the taking of Herat, in the mosque, at the very first Friday prayer! This fact in itself shows that the reform envisioned not only economic goals, but political aims as well. It is clear that it promised stability in the context of the negative fluctuations of the preceding period.

The elements of the reform that were registered by Khwāndamīr were not put into practice at once, and do not exhaust the full substance of the reform; the reform was refined and supplemented. Though begun in 913 A.H., only in 914 did it organize, on a state-wide scale, the minting and circulation of *tangacha*s. But the reform involved more than silver coins. All the data concerning the reform's substance and results may be grouped in the following 'items.'

Item 1: the proclamation—in Herat, the capital of the Timurids—about the minting of *tangacha*s in the name of the founder of a new dynasty, Shībānī Khān, which had political significance: this represented the most unambiguous and graphic 'documentation,' in the Muslim world, of the end of an old dynasty and the accession of a new one. The state-wide announcement that silver *tangacha*s would henceforth be "adorned by the imperial name"—i.e., with the name of Shībānī Khān—was made (according to Khwāndamīr) in Muḥarram 913, and thus at the very beginning of the year. The minting of *tangacha*s in the name of Shībānī Khān was indeed begun that year, and at present coins of Herat, Samarqand, and Bukhara are known with this date.

Item 2: 'coin documentation' of the new title of Shībānī Khān. This title ("*imām* of his time and vicegerent of [God] the Compassionate"), with a clearly expressed theocratic conception, was also proclaimed in the *khuṭba* on the first Friday of 913 A.H.

following the taking of Herat; and in the same year, 913, it appeared on the *tangacha*s minted in the name of Shībānī Khān, but not on all coins of this year. It was included in the titulature on the *tangacha*s of Herat from 913 A.H. (Type 4). On the *tangacha*s of Bukhara and Samarqand from 913 A.H. (Types 2-3), by contrast, appears the earlier, *first* title, a more modest one. The new, *second* title received state-wide use not from the beginning of 913 A.H., but somewhat later. In coin inscriptions it was connected with the post-reform, state-wide Type 4; on *tangacha*s of Type 4 from all presently known mints (including Bukhara and Samarqand), from 914 A.H., it is precisely this new, *second* title, that appears.

Item 3: the unification of the *type* of the *tangacha*s for the entire state (Type 4). Type 4 was produced in 913 A.H., evidently in Herat. In the course of implementing the reform, *tangacha*s of this type began to be issued by other mints (at present 14 sites have been identified; see Table 1). The example of Mavarannahr, where in 913 A.H. *tangacha*s of completely different types (Types 2-3) were issued, allows us to suppose that this most important item, about the *unification of the type* of coins on a state-wide scale, either was not envisioned in the initial elaboration of the reform, or required some time for its practical realization. In other words, Type 4 achieved *state-wide* status either in the second half of 913 A.H., or in 914 A.H.; in 914, *tangacha*s of Type 4 were issued at all mints, and the minting from this year was also the most plentiful. The implementation of the reform through Type 4, and the lack of any variation in type until 916/1510 (the year of Shībānī Khān's death), show that the reform provided for the state-wide circulation of silver coins at a unitary rate (independent of the place where each was issued), without rate-related machinations by Shībānid appanage-holders or regroupings of rates with fiscal goals in mind.

Item 4: the stipulation of a new weight standard for *tangacha*s in the name of Shībānī Khān. In view of Khwāndamīr's testimony and the results of studying the real and average weight of the post-reform silver coins of Shībānī Khān (Type 4), it is clear that the weight standard of his *tangacha*s equaled a *mithqāl* and half a *dāng* of a *mithqāl* (4.8 + 0.4 = 5.2 g). The reform of Shībānī Khān thus increased the weight standard by half a *dāng* relative to the late-Timurid weight standard (one *mithqāl*). The scale of the increase, however, was not coincidental or arbitrary; Shībānī Khān rejected only the later tradition of the Timurids, and returned to the final weight standard of the popular *tangachas* of Shāhrukh (807/1405–850/1447).

Item 5: policy regarding copper *dīnārs*. This item was not intended initially, but represents a positive development of the reform. Its substance was the unification of the weight standard for both silver and copper coins, which gives the reform a particularly comprehensive form in circumstances when the rate of silver *tangachas* was fixed in terms of copper *dīnārs*. This element was discovered as a result of studying the copper *dīnārs* of Bukhara and Samarqand from 914/1508-09. The coin inscriptions, and the real and average weight of these coins, showed convincingly that in 914/1508-09, the weight standard of these copper *dīnārs* equaled a *mithqāl* plus half a *dāng* of a *mithqāl*, or 5.2 g. For this reason it is now possible to affirm with certainty that in Mavarannahr, the reform of Shībānī Khān was accomplished precisely in 914 A.H. through the unification of the weight standard for coins of two metals; and this was a policy that also reflected local traditions.

Item 6: determination of the *rate* of the *tangachas* that were to be minted in the name of Shībānī Khān. Khwāndamīr indicated their *rate* not in copper *dīnārs* (the traditional and reliable method), but in small silver coins—*kepekī dīnārs*. One of the prospective *tangachas*, according to Khwāndamīr, would be equal to six *kepekī dīnārs*. An analysis of this report by Khwāndamīr confirms its erroneous character. A more convincing conjecture is that the word "*nīm*" ("half") has been omitted from the text, and that the *tangachas* of Shībānī Khān were initially made equal not to six, but to six and a half, *kepekī dīnārs*.

Item 7: permission for the continued circulation of "former" *tangachas*—i.e., the Timurid one-*mithqāl* variety—but with a reduction of their rate. Before Shībānī Khān's reform, according to Khwāndamīr, they were equal to six *kepekī dīnārs*; the reform made them equal to five *kepekī dīnārs*, and thus lowered their purchasing power by one-sixth. This report is reliable, and may be checked through copper *dīnārs*. Prior to the reform, the *kepekī dīnār* weighing one-sixth *mithqāl* (0.8 g) was equal to six copper *dīnārs*, meaning that the one-*mithqāl* Timurid *tangacha* equaled 36 copper *dīnārs*; after the reform, the very same *tangachas*, reduced in value to five *kepekī dīnārs*, should have been equal to 30 copper *dīnārs*. Precisely such a reformed equivalence between Timurid *tangachas* and copper *dīnārs* is confirmed by other evidence.

Item 8: the comparative status (rate) of the two groups of *tangachas*. The reform established the coexistence of the new *tangachas* of Shībānī Khān and the "former" Timurid *tangachas*, and defined their official rates differently. For the *tangacha* of Shībānī Khān, the 'full' rate was stipulated, corresponding to their metal; for the "former" Timurid *tangachas*, an artificially reduced rate was set, with a significant undervaluation of the silver they contained. The possibility of such a model for the coexistence of two groups of silver coins is reliably confirmed by an analogy: the organization of the circulation of "new" and "old" *tangas* in the Shībānid state (the fixed rate of the "old" coins was always reduced by 10%).

Item 9: the scale of prices. The post-reform minting of silver coins included the issue of fractions of the basic denomination. The post-reform type of the coins of the basic denomination and of those of half the basic denomination was identical (Type 4); they differed only in their size, weight, and inscriptions. In other words, the issue of coins in the basic denomination and of coins one-half of the basic denomination represented a single act, actualized in the single Type 4. Post-reform coins of Shībānī Khān equal, evidently, to two-thirds of the basic denomination are also known, but they are of a different type (Type 6); this should be recognized as a correct decision, since the uniformity of two fractions (at half and two-thirds the basic denomination) that were relatively close in weight would have caused practical difficulties in distinguishing between them.

Item 10: the post-reform countermarks of Shībānī Khān. Among the many anonymous countermarks with the term *shīrmard*, countermarks of Type 3 (Fig. 1/3) are attributable to an action carried out after 913 A.H. in many mints. Countermarks of Type 3 divided Timurid *tangachas* into two groups with respect to their rate: *tangachas* without countermarks (whose rate equaled 30 copper *dīnārs*), and *tangachas* with countermarks (with an unknown, but higher, rate). The substance of the reform as initially developed provided for the legal coexistence of *two* groups of *tangachas*, of different weights and different rates. The countermark of Type 3 (which undoubtedly brought income to the treasury) was either the result of further elaboration of the reform, or a separate fiscal measure. In either case, this was a third group of *tangachas*, with its own official rate.

Item 11: the decreed issue of gold coins (*ashrafī*). The place (or places) of their issue remains unknown, and they lack precise dates as well, but they belong to the post-reform period (judging from the *titles* of Shībānī Khān and the *type* of the *ashrafis*); for this reason the issue of *ashrafis* should be regarded as the result of further elaboration of the reform. However, gold coins did not play a substantial role in trade during the 16th century, and after Shībānī Khān, they were not minted at all in the Shībānid state for many decades.

Following the implementation of the basic, original substance of the reform of Shībānī Khān and of its supplementary measures, the composition of the bulk mass of money provided for all levels of monetary trade. Trade in expensive goods was based on silver coins (*tangacha*s, *tanga*s) of different values: the high-weight (5.2 g) *tangacha*s of Shībānī Khān (Type 4); Timurid one-*mithqāl tangacha*s (with a weight standard of 4.8 g) without countermarks, and the same with countermarks of Type 3; and fractions of the basic denomination. The most substantial achievement of the reform was the equal, state-wide circulation of *tangacha*s of Type 4 (independent of their place and year of issue). Such a stable situation in monetary circulation and trade was a rare occurrence; subsequently, in the state of the Shībānids, throughout the 16th century, not a single ruler managed to repeat this success.

The policy with regard to copper coins, as it appears according to the coinage of central Mavarannahr (Bukhara and Samarqand), provided for two results: the liquidation of all the negative effects that had accumulated in the minting and circulation of copper coins during the preceding period (910-913 A.H.); and the provision, to the market, of a new copper *dīnār* (the basic denomination in copper minting) within the framework of the reform, on the basis of a unification of the weight of silver and copper. The post-reform circulation of copper coins in central Mavarannahr was organized in the best possible way, with consideration of the role of social psychology in the process of stabilizing the market following major shocks. This was extraordinarily important, if one considers that the second half of the 15th century and the first quarter of the 16th was a special period, marking a 'peak' in the development of retail trade and the production of small-scale goods,[75] which were fully accommodated precisely by copper coins.

* * *

[75] Davidovich, *Istoriia denezhnogo obrashcheniia srednevekovoi Srednei Azii*, pp. 310-322.

The study of the substance of the reform and of the post-reform monetary circulation remains incomplete, since there is not yet sufficient material with which to answer several questions. First among the issues left unresolved for now because of the state of the source base is the status of the post-reform minting and circulation of copper coins beyond the confines of Mavarannahr.[76]

There is no doubt that the post-reform model for the coexistence of the *tangacha*s of Shībānī Khān with the "former" Timurid *tangacha*s (both without countermarks and with countermarks of Type 3) in Khurāsān and Mavarannahr was identical: the official rate of the Timurid *tangacha*s was artificially reduced. But this does not exclude regional variants of the relationship between silver and copper coins. Norms revealed by documents (a *mithqāl* of silver equaled first 18 copper *dīnār*s, then 36; after the announcement of the reform, the one-*mithqāl tangacha* was made equal to 30 copper *dīnār*s) might well lack state-wide significance. Mavarannahr could have had its own traditional norms of equivalence between silver and copper coins in a stable situation. For example, according to the *vathīqa* cited above,[77] prepared on 3 Dhū'l-Qaʿda 915/12 February 1510, an object in the *tümen* of Ura-tepe (in present-day Tajikistan) was sold for 800 *tanga*s, each of which was equal to ten full-rate copper *dīnār*s. Which *tanga*s are meant in this document? If they were coins of half the basic denomination, then the latter would be equal to 20 copper *dīnār*s; if they were coins of one-third the basic denomination, then the latter would be equal to 30 copper *dīnār*s (as in Khurāsān). Later on in Mavarannahr under the Shībānids,[78] the one-*mithqāl* silver coin that is called "new" in documents (each latest issue) was for many decades officially made equal precisely to 20 copper *dīnār*s, and then, only in the last third of the century, to 30. Apparently, this question would be resolved by a document prepared in Mavarannahr some time between 913 and 916 A.H. and containing a description of the *tangacha* in the basic denomination.

The place, time, and significance of the minting of silver coins of Type 5 (in the basic denomination) also remains unclear, inasmuch as

[76] Even for the territory of the subregion of Ḥiṣār, the composition of the money supply in the sphere of the circulation of copper coins is unknown; see Davidovich, *Istoriia denezhnogo obrashcheniia srednevekovoi Srednei Azii*, pp. 222, 226, 301.

[77] Egani and Chekhovich, "Regesty sredneaziatskikh aktov," p. 50, No. 3.

[78] See Davidovich, "K voprosu o kurse."

*tangacha*s in the basic denomination, of Type 4, were issued until 916 A.H., inclusively, and at many mints.

Deeper investigation, on a broader source base, will in all likelihood make it possible to examine all or some of these questions, but will almost unavoidably pose new ones. The process of understanding is always a multi-stage affair; difficulties increase when the basic information must be drawn from such sources as coins and documents. The accumulation of both kinds of sources is independent of the researcher, and at present does not facilitate an understanding of certain aspects of the reform of Shïbānī Khān and of the post-reform monetary circulation.

RECONSTRUCTING BALKH: THE *VAQFĪYA* OF 947/1540[1]

R. D. McChesney

New York University

The value of *vaqf* deeds (*vaqfīyas*, *vaqf-nāmas*) for reconstructing the social and physical environments of earlier times in the Islamicate world has long been recognized. Scholars such as Ol'ga D. Chekhovich, Leonor Fernandes, Soraiya Faroqhi, Abraham Marcus, David Powers, André Raymond, Maria Subtelny, Ol'ga A. Sukhareva, and many others have used evidence from *vaqf* documents to bring back to life long-vanished urban landscapes and social networks.

Nowhere perhaps is such information—preserved on paper in archives—more important than where the physical evidence it represents is now inaccessible, either buried beneath immovable accretions or isolated by political circumstances. One such place is the site of the former city of Balkh in north-central Afghanistan. When the site of ancient Balkh was open to excavation, it attracted the interest of scholars searching for the Hellenic, particularly Alexandrine, and Buddhist past.[2] For at least the past quarter century or so it has not been possible to research Balkh *in situ* because of political conflict, a factor which

[1] I would like to thank Erkin Abdullaev, Director of the Central State Archive of the Republic of Uzbekistan, for permission to publish the *vaqfīya* in facsimile. The present paper would not have been written but for the generous assistance of Maria Eva Subtelny, who encouraged the work at several points with careful readings and always insightful comments. For this the author is truly grateful. Yuri Bregel also indirectly encouraged the work when, as rapporteur on a panel on *vaqf* at the 1997 Middle East Studies Association Annual Conference, he politely but firmly noted that the lack of published documents made generalizations about *vaqf* in Central Asia problematic if not suspect.

[2] The published record of excavations is tiny. The Délégation Archéologique Française en Afghanistan excavated in the citadel in 1924-25 (see A. Foucher, *La vieille route de l'Inde de Bactres à Taxila* [Paris: Les Éditions d'art et d'histoire, 1942], vol. I, pp. 98-121). Rodney S. Young dug several sondages in the southwest wall of Balkh (the wall referred to in the present *vaqfīya* as the "new wall" (*ḥiṣār-i jadīd*), but his object was the Hellenistic past and the findings from 'Islamic layers' were of no apparent interest (see R. S. Young, "The South Wall of Balkh-Bactra," *The American Journal of Archaeology*, 59 [1955], pp. 267-276).

prevents access for the foreseeable future as well. Consequently what little has been written about Balkh has been derived from the fairly sketchy and impressionistic descriptions found in narrative sources (authored by indigenous writers as well as visitors).[3] Each of these texts presents its own set of problems for the reader/researcher. Interpretation of the information each offers first requires knowledge of the motives that led to production of the text. Sometimes military and political interests were the motivating factors (for example, the texts produced by British and Russian officials in the 19th and 20th centuries). Other texts were produced to highlight and publicize (and aggrandize) the power or virtues of an indigenous figure.

The importance of detailed information from legal documents, generally written to record some kind of exchange transaction, can hardly be overstated. These too, of course, are produced within a context and framework and require understanding of that framework but they have the not insignificant virtue, at least as far as the contemporary researcher is concerned, of precision: precision in nomenclature, physical description, and the definition of economic and social relationships.

For Balkh, information on its pre-nineteenth century urban plan and social makeup is, as I have discussed elsewhere, extremely slim. Moreover, the abandonment of the site as urban center in the course of the

[3] On the textual sources see A. M. Mukhtarov, *Pozdnesrednevekovyi Balkh (Materialy k istoricheskoi topografii goroda v XVI-XVIII vv.)* (Dushanbe: Donish, 1980), pp. 8-16 (translated by R. D. McChesney with Nadia Jamal and Michael Lustig, "Balkh in the late Middle Ages," *Papers on Inner Asia*, No. 24 [Bloomington, Indiana: Research Institute for Inner Asian Studies, 1993], pp. 6-12); B. A. Akhmedov, *Istoriia Balkha (XVI-pervaia polovina XVIII v.)* (Tashkent: Fan, 1982), pp. 4-13; Zeki Velidi Togan, in his "The Topography of Balkh down to the Middle of the Seventeenth Century," *Central Asiatic Journal*, 14 (1970), pp. 277-288, attempts a sketch map of the city based on Maḥmūd b. Amīr Walī's section in the fourth part of the sixth volume of *Baḥr al-asrār fī manāqib al-akhyār*, MS India Office Ethé No. 575. Neither Mukhtarov nor Akhmedov made use of unpublished legal documentary sources despite the fact that Davidovich's references to this *vaqfīya* at least (see below) were presumably available to them. Mukhtarov cites the State Archive of Uzbekistan (the repository of the 1540 *vaqfīya*) as one of his sources but there is no evidence in his study that he actually worked there. The one document he cites from the archives, Subḥān Qulī Khān's *madrasa vaqfīya*, had already been published at the time he was writing and he presumably used the published version (A. D. Davydov, "Imenie medrese Subkhankuli-khana v Balkhe (po vakfnoi gramote XVII v.)," *Kratkie Soobshcheniia Instituta Vostokovedeniia*, 37 [1960], pp. 82-128).

19th century for the nearby site of the shrine of ʿAlī b. Abī Ṭālib (Mazār-i Sharīf) also severed much of the oral tradition which informed the written. The significance of the present document for re-constructing Balkh when it stood as the principal urban center of the great plain lying between the Amū Daryā (Oxus River) to the north, the Hindu Kush mountains to the south, the basin of the Harī Rūd (Herat River) to the west and the heights of the Pamirs to the east becomes clearer against this background.

E. A. Davidovich first drew attention to this document in 1961 and again in 1982, and Galiba Dzhuraeva (Juraeva) provided a synoptic account of some of its features in an article published in 1995.[4] Davidovich drew on it to help clarify certain monetary and land ownership issues. Juraeva extended the discussion of the document by identifying the unnamed author and donor of the *vaqf*. She also briefly described the public beneficiary of the *vaqf* (this was a typical 'mixed endowment' in which both public and private purposes are served), enumerated the properties and defined a number of terms that appear in the document.

The purpose of the present article is to make the entire document available, to draw attention to its value, not only for the information it provides about a now-vanished urban landscape, but also for what it tells us of the document itself as object and textual production.

THE DOCUMENT: COPIES AND ORIGINALS

The *vaqfīya* is typical of large-scale endowment deeds of 15th-17th century Central Asia. In the first place it is a copy of the 'original.' (The question of what constitutes 'original' in the case of a legal document requires lengthy treatment and cannot be addressed here. Suffice it to say that in some sense all hand-written documents are 'originals' and in some sense no document is 'original.') Very few of the *vaqfīyas* in

[4] E. A. Davidovich, "Materialy dlia kharakteristiki èkonomiki i sotsial'nykh otnoshenii v Srednei Azii XVI v.," *Izvestiia otdeleniia obshchestvennykh nauk Akademii Nauk Tadzhikskoi SSR*, 24 (1961), p. 41 (of which an English summary, "Some Social and Economic Aspects of 16th Century Central Asia," appeared in *Central Asian Review*, 12 [1964], pp. 265-270); *idem*, "O sotsial'nom i zhiznennom urovne riadovykh predstavitelei dukhovensta (po vakf-name XV-XVII vv.)," *Bartol'dovskie chteniia 1982*, p. 19; and G. A. Dzhuraeva, "Vakfnyi dokument 1540 g.," *Vostochnoe istoricheskoe istochnikovedenie i spetsial'nye istoricheskie distsipliny*, vyp. 3 (1995), pp. 190-198.

the possession of the State Archive in Uzbekistan are those drafted at the precise moment a transaction was concluded. The catalogue of the archival collection I-323 lists many documents as "original" (*podlinnik*) but by this is meant a document contemporary with the transaction and bearing the seals of people who witnessed the transaction as distinct from a "copy" (*kopiia*), a later document transcribed from an 'original' or an earlier copy. But we know from the internal evidence of this *vaqfīya* that it was considered prudent and necessary to produce numerous copies of the document both at the time of the transaction and in future. The purpose was both to preserve the document and to ensure that all interested parties had access to its terms.

In the second place the *vaqfīya* is typical in terms of its size. It is a large scroll (measuring almost a foot wide and 18 feet long) made up by pasting together a number of sheets of paper (an examination of the photocopy indicates at least fourteen). Rather than assembled as codices, the *vaqfīya*s in the State Archive of Uzbekistan that this writer has examined have all been scrolls. The scroll form would seem to be related to a scribal convention. Although there has been no definitive study yet, it appears to me that limiting the writing to one side of the sheet of paper was a legal document-writing convention of the 16th- and 17th-century Central Asian chanceries. When the document required more than one side, a second, third, fourth, etc. sheet of paper would be glued to the foot and the writing continued. This writer has not yet come across instances, at least in 16th- and 17th-century documents, where the text of the document continues on the reverse. It was also conventional in documents requiring more than one side of a sheet but less than two, to continue the text in the right hand margin, beginning at the foot, the text upside down and written on the diagonal. In this document another stylistic convention (also widely used) was to finish a horizontal line of text by moving to the vertical at the very end of each line until the last inch or so of space between lines was filled.

The reverse of the document had its own uses. One, as we will see here, was as a place for notes regarding matters pertinent to the transaction recorded on the obverse, in this case properties relevant in some way to this *vaqf* transaction but not a part of it. The back of a document was also a place for an archivist to place library marks that, when the document was rolled (if not encased in a leather end-flap), made it easy to identify and retrieve from a shelf, niche, or trunk.

The present copy is backed with fabric. This is of some significance because for the moment it makes it impossible to verify the several references to items noted "on the back of" (*dar ẓahr-i* or *dar aẓhar-i* [*sic*]) the document. With no physical evidence to the contrary, I would speculate that those notes on the reverse of the document appear only on the contemporary copies. In producing the later copies, made for reasons to be discussed below, the scribes might have only felt it necessary to copy the 'original' text since the institutions noted on the reverse were presumably fully described in their own *vaqfīyas*. But this, of course, is pure speculation on my part.

PRESERVATION AND REPRODUCTION

The document contains its own recipe for preservation. Every year at the celebration of the Prophet's birthday (12 Rajab), the trustee of the *vaqf* was required to read the entire *vaqfīya* aloud at a public gathering. This presumably would ensure continuing access to the terms of the *vaqfīya* for all concerned parties. Furthermore, every ten years, a new copy of the *vaqfīya* was to be made. This is one of the founder's original stipulations (see lines 129-130).[5] Besides the public recitation of the document and the decennial reproduction of it, a further directive for preservation of the document has been added, perhaps at the behest of the founder himself. In the document as we find it today, this text is on a separate sheet, pasted to the foot of the *vaqfīya*, rather than in the ample space left at the end of the *vaqfīya* itself. In some earlier incarnation it may have been one of the supplementary notations on the reverse. This note states that there are six copies of the *vaqfīya* held in different locations: two in Bukhara, one at the Khwāja Muḥammad Pārsā library[6] and one at the home of a certain "Ḥażrat-i Shaykh al-ᶜĀlam" (identity unknown); two in Balkh, both at the homes of judges, Qāżī Mālmal and

[5] This stipulation was probably widely used. In the 1890s, a Russian official examining the documents of the Aḥrārid *vaqf* in Samarqand noted that the *mutavallīs* explained the absence of an authenticating seal by the fact that the charter document was copied every ten years as the 15th century *vāqif* had stipulated (see Jo-Ann Gross, "The *Waqf* of Khoja ᶜUbayd Allah Aḥrār in Nineteenth Century Central Asia: A Preliminary Study of the Tsarist Record," *The Nakshibendis in Western and Central Asia: Change and Continuity*, ed. Elizabeth Ozdalga (Richmond, Surrey: Curzon, 1999), pp. 55-56).

[6] See the study of this library by Maria E. Subtelny, "The Making of Bukhārā-yi Sharīf: Scholars and Libraries in Medieval Bukhara (The Library of Khwāja Muḥammad Pārsā)," in the present volume.

Qāżī Ṣāliḥ; a fifth copy in Samarqand in the house of the "attendants" (*mulāzimān*) of Khwāja Bahāʾ al-Dīnī (or al-Dīn); and the sixth at the home of Muḥammad Ṣādiq Shaykh in Shahr-i Sabz. (One assumes as well that the settlor, his descendants, and the successors to the trusteeship would also have had copies.) This appended text then goes on to say that if any of these copies is lost another copy should be made. If we then factor in the settlor's own instructions, it should have meant that every ten years six (probably more) new copies would have been made and sent out to the separate repositories.

Was such a practice usual and was it ever fully implemented and maintained? The one comparable case that comes imediately to mind is the directive that the thirteenth-century historian and Ilkhanid minister, Rashīd al-Dīn, gave for the preservation and reproduction of his many works.[7] But no doubt there are other such cases awaiting discovery. The circumstantial evidence here suggests that the intention was not fulfilled. In the first place, there are only two known surviving copies of the *vaqfīya* (one very clearly copied from the other). The endowment itself does not appear to have been long-lived, which may account for the small number of documents. There are subsequent references to the *madrasa* part of the complex but none later than the 16th-century that I have found, and the name of the quarter in which it was situated, Chaqar-i Mūsā Shaykh, also disappears or another name supersedes it. The fact that the latest of the copies is probably 19th-century should not be taken as evidence that the *vaqf* was still functioning. Preserving the documents may simply have been thought to be a worthwhile act in itself whether or not the foundation still operated. All we can say at this point is that a system for preservation of the document was of considerable concern to people involved with the *vaqf* and this system had multiple redundancies built into it by the time the present copy was drafted.

It appears that the document was part of the repository known as the "Qoshbegī archive," which was moved from Bukhara to Tashkent

[7] E. G. Browne, *A Literary History of Persia* (Cambridge: Cambridge University Press, 1920; repr. 1964), vol. III, pp. 77-80. Browne's summary of Rashīd al-Dīn's efforts to preserve his works is based on Quatremère's translation of the *Jāmiᶜ al-tavārīkh* (*Histoire des Mongols de la Perse écrite en persan par Raschid-eldin*, ed. & tr. Étienne Quatremère [Paris, 1836]). Although it is not entirely clear in Browne, these instructions appear to be contained in a document separate from the *Jāmiᶜ al-tavārīkh* (see Browne, III, p. 77).

sometime after 1924. The actual *vaqfīyas* from that repository apparently were collected in Fond I-323 while the rest of the mass of Persian material kept by the Qoshbegī, much of it *vaqf*-related, now lies in Fond 126 ("Upravlenie Kush-Begi Emira Bukharskogo").[8] There would seem to be a good likelihood therefore that the present document came from the Pārsā Library in Bukhara and was one of the copies sent there for safekeeping. In fact the circumstantial evidence suggests that both extant copies came from Bukhara and perhaps both from the Pārsā Library.

THE TWO COPIES OF THE *VAQFĪYA*

The State Archive of Uzbekistan possesses two copies of the document. These are catalogued as *Fond* I-323, *opis'* 1, No. 956 and No. 1216.[9] In the unpublished catalogue of the collection, the founder of the *vaqf* in both cases is named "Khodzha Mukhammad Kanot" (i.e., Kanāt) although the short identical description that appears with both entries says "the name of the founder . . . is unknown." Juraeva, who compared the two surviving copies, concluded that the later was copied directly from the earlier as both share the identical lacunae and defectiveness.

THE QUALITY OF THE COPYING

The copy used here (No. 1216) was done in a professional-looking *naskh* copperplate. Its professional look, however, masks considerable orthographic carelessness. While the script is of fairly high quality,[10] the scribe's attention must have wandered at times. On line 18 the

[8] See Z. N. Agafonova and N. A. Khal'fin, *Putevoditel' (Tsentral'nyi Gosudarstvennyi Istoricheskii Arkhiv UzSSR)* (Tashkent, 1948), pp. 30-32.

[9] The catalogue of the *fond*, Kollektsiia Vakufnykh Dokumentov (compiled by I. Miradylov: see O. A. Sukhareva, *Kvartal'naia obshchina pozdnefeodal'nogo goroda Bukhary* [Moscow: Nauka, 1976], p. 4) describes the documents identically. No. 956 was transcribed later, according to Juraeva, "Vakfnyi dokument," p. 191, and has a seal imprint with the date 1309/1891-92, although this can only be a *terminus ad quem* for the date of the copy. I have not examined No. 956 and have seen No. 1216 only in a photcopy, slightly reduced in size from the original.

[10] Comparing it, for example, to the illustrations in the enormously useful article "Calligraphy," by Ghulām-Ḥusayn Yūsofī, in the *EIr*, IV, pp. 680-718.

scribe copied *ẓahr* as *aẓhar*. In line 29, in writing *rāhraw*, he forget to inscribe the 'h' (*hā*ʾ) and when the error was later noticed he or someone else went back and hung a tiny *hā*ʾ off the top of the *alif*. He omitted the word *aʿyān* in line 35 in the phrase "*tamāmī ʿamala va aʿyān-i qāʾima*," and in line 39 misspelled *akhta-khāna* as *akhtāna*. While writing line 89 he somehow lost his place, and recopied the phrase "*wa fī maḥṣūlātihā*" (a phrase that occurs at the beginning of the line), before he had completed writing out the maxim "*yataṣṣarafu fīhā wa fī maḥṣūlātihā kayfa yashāʾ wa ayna yashāʾ wa yuṣarrifuhā*" (repeating at this point the phrase "*wa fī maḥṣūlātihā*") "*ilā man yashāʿ*." This error apparently presented a dilemma when he realized what he had done. Now more than halfway through copying the document, the scribe probably first berated himself for his carelessness and then decided it was impossible, for whatever reason, to start over (perhaps he had already wasted too many sheets of paper) and so the errant words are lightly crossed out. From here on the problems multiply. He misspells *tanqīṣ* as *tanṣīṣ* (line 90), *rawghan* as *raghan* (line 137), and writes "*bi-ṭarīq-i mann*[an] *niṣf*" instead of "*bi-ṭarīq-i munāṣif*" (line 98). In line 110 he forgets the counting word *ʿadad* and either his or another hand later wrote it in above the line. In line 112 he repeats the entire preceding sentence regarding the appointment of a *muʾadhdhin* and then omits the phrase "*khams nīz az īn*" (later superscribed) in line 113. In line 120 he writes *mīlād* for *mawlid* and at line 122 *sirīnī* for *shīrīnī*. There are other scribal problems though perhaps not his errors. The Qurʾān as quoted in line 15 deviates from the reading as found in the standard version.[11] The note that appears at the very end and sets forth the terms for copying and depositing the *vaqfīya* in Bukhara, Balkh, Samarqand, and Shahr-i Sabz refers to the Khwāja Muḥammad Pārsā library as a *katīb-khāna* (line 174). Numerous other errors and omissions are to be found but these are representative of the general carelessness the document displays.

THE FOUNDER

Based on references in the unpublished *Majmaʿ al-gharāʾib* of the 16th century Balkh native and resident Sulṭān Muḥammad and in the

[11] *Qurʾān Karīm bi-tafsīr al-Imāmayn al-Jalālayn* (Damascus, 1964), and Muḥammad Fuʾād ʿAbd al-Bāqī, *al-Muʿjam al-mufahras li'l-Qurʾān al-Karīm* (Beirut: Dār al-Kutub al-Miṣrīyah, 1945?), p. 748.

Bābur-nāma, Juraeva identified the founder or settlor as Khwāja Kamāl al-Dīn Kunak (Qunāq).

The question of the founder/settlor's identity arises because the beginning of the document, where the settlor's name would normally appear, is missing. In the document itself, the settlor refers to property owned by his son, Khwāja Mawlānā (line 27) and later (line 139) to three mosques which his uterine (*aʿyānī*) brother, "Khwāja Muḥammad Qunāq" had built and then endowed as *vaqf*. The settlor's own name, however, is missing.

The evidence that makes it possible to identify the founder has been partially noted by Juraeva in her citation of the *Bābur-nāma*. On 2 Jumādā II 935/February 11, 1529, Bābur dismissed a certain Kamal al-Dīn ("Qīāq" in Beveridge, "Qanaq" in Thackston, and "Qunāq" in Mano[12]). This Kamāl al-Dīn had himself just received a messenger from his own lord, Kīstan-Qarā Sulṭān, the Jānī-Begid appanage-holder at Balkh. As the translations (both the Persian and the English) reproduce the Chaghatay text, Bābur writes that he was privy to a message from Kīstan-Qarā to his own liege man (*nawkar*) in which the *sulṭān* complains about the behavior of *beg*s on the Balkh border and their ties to Kamāl al-Dīn.

The *Bābur-nāma* thus establishes the existence of a high Uzbek official connected to Balkh in 1529 named Kamāl al-Dīn, with the same name (Qunāq) the settlor uses when he mentions his brother. Besides this evidence, Juraeva cites a note in a manuscript of the unpublished *Majmaʿ al-gharāʾib* that a certain Khwāja Kamāl al-Dīn Qunāq (Kunak in Juraeva) built a *madrasa* and bath in Balkh in "Chaqar." The author of *Majmaʿ al-gharāʾib*, Sulṭān Muḥammad, a *muftī* and the son of Darvīsh Muḥammad, wrote his work in 977/1563. He and his father before him were leading citizens of Balkh, and when the Jānī-Begid Pīr Muḥammad came to power in 963/1556, Sulṭān Muḥammad began work on the *Majmaʿ* in response to the former's desire for information about the city. The *Majmaʿ*, completed some four years after Pīr Muḥammad's death,

[12] Ẓahīr al-Dīn Bābur, *The Bābur-nāma in English (Memoirs of Babur)*, tr. Annette Susannah Beveridge (London: Luzac, 1922; repr. 1969), p. 649; *idem*, *The Baburnama: Memoirs of Babur, Prince and Emperor*, tr. Wheeler M. Thackston (New York/Oxford: Oxford University Press, 1996), p. 415; *idem*, *Bābur-nāma (Vaqāyiʿ)*, critical edition based on four Chaghatay texts with introduction and notes by Eiji Mano, 2 vols. (Kyoto: Skyodo, 1995), I (text), p. 576, II (concordance with vocalization), p. 248.

reveals the author as a man proud of his city and the public works that political figures had constructed there in the last half of the 15th and first half of the 16th centuries. The completion of one of the projects, a 'royal bath' commissioned by Kīstan Qarā in 934/1527-28, was memorialized in a chronogram, "*ḥammām-i ṭāhir-i Balkhī*" = 946 (if the word *ḥammām* is read *ḥamām*), composed by Sulṭān Muḥammad's father.[13] The writer describes Kamāl al-Dīn's own bath as having been built near the *madrasa* and as also having been completed in 946/1539 (one year before the establishment of the endowment), while the *madrasa* had been completed some time before.[14]

But there is even more evidence linking the *madrasa* to Kamāl al-Dīn Qunāq. Writing about the same time as Sulṭān Muḥammad (in the 1560s), Khwāja Bahāʾ al-Dīn Ḥasan "Nithārī" Bukhārī shows that the *madrasa* and the *vaqf* supporting it were in operation, at least for a while. Speaking of a teacher of his, Amīr Mahdī al-Ḥusaynī, Nithārī writes, "He taught at the *madrasa* of Khwāja Kamāl al-Dīn,[15] and agreed to teach this humble one *Chaghmīnī*."[16] Nithārī then goes on to say that al-Ḥusayni had been murdered in Balkh and buried at "the *mazār-i shāh*" (probably referring to the shrine of ʿAlī b. Abī Ṭālib east of Balkh).[17] Although Nithārī does not specifically place the *madrasa* of Kamāl al-Dīn in Balkh, the circumstantial evidence of his teacher's being murdered and buried there as well as the manuscript variant that gives "Fatāq" as part of Kamāl al-Dīn's name seems fairly

[13] Sulṭān Muḥammad, *Majmaʿ al-gharāʾib*, MS Tashkent, IVANUz, No. 1494, f. 16b.

[14] Dzhuraeva, "Vakfnyi dokument," pp. 191-192.

[15] Bahāʾ al-Dīn Ḥasan Nithārī Bukhārī, *Mudhakkir al-aḥbāb*, ed. Syed Muhammad Fazlullah (New Delhi, 1969), pp. 373-374. The editor of the text here gives a variant reading in a footnote: "Kamāl al-Dīn Fatāq" (*sic*—a simple transposition of the pointing of "Qunāq"), p. 373.

[16] "*Chaghmīnī*" is shorthand for Sayyid al-Sharīf al-Jurjānī's commentary on Maḥmūd b. Muḥammad al-Chaghmīnī al-Khwārazmī, *al-Mulakhkhaṣ fi'l-hayʾa*. Both commentary and original were in Arabic and the commentary was standard reading at this time for students of astronomy.

[17] The shrine of ʿAlī b. Abī Ṭālib had been the object of considerable patronage by Sulṭān Ḥusayn Bāyqarā sixty years earlier; see my *Waqf in Central Asia* (Princeton, 1991), pp. 39-45, and the review by Maria Eva Subtelny, *Journal of Near Eastern Studies*, 55/1 (1996), pp. 49-52.

persuasive. The editor of Nithārī's work had no doubt that the *madrasa* was in Balkh.[18]

Although Juraeva does not note this, Sulṭān Muḥammad has a good deal to say about Kīstan Qarā's urban renewal projects. These included reconstruction of the walls of the "Qalᶜa-i Hinduvān"[19] (the name for the inner city) which at the southeast quadrant abut the Chaqar-i Mūsā Shaykh Quarter, the site of the *madrasa*-mosque complex and much of the endowed property. Together the *vaqfīya* and the *Majmaᶜ* point to a major redevelopment of the city under the regime of Kīstan Qarā (r. 1526-1544).

THE INFORMATION ON THE REVERSE OF THE *VAQFĪYA*

Throughout the text (lines 18, 49, 117, 137-149) there are many references to matters mentioned or defined "on the reverse of this *vaqfīya*" (*dar ẓahr-i īn vaqfīya*). The term *ẓahr* is contrasted with the term *ṣadr* (the body or obverse of the document).[20] All the references on the reverse are to public structures already built and conveyed as *vaqf* by the settlor and his brother, Khwāja Muḥammad Qunāq, and which now were to derive some of their support from the income produced by the properties endowed in the 1540 *vaqfīya*. Those properties included three mosques which his brother had built (line 139) and four mosques

[18] Nithārī, *Mudhakkir*, ed. Fazlullah, introduction, p. 7. The late-17th- and early-18th-century compiler of chronograms, Sharaf al-Dīn "Rāqim" b. Nūr al-Dīn, also names "Khwāja Kamāl al-Dīn Qunāq" as the builder of a bath in Balkh to support his *madrasa*. But Rāqim dates the bath to 956/1549 (*Tārīkh-i Mīr Sayyid Sharīf Rāqim*, or *Tārīkh-i Rāqimī*, MS Royal Asiatic Society, Morley, No. 163, f. 135b; see also Baron Victor Rosen, *Collection Scientifique de l'Institut des Langues Orientales*, III, *Manuscrits persans* [St. Petersburg, 1886], p. 128). The name Qunāq is also recorded by Foucher, *La vieille route de l'Inde*, vol. 1; Plate XXII is a stupa at "Asyab-e Konak" ("Qunāq's water mill," perhaps the name locals gave the stupa itself?), on the very southern edge of Balkh (see map, p. 59).

[19] Sulṭān Muḥammad, *Majmaᶜ*, f. 16a.

[20] The non-technical meaning of *ṣadr* is "front, forepart, upper part." Maria Subtelny has raised the question with me as to whether in a document *ṣadr* rather means "beginning" of the document, the part following the *invocatio* that contains the crucial information and ends before any appendixes, codicils, attestations, affidavits, or the like. On the other hand, W. P. Heinrichs, in his article on "*ṣadr*" in *EI²*, VIII, p. 748, defines the term in the context of epistolography as "introductory formulae" or "preface;" this does not correspond well with its use in this *vaqfīya*, where it refers to the designated part of the document in which substantive matters are set out.

(line 138), an ablution station, and two *ribāṭ*s[21] (lines 18, 146) which he himself had built and endowed. The trustee of the 1540 endowment was to pay at least part of the salaries of the *imām*s and *mu'adhdhin*s of the seven mosques. Each of the seven *imām*s was to be paid forty *tanga*s per annum and each *mu'adhdhin* twenty. This, presumably, was supplementary to the income derived from the earlier endowments and appropriated for their salaries, since the *imām* of the congregational mosque was granted a salary of 180 *tanga*s and each *mu'adhdhin*, forty. Conceivably the smaller mosques paid the *imām* less, but unless the duties were significantly different, one would not expect the *mu'adhdhin*s to be paid at such disparate scales.

Besides supplementing the salaries of the *imām*s and *mu'adhdhin*s, the 1540 *vaqf* also appointed an apparently new position for the *ribāṭ*s mentioned on the document's reverse. The document stipulates a custodian, at an annual salary of 100 *tanga*s, to open the *ribāṭ*s in the morning, lock them up at night, and daily sweep them out. The 1540 *vaqfīya* draws the line, however, at any expenditures from its own revenues for renovation and repair of these mosques and *ribāṭ*s and the ablution station (line 149).

A FEW OBSERVATIONS ON THE CONTENTS OF THE *VAQFĪYA*

The *vaqfīya* has five distinct parts. The first is a prolegomenon (missing from the surviving copies) in which a kind of 'legislative intent' is established by the settlor's naming himself and giving a statement of purpose. Next comes a definition of the beneficiary (*mawqūf ʿalayh*) which here is partly missing (lines 1-19). Third is a listing of all the properties which make up the income-generating part of the endowment (lines 20-87). Fourth are the settlor's stipulations and conditions (*shurūṭ*) governing administration of the *vaqf* (lines 87-165) and fifth is the pro forma suit that the settlor initiates and that establishes the legal inviolability of the endowment (lines 165-172). This document contains

[21] The term *ribāṭ* probably refers here to hospices or guesthouses. Although used elsewhere as a synonym for caravanserai, the use of both terms in this document would seem to indicate distinct meanings. For other uses of the term *ribāṭ* in Bukhara during the same period, see my "Some observations on 'garden' and its meanings in the property transactions of the Juybari family in Bukhara, 1544-77," *Gardens in the Times of the Great Muslim Empires: Theory and Design*, ed. Attilio Petruccioli (Leiden: Brill, 1997), p. 104.

a sixth section, written in a different hand and on a separate sheet pasted to the end of the scroll, which names the repositories of the document and gives instructions for replacing copies that are lost.

The public beneficiary is a congregational mosque/*madrasa*/ablution station complex in the Chaqar-i Mūsā Shaykh quarter, probably, as suggested above, part of the urban redevelopment scheme spearheaded by the Jānī-Begid/Shībānid appanage-holder, Kīstan-Qarā Sulṭān. Supporting it is a substantial fund of properties including two caravanserais, sixty-one shops, a large public bath, and three residential compounds (*ḥavīlī*). These properties were located mainly in three of the city's quarters (*kū*, *gudhar*), Chaqar-i Mūsā Shaykh, Sallākh Khāna, and Āsyābād. In addition there is one property (five attached shops) that is described as "outside the old walls" (*ḥiṣār-i qadīm*, i.e., the 'inner city') and "near the ʿIrāq Gate" (lines 58-60). Another shop is also

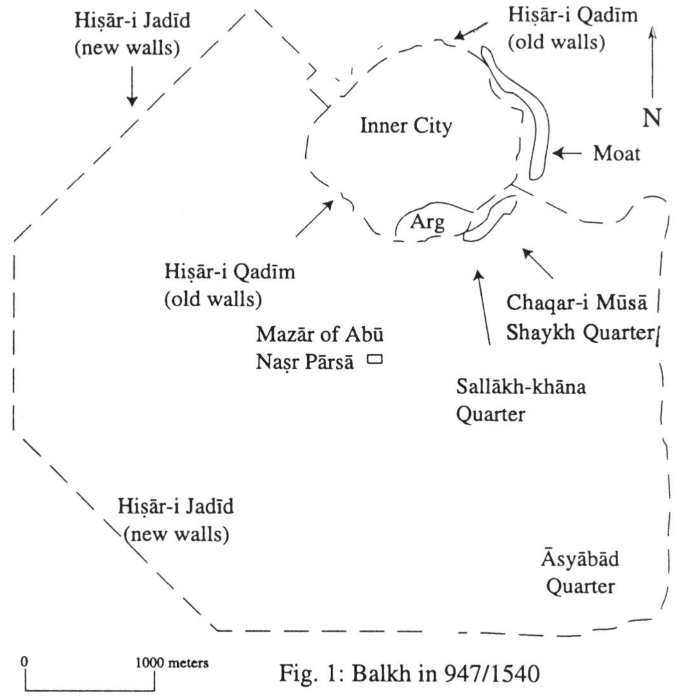

Fig. 1: Balkh in 947/1540

described as standing "outside the old walls" and "inside the new" in the Clothes Market (*bāzār-i jāma-furūshān*) (lines 60-63). Another property consisting of two shops and a residential compound (*ḥavīlī*) stood in "Sar-i Pul-i Dūāba," perhaps outside the alignment of the new walls (lines 63-66). Lastly "an undivided half" of a mill was located in Shakhshār, a "designated village" (*qarya-i muʿayyan*).[22]

Rather than attempt to make sense of the endowment in narrative form, I have put the information on the endowed properties in the three city quarters into a series of figures (Figs. 2-6, accompanying the translation) which, though admittedly schematic and not as precise as they might seem, at least give some idea of spatial relationships and the mixture of uses in the different quarters of the city. The settlor says (line 17) that he has made "everything he possessed" *vaqf*. What the mapping of the property listings shows is that in Sallākh Khāna and Āsyābād the properties were concentrated more or less in one locale, while in Chaqar-i Mūsā Shaykh they were scattered throughout the quarter, in six different and, as far as I can tell, non-contiguous locations.

The document reveals a number of social aspects that warrant comment. First is the extensiveness of private property ownership in Balkh. Besides the settlor, his brother, and son, the document names thirty-six other property owners (see Table 1, following the translation), and what is striking about them is that virtually none (judging by their names) would appear to be part of what we might think of as the elite—

[22] Although the three quarters—Chaqar-i Mūsā Shaykh, Sallākh Khāna, and Āsyābād—can be fairly easily located, these latter places are somewhat more difficult to identify. Mukhtarov, *Pozdnesrednevekovyi Balkh*, p. 40, seems to place the ʿIrāq Gate in the walls of the inner city (*ḥiṣār-i qadīm*). The description of the property would further locate the ʿIrāq Gate in the eastern or southeastern side of the inner city walls, since it puts the moat of the inner walls to the northwest of the property. This property should then have been in the vicinity of the Chaqar-i Mūsā Shaykh Quarter. Sar-i Pul-i Dūāba and Shakhshār elude precise location for the moment. Gazetteers from four periods—(1) the late 17th century (M. A. Salakhetdinova, "K istoricheskoi toponomike Balkhskoi oblasti," *Palestinskii sbornik*, 21 [1970], pp. 222-228); (2) 1871 (F.[ayz] B.[akhsh], *Translation of a Report on Badakhshan, Balkh and Bokhara*, Records of the Government of the Punjab and its Dependencies [Lahore: Civil Secretariat Press, 1871], pp. 5-8); (3) 1914 (Ludwig Adamec, ed., *Gazetteer of Afghanistan*, vol. IV [Mazar-i Sharif and North-Central Afghanistan] [Graz, 1979], pp. 250-260); and (4) 1975 (Afghanistan, Prime Ministry, *A Provisional Gazetteer of Afghanistan*, vol. II [Kabul: Afghan Demographic Studies, Central Statistics Office, 1975], pp. 887-927)—do not mention these places under these names.

sulṭāns, *amīrs*, or intellectuals. There are two market inspectors (*muḥtasibs*) among the owners, a military man (*chuhra*), and another probable military figure (Yārī Bahādur the son of Jānī Bahādur and the grandson of Tengrī Berdī Bahādur, who is only a lessee of state land), but by and large the group of owners is made up of craftspeople and tradesmen (greengrocers, bakers, dyers, a landscape architect or horticulturalist, a weaver, a pursemaker, and a butcher). This picture of a propertied petty bourgeoisie is fully in keeping with the picture of property ownership that emerges from the nearly contemporary Jūybārī sale documents (1544-1577).

Another significant bit of sociological evidence the document contains is the number of property owners whose names suggest origins in other towns and cities in Central Asia, that is if we assume the locational *nisba* name of some of these individuals is meant to convey the idea that the person is in some way to be associated with the named towns. These *nisbas* show six people with a Balkh affiliation, three with a Marv connection, one from Kūlāb (the grandson of a man who had the *nisba* "Balkhī"), one Bukhārī, one Haravī (of Herat), and one Samarqandī. The idea that such locational *nisba* names identify place of origin has circulated in modern historiog-raphy for some time, but here one needs to take into account the facts that (1) the majority of property owners are not identified by such a name and (2) of those that are, the greatest number use the *nisba* "Balkhī," presumably unnecessary for someone actually living in Balkh. It is possible that the *nisba*-name "Balkhī" was used to designate a native of Balkh when many residents of the town were not natives. But it may be that the *nisba* name and its application was wholly an individual matter and simply the name by which someone was known at a given time without any other firm connotation.

Finally, one is struck by the fact that only one woman, Bībī Ṣafīya the daughter of Shāh Muḥammad Balkhī, is named as a property owner, among the total of nearly forty individuals named here. This is quite a different ratio from the 30% or so of property owners named in the Jūybārī sale documents who are women. It may well be the sample here is small and not representative of the city as a whole.

TRANSLATION[23]

Vaqfīya-i masjid-i jāmiʿ-i Balkh[24]
(Central State Archive, Republic of Uzbekistan,
Fond I-323, Doc. No. 1216)

[1] [first half of line missing] . . . and the standing assets (*aʿyān-i qāʾima*) of the congregational mosque comprising the *miḥrāb* and the *minbar* and whatever (*har ki* ?) . . .
[2] [first half of line missing] . . . [two words unclear] the whole of unfired brick (*khisht-i khām*) and the entirety (*hamagī va tamāmī*) of the improvements and standing assets (*aʿmāl va aʿyān-i qāʾima*) of two ablution stations (*dū ḥujra-i siqāya*)
[3] [first third of line missing] . . . [first two or three words unclear—located partly ?] inside the northern wall of this congregational mosque and partly outside this wall
[4] [first third of line missing] [of] this [mos]que (. . . *d-i madhkūr*) from inside these two stalls (*az darūn-i īn dū ḥujra ast*) for all Muslims residing in (*bar ʿāmma-i musulmānān-i sākinān*)
[5] in the "Cupola of Islam," Balkh—May God preserve it from harm—and for others whenever they may wish to perform their ritual purification and ablutions (*ṭahārat va ghusl*)
[6] every day the five prayers should be conducted in the congregational mosque and on Friday the Friday prayer. The entirety of the improvements and standing assets of a college (*madrasa*) consisting of
[7] thirty rooms (*sī ḥujra*) with domed roofs and thirty rooms (*sī ghurfa*)[25] and [word unclear] *dīvān* and walls (*dīvār*), the entirety [built] of unfired brick, for students of the traditional [religious] sciences

[23] Translation notes: My interpolations are contained within square brackets. Numbers in square brackets represent individual lines of the document as it exists today. Numbers in curved brackets { } are used to set off individual items in a list (here, the properties donated and the conditions set), and are not part of the original.

[24] The document is defective here. It is unclear how many lines before the first surviving line are missing.

[25] It is not clear what the difference between a *ghurfa* and a *ḥujra* is. If we look at a contemporary *madrasa* from Bukhara, the Mir-i ʿArab, one might infer that a "*ḥujra* with a domed roof" was a second-story room, and a *ghurfa* therefore a first- or ground-floor room.

Fig. 2: The Object of the *Vaqf* in Chaqar-i Mūsā Shaykh

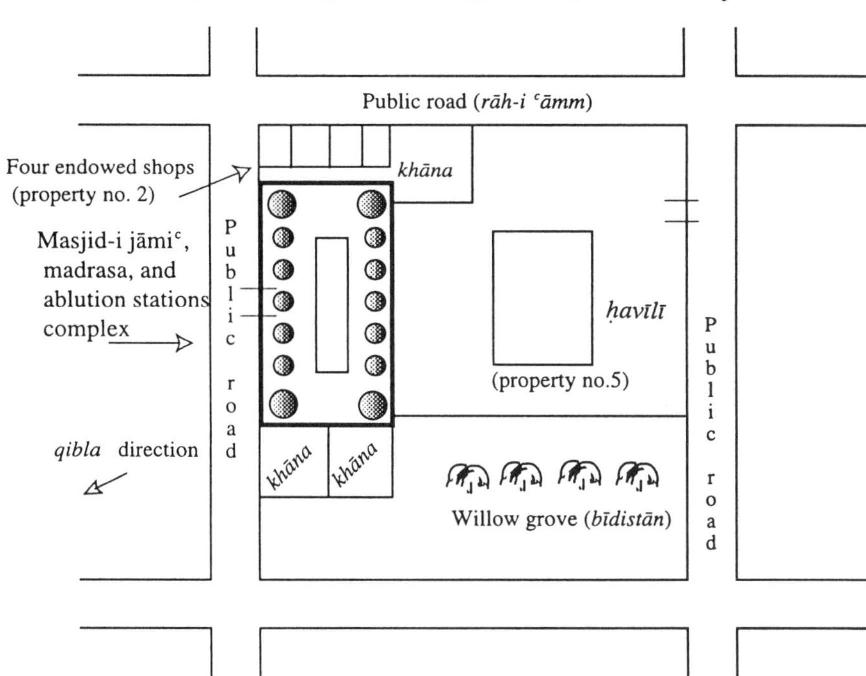

(*bar ṭalaba-i ᶜulūm-i mutadāvila*), ultimately [the endowment is] for needy Muslims. This (a word is missing—perhaps *madrasa*?) [8] and congregational mosque and ablution stalls are attached (adjacent) and are located on land [of my own?] (*dar zamīn-i*) [*milk-i khūd*?][26] [two or three words missing] [located outside] the old walls and inside the new walls[27]

26 After the word *zamīn*, there is a lacuna of perhaps two or three words between it and *ḥiṣār*.

27 The contrast *ḥiṣār-i qadīm*/*ḥiṣār-i jadīd* refers to the "old walls," the walls around the inner city which contained the citadel (*arg*) within it, and the "new walls," the alignment that enclosed the outer city (see the map at fig. 1).

[9] of the city in Chaqar-i[28] Mūsā Shaykh Quarter (*dar kūy-i Chaqar-i Mūsā Shaykh*). The above-mentioned settlor (*vāqif*) built the college, congregational mosque and ablution stations and with the permission of "the one who has authority" (*bi-idhn-i man lahu al-wilāya*[29]) [made it an endowment].
[10] The entire (complex of) college, congregational mosque, and ablution stations is bounded by these boundaries: on the west by a public road, on the north partly by . . . [words missing]
[11] and partly by a shop which is in the possession of the settlor, the improvements (*ʿamala*) of which are among the endowed properties for the congregational mosque, college and ablution stations

[28] A contemporary source for the word *chaqar* is the *Bābur-nāma*, written 15–20 years before this *vaqfīya*. In the Mano edition of this work the word appears as *chāqār* (pp. 37, 70), both times in almost the same context: "*tāsh qūrghān-dā chāqār-dā īldīlār*" (p. 37) and "*tāsh qūrghānīda chāqār-dā bīr madrasa sālīb tūr*" (p. 70). The late 16th century Persian translation by Khānkhānān, made for Bābur's grandson Akbar, in the first instance does not translate it at all ("*mādar va mādar-i kalān-i man dar qalʿa-i sangīn dar chāqār būdand*" [W. M. Thackston, ed. and tr., *Bâburnâma* (Cambridge, Massachusetts, 1993; Sources of Oriental Languages and Literatures, 18 [with the Chaghatay text in transcription, the edited text of the Persian translation by ʿAbd al-Raḥmān Khān-khānān, and English translation]), Part 1, p. 48]), and in the second translates it as "*bar-āmad*" (*dar bar āmad-i qalʿa-i sangīn madrasa andākhtah*" [ed. Thackston, Part 1, p.94]). "*Bar āmad*" seems a curious choice, for it connotes a place to which one ascends or at which one comes out (see ʿAlī Akbar Dihkhudā, ed.,*Lughat-nāma* [Tehran, 1337/1959–1352/1975], *s.v.* "*bar āmad jāy*"). Beveridge's English translation has two variants ("they [Babur's mother and grandmother] were living in the *Gatehouse* of the outer fort" [p. 43], and "a College, built at the *exit* [*chāqār*] of the walled town" [p. 78]), as does the Thackston translation ("My mother and grandmother were in the gatehouse in the outer fortress" [p. 59], and "a *madrasa* constructed in the gateway to the outer wall of Samarkand" [p. 84]). In her explanation of the term, Juraeva ("Vakfnyi dokument," p. 197, note 6) says the meanings she found were "an inn or hospice," and "a fortified place surrounded by a wall outside the citadel." She believes the latter meaning is most appropriate and similar to the use of the term in the *Bābur-nāma*. The Russian translation of the *Bābur-nāma* as cited by Juraeva does indeed translate the term in that fashion ("*v ukreplennom meste*"), although this is quite different from the English translations. Gerhard Doerfer, *Turkische und mongolische Elemente im Neupersischen*, 4 vols. (Wiesbaden, 1963-1975), I, pp. 307-308 [No. 179], and III, p. 78 [No. 1091] and p. 81 [No. 1099], gives the readings *chaqar* (179), *chuqur*, and *chuqūr* (Nos. 1091, 1099); he defines the first, *chaqar* (No. 179, of Mongol origin), as "Ort ausserhalb einer Zitadelle, wo Handwerker und sonstige dem Fürsten dienende Familien wohnen," a definition that fits the use of the term in the present *vaqfīya* particularly well (see below where the location of the Chaqar-i Mūsā Shaykh Quarter is discussed).

[29] The person who has *wilāya* in an administrative context is the governor or ruler, the *wālī*.

[12] and which will be discussed in due course. The eastern boundary adjoins a residential compound (*ḥavīlī*) in the possession of the settlor and that too is one of the properties endowed for this
[13] property and will be mentioned in due course. The southern boundary partly abuts the house (*khāna*) of Ḥājjī Muḥammad son of Shaykh Junayd al-Balkhī and partly a house belonging to Shāh Berdī
[14] son of Mawlānā Bazmī [Barmī?]. [This complex] with all its appurtenances, additaments, accessories, and accompaniments (*tavābiʿ va lavāḥiq va mużāfāt va mansūbāt*) whether few or many, great or small, [the settlor] has endowed as a valid *vaqf* (*waqf*^an^ *ṣaḥīḥ*^an^)
[15] and a permanent operative permissible charitable donation (*ṣadaqat*^an^ *jāʾizat*^an^ *nāfidhat*^an^ *muʾabbadat*^an^) which may neither be sold nor given away nor mortgaged nor pledged in a dowry nor inherited nor owned as private property in any way whatsoever "Until [We] inherit the Earth and whosoever is upon it"[30]
[16] "and it."[31] After the settlor set this property aside from [the rest of] his own private property (*maḥdūd-i madhkūr-rā az milk-i khūd ifrāz namūd*) and made it a binding legal endowment (*vaqf-i sharʿī lāzim*), he wanted this benefice (*khayr*) of his
[17] to be operative and effective (*ravājī va madārī bāshad*) [and so] he then endowed and bestowed it as a charitable donation (*vaqf kard va taṣadduq namūd*). Immediately he fulfilled it [his wish] willingly [making] everything that he possessed under *sharīʿa* law [an endowment] for the above-mentioned specified property as well as for the mosques, ablution station, and hospice (*ribāṭ*)
[18] that are defined on the reverse (*dar aẓhar* [*sic*]) of this endowment deed [endowing] those [properties] which are rightfully his own property (*ki ḥaqq va milk-i ū būd*) and which he had in his own possession and under his own proprietary jurisdiction (*dar taḥt-i taṣarrufā[t]-i mālikānah-i khūd dāsht*) at the time this endowment was made, "free of anyone else's right and
[19] of anything else which would negate the permissibility of the *vaqf* and what makes it binding" (*khāliy*^an^ *ʿan ḥaqq al-ghayr wa ʿammā*

[30] Qurʾān 19:40 (*Tafsīr al-Jalālayn* [Damascus, 1964]. The text here is a corrupted (?) version of the standard reading which is "*innā naḥnu narithu'l-arḍ wa man ʿalayhā . . .*" The text is clearly written and pointed "*ilā an yarithu al-arḍ wa man ʿalayhā.*"

[31] *wa-hiya . . .* Not apparently the continuation of Qurʾān 19:40: *wa ilaynā yurjaʿūna.*

yamnaʿu jawāz al-waqf wa luzūmahu): the entire improvements, standing assets, and demesnes (*ẓiyāʿ*) [two or three words missing] which are located in the province (*vilāyat*) of the "Cupola of Islam,"
[20] Balkh. These include:
{1} The improvements and standing assets of a bath (*ḥammām*) comprising a wooden-roofed changing room (*jāma khāna*), a place for washing one's feet (*pāy shū . . .*), a [three or four words missing here] -room (*-khāna*), a connecting room (*miyān sarā*),

Fig. 3: Chaqar-i Mūsā Shaykh *Vaqf* Properties

No. 1: A bath

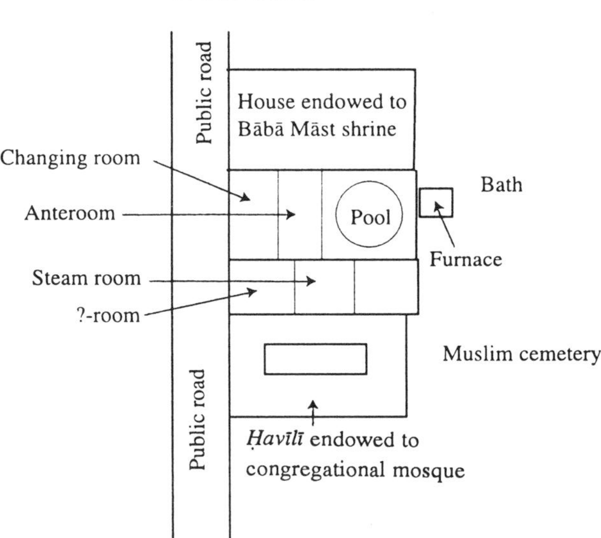

Nos. 3, 5: Shops

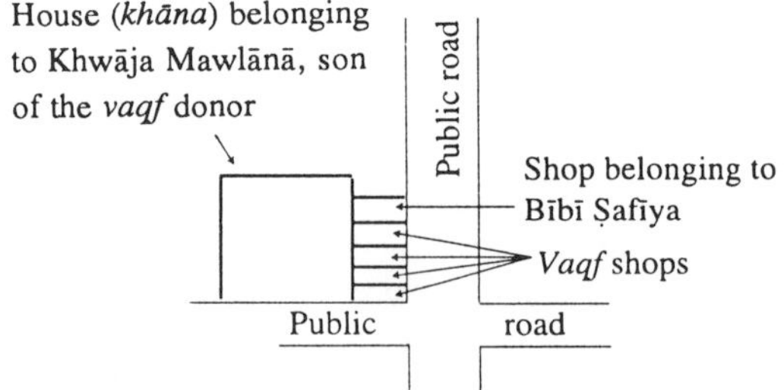

[21] a steam room (*garm khāna*), a circular pool (*ḥawż-i charkhī*), three additional rooms, and two raised platforms facing each other (*dū ṣuffa-i rū ba-rū*), the whole roofed with baked brick; a furnace for heating the water (*gulkhan*), a place where towels hang (? *maṭraḥ-i rumā(l* ?)[32] and [two or three words missing].
[22] This bath is located in Chaqar-i Mūsā Shaykh Quarter and is bounded by these boundaries: on the west by a public road; [on the north]
[23] by a house which is an endowment for the shrine (*mazār*) of Bābā Mast;[33] on the east by a Muslim cemetery (*maqbara-i musulmānān*) which is on elevated ground (*makān-i arfaʿ*);[34] and on the south by
[24] a residential compound (*ḥavīlī*) which is [part of] the endowment for the aforementioned congregational mosque.
{2} The entire improvements and standing assets of four adjoining shops (*dukkān*) in the same quarter and bounded
[25] by these boundaries: on the west by the public road, and access is from this side (*wa minhu al-madkhal*); on the north the same as the west; on the east by a residential compound (*ḥavīlī*) which is an endowment of the aforementioned congregational mosque; and on the south by the walls
[26] of the aforementioned *madrasa.*
{3} The improvements and standing assets of five attached shops (*panj dar*[35] *dukkān muttaṣil ba-yakdīgar*) in the same quarter bounded by these boundaries: on the west by the house(s? *khana* [*hā*?]) of

[32] See Heinz Grotzfeld, *Das Bad im arabisch-islamischen Mittelalter* (Wiesbaden: Otto Harrassowitz, 1970), Tafel 1.

[33] Legend had it (as recently as the 1970s) that there were four shrines of "*bābā*s" in Balkh, one of them the Bābā Mast. Its location is/was in the outer city, in the general vicinity of the Chaqar-i Mūsā Shaykh quarter, if not in it. See Mukhtarov, "Balkh in the Late Middle Ages," tr. McChesney *et al.*, p. 26.

[34] The qualifying formula "*ki makān-i arfaʿ-ast*" ("which is an elevated place") appears so frequently in references to cemeteries that perhaps it should be understood metaphorically rather than literally. On the other hand, topographical elevations are often used for burial places in Central Asia—perhaps both for the practical reason that they are unsuitable for irrigation and thus agriculture, and as a sign of being closer to God—and so the references may have a literal sense as well.

[35] Juraeva's definition of the use of the term as signifying a shop with only one door ("Vakfnyi dokument," p. 192) is, I believe, mistaken. The term *dar* is a counting word used here exclusively for shops, and elsewhere, as she notes, for another architectural unit, the *khānah*. It is analogous to *ʿadad* used in this document for coins and loaves of bread, and in other contexts *dānah* and *tā* for small items.

[27] Khwāja Mawlānā the son of the settlor (*vāqif*); the northern boundary abuts a shop belonging to a woman named Bībī Ṣafīyah, the daughter of Shāh Muḥammad Balkhī; the eastern and southern boundaries abut the public road.
[28] {4} The entire assets of a shop for cooked food (*yak dar dukkān-i ṭabbākhī*) located in the same quarter and bounded by these boundaries: on the west by a residential compound belonging to Khwāja Mawlānā,
[29] the aforementioned; on the east by the public road; the north like the west; and the south by the access way (*rāhraw*) and [to?] the residential compound of Khwāja Mawlānā.
[30] {5} The entire improvements and standing assets of a residential compound (*ḥavīlī*) comprising three units (*sih dar khāna*) [three connected courtyard houses, or perhaps three separate units around a common courtyard?] with wooden ceilings (*chūb pūsh*), a vestibule or connecting corridor (*dālān*), and a second story room with a wooden ceiling (*bālākhāna-i chūb pūsh*) and bounded by these boundaries: on the west
[31] by the above-mentioned college (*madrasa*); on the north and east by the public road; and on the south by a willow grove (*bīdistān*) owned by Shaykh ʿAlī, pursemaker (*kīsa-dūz*) and the son of Khwāja Shams Balkhī.
[32] {6} The entire standing assets of two shops (*dū dar dukkān*) which are located in the same quarter, one of which is an oil press (*rawghangarī*) and the other a dyer's (*rangrīzī*), bounded by these boundaries: on the west by a shop
[33] belonging to Qāsim son of Khammār (? *kh.mār*) Aqā, by the residential compound of Shāh Muḥammad son of Ḥasan ʿAlī Balkhī, and by a shop belonging to Muḥammad, the greengrocer and son of ʿAlī al-Balkhī; on the north by the public road; on the east by state land (*zamīn-i mamlaka-i pādshāhī*)
[34] which is in the possession of (*ba-taṣarruf-i*) this settlor; and on the south by state land part of which is in the possession of Ḥāfiẓ Fānī the son of Ḥāfiẓ Darvīsh al-Haravī,
[35] and part of which is in the possession of this settlor.
{7} The entire improvements and standing (assets) (*ʿamala va qāʾima*) of a shop located in the same quarter and bounded by these boundaries: on the west by lands belonging to the crown (*zamīn-i khāliṣa-i*
[36] *pādshāhī*) which are in the possession of the settlor; on the north

Fig. 4: Other Chaqar-i Mūsā Shaykh Properties

No. 4: Cooked food shop (*dukkān-i ṭabbākhī)*

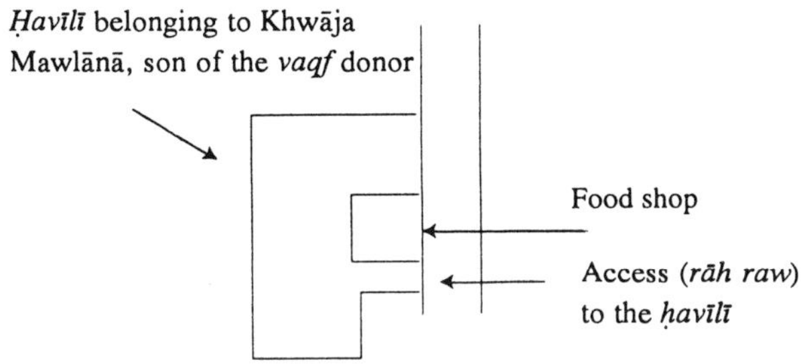

No. 6: Two shops

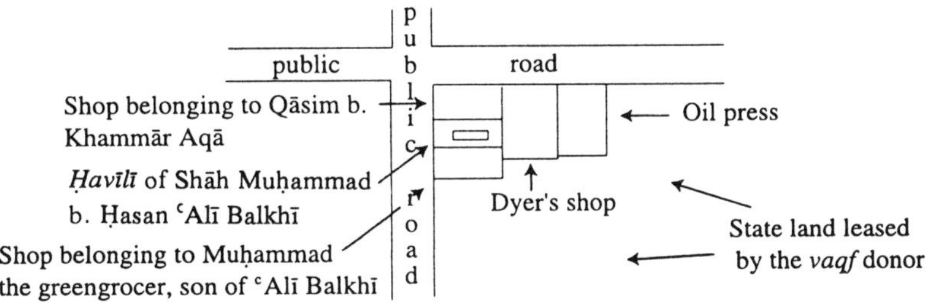

Nos. 7, 8: A mill and a shop

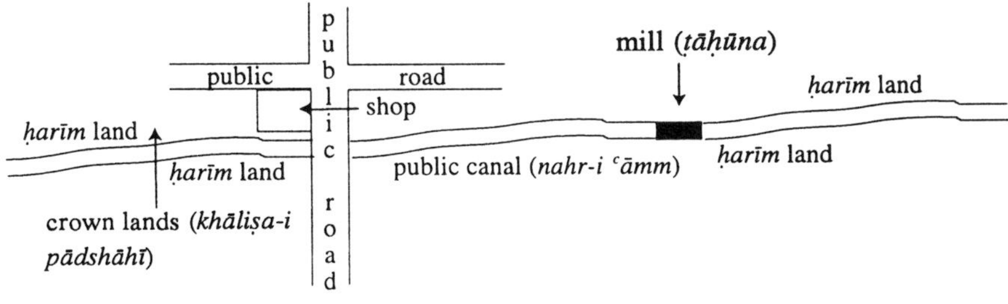

and east by the public road and on the south by reserved land (*ḥarīm*) along the public water channel (*nahr-i ʿāmm*) situated in this quarter.
{8} The entirety of
[37] the improvements and standing assets of one round millstone, including all wooden, iron, and stone implements, located in the aforementioned quarter and bounded by these boundaries: on the west and east
[38] by crown land (*mamlaka-i pādshāhī*) held by the settlor, and on the north and south in part by reserved land along the public water channel located in this quarter,
[39] and in part by the middle (*baṭn*) of that channel.
{9} The entire improvements and standing assets of a caravanserai comprising forty-nine rooms and a stable (*akhtāna* [*sic*]) entirely roofed with unfired brick (*majmūʿ musaqqaf ba-khisht-i khām*) and the entire
[40] improvements (*hamagī ʿamala*) of a residential compound attached to the caravanserai comprising two [separate] units (*dū dar khāna*), one of which has a domed roof and the other a wooden roof. The caravanserai and compound are located
[41] outside the old walls (*qalʿa-i qadīm*) of the city and within the new walls (*ḥiṣār-i jadīd*) in the Sallākh Khāna (Slaughterhouse) Quarter,[36] and are bounded by these boundaries: on the west by the old walls of the [inner] city;
[42] on the south by a public road; on the east by shops which are an endowment for the beneficiary (*mawqūf ʿalayhi*) [of this endowment]; and on the north partly by a residential compound (*ḥavīlī*) belonging to Khān Muḥammad the son of Yār Muḥammad the son of
[43] ʿAbdullāh al-Marvī, partly by a residential compound belonging to Mawlānā Muḥammad Bāqir the son of Mawlānā Muḥammad al-Qāżī al-Bukhārī, partly by a house (*khāna*) belonging to Tursūn Kulābī the son of Ṣadr al-Dīn the son of Nūr al-Dīn al-Balkhī,
[44] and partly by a house belonging to Dūst Muḥammad the son of Abū Saʿīd the son of Nūr Saʿīd al-Balkhī.
{10} The entire improvements and standing assets of sixteen attached shops (*shanzdah dar dukkān muttaṣil ba-yakdīgar*)

[36] Foucher, *La vieille route de l'Inde*, vol. I, Plate V (f) is a photograph of what the author labels "le vieux caravanserai." He sites the caravanserai (map, p. 59) in what would have been the Sallākh Khāna Quarter. As late as the 1960s the foundations of a large caravanserai in that location were still visible in aerial photographs.

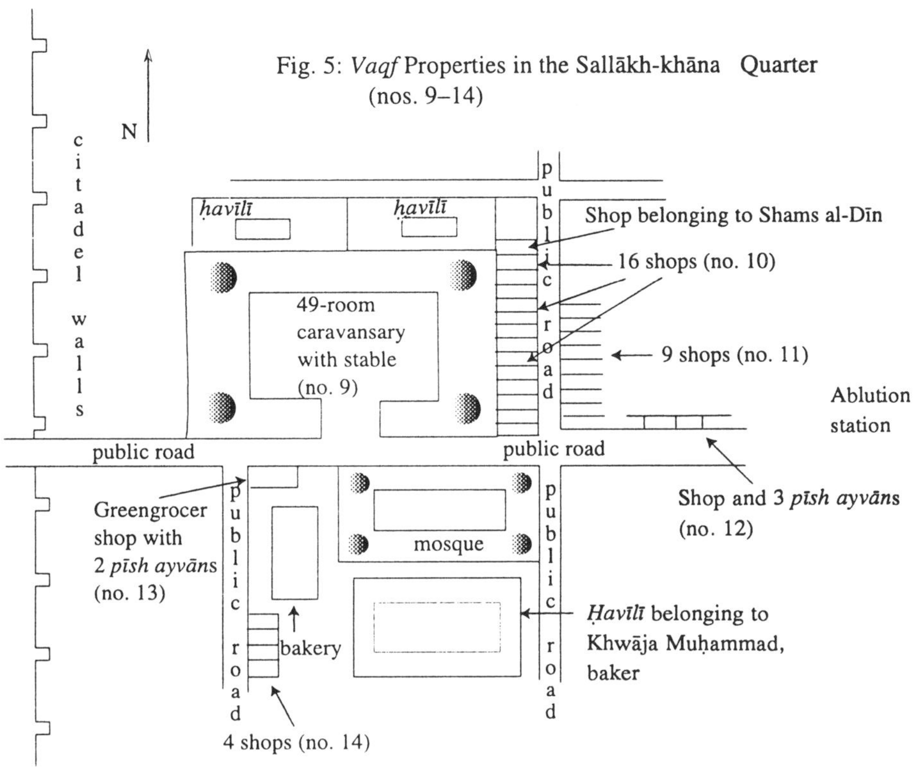

Fig. 5: *Vaqf* Properties in the Sallākh-khāna Quarter (nos. 9–14)

[45] bounded by these boundaries: on the west by the caravanserai mentioned above; on the north by the shop of Shams al-Dīn the son of Ustād Rajab Shibarghānī;
[46] on the south and east by a public road.
{11} The entire assets of nine attached shops (*dar dukkān*) located opposite (*dar maḥādhī*) the caravanserai
[47] aforementioned and bounded by these boundaries: on the west by a public road; on the north by the oil shop (*dukkān-i rawghangarī*) of Mastī Lang [Mastī the Lame] the son of Saᶜīd Balkhī;
[48] on the east by a shop belonging to the settlor, the improvements of which will be mentioned as part of the endowment made on behalf of the object [of this endowment deed],
[49] and partly by the ablution station which on the reverse (*dar ẓahr-i*) of this *vaqf* deed has been defined as one of the objects of the endowment; and on the south in part by a public way

[50] and in part by a terrace or raised forecourt (*pīsh-ayvān*[37]) which belongs to one of the objects of the *vaqf*.
{12} The entire improvements of three terraces (*pīsh-ayvān*) and one shop (*yak dar dukkān*) all attached to each other.
[51] These too are located near the caravanserai and are bounded by these boundaries: on the west by the nine shops described above; on the south
[52] by a public road; on the east by the above-mentioned ablution station; and on the north as on the west by the demarcated and aforementioned shops.
[53] {13} The entire improvements of a greengrocer's shop (*yak dar dukkān-i baqqāl*) which faces (*rū ba-rū-yi*) the caravanserai and two terraces attached to this greengrocer's shop,
[54] the entirety bounded by these boundaries: on the west and north by public roads; on the east by a mosque which is one of the objects of this endowment
[55] and which is defined (*maḥdūd*) on the reverse (*dar ẓahr-i*) [of this document]; on the south by a shop belonging to Khwāja Muḥammad a baker and the son of Fakhr al-Dīn, son of Khwāja Aḥmad, and by a bakery (*tannūr khānah*)
[56] belonging to the aforementioned Khwāja Muḥammad.
{14} The entire improvements of four attached shops (*chahār dukkān muttaṣil ba-yakdīgar*) [also] located near the caravanserai and bounded
[57] by these boundaries: on the west by a public road; on the north by the bakery of the aforementioned Khwāja Muḥammad; on the east and south by
[58] the residential compound belonging to the aforementioned Khwāja Muḥammad [the baker].
{15} The entire improvements of five attached shops located outside the old walls (*ḥiṣār-i qadīm*) near the ʿIrāq Gate (*darvāza-i ʿIrāq*)
[59] and bounded by these boundaries: on the west and north by the moat (*khandaq*) of the old walls; on the east by a public road; and on the south by

[37] Dihkhudā, *Lughat-nāma*, defines it as "a raised space or high terrace (*mahtābī*) in front of an *ayvān* and having no roof. Courtyard of a house." In the 1930s, Elizabeth Bacon described this same raised terrace, made of packed earth, as an "aivan" (see her *Central Asia under Russian Rule* [Ithaca, New York: Cornell University Press, 1966; repr. 1980], p. 61).

[60] a shop belonging to Sulṭān Muḥammad *kharkār* (?)[38] the son of Jān Muḥammad.
{16} The improvements of a shop (*yak dar dukkān*) with three connected rooms (*maʿa sih dar khāna*[39] *muttaṣil ba-yakdīgar*) located outside the old walls (*ḥiṣār-i qadīm*) of the city
[61] and inside the new walls in the Clothes Market (*bāzār-i jāma-furūshān*) and bounded by these boundaries: on the west by a public road; on the north by a shop
[62] belonging to Banda ʿAlī the son of Muḥammad the dyer (*rangrīzī*) the son of Ūstād [*sic*] ʿAlī Balkhī; on the east by state land which is in the possession of the settlor;
[63] and on the south by a shop belonging to Khwāja Mīr ʿAlī the son of Sulṭān Maḥmūd Haravī the son of ʿAbdullāh.
{17} The entire standing improvements of two shops (*dū dar dukkān*) and one residential compound (*yak dar ḥavīlī*) consisting
[64] of one unit (*yak dar khāna*). [The shops and *ḥavīlī*] are attached and are located in Sar Pul-i Dūāba and are bounded [by these boundaries]: on the west and south
[65] by a public way; on the east by a bread bakery (*dukkān-i khabbāzī*) belonging to Ūstād Yārī the son of Ustād Tāj al-Dīn [the son of?] Ustād Muḥammad al-Balkhī; and on the north
[66] by a residential compound belonging to Mawlānā ʿAbdullāh the son of Mawlānā Maḥmūd, and by a residential compound belonging to Shīrum the son of Ustād ʿAbdullāh the dyer (*ṣabbāgh*).
{18} All the improvements and all the improvements and standing assets (*hamagī ʿamala va tamāmī ʿamala va aʿyān-i qāʾima*) of a cara-
[67] vanserai consisting of seventy-six rooms and a stable (*akhta-khāna*) located outside the old walls and inside the new walls (*ḥiṣār-i jad* [*sic*]) [of Balkh] in Āsyābād Quarter and bounded by these [boundaries]:
[68] on the west by state land held by the honorable Mawlānā Ḥājjī ʿAlī the market inspector (*muḥtasib*) and son of Mawlānā Ḥasan; on the south by

[38] It is unclear what the word here signifies. The *Lughat-nāma* has two definitions of the word: "one who works hard (without tiring)," and "one whose works involves carrying wood and manure with a donkey or horse." It is not evident which, if either, is meant here. R. G. Mukminova, author of *Ocherki po istorii remesla v Samarkande i Bukhare v XVI veke* (Tashkent: Fan, 1976), gives an extensive listing of occupational titles for the period, but has no entry for *kharkār*.

[39] The word *dukkān* precedes *khāna* but has been crossed out.

[69] a field planted in clover (*bāgh-i vīrūnjqahzār*) belonging to Mīr Muḥammad, [also] a market inspector and son of Mawlānā Darvīsh Muḥammad Samarqandī the son of Mawlānā Ḥasan, and by
[70] state land held by Pahlavān Shāh Muḥammad, who is also known as Pahlavānzāda, the son of Pahlavān Maḥmūd the gardener (*bāghbān*);[40] on the east
[71] by the Muslim Men's and Women's Cemetery (*maqbara-i muslimīn va muslimāt*), which is on elevated ground, and by houses belonging to Yārī Bahādur the son of Jānī Bahādur the son of Tengrī Berdī
[72] Bahādur, the house of Shaykhum Chuhrah the son of Mīrum Chuhrah the son of Nūr Chuhrah, the residential compound of the aforementioned Shāh Muḥammad, the residential compound of Ustād ᶜAlī, a weaver (*bāfanda*)
[73] and the son of ᶜAbdullāh the son of ᶜAbd al-Raḥīm, by the house and shop (*dukkān*) of Ustād Sangīn a dyer (*ṣabbāgh*) and the son of Khwāja Kalān the son of Khwāja Khurd, by the house of Zayn al-Dīn the son of
[74] Dūst, a greengrocer, the son of Jān Muḥammad, by the residential compound of Jamāl al-Dīn Khwāja the son of Abdāl the son of[41] Kamāl Khwāja, and by the house of Yār Muḥammad Jangī the son of Mīr Muḥammad the son of Pīr Muḥammad Marvī;
[75] on the north by state land in the possession of Tīlāvalī Bahādur the son of Tengrī Qulī Bahādur the son of ᶜAbdullāh,
[76] by state land in the possession of Ḥasan ᶜAlī, a vegetable farmer (*sabzkār*), the son of ᶜAlī Sīstānī the son of ᶜAbdullāh, by shops which
[77] will be enumerated as part of the endowment, by houses belonging to Ustād Khudāy Qulī, a butcher, the son of Maḥmūd the son of Muḥammad Marvī, and by a shop
[78] belonging to the abovementioned Khudāy Qulī.
{19} The entire assets of three attached shops bounded by these boundaries: to the west and north by
[79] the reserved land along a public water channel; on the east by a right-of-way (*rāhraw*) to the second named caravanserai; and on the south [also] by the second caravanserai
[80] mentioned above.

[40] Or landscaper; see M. E. Subtelny, "Mīrak-i Sayyid Ghiyās̱ and the Timurid tradition of Landscape Architecture," *Studia Iranica*, 24 (1995), pp. 19-60, on the position and profession of a famous *bāghbān*.

[41] The words "Abdāl the son of" are written above the line.

Fig. 6: Āsyābād Quarter (Nos. 18, 19, 20)

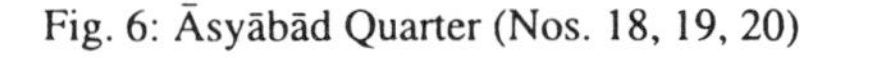

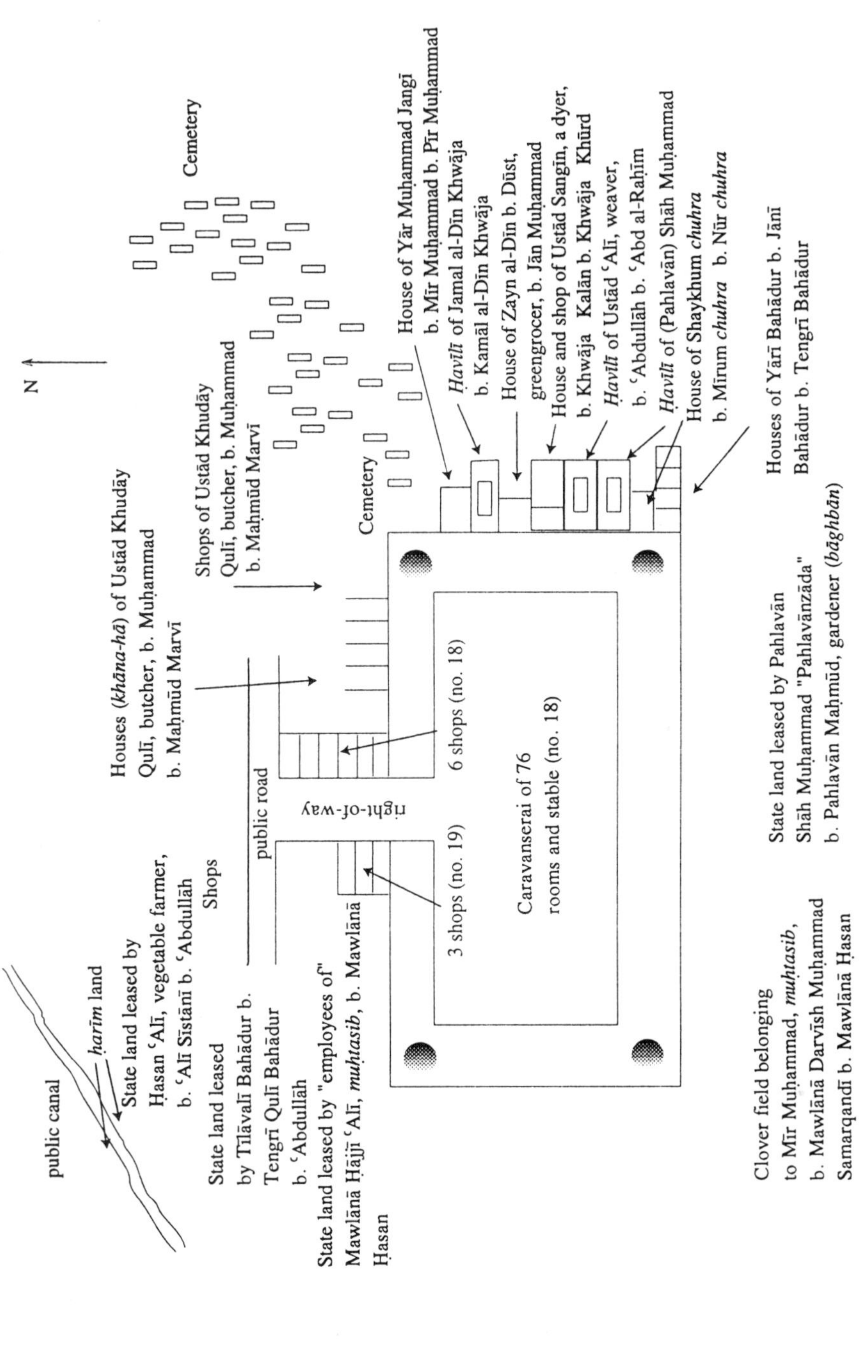

{20} The entire assets of six attached shops bounded by these boundaries: on the west by the right-of-way to the caravanserai
[81] the aforementioned; on the south also by that caravanserai; on the east by the Muslim Cemetery which is on elevated ground;
[82] and on the north by the public road.
{21} An undivided half (*niṣf-i mus[h]āʿ*) of a round millstone including (all) the implements, whether of
[83] wood, iron, or stone, situated in Shakhshār, which is a delimited [known] village (*ki qarya-i muʾayyan ast*), one of the villages of [Balkh]. [The millstone] is bounded by these boundaries: on the west
[84] and east by state land in the possession of the settlor; on the north and south
[85] in part by the reserved land along the public water channel, and in part the middle (*baṭn*) of that channel.
[The donor makes all these] properties, with their boundaries and rights, their appurtenances and additaments, and the aforementioned properties
[86] whether small or large, however minute, an obligatory (*marʿī*), legal, binding, valid endowment in such a manner that it may neither be sold, nor donated as gift (*lā yūhab*), nor pawned,[42] nor given as dower (*lā yumhar*), nor be conveyed (*lā yuntaqal*)
[87] from ownership to ownership (*min milk*in *ilā milk*in) by any legal means whatsoever; and he makes the ultimate purpose of these endowments to be for the sake of needy Muslims.
The settlor—may his glory endure—stipulated:
[88] {1) that the trustee (*mutavallī*) of the defined endowments, every one from first to last, will be he himself, wholly and independently, as long as he shall live
[89] to possess it and its yield, [acting] how and where he wishes and disposing of it ("and its yield," *wa fī maḥṣūlātihā* [written but deleted with light pen strokes]) to whomever he wishes and from whomever he wishes (*liya* [*sic*] *man yashāʾ wa ʿamman yashāʾ*) and to change its appropriations (*maṣārif*)
[90] and stipulations and to decrease [*tanqīṣ*, but written *tanṣīṣ*] and increase the stipends and [to put] the "reins of bestowing and dispossessing" (*ʿinān-i iʿṭāʾ va ḥirmān*) and the "reins of increase and decrease" for whomever he wishes and however he wishes

[42] The text reads *lā yuzhar*, but this is probably an orthographic error for *lā yurhan*.

[91] in [all] these matters into his own capable hands and for his own benefit (*ba-kaff-i kifāyat va qabża-i maṣlaḥat-i khūd*), so that no one should raise any objection against him about any aspect of [his] competence.
He [also] stipulated:
[92] {2} that whoever of his children, his children's children, and his children's children's children, generation after generation (*baṭn*^{an} *baʿda baṭn*^{in} *wa qarn*^{an} *baʿda qarn*^{in}), be most worthy and capable (*aṣlaḥ va akfā*),
[93] he should be the trustee of these endowments. If none—God forbid—should survive of the lineage and stirps (*nasl va aʿqāb*) of the settlor, or there should remain such but he be in another country (*dar vilāyat-i dīgar*)
[94] and it be impossible for him to come to this country (*ba-īn vilāyat*), then the option rests with the ruler, the *qāżī*, or the viceroy (*khalīfa-i pādshāh*) of this region to select someone as trustee from among the relatives (*aqribāʿ*) of
[95] the settlor. And should there be no one from among his relatives, then they should make an upright, pious, and trustworthy man (*mard-i amīn ṣāliḥ mutadayyin*) trustee.
[96] Anyone who becomes trustee from these last two categories [should take] annually as his trustee's salary (*ḥaqq al-tawliya*) out of the income (*irtifāʿāt*) of these endowments two hundred *tangacha*s
[97] [of the type] currently in circulation, weighing one *mithqāl* and of pure silver (*tangacha-i sara pākīza yak-mithqālī rāyij al-vaqt*), and three hundred *mann*s of farmer-approved, whole unadulterated grain (*ghalla-i pākīza-i sīrdāna-i dihqān-pasand*) by the weight standard of the "Cupola of Islam,"
[98] Balkh—the *mann* being half of wheat and half of barley.[43]
The settlor [also] stipulated:
{3} that the income of the endowments should be expended as follows:
[99] {a} First for construction and necessary repairs (*awwal*^{an} *ba-ʿimārat va murammat-i żarūrīya*) of the properties.
{b} Annually, from any excess, ten percent of the income (*ʿushr-i maḥṣūl*) should be given to an accomplished man (*mard ṣāḥib-i kamāl*)

[43] Here the text has *az gandum va jaw ba-ṭarīq-i mann*^{an} *niṣf*, which probably should be read *ba-ṭarīq-i munāṣif*.

[100] who should teach the legal sciences (*ʿulūm-i sharʿīya*) each week on Saturday, Sunday, Monday, and Tuesday in the aforementioned *madrasa*.[44]
[101] {c} An additional ten percent should be paid to his [the settlor's] children, his children's children, and his children's children's children, generation after generation (*baṭn*an *baʿda baṭn*in *wa qarn*an *baʿda qarn*in), whoever they might be,
[102] "to the males the share of two females."[45]
{4} There should be a Qurʾān-reciter (*ḥāfiẓ*) of good voice, who reads well, has memorized the Qurʾān and recites it accurately.
[103] {5} In the mosque he should serve as the preacher (*khaṭīb*), the *muṣaddir*,[46] and the leader of the Friday prayer (*imām-i jumʿa*). For the duties of preaching and prayer-leading the sum of 100 *tangacha*s
[104] [of the type] currently in circulation weighing one *mithqāl* and of pure unalloyed silver (*tangacha-i nuqra-i sara pākīza yak-mithqālī rāyij al-vaqt*) should be taken. The *muṣaddir* likewise should annually be paid at the rate of 100 *tangacha*s of the described type. If two persons
[105] should undertake these two responsibilities, then each should receive 100 *tangacha*s as described.
{6} There should also be six Qurʾān-reciters (*ḥāfiẓ*, pl. *ḥuffāẓ*) of good voice, who read well and who have [fully] memorized the Qurʾān
[106] and recite it accurately. Every Friday, prior to the Friday worship in the congregational mosque, they will recite one of the thirty sections of
[107] the Glorious Qurʾān. Each of these reciters will annually receive the sum of seventy-two *tangacha*s of the type described.

44 The man who taught Ḥasan Nithārī astronomy, Amīr Mahdī al-Ḥusaynī, was an early, if not the first, appointee to this post (see above).

45 "*li'l-dhakar ḥaẓẓ al-unthayayni*," an almost verbatim citation of Qurʾān 4:11, "*li'l-dhakar mithla ḥaẓẓ al-unthayayni*," a fundamental principle of the *sharʿī* law of succession. Although the *vāqif* is not bound by the Qurʾānic rules on succession (*mīrāth*), it was common practice in *vaqf*s where a family member was a beneficiary to use the Qurʾānic standard.

46 Maria Eva Subtelny, "A Timurid Educational and Charitable Foundation: The Ikhlāṣiyya Complex of ʿAlī Shīr Nawāʾī in 15th Century Herat and its Endowment," *Journal of the American Oriental Society*, 111/1 (1991), p. 59, line 5 of the Chaghatay text, where the term is used for the lead *ḥāfiẓ*, presumably the chief or lead *ḥāfiẓ* in a particular institution.

[108] Should any one of these reciters abandon his responsibilities (*tark-i mulāzamat*) for a continuous month without a legitimate excuse (*bī ʿudhr-i sharʿī*), he should not collect his stipend. One of the reciters, of good voice who reads well,
[109] and who accurately recites the Qurʾān [from memory], should always be present for the five daily prayers in this congregational mosque, as instructed by the *imām*.
[110] {7} The annual salary of the *imām* [as distinct from the *imām-i jumʿa*?] should be 180[47] *tangacha*s of the type described, on condition that he not solicit the "holiday tax" (*ʿīdī*) from any person of the congregation or otherwise.
[111] {8} A *muʾadhdhin* possessing a good voice, who can accurately enunciate the first and second summonings to prayer (*ādhān va iqāmat*) every Friday, should do the recitation (*muqrī-garī*) and the first and the second summonings to the Friday prayer.
[112] He should get an annual salary of forty *tangacha*s of the described type.[48]
[113] Also at the times of the five [daily] prayers, he should perform the first and second summonings, and (for this) should receive an annual salary of 120 *tanga*s
[114] of the described type, on condition too that he not try to solicit the holiday tax (*ʿīdī*) from the congregation, or anything else.
{9} [There should also be] one trustworthy pious Ṣūfī fellow (*yak nafar mard-i ṣūfī ṣāliḥ mutadayyin*) who
[115] will undertake to sweep and serve as caretaker (*khādim*) of the congregational mosque and the *madrasa* mentioned at the beginning (*fī'l-ṣadr*) [of this document] winter and summer, and in winter [clear] snow from the roof domes (*pushtahā-yi bām*),
[116] and each year receive a salary of sixty *tanga*s of the described type, on condition that he take good care of the felt carpets (*namad*), the plush carpets (*būb*), and the brooms (*jārūb*).
{10} [Also there should be] one
[117] reliable person who would carry water for ritual purification and ablutions (*ṭahārat va ghusl*) to the Believers (*musulmānān*) from the well of the ablution station (*siqāya*) mentioned on the reverse (*dar ẓahr*) of

[47] The counting word "*ʿadad(-i)*" has been written above the word *tangacha*.

[48] The sentence beginning "A *muʾadhdhin* possessing a good voice . . ." is repeated at this point.

this document; but no one should be assigned for [disposing of?] the waste (*muʿaṭṭal*) water.
[118] From the first light of day (*az ṣubḥ-i ṣādiq*) until the night prayer (*namāz-i khuftan*), the door to the ablution station should be [kept] unlocked. [The watercarrier's] annual salary will be 100 *tanga*s of the described type,
[119] on condition that he not act boorishly (*durushtī va kaj-khūy nakunad*) nor demand anything from anyone.
{11} The settlor also stipulated that the trustee of these endowed properties
[120] should annually appoint an upright and pious man who, on the first day of Rabīʿ al-Awwal would open *Kitāb-i mīlād* [*sic*] of the Prophet[49]—May the prayers and peace of God be upon him—
[121] in the congregational mosque, and every day read part of the life of the Prophet, finishing on the twelfth.
{12} And for
[122] the twelfth [of Rabīʿ al-Avval[50]] the trustee should buy, from the income (*irtifāʿāt*) of the endowment, two medium-sized sheep, eight *manns*[51] of rice, one *mann* (?) of a sweet substance [reading *shīrīnī* instead of *shirīnī*], one *mann* of sheep's-tail fat (*yak-mann dunba*),
[123] half a *mann* of sugar (*qand*), half a *mann* of chick peas (*nukhūd*), all according to the weight standard of the "Cupola of Islam," Balkh. A rice dish (rice pudding?—*qalya birinj*) and a sweet with sugar (*ḥalwāy*

[49] Presumably the writer (or copyist) meant *mawlid* for *mīlād*. The kinds of ceremonies performed and the types of literature read on the occasion of the Prophet's birthday are described in J. Knappert, "Mawlid," *EI²*, VI, pp. 895-897.

[50] The day on which the anniversary of the Prophet's birth is celebrated.

[51] Throughout, the document refers to weights (*mann, sīr, kharvār*) in terms of the weight standard of Balkh (*ba-vazn-i qubbat al-islām Balkh*). We have no contemporary information on the weight standard of Balkh. As Davidovich shows in her discussion of the sources for the Mawarannahrid *mann* (*Materialy po metrologii srednevekovoi Srednei Azii* [Moscow: Nauka, 1970], pp. 85-94), there was enormous variation in the size of the *mann*. Generally speaking, in the 16th and 17th centuries at least, the relationships between units of weights remained fairly constant: thus 40 *sīr* = 1 *mann*, 10 *mann* = 1 *kharvār*. Information from late 19th century sources collected by the British from the Balkh region show a very different relationship: 16 *sīr* to the *mann* and 3 *mann* to the *kharvār* (Ludwig W. Adamec, ed., *Gazetteer of Afghanistan*, vol. IV: *Mazar-i Sharif and North-Central Afghanistan* [Graz: Akademische Druck-u. Verlagsanstalt, 1979], p. xi).

ba-qand) and a sweet with the *shīrīnī* should be cooked. Over the surface of the rice dish
[124] sugar should also be [sprinkled]. He should buy two hundred loaves of narrow [flat?] bread (*nān-i tang*), four loaves of which weigh one *sīr* by Balkh weight, and should make all [the food] available at the congregational mosque.
[125] All the friends and people [connected with the complex and its endowment?], pillars of the community, and Qur'ān reciters (*mawālī va ahālī va a'yān va ḥuffāẓ*) should be assembled, and after they recite the thirty parts and [thus] perform a complete recitation of the Qur'ān, the food should be brought out (*īn ṭa'ām-hā-rā bi-kashand*)
[126] and divided amongst them. When the grape and melon season (*maḥall-i angūr va kharbūza*) coincides with this gathering (*majlis*), grapes and melons should also be provided. If it is summer
[127] (the trustee) should make ice water from a *kharvār*[52] of ice or snow and distribute it to those at the gathering. Also every Friday during the six months of summer, in every congregational mosque,
[128] whether in the inner or outer city, he should make ice water from a *kharvār*'s worth of ice and distribute it, if ice is easy to come by in the city (*agar dar shahr yakh ba-suhūlat paydā shavad*).
{13} To the reciter (*khwānda*)
[129] of the [Prophet's] *mawlid* [the trustee of the endowment] should give two articles of clothing of moderate cost, one a *farajī* and the other a *qabā*,[53] the price of both together (*har dū*) being twelve *tangas*.
{14} At the conclusion of
[130] the *majlis*, the reciter of the birthday reading (*qārī mīlād*) should also read out the endowment charter (*vaqfīya*).
{15} It is also incumbent upon the legal trustee (*mutavallī shar'ī*) to make a new and fresh copy of the endowment charter every ten years
[131] and likewise

[52] Literally "donkey-load," a unit of weight (in Bukhara during this period) of about 250 kilograms (see E. A. Davidovich, *Materialy po metrologii*, pp. 105-106).

[53] Both terms refer to a long outer garment or coat. A *farajī* is described as "a woolen *qabā'* loose and unbelted with long full sleeves" (Ghulām Ḥosayn Yūsofī, "Clothing, xxii: Historical Lexicon of Persian clothing," *EIr*, V, p. 859); the *qabā'* is a "long outer cloak buttoned down the front" (p. 862).

{16} every time the Qur'ān reciters [assigned to?] the reserved area of the mosque (*maqṣūra*) complete a recitation of the entire Word of God, [the trustee should distribute] three *manns* of raisins, and two of shelled [?] pistachios (*pista maghz*), by the Balkh weight standard,

[132] to the Qur'ān reciters and the congregation (*ḥużżār*) at the congregational mosque.

{17} Likewise, it is incumbent on him that, at the Festival of the Sacrifice[54] (*ʿīd-i qurbān*), with money (*maḥṣūlāt*) from the endowments,

[133] he buy a fattened cow (*gāw-i farbih*), slaughter it in the prescribed fashion (*qurbānī va dhibḥ namāyad*), cook the meat, buy 100 [loaves of] flat [bread] at the above-mentioned weight [one-quarter *sīr*, see line 124], and distribute it to the needy.

[134] The people associated with the *madrasa* (*ahl-i madrasa*) and the neighbors (*hamsāya-hā*) of the congregational mosque should not be turned away. The head and hide (*kalla va pūsht*) (of the cow) should be given to the caretaker (*khādim*) of the congregational mosque.

[135] {18} The settlor also stipulated that the legal trustee should buy a slave who is an oil presser (*ghulām-i rawghangar*). He [the trustee] should put the oil press (*jawār-i rawghangarī*)

[136] described earlier [see line 32] into operation [lit., make it turn], and give the slave as much stock (*rās al-māl*) as he is capable of handling, so that he may [conduct business?] as an oil presser (*tā ba-kas rawghangarī qiyām namāyad*). From this oil press

[137] he should supply oil for the lamps needed in the congregational mosque and in the rooms of the college. [He should also supply] oil for lamps needed in the other mosques that are defined (*maḥdūd*) on the reverse (of this document).

[138] These include four mosques which the settlor built and conveyed as a binding legal endowment, and

[139] three other mosques which the uterine brother (*barādar-i aʿyānī*) of the settlor, the late Khwāja Muḥammad Qunāq, built and

[140] conveyed as a binding legal valid endowment. The aforementioned settlor stipulated in the body (*fī'l-ṣadr*[55]) [of that endowment

[54] The tenth day of the twelfth month, Dhū'l-Ḥijjah.

[55] Here is an instance where translating *fī'l-ṣadr* as "in the beginning of the document" does not work. The stipulations (*shurūṭ*) section of a *vaqfīyah* follows the descriptions of the beneficiary (*mawqūf ʿalayh*) and the endowed properties (*mawqūfāt*) and, as here, is often far into the document itself.

deed] that the legal trustee [should disburse] from the income of these endowments an annual sum of
[141] forty *tanga*s of the described type to the *imām*s of each of the seven mosques as salary, and to the *mu'adhdhin* of each of the mosques
[142] the sum of twenty *tanga*s of the described type.
{19} And to each of the mosques mentioned on the reverse [of this document] [the trustee should provide] felt carpets (*namadān*) of a size which accommodates two rows of people (*mardum-i dū ṣaff*) for prayer.
[143] {20} [He should also provide] woven mats (*buryā-ān*) of a size which accommodates three rows of people to pray on them. To all the mosques enumerated on the reverse [of the document] (*fī'l-ẓahr*), beginning with the inception (*taḥvīl*) of [the month of] Qaws[56]
[144] until the inception of [the month of] Jawzā,[57] he should provide ten *sīr*s of lamp oil monthly if the prayers are being conducted inside the mosques. If the prayers are performed out-of-doors,
[145] there will be no need for lamp oil.
{21} Annually he should allocate four brooms for each mosque
[146] and provide them.
{22} The settlor also stipulated that the sum of 100 *tanga*s of the described type [should be paid] to a reliable person who, at each of the two hospices (*ribāṭ*s) mentioned on the reverse (*madhkūr* [*dar*?] *ẓahr*) [of the document],
[147] should serve as custodian (*khidmat mīkard*) and in the morning and the evening should open and close [these buildings] and sweep them out.
[148] {23} The settlor also stipulated that [the expense] of building and repairing the congregational mosque, the *madrasa*, and the other endowments described
[149] at the beginning of (*fī'l-ṣadr*) [of this document] should be taken from the income of the endowment. Regarding the building and repairing of the properties mentioned on the reverse [of the document], these should not be taken from the income of this endowment.
[150] {24} He also stipulated that unless there is surplus remaining after the construction and repair of the congregational mosque, the *madrasa*,

[56] The ninth month on the solar/zodiacal calendar, still in use in Afghanistan. Qaws is Sagittarius, in 1540 beginning about 10 November.

[57] Gemini, beginning about 10 May.

and the other endowed properties mentioned in the body (*mawqufāt-i ṣadr*) [of the document], nothing should be spent on anyone (*ba-hīch kas-rā maṣārif-i chīzī nadahad*).

[151] {25} He also stipulated that none of the income-producing property (*mustaghallāt*) should be granted to any person of power (*mutaghallibī*) or to anyone from whom it might be difficult to extract the rent (*kasī ki giriftan-i badal-i ijārat azū mutaʿassir bāshad*).

[152] He should lease [only] to one person via a single lease contract, the term of which should not exceed one year.

{26} The settlor also stipulated that the trustee of this endowment

[153] should pay on a monthly basis the salaries of those designated to receive salaries. Whatever might be left over after paying these salaries [should be given] to the sixty students (*ṭālib-i ʿilm*) who reside in the *madrasa*

[154] and there occupy themselves in seeking to acquire a knowledge of the sciences from the professor (*mudarris*) of the *madrasa*. But this is on condition that

[155] during the term of study they should be in residence at the *madrasa* and nowhere else, that they not take part in games, or play, or anything that is not permitted by the *sharīʿa*, and that they

[156] not miss any of the group prayers if they live at home. This stipend, also on a monthly basis and equally divided, with the concurrence and

[157] approval of the professor, should be paid to these students. As long as the students are from abroad (*tā zamānī ki ṭālib-i ʿilmān-i musāfir bashand*), the room should not be given to anyone else (*ba-kas-i dīgar ḥujra nadahand*).

[158] But if among the students there is no one from abroad, the trustee has the option to bestow the *ḥujra*-room on any student he wishes[58] (*agar az ṭālib-i ʿilmān-i musāfir kasī nabāshad ān zamān ikhtiyār pīsh-i mutavallī bāshad ba-har ṭālib-i ʿilm ki khwāhad ḥujra dahad*).

[58] Line 157 might possibly be read "as long as the students are travelling (away from the school) the room and stipend should not be given to anyone else," but given the fairly unambiguous meaning of line 158, it seems clear that "students from abroad" must be meant here, i.e., that preference must be given them in the assignment of rooms and stipends.

[159] {27} The settlor also stipulated that [he as] the trustee may make any expenditure he wishes on this endowment and he may amend or delete any stipulation that he has made. This
[160] is his discretionary right (*ikhtiyār*). But after him, no other person shall have this option. Nor do any of the "trustees-general" (*mutavalliyān-i ʿāmm*)[59] or "clerical chiefs" (*ṣudūr-i ʿiẓām*) of the "Cupola of Islam,"
[161] Balkh—May God preserve it from all harm—have the right to interfere (*majāl-i dakhl va taṣarruf*) in these endowments; and anyone who changes any of these stipulations,
[162] may he endure the curse of God and all the angels and all men until the Day of Resurrection, and be counted among the oppressors and tyrants,
[163] and [may he suffer] serious disease and the wrath of the Lord [the Prophet Muḥammad] in this world and in that [next] world, [and may he endure] the lowest depths of Hell (*darakāt-i dūzakh*), eternal torment, and
[164] everlasting suffering, and be like Nimrod and Pharaoh and Shaddād and Abū Jahl.[60]
[165] And may he remain forever cut off from the intercession of the Prophet—upon whom be the prayers and peace of God.
The settlor, after setting aside the endowments enumerated
[166] in the body [of the document] from the rest of his private property, and after turning them over to a man whom he made trustee of these endowments on his behalf, then, because of the non-
[167] binding nature [of the endowment] and the lack of a judicial decree (*ʿadam-i . . . qażīyat*) retrieved them from the aforementioned trustee and re-possessed them as his own private property. [Thereupon]

[59] The reference here is to the politicians and state officials. It was not uncommon for sovereigns for symbolic reasons to name themselves *mutavallī ʿāmm* or *mutavallī-bāshī* of significant endowments as this one was. See my *Waqf in Central Asia*, pp. 14, 295-296.

[60] In Muslim lore Abū Jahl was a boyhood friend of the Prophet Muḥammad who, when he grew up, led the opposition to the Muslims in Mecca (before their move to Medina). He was later killed at the Battle of Badr fighting the Muslims led by Muḥammad (see W. Montgomery Watt, "Abū Djahl," *EI²*, I, p. 113). Nimrod, Pharaoh, and Shaddād (the son of ʿĀd) are figures in the Isrāʾīliyyāt lore that appears in the Qurʾān and *qiṣaṣ al-anbiyāʾ* literature who suffered sanguinary and exemplary punishments for their sins.

His Excellency, the Qāżī of Islam, presiding (*nāfidh al-umūr wa'l-aḥkām*)
[168] in the "Cupola of Islam," who will adorn the end of this piece of writing with his noble seal, knowledgeable in the differences in legal opinions among (*ʿālim būd ba-maḥall-i khilāf-i*)
[169] scholars exercising independent judgement (*mujtahidīn*) and in the points on which religious scholars differ (*wa* [*ba-*] *mavāżiʿ-i ikhtilāf-i ʿulamāʾ-i dīn*), subsequent to the pro forma dispute (*mukhāṣamah-i sharʿīya*) between the settlor and this trustee, issued a legally valid decree
[170] to the settlor, following judicial procedures, affirming first the validity of these endowments and secondly their binding nature; and thus these endowments became
[171] secondarily [i.e., at this second procedural level, after first being made *vaqf* and then being re-possessed] legally binding, valid, effective, eternal, and everlasting and recorded in a *sijill*. "Whoever should attempt to alter it, after hearing the terms of it, verily the sin of it is against those who change it. Surely God
[172] is all-hearing all-knowing."[61] All that is recorded in this valid endowment deed has been witnessed by a large number of reliable witnesses (*thiqāt*) and notaries (*ʿudūl*).
[173] Dated the month of Jumādā al-Thānī the year Nine Hundred and Forty-seven.

[Separately—originally on the reverse (?):]

[174] May it not be hidden that two copies of this endowment deed (*vaqfīya*) are in the city of Bukhara, one in the library (*katīb-khāna* [*sic*]) of Ḥażrat Khwāja Muḥammad Pārsā—May God sanctify his glorious secret—and the other in the house of
[175] Hażrat Shaykh al-ʿĀlam—May God sanctify his glorious secret. Another copy exists in Samarqand at the home of the servitors (*mulāzimān*) of His Excellency (*janāb khwāja-i ṣādiq*) Khwāja-i Bahāʾ al-Dīnī,
[176] and another in the *vilāyat* of Shahr-i Sabz at the home of His Excellency (*ʿālī-ḥażrat hidāyat dastgāh*) Muḥammad Ṣādiq Shaykh.

[61] Qurʾān 2:181, "*fa-man baddalahu baʿda mā samiʿahu fa-innamā ithmuhu ʿalā'l-ladhīna yubaddilūnahu innā'llāha samīʿun ʿalimun.*" The preceding verse in the Qurʾān (2:180) obliges a person approaching death to make a a last will and testament (*waṣīya*) in favor of one's parents and kin to dispose of any possessions.

Two other copies are in Balkh, one
[177] at the home of His Honor (*janāb irshād-maʾābī*) Qāżī Ṣāliḥ, and the other at the home of Qāżī Mālmal. Another copy is with the settlor. God forbid,
[178] but if one of these should go missing (*agar yakī az īnhā ghāyib shavad*), recourse should be had to these places (*ba-rujūᶜ ba-mavāżiᶜ-i madhkūra kard shavad*).

Table 1: Balkh Property Owners in 1540

Name	Property
Ḥājjī Muḥammad b. Shaykh Junayd al-Balkhī	*khāna* (house)
Shāh Berdī b. Mawlānā Bazmī	*khāna*
Khwāja Mawlānā (Qunāq—son of the *vaqf* founder)	*khāna-hā* (houses) *ḥavīlī* (compound)
Bībī Ṣafīya bt. Shāh-Muḥammad Balkhī	*ḥavīlī*
Shaykh ʿAlī (pursemaker) b. Khwāja Shams Balkhī	willow grove
Qāsim b. Khamār Āqā	*dukkān* (shop)
Shāh-Muḥammad b. Ḥasan ʿAlī Balkhī	*ḥavīlī*
Muḥammad (greengrocer) b. ʿAlī al-Balkhī	*dukkān*
Ḥāfiẓ Fānī b. Ḥāfiẓ Darvīsh al-Haravī	state land (lessee)
Khān-Muḥammad b. Yār-Muḥammad b. ʿAbdullāh al-Marvī	*ḥavīlī*
Mawlānā Muḥammad Bāqir b. Mawlānā Muḥammad al-Qāżī al-Bukhārī	*ḥavīlī*
Tursūn Kūlābī b. Ṣadr al-Dīn b. Nūr al-Dīn al-Balkhī	*khāna*
Dūst Muḥammad b. Abū Saʿīd b. Nūr Saʿīd al-Balkhī	*khāna*
Shams al-Dīn b. Ustād Rajab Shibarghānī	*dukkān*
Mastī Lang b. Saʿīd-i Balkhī	oil shop (oil press?)
Khwāja Muḥammad (baker) b. Fakhr al-Dīn b. Khwāja Aḥmad	*dukkān* *tannūr-khāna* (bakery) *ḥavīlī*
Sulṭān-Muḥammad *kharkār* (?) b. Jān-Muḥammad	*dukkān*
Banda-i ʿAlī Muḥammad (dyer–*rangrīzī*) b. Ūstād ʿAlī Balkhī	*dukkān*

Name	Property
Khwāja Mīr ʿAlī b. Sulṭān-Maḥmūd Haravī b. ʿAbdullāh	*dukkān*
Shīrum b. Ustād ʿAbdullāh (dyer–*ṣabbāghī*)	*ḥavīlī*
Mawlānā Ḥājjī ʿAlī (market inspector) b. Mawlānā Ḥasan	state land (lessee)
Mīr Muḥammad (market inspector) b. Mawlānā Darvīsh Muḥammad Samarqandī b. Mawlānā Ḥasan	clover field
Pahlavān Shāh-Maḥmūd (Pahlavānzāda) b. Pahlavān Maḥmūd(landscape architect/ horticulturalist—*baghbān*	state land (lessee)
Yārī Bahādur b. Jānī Bahādur b. Tengrī Berdī Bahādur	*khāna-hā*
Shaykhum *chuhra* b. Mīrum *chuhra* b. Nūr *chuhra*	*khāna*
Shāh-Muḥammad (b. Ḥasan ʿAlī Balkhī)	*ḥavīlī*
Ustād ʿAlī (weaver) b. Khwāja Kalān b. Khwāja Khurd	*khāna* *dukkān*
Zayn al-Dīn b. Dūst (greengrocer) b. Jān-Muḥammad	*ḥavīlī*
Jamāl al-Dīn Khwāja b. Kamāl Khwāja	*ḥavīlī*
Yār-Muḥammad Jangī b. Mīr Muḥammad b. Pīr Muḥammad Marvī	*khāna*
Tīlā Valī Bahādur b. Tengrī Qulī Bahādur b. ʿAbdullāh	state land (lessee)
Ḥasan ʿAlī (vegetable farmer—*sabzkār*) b. ʿAlī Sīstānī b. ʿAbdullāh	state land (lessee)
Ustād Khudāy Qulī (butcher) b. Maḥmūd b. Muḥammad Marvī	*khāna-hā* *dukkān*

FACSIMILE OF THE *VAQFĪYA*

Central State Archive of the Republic of Uzbekistan, Fond I-323, No. 1216

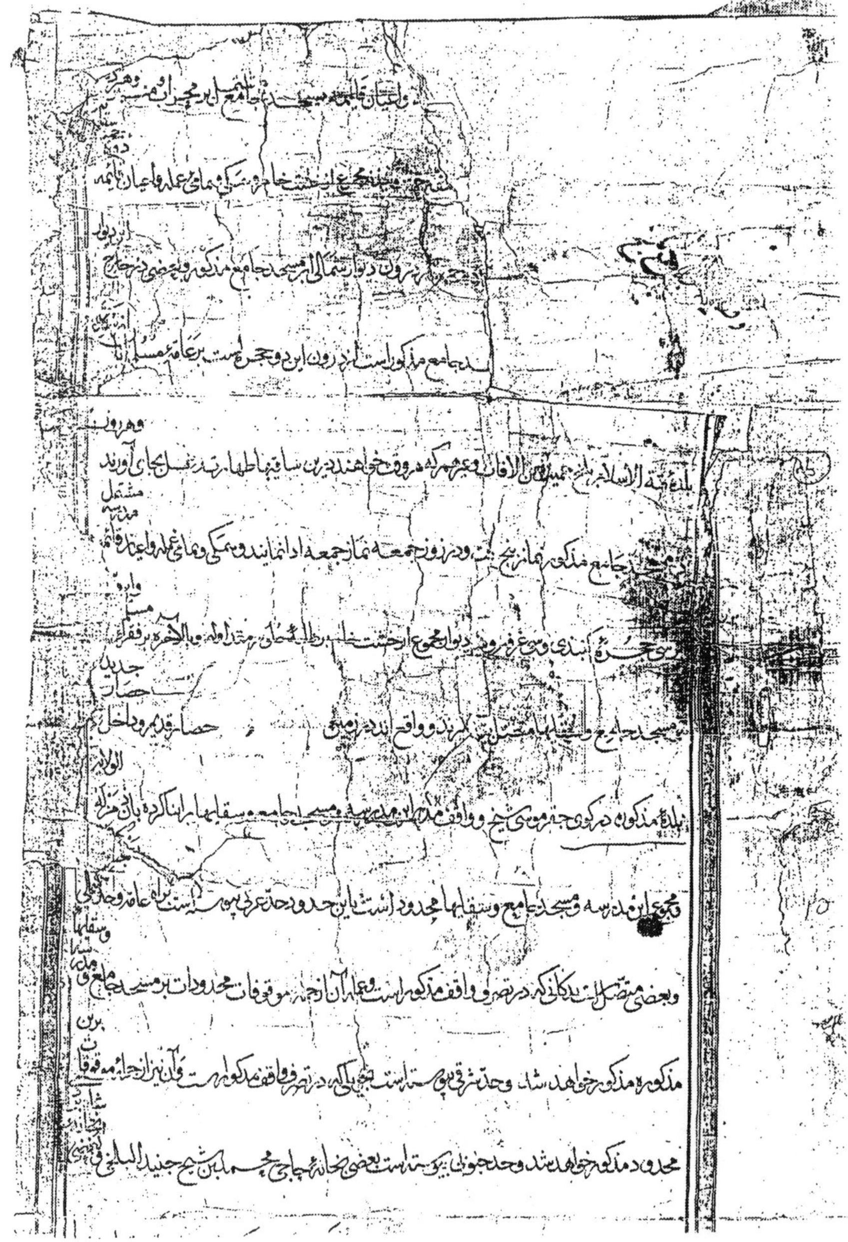

ن مولانا بابری با جمیع توابع ولواحق ومضافات ومنسوبات محدود مذکوره من القلیل والکثیر والنقیر والقطمیر وقفا صحیحا

وصدقة جاریة نافذة موبدة بحیث لا یباع ولا یوهب ولا یرهن ولا یمهر ولا یورث ولا یملک بوجه من الوجوه الی ان یرث الله

وبعد از آنکه واقف مذکور محدود مذکوره را از ملک خود افراز نمود ووقف لازم شرعی کرد خواست که این خیرات

ومیداری باشد پس وقف کرد وتصدق نمود در حال صحت وجمیع تصرفات شرعیه خود طائعا این محدود مذکوره را

له دار ظهر این وقفیه محدود شد [illegible] نمود که حق وملک او بود وتحت تصرف مالکانه خود داشت [illegible]

[illegible] جواز الوقف ولزومه همگی وتمامی عمله واعیان قایمه وصحیح [illegible] واقع است در ولایة قبة الاسلام

بلخ مذکور [illegible] همگی وتمامی عمله واعیان قایمه مشتمل بر جامه خانه چوب پوش وپای [illegible]

وگرم خانه وحوض [illegible] خانه دیگر ودو صفه وبرون ومجموع مسقف بخشت پخته وگلخن ومطرح [illegible]

وواقع این حمام در کوی جعفر موسی شیخ مذکور محدود باین حدود حد غربی متصل براه عام

پیوسته است بخانه وقف [illegible] حد شرقی متصل بمقبره مسلمانان که مکان ارفع است [illegible]

بحویلی وقف مسجد جامع مذکور ومنها همگی عمله واعیان قایمه چهار دکان متصل بیکدیگر [illegible] مذکور محدود

باین حدود حد غربی براه عام ومنه المدخل وشمالی کالغربی وشرقی متصل بحویلی وقف مسجد جامع مذکور وحد جنوبی

مدرسه مذکوره ومنها تمامی عمله واعیان قایمه پنج دکان متصل بیکدیگر در کوی مذکور محدود باین حدود

خواجه مولانا اولاد واقف مذکور وحد شمالی متصل بدکان مسماة بی بی صفیه بنت شاه محمد بلخی وحد شرقی [illegible]

[illegible]

ومنها همگی وتمامی عمله یک دربکان طباخی که واقع است در کوی مذکور محدود باین حدود حد غربی متصل بحویلی خواجه مولانا

مذکور وحد شرقی پیوسته براه عام وحد شمالی کالغربی وحد جنوبی متصل بر آب رو بحویلی خواجه مولانای مذکور ومنها

همگی عمله واعیان قایمه یک حویلی مشتمل بر سه درخانه چوب پوش ودالان وبالاخانه چوب پوش محدود باین حدود حد غربی

پیوسته بمدرسه مذکوره وشمالی وشرقی پیوسته براه عام وجنوبی پیوسته بهدستان شیخ علی کسه دوز ابن خواجه شمس بلخی

ومنها همگی اعیان قایمه دو دربکان که واقع است در کوی مذکور یکی زرگری ودیگری [illegible] محدود باین حدود حد غربی پیوسته بعضی بدکان

قاسم بن خواجه [illegible] بحویلی شاه حسین بن علی بلخی وبعضی بدکان محمد بقال بن علی البلخی وحد شمالی پیوسته براه عام وحد شرقی پیوسته بزمین مملکه

پادشاهی که بتصرف واقف مذکور است وجنوبی پیوسته بزمین مملکه که بعضی آن بتصرف حافظ فانی ابن حافظ درویش الهروی است

وبعضی بتصرف واقف مذکور ومنها همگی وتمامی عمله وقایمه یک دکان که واقع است در کوی مذکور محدود باین حدود حد غربی پیوسته بزمین خالصه

پادشاهی که بتصرف واقف مذکور است وشمالی وشرقی پیوسته براه عام وجنوبی متصل بحریم نهر عام که واقعست در کوی مذکور ومنها همگی وتمامی

عمله واعیان قایمه یک حجره طاحونه دایر ومشتمل بر آلات حجریه وحدیدیه وخشبیه که واقعست در کوی مذکور محدود باین حدود حد غربی [illegible]

متصل بزمین مملکه پادشاهی که بتصرف واقف مذکور است وحد شمالی وجنوبی متصل بعضی بحریم نهر عام که واقعست در کوی مذکور

وبعضی ببطن آن نهر ومنها همگی وتمامی عمله واعیان قایمه کاروانسرای مشتمل بر چهل وهفت حجره ویکی آبخانه مجموع مسقف بخشت خام وهمگی

عمله یک حویلی متصل بکاروانسرای مذکور ومشتمل بر دو درخانه یکی گنبدی ویکی چوب پوش واین کاروانسرا واین حویلی واقع است

[illegible] که ودکانها حصار [illegible] در کوی [illegible] خانه محدود باین حدود حد غربی آن [illegible]

در خارج قلعهٔ قدیم بلدهٔ مذکوره و داخل حصار جدید در کوی سلاخ خانه محدود باین حدود حد غربی آن پیوسته بدیوار حصار مذکور

و جنوبی متصل براه عام و شرقی آن پیوسته است بدکان که وقف بر موقوف علیهما مذکوره و شمالی پیوسته است بعضی بحویلی حاجی محمد بن یار محمد بن

عبد الله المروی و بعضی بحویلی مولانا محمد باقر بن مولانا محمد القاضی البخاری و بعضی بخانه ترسون کلانی ابن صدر الدین بن نور الدین البلخی

و بعضی پیوسته بخانه دوست محمد بن ابو سعید بن نور سعید البلخی و منها همگی عمله و اعیان قایمه شانزده دکان متصل بیکدیگر

محدود باین حدود حد غربی آن پیوسته است بکاروانسرای مذکوره و حد شمالی آن پیوسته است بدکان شمس الدین بن استاد خواجه شیر غازی

و جنوبی و شرقی پیوسته است براه عام و منها همگی و تمامی عمله نه دکان که متصل است بیکدیگر و واقع است در محاذی کاروانسرای

مذکوره محدود باین حدود حد غربی آن متصل است براه عام و شمالی پیوسته است بدکان روغنگری منسوب بلنگر ابن سعید بلخی

و حد شرقی پیوسته است ببعضی بدکان واقف مذکور که عمله این دکان از جمله موقوفات بر موقوف علیهما مذکوره مذکور خواهد شد

و بعضی پیوسته است بسقایه که در ظهر این وقفیه از جمله موقوف علیهما محدود شد و جنوبی آن پیوسته است بعضی براه عام

و بعضی به پیش ایوان که بر موقوف علیهما مذکوره محدود خواهد شد و منها همگی عمله پیش ایوان و یک دره دکان متصل بیکدیگر

آن نیز واقع است در قریب کاروانسرای مذکوره محدود باین حدود حد غربی آن پیوسته به دکان محدود مذکوره و جنوبی

آن پیوسته است براه عام و حد شرقی آن متصل است بسقایه مذکوره و شمالی آن پیوسته است بدکان الغربی بدکان محدود

مذکوره و منها همگی عمله یکدره دکان بقال که واقع است روبروی کاروانسرای مذکوره و دو پیش ایوان متصل باین دکان

[illegible] محدود باین حدود حد غربی و حد شمالی متصل براه عام و حد شرقی [illegible]

مجموع محدود باین حدود حد غربی و حد شمالی متصل براه عام و حد شرقی ان پیوسته بمسجدی که داخل موقوف علیها

گردد ظهر محدود شده و جنوبی آن پیوسته است ببعضی بدکان خواجه محمد خباز بن فخر الدین خواجه احمد و ببعضی بشوره خانه

خواجه محمد مذکور و منها همگی عمله چهار دکان متصل بیکدیگر که واقع است در قریب کاروانسرای مذکور محدود

باین حدود حد غربی آن پیوسته براه عام و شمالی ان پیوسته است بدکان خبازی خواجه محمد مذکور و شرقی و جنوبی ان پیوسته است

بحویلی ان خواجه محمد مذکور و منها همگی عمله پنج دردکان متصل بیکدیگر که واقع است در خارج حصار قدیم بلده مذکور قریب بدروازه عراق

محدود باین حدود حد غربی و حد شمالی ان پیوسته بخندق حصار قدیم بلده مذکوره و حد شرقی آن پیوسته است براه عام و حد جنوبی آن پیوسته است

بدکان سلطان محمد خرکار بن جان محمد و منها همگی عمله یکدردکان مع سه دردکان خانه متصل بیکدیگر که واقع است در خارج حصار قدیم بلده مذکور

در درون حصار جدید در بازار جامه فروشان محدود باین حدود حد غربی ان پیوسته براه عام و حد شمالی آن پیوسته است بدکان

بنده علی بن محمد بکر بن استاد علی بلخی و حد شرقی ان پیوسته است بزمین مملکه بادشاهی که در تصرف واقف مذکور است

و حد جنوبی ان پیوسته است بدکان خواجه میر علی بن سلطان محمود هروی بن عبد الله و منها همگی عمله قائمه دو دردکان و یکدر حویلی مشتمل

بر یکدرخانه و متصل بیکدیگر که واقع است در سر پول دو آبه و محدود است باین حد غربی و جنوبی ان پیوسته است

براه عامه و حد شرقی ان پیوسته است بدکان نجاری استاد باری بن استاد تاج الدین استاد محمد البلخی و حد شمالی آن پیوسته است

ببعضی بحویلی مولانا عبد الله بن مولانا محمود و ببعضی بحویلی شیر مرد بن استاد عبد الله صباغ و منها همگی عمله و تمامی عمله قائمه واقعه

و آسیای مشتمل بر هفت دانه و شش حجره و ختله خانه که در اقطاعات در خارج حصار قندهار بلده و درون حصار حدود نهر اسیاب و محدود بعضی است سو آن

و حد جنوبی آن بزمین مملکه بادشاهی که بتصرف خدمت مولانا حاجی علی بن محتسب بن مولانا حسن است و حد جنوبی

بباغ و بیرون جفد زار مولانا امیر محمد محتسب بن مولانا درویش محمد سمرقندی ابن مولانا حسن و بعضی پیوسته آن

بزمین مملکه بادشاهی که بتصرف پهلوان شاه محمد معروف به پهلوان زاده بن پهلوان محمود باغبان است و حد شرقی بردی

پیوسته است بعضی بمقبره مسلمین و مسلمات آن مکان رفیع است و بعضی بخانهای یاری بهادر بن جانی بهادر بن تنکری بافنده

بهادر و بعضی بخانه شیخم جهره بن میرم جهره بن نور جهره و بعضی بحویلی شاه محمد مذکور و بعضی بحویلی استاد علی

بن عبد الله بن عبد الرحیم و بخانه و دکان استاد سنکین صباغ بن خواجه کلان بن خواجه خرد و بعضی بخانه زین الدین بن

دوست بقال بن جان محمد و بعضی بحویلی جمال الدین خواجه بن کمال خواجه و بعضی بخانه یار محمد جنکی بن میر محمد بن پیر محمد مروی

و حد شمالی آن پیوسته است بعضی بزمین مملکه بادشاهی که بتصرف تیلا ولی بهادر بن تنکری قلی بهادر بن عبد الله است

و بعضی بزمین مملکه بادشاهی که در تصرف حسن علی سبزکار بن علی شیستانی بن عبد الله است و بعضی بدکاکین که

از جمله موقوفات محدود خواهد شد و بعضی بخانهای استاد خدایقلی قصاب بن محمود بن محمد مروی و بعضی بدکان

خدایقلی مذکور و منها رهمگی و تمامی عمله سه در دکان متصل بیکدیگر محدود باین حدود حد غربی و شمالی آن پیوسته است

بجوی نهر عام و حد شرقی آن پیوسته است براه رو کاروانسرای محدود ثانی و حد جنوبی آن پیوسته است بکاروانسرای دویم

مذکور و منها همگی عمله شش در دکان متصل بیکدیگر محدود باین حدود حد غربی آن پیوسته است براه رو کاروانسرای

مذکور حد جنوبی آن پیوسته است بکاروانسرای مذکور حد شرقی آن پیوسته است بمقبرهٔ مسلمانان که مکان رفیع

حد شمالی آن پیوسته است براه عام و منها همگی و تمامی نصف مسلخ یکجهت طاحونه دایر مشتمل بر اسباب و ادوات حجره

و جدیده و خشبیه که واقع است در موضع شخشارک که قریه معین است از قرای بلده مذکوره محدود باین حدود حد غربی

و حد شرقی آن پیوسته است بزمین مملکه پادشاهی بتصرف واقف مذکور است و حد شمالی آن پیوسته است وجنوبی

بعضی بحریم نهر عام و بعضی ببطن نهر عام با جمیع حدود و حقوق و توابع و لواحق مضافات و محدودات مذکو 45

من القلیل و الکثیر و النقیر و القطمیر وقفا صحیحا لازما شرعیا مرعیا بحیث لا یباع و لا یوهب و لا یرهن و لا یمهر و لا ینتقل

من ملک الی ملک بوجه من الوجوه الشرعیه و جعل آخره هذا الاوقاف علی الفقراء المسلمین و شرط کرد واقف مذکور

مادام حیوته دام عمره که متولی این موقوفات محدوده مذکوره من الاول الی الاخر خود باشد علی سبیل العموم و الاستقلال

یتصرف فیها و فی محصولاتها کیف یشاء و این یشاء و یصرفها و فی محصولاتها الی من یشاء و عمن یشاء تغییر مصارف

و شرایط و تنصیص و ازدیاد وظایف و عنان اعطا و حرمان و زمام زیادت و نقصان از هر که باشد و هر جه خواهد 90

در این امور بکف کفایت و قبضهٔ مصلحت خود نهاد چنانچه کسی را بروی بهیچ نوع و لا اینا اعتراض نباشد و شرط کرد که

بعد از وی از اولاد وی و اولاد اولاد وی و اولاد اولاد اولاد وی بطنا بعد بطن و قرنا بعد قرن هر کدام اصلح و اکفی باشد

متولی این موقوفات مذکوره باشد و اگر از نسل و اعقاب واقف مذکور کسی نماند العیاذ بالله یا آنکه باشد لیکن در ولایت دیگر باشد کسی

آمدن او باین ولایت متعذر شده باشد پادشاه یا قاضی و یا خلیفه پادشاه این ولایت را اختیار باشد که از اقربای سازند

سازند

واقف مذکور کسی را متولی این موقوفات سازند و اگر از اقربای نیز کسی نباشد مردان صالح متدین را متولی

تنکچه
دو بیست

و هر کدام از این دو قسم آخر که متولی باشد هر سال حق التولیه از ارتفاعات موقوفات مذکور مبلغ

الاسلام

سره پاکیزه یکمثقالی رایج الوقت و مقدار سیصد من غله پاکیزه سیر دانه دهقان پسند بوزن قبة

کرده شود

بلخ از گندم و جو بطریق مناصفه گیرد و شرط کرد واقف مذکور که آنچه از این موقوفات حاصل شود صرف

کمال
جب

اولا بعمارت و مرمت ضروریه محدودات مذکورات و آنچه فاضل آید هر سال عشر محصول را بیک مدرس صاحب

شود

که در مدرسه محدود مذکور هر هفته روز شنبه و یکشنبه و دوشنبه و سه شنبه درس علوم عربیه گوید داده

و یک عشر دیگر را اولاد واقف مذکور و اولاد اولاد او و اولاد اولاد اولاد او بطنا بعد بطن و قرنا بعد قرن هر کس باشد

باشد
میخوانده

للذکر مثل حظ الانثیین گیرند و یکنفر حافظ خوش خوان خوش آواز که قرآن را یاد داشته باشد و درست

تنکچه
عدد

در مسجد جامع مذکور خطیب و مصدر و امام جمعه باشد و بجهت خطابت و امامت هر سال مبلغ صد

این
نش

نقره سره پاکیزه یکمثقالی رایج الوقت گیرد و بجهت مصدری نیز هر سال مبلغ صد عدد تنکچه موصوفه بگیرد و اگر دو

باشند
داشته

دوام قیام نمایند هر کدام صد تنکچه موصوفه گیرند و شش نفر حافظ خوش خوان خوش آواز که قرآن را یاد

و درست میخوانده باشند و هر روز جمعه پیش از نماز جمعه در مسجد جامع محدود مذکور یکجزو از سی جزو

قرآن مجید میخوانده باشند هر یک از این حفاظ هر سال مبلغ هفتاد و دو عدد تنکچه موصوفه گیرند

که
ش آواز

یکماه
و از این حفاظ هر کدام بی استمهالی عذر شرعی ترک ملازمت کنند وظیفه نگیرند و یک نفر حافظ خوش خوان خو

باشد قرآن را درست میخواند باشد بامر امامت صلوة خمسه دیرین مسجد جامع محدود مذکور اقامت نماید

وظیفه امامت هر سال مبلغ صد و هشتاد تنکچه عدد موصوفه کیرد باین شرط که از هیچ کس از مردم جماعت عیدی وغیره طمع نکند

و یکنفر موذن خوش آواز که آذان و اقامت را درست می کفته باشد هر روز جمعه مقری کری کند و اذان و اقامت نماز جمعه

کوید و هر سال مبلغ چهل تنکچه موصوفه کیرد و یکنفر موذن خوش آواز که آذان و اقامت را درست میکفته باشد هر روز جمعه

مقری کری کند و اذان و اقامت نماز روز جمعه کوید و در اوقات صلوات خمس نیز اذان و اقامت کوید و وظیفه هر سال صد و بیست تنکه

موصوفه کیرد باین شرط که او نیز از مردم جماعت عیدی و چیزی دیگر طمع نکند و یکنفر مرد صالح صوفی متدین که زمستان و تابستان

بجاروب کشی و خادمی مسجد جامع و مدرسه محدود مذکور فی الصدر قیام نماید و در زمستان پشتهای بام را از برف

پاک سازد و هر سال مبلغ شصت تنکچه موصوفه کیرد باین شرط که محافظت … و بوریا و جاروب کما ینبغی بجای آرد و یکنفر مرد

امین که از چاه سقایه که در ظهر محدود شده برای مسلمانان آب کشد که طهارت کنند و غسل بجای آورند و کسی بجهت آب معطل

نسازد و از سر صبح صادق تا نماز خفتن در سقایه مذکوره را نبندد و هر سال وظیفه او صد تنکه موصوفه

باشد باین شرط که درشتی و کج خلقی نکند و از کسی چیزی نطلبد و نیز شرط کرد واقف مذکور که متولی این اوقاف

هر سال مرد صالح متدین را تعیین نماید که در غره شهر ربیع الاول کتاب میلاد حضرت رسالت پناه را صلی الله علیه وسلم

افتتاح کند در مسجد جامع مذکوره و هر روز پاره از احوال آنحضرت میخوانده باشد و در روز دوازدهم تمام کند و در روز

دوازدهم متولی مذکور از ارتفاعات این اوقاف دو کوسفند متوسط القیمه بخرد و هشت من برنج و هر یکمن شیرینی و یکمن روغن

بخ

وبمدرسه

دوازده من متولی مذکور از ارتفاعات این اوقاف دو گوسفند متوسط القیمه بخرد و هشت من برنج و هر یک من

و نیم من قند و نیم من نخود مجموع بوزن قبة الاسلام بلخ و قلیه برنج و حلوای بقند و حلوای پشرهنی بزد و بر روی قلیه برنج

قند نیز بپاشند و دویست عدد نان تنک بخرد که هر چهار نان ده سیر باشد بوزن بلخ و در مسجد جامع حاضر سازد

و جمیع موالی و اهالی و اعیان و حفاظ را جمع ساخته و بعد از آنکه سی پاره بخوانند و قران ختم کنند این طعامها

بکشند و بر ایشان قسمت نمایند و در مجلس انگور و خربزه فراخور مجلس انگور و خربزه نیز بکشند و اگر تابستان باشد

یک خروار یخ یا برف را ایجاب ساخته باهل مجلس بدهد و در تابستان شش ماه نیز در هر روز جمعه در هر یک از مساجد

جامعه بیرون و درون شهر یک خروار یخ بجاب سقایه مردم بدهد اگر در شهر یخ بسهولت پیدا شود و خواننده

میلاد را دو جامه متوسط القیمه یک فرجی و دیگری قبا قیمت هر دو دوازده تنکه باشد بدهند و در آخر

مجلس قاری میلاد باید که وقفیه را نیز بخواند و نیز باید که متولی شرعی بعد هر ده سال وقفیه را نو و تازه سازد

و نیز باید که متولی شرعی هر بار که حافظان مقصوره کلام الله ختم کنند سه من کشمش و دو من پسته مغز بوزن بلخ

بحفاظ و حضار مسجد جامع مذکور قسمت نماید و نیز باید که در هر عید قربان از محصولات این اوقاف

یک گاو فربه بخرد بجهت قربانی و ذبح نماید و گوشت از ابخته و صد تنکه وزن او مذکور شده بخرد و بفقرا قسمت نماید

و اهل مدرسه و همسایهای مسجد جامع محروم نگذارد و کله و پوست بخادم مسجد جامع و مدرسه مذکور

بدهد و نیز شرط کرد واقف مذکور که متولی شرعی از حاصلات این اوقاف یک غلام روغنگر بخرد و جوار رود عنکری برکه

جوار رود عنکری

محدود شد گردان سازد و بقدر الوسع این غلام را راس المال بدهد تا بکسب روغنگری قیام نماید و اوان

محدود

روغن چراغ لابدی مسجد جامع و چراغ مدرسه مذکوره را بدهد و روغن چراغ لابدی مساجدی که در ظهر محدود
شده نیز بدهد و از الجمله چهار مسجد است که آنرا واقف مذکور بنا کرده و وقف لازم شرعی کرده و از آنجمله
سه مسجد دیگر را برادر اعیانی واقف مذکور جناب مغفرت مآب مرحمت انتساب خواجه محمد قنات بنا کرده
و وقف صحیح لازم شرعی کرده است و شرط کرده واقف مذکور فی الصدر که متولی شرعی هر ساله از حاصل این اوقاف
با امام هر یک از این هفت مسجد که مذکور شد وظیفهٔ امامت مبلغ چهل تنکه موصوفه و به مؤذن هر کدام از این مساجد
مبلغ بیست تنکه موصوفه بدهد و بجمیع مساجد که در ظهر مذکور شده نمدان مقداری که مردم دو صف بر و نماز
گذارند بدهد و بوریا آن مقداری که سه صف بر و نماز گذارند بدهد و بجمیع مساجد محدود فی الظهر از قوس
تا تحویل جوزا هر ماه ده سیر روغن چراغ بدهد اگر نماز را در درون مسجد میگذارده باشند و اگر در بیرون مسجد نماز
میگذارده باشند احتیاج بروغن چراغ نخواهد بود و جاروب مساجد را هر سال چهار جاروب مرتب دارد
و بدهد و نیز شرط کرد واقف مذکور که هر سال مبلغ صد تنکه موصوفه بیک امین که در هر یک از این دو رباط مذکور
ظهر خدمت میکرده باشد و صباح و شام در این رباط را بسته و میگشاده باشد و جاروب کشی این رباط
میکرده باشد بدهد و نیز شرط کرد واقف مذکور که عمارت و مرمت مسجد جامع و مدرسه و سایر موقوفات محدود
فی الصدر از حاصل این اوقاف باشد فاما عمارت و مرمت محدودات فی الظهر از حاصل این اوقاف نباشد
و نیز شرط کرد که تا از عمارت و مرمت مسجد و مدرسه و سایر موقوفات صدر چیزی فاضل نیاید هیچ کس از مصارف چیزی

[illegible]

ندهد و نیز شرط کرد هیچ یک از ین مستغلات را بمتغلبی و کسی که کرفتن بدل اجارت از و متعسر باشد ندهد

و بیک کس بیک عقد اجارت زیاده از یک سال با جارت ندهد و نیز شرط کرد واقف مذکور که متولی این اوقاف

وظایف ارباب وظایف مذکوره را ماه بماه بدهد و آنچه ازین وظایف مذکوره فاضل آید بشصت نفر طالب علم که در مدرسه

مذکوره ساکن باشند و بطلب تحصیل علوم نزد مدرس این مدرسهٔ مذکوره مشغول بوده باشند بدهند باین شرط که

در ایام تحصیل بی عذر شرعی در غیر مدرسه ساکن نباشند و بلهو و لعب و امر نامشروع مباشرت نمی نموده باشند

و ترک نماز بجماعت نمی کرده باشند در زمانی که در خانهٔ خود باشند و این وظیفه را نیز ماه بماه و بر سبیل تسویه

بی تفوق و استصواب مدرس بر طلبهٔ مذکوره قسمت نماید و تا زمانی که طالب علمان مسافر باشند بکس دیگر حجره

ندهند و اگر از طالب علمان مسافر کسی نباشد آن زمان اختیار به بیش متولی باشد بهر طالب علم که خواهد حجره دهد

و نیز شرط کرد واقف مذکور که هر نوع تصرفی که خواهد درین اوقاف کند و هر شرطی را که خواهد زیاده و کم سازد و این

اختیار او را باشد و بس و غیر او هیچ آفریده را این اختیار نباشد و هیچکس از متولیان عام و صدور عظام قبة الاسلام

بلدهٔ بلخ راحمیت عن الافات درین اوقاف مجال دخل و تصرف نباشد و هر کس که شرطی را ازین شروط مذکوره

تغییر دهد تا قیام قیامت در لعنت خدای تعالی و جمیع ملایکه و آدمیان باشد و از جملهٔ ظالمان و عاصیان

باشد و در سخط و غضب حضرت خداوندی باشد درین دنیا و در آن جهان در درکات دوزخ و بتعذیبات

ابدی و عقوبات سرمدی مبتلا کردد و از اقران و امثال نمرود و فرعون و شداد و ابوجهل باشد و از شفاعت

حضرت رسالت پناه صلی الله علیه وسلم محروم ماند و واقف مذکور بعد از آنکه موقوفات مذکور را

عدم

وبعلت

فی الصدر را از سایر املاک خود افراز نموده بود و بکسی که از قبل خود متولی این موقوفات ساخته بود تسلیم کرده

لزوم و قضیت بان این موقوفات را از متولی مذکور واسته و بملکیت تصرف نموده بود حضرت قاضی الاسلام نافذ الامر

خلاف

والاحکام قبة الاسلام بلده مذکوره الذی سشوح ذیل هذه المسطور بتوقیع الشریف در وقتی که عالم بود بمحل

مجتهدین و مواضع اختلاف علماء دین بعد از وقوع مخاصمه شرعیه میان واقف مذکور و متولی مذکور حکم صحیح شرعی

کرد دظهر رافع شرعیه بر واقف مذکور بصحت این اوقاف اولا و بلزومها ثانیا فصارت هذه الاوقاف صحیحة

لازمة شرعیة ثابتة نافذة مؤیدة مخلدة مسجلة فمن بدله بعد ما سمعه فانما اثمه علی الذین یبدلونه والله

واسع علیم و بر جمیع ابخدرین و ففیته شرعیه مذکور و مسطور شد اشهاد نمود جمع کثیر از ثقات و عدول

واقع شد وکان ذلک بتاریخ شهر جمادی الثانی سنه سبع واربعین وثمانمائه

بنویسند نماند که دو عدد وقفیه در شهر بخارا است یکی در کتبخانهٔ حضرت خواجه محمد پارسا قدس الله سره العزیز و یکی در کتبخانهٔ

١٦ حضرت شیخ العالم قدس الله سره العزیز است و یکی دیگر در شهر سمرقند است در خانهٔ ملا [illegible]

و یکی دیگر در ولایت شهر سبز است در خانهٔ عالیحضرت هدایت دستگاه محمد صادق شیخ و دو عدد دیگر در بلخ یکی

در خانهٔ جناب ارشاد مآبی قاضی صالح و دیگری در خانهٔ قاضی مال و یکی دیگر نزد وقف مذکور است العیاذ بالله

١٨ اگر یکی از اینها غایب شود رجوع بمواضع مذکوره کرده شود م

THE SAYYID ATĀʾĪ PRESENCE IN KHWĀRAZM DURING THE 16TH AND EARLY 17TH CENTURIES

Devin DeWeese

Indiana University

The figure of Sayyid Ata casts a long, and broad, shadow in the history of Central Asia, from his lifetime (evidently in the late 13th and early 14th centuries) down to the present. He was credited with initiating the conversion to Islam of the peoples of the Dasht-i Qïpchāq, in narratives recorded from the 15th century to the 20th; he was incorporated into the Sufi *silsila* of the Yasavī order, beginning from the 15th century at least; he was regarded as the saintly ancestor of families who gained prominence both in Sufism and in political affairs, throughout Central Asia, and who maintained their self-consciousness as descendants of Sayyid Ata, from the 15th century through the 19th; his shrine in northern Khwārazm served as a pilgrimage place from the early 16th century, if not earlier, down to the present; and he is remembered as a saint and culture hero in oral tradition recorded among the Uzbeks, Türkmens, Qazaqs, and Qaraqalpaqs.

I have discussed in another article one important aspect of the familial legacy of Sayyid Ata, namely the specific post—that of the *naqīb*—that was regarded, for a time, as the hereditary prerogative of Sayyid Ata's descendants within the Chinggisid polities of the 'Shībānids' and 'Ashtarkhānids,' who ruled in Mavarannahr from the 16th century to the 18th.[1] As noted there, available sources on the Chinggisid polity of Khwārazm during the same period do not expressly link the post of *naqīb* with the descendants of Sayyid Ata, and in fact offer far less information on the familial legacy of Sayyid Ata than we find in sources produced in Bukhara or Balkh. Yet Khwārazm clearly holds a central place in the development of traditions about Sayyid Ata, and is an important locus of the Sayyid Atāʾī legacy in terms of the saint's shrine, of his role in Sufi transmission, and of his folkloric

[1] "The Descendants of Sayyid Ata and the Rank of *Naqīb* in Central Asia," *Journal of the American Oriental Society*, 115 (1995), pp. 612-634.

impact; as we will see, moreover, Sayyid Atāʾī descent groups were also prominent in Khwārazm at least as early as such groups gained notoriety in Mavarannahr, and one important source, from the early 17th century, insists that the family indeed originated in Khwārazm, and spread to Mavarannahr only as a result of an internal quarrel.

The present contribution, offered in honor of one who has done so much to illuminate the history of Khwārazm, and of Central Asia in general, during the period in which the Sayyid Atāʾī legacy developed, is intended to explore the information we have, from various sources, on the activity of descendants of Sayyid Ata in Khwārazm during the 16th and early 17th centuries.

SAYYID ATA'S SHRINE IN KHWĀRAZM

The tradition that Sayyid Ata died in Khwārazm and was buried there provides one reasonable basis for assuming that his descendants would have dwelled in the same region; that tradition is not attested in our sources, however, until the 16th century. The earliest account of Sayyid Ata's Islamizing activity in the Jöchid *ulus* ends with the saint accompanying his convert-disciples from the Dasht-i Qïpchāq to Mavarannahr; in the best-known account of his place in the Yasavī *silsila*, in the *Rashaḥāt-i ʿayn al-ḥayāt*, Sayyid Ata is linked only with Bukhara (where he is said to have studied) and with Tashkent (where he was trained by Zangī Ata); and the scattered references to Sayyid Ata dating before the time of the *Rashaḥāt*'s account allude to his presence (posthumous, in one case) in various sites in Mavarannahr.[2] The story explicitly linking Sayyid Ata with the *amīr* Nanghidāy (or Naghaṭay, or Naghdāy), known from earlier sources as a prominent figure at Özbek Khān's court and as the ancestor of a lineage of rulers of Khwārazm known as the 'Qonghrat Sufi' dynasty, despite the likelihood of its historical basis, is not actually recorded until the work of the Khivan historian Muʾnis from the early 19th century.[3]

[2] See my survey of the sources on Sayyid Ata in "Atāʾīya," *Encyclopaedia Iranica*, II (fasc. 8, 1987), pp. 904-905; a fuller study of the Sayyid Atāʾī legacy, in the context of the Yasavī Sufi tradition, is in preparation.

[3] Shīr Muḥammad Mīrāb Munis and Muḥammad Rizā Mīrāb Āgahī, *Firdaws al-iqbāl: History of Khorezm*, ed. Yuri Bregel (Leiden: E. J. Brill, 1988), pp. 204-206; and now the English translation, Shir Muhammad Mirab Munis and Muhammad Riza Mirab Agahi, *Firdaws al-iqbāl: History of Khorezm*, tr. Yuri Bregel (Leiden: E. J. Brill, 1999), pp. 88-89. See also the discussion in my *Islamization and Native Religion in the Golden Horde: Baba Tükles and Conversion to Islam in*

To be sure, a Turkic hagiographical work focused primarily on the Yasavī saint Ḥakīm Ata—who is shown in standard presentations of the Yasavī *silsila* as the disciple of Aḥmad Yasavī and the master of Zangī Ata—does affirm that Sayyid Ata was buried near the shrine of Ḥakīm Ata, in the Khwārazmian locality known as Bāqïrghān. This work, known as the *Ḥakīm Ata kitābï*, first recounts how Sayyid Ata in effect usurped the position of *mujāvur* (caretaker) at Ḥakīm Ata's shrine, and then explains that upon Sayyid Ata's death, the spirits of Bāqïrghān struggled over his body with the spirits of the Kaᶜba; the spirits of Bāqïrghān were victorious, and so Sayyid Ata was buried there.[4] While the mythic quality of this story neither establishes nor precludes its antiquity, of course, its attestation of the simple fact of Sayyid Ata's burial at Bāqïrghān is significant. Nevertheless, the *Ḥakīm Ata kitābï* cannot be dated with any precision; it includes narratives that are quite old and can be traced in other sources datable to the 15th century, but in its extant form it can hardly be older than the end of the 17th century.

It is not until the middle of the 16th century that we find our first clearly datable references to Sayyid Ata's shrine in Khwārazm. Two hagiographical works devoted to the Kubravī saint Ḥusayn Khwārazmī refer to the latter's contemplative seclusions (in the late 15th century, before he met his principal master in the Kubravī *silsila*) at "Bāghïrghān Ata," where were found the shrines of Sayyid Ata, Ḥakīm Ata, and Ḥubbī Khwāja (the latter is identified, in the *Ḥakīm Ata kitābï*, as a son of Ḥakīm Ata). One work describes the site as extremely isolated, but notes that it had a well and a mosque, that it was always staffed with *mujāvur*s, and that many people came to it from Khwārazm (presumably meaning the city of Urgench, or perhaps simply the entire region of Khwārazm) in order to perform the circumambulation of the graves.[5]

Historical and Epic Tradition (University Park: Pennsylvania State University Press, 1994), pp. 102-103.

[4] K. G. Zaleman, "Legenda pro Khakim-Ata," *Izvestiia Akademii nauk* (St. Petersburg), 9/2 (1898), pp. 105-150 [pp. 119-122, narrative No. 11].

[5] The earlier of the two hagiographies, the *Miftāḥ al-ṭālibīn* (written by one of the shaykh's disciples), does little more than mention the saints buried at "Baqīrghān" (MS Aligarh Subhanallah 297.7/13, ff. 48a-b; in his description of one manuscript copy of this work, Bartol'd noted its mention of these shrines ["Otchet o komandirovke v Turkestan," *Sochineniia*, VIII (Moscow, 1973), p. 147]). The fuller description comes from the somewhat later *Jāddat al-ᶜāshiqīn*, written by a son of Ḥusayn Khwārazmī (MS Aligarh Subhanullah No. 297.71/1, ff. 27b-28a). On Ḥusayn Khwārazmī and the sources on his career, see my "The Eclipse of the Kubravīyah in Central Asia," *Iranian Studies*, 21/1-2 (1988), pp. 45-83 [pp. 69-74].

The shrines of Sayyid Ata and Ḥakīm Ata were also visited, in the mid-1550s, by the Ottoman admiral Sīdī ʿAlī Raʾīs, but his account does no more than mention them among the shrines of Khwārazm.[6]

The shrines at Bāqïrghān are mentioned in sources from subsequent centuries, and still exist, but it is undoubtedly of some significance that we first hear of them at approximately the same time that we begin to hear of families claiming descent from Sayyid Ata and residing near Bāqïrghān, as in the accounts reviewed below. While Sayyid Ata's own activity in Mavarannahr is reflected in 15th-century sources, as noted, and descendants of his living in that region are known from late Timurid times (though they are mentioned only in sources from the early 16th century), we find no tradition of comparable antiquity about a shrine or even *qadamgāh* (i.e., a place visited by a saint rather than his burial place) of Sayyid Ata anywhere in Mavarannahr; the identification of a shrine in old Paykand as that of Sayyid Ata's *son* is first attested only much later (in the 19th century), while another Sayyid Atāʾī burial ground in a village of Bukhara, mentioned in the 17th century, clearly owes its existence to the establishment of Sayyid Atāʾī families near Bukhara (an event that itself evoked explanatory anecdotes, one of which is noted below). It is thus reasonable, in such cases, to presume that a self-defined descent group took shape first, and only later established a shrine for its eponymous ancestor—a pattern especially prevalent, it would seem, when the descent group moves to a new region, away from the area in which it took shape, and seeks to mark its newly adopted space by, in effect, implanting its 'ancestor' in the new region as well; such a pattern is undoubtedly at work in the emergence of the shrine ascribed to Sayyid Ata's son in old Paykand.

On the other hand, a significant lapse of time between the attestation of a saint's shrine tradition and the mention of familial groups claiming descent from that saint may signal the likelihood of a later, retrospective construction of familial traditions, rooted in part in the benefits accruing to those who control the shrine;[7] we might thus argue that in some cases,

[6] *Mirʾāt al-mamālik*, ed. Aḥmad Jawdat (Istanbul, 1313/1895), p. 71; A. Vambéry, tr., *The Travels and Adventures of the Turkish Admiral Sidi Ali Reïs in India, Afghanistan, Central Asia, and Persia, during the Years 1553-1556* (London: Luzac & Co., 1899), p. 79.

[7] Such a scenario is argued, in connection with putative descent groups linked to Khwāja Aḥmad Yasavī, in my "The Politics of Sacred Lineages in 19th-Century Central Asia: Descent Groups linked to Khwaja Ahmad Yasavi in Shrine Documents and Genealogical Charters," *International Journal of Middle East Studies*, 31/4 (1999),

the emergence of descent-groups linked to a particular saint may depend on the prominence of the saint's shrine well before we hear of the saint's putative descendants. In the case of Bāqïrghān, however, the nearly simultaneous, and relatively early, attestations of a shrine tradition and of descent groups linked to Sayyid Ata may suggest a more deeply rooted tradition of Sayyid Ata's association with Bāqïrghān in Khwārazm;[8] and such a tradition, affirming also the Khwārazmian locus

---

pp. 507-530. In the present context it is important to note that we have much earlier attestation of descent groups linked to Sayyid Ata than we have in the case of descent groups linked to Aḥmad Yasavī.

[8] We may stress that *other* Sayyid Atā'ī centers in Khwārazm need not be of comparable antiquity, and may reflect the second of the patterns noted here. The specific tradition that Sayyid Ata himself built a Sufi *khānqāh* in a town of Khwārazm that came to be known for that reason as 'Khānqāh' (present-day 'Khanka,' east of Khiva), is evidently not recorded before the 19th century (it is mentioned in the hagiographical compendium of Mīr Musayyab Bukhārī, completed in 1263/1846-47, which survives in a single manuscript [No. 854] preserved in the collection of the Oriental Department at St. Petersburg University [described in A. T. Tagirdzhanov, *Opisanie tadzhikskikh i persidskikh rukopisei Vostochnogo otdela Biblioteki LGU*, t. I, Istoriia, biografii, geografiia (Leningrad: Izd-vo Leningradskogo Universiteta, 1962), pp. 362-368, No. 150], ff. 469b-470a); it undoubtedly reflects the presence of families claiming descent from Sayyid Ata in the region of Khanka (on these groups, see G. P. Snesarev, *Relikty domusul'manskikh verovanii i obriadov u uzbekov Khorezma* [Moscow: Nauka, 1969], p. 289). The Khivan historian Mu'nis, who was writing in the early 19th century, and who was well aware of the shrines of Sayyid Ata and Ḥakīm Ata in northern Khwārazm, near Qonghrat, mentioned also a *qadamgāh* of Sayyid Ata near Khānqāh (*Firdaws al-iqbāl*, ed. Bregel, pp. 667, 797-798 on the shrines in the north, p. 237 on the *qadamgāh*; tr. Bregel, pp. 310-311, 368, and p. 106); in an earlier Russian translation of this passage, the *qadamgāh* was misleadingly called the *mazār* of Sayyid Ata (*Materialy po istorii turkmen i Turkmenii*, t. II [*XVI-XIX vv., Iranskie, Bukharskie i Khivinskie istochniki*], ed. V. V. Struve, A. K. Borovkov, A. A. Romaskevich, and P. P. Ivanov [Moscow/Leningrad: Izd-vo AN SSSR, 1938], p. 342). It was also near the town of Khānqāh that a shrine, noted in 19th-century sources, was ascribed to Sayyid Muḥammad Māhrūy, who was by some accounts a son, and by others a grandson, of Sayyid Ata; it is mentioned by Mu'nis (*Firdaws al-iqbāl*, ed. Bregel, pp. 457, 695; tr. Bregel, pp. 222, 323), in an anonymous Turkic work written in 1228/1813, on the occasion of a grand assembly of Sufi communities in Khwārazm, convened by Qutluq Murād *ïnāq*, elder brother of the Khivan ruler Muḥammad Raḥīm Khān (*Risāla-i khalvat-i ṣūfīhā*, MS Tashkent, Institute of Oriental Studies of the Academy of Sciences of the Republic of Uzbekistan [Institut vostokovedeniia Akademii nauk Respubliki Uzbekistan, hereafter "IVANRUz"], No. 7610 [described in *Sobranie vostochnykh rukopisei Akademii nauk Uzbekskoi SSR*, 11 vols. (Tashkent, 1952-87; hereafter "*SVR*"), III, p. 381, No. 2720], p. 10), and in a 19th-century shrine guide for Khwārazm, written in Turkic verse (*Khwārazm taʿrīfi*,

of Sayyid Atāʾī familial origins, is found in an important 'internal' Sayyid Atāʾī source from the early 17th century.

THE LINEAGE OF SAYYID JAMĀL AL-DĪN

In many ways our most substantial source on the Sayyid Atāʾī legacy in Khwārazm is the *Manāqib al-akhyār*, a hagiographical work completed in 1036/1626, most likely in India, by Muḥammad Qāsim "Rivān;" the work deals with the life of the author's father, Sayyid Jamāl al-Dīn of Khwārazm, known as "Khwāja Dīvāna Sayyid Atāʾī" (d. 1016/1607). As I have discussed elsewhere,[9] this work recounts the Islamizing activity of Sayyid Ata himself, and traces a lineage of combined natural and spiritual descent down to Sayyid Jamāl al-Dīn: Sayyid Ata > Sayyid ʿAbdullāh Zarbakhsh > Sayyid Vilāyat Khwāja > Sayyid Quraysh Khwāja > Sayyid Ismāʿīl Khwāja > Sayyid Pādshāh Khwāja, known as "Parda-pūsh"[10] ('clothed in a veil') > Sayyid Jamāl

MS IVANRUz No. 7700 [uncatalogued], ff. 52b-53a) (on the relocation of this shrine to Khiva in 1304/1887, see the discussion in *Firdaws al-iqbāl*, tr. Bregel, pp. 620-621, n. 706). In addition to the former shrine of Muḥammad Māhrūy, a mosque of "Seid-Ata," said to date from 1179/1766, is found in the town of Khanka; see L. Man'kovskaia and B. Bulatova, *Pamiatniki zodchestva Khorezma* (Tashkent: Izd-vo Gafura Guliama, 1978), pp. 69, 134-135, ill. pp. 136-137, Nos. 126-129 (the authors mention a verse, carved on the gates of the mosque, dating the founding of the town of Khānqāh to 758/1357). The 19th-century shrine guide referred to above also mentions a shrine of "ʿAbdullāh Zarbakhsh," identified as a son of Sayyid Ata, in Kuhna Urgench (*Khwārazm taʿrīfi*, f. 75b; the shrine of Sayyid Ata himself is discussed in this work at ff. 81b-82a, 86b-88a). It is this same ʿAbdullāh Zarbakhsh (the 'son' of Sayyid Ata mentioned most prominently in genealogical materials recorded in Mavarannahr) who is said, in the 19th-century work of Mīr Musayyab, to have been buried in old Paykand.

[9] See my "A Neglected Source on Central Asian History: The 17th-Century Yasavī Hagiography *Manāqib al-akhyār*," in *Essays on Uzbek History, Culture, and Language*, ed. Denis Sinor and Bakhtiyar A. Nazarov (Bloomington: Research Institute for Inner Asian Studies, 1993; Uralic and Altaic Series, Vol. 156), pp. 38-50.

[10] This epithet might also be read "*burda-pūsh*," i.e., "wearing a mantle," alluding to the famous *burda* of the Prophet. However, while the two manuscripts of the *Manāqib al-akhyār* use both *bā* and *pā*, they clearly do not distinguish between them systematically, so that with reference to Sayyid Pādshāh Khwāja alone, his epithet appears in the forms "*burda-pūsh*," "*parda-pūsh*," and "*parda-būsh*" in the India Office copy, and always in the form "*parda-būsh*" in the Rampur copy (which writes his name always as "*bādshāh*"); the second element, of course, can only be "*pūsh*," and the most likely reading is "*parda-pūsh*" (MS India Office, Ethé 644 [described in Hermann Ethé,

al-Dīn. Little is said, in fact, about the lives of the intervening figures in this lineage, but the work clearly implies that all of them were active in Khwārazm; it affirms that Sayyid Ata himself died and was buried in Khwārazm (where his shrine, according to the author, was a popular pilgrimage site), and that Sayyid Jamāl al-Dīn's father, Sayyid Pādshāh Khwāja, was the spiritual guide of Khwārazm in the "*silsila-i jahrīya-i yasavīya.*"

The latter comment is of interest insofar as it leaves no doubt about the self-consciously "Yasavī" affiliation of this Sayyid Atā'ī lineage, at least by the 16th century; while it is plausible to suppose that the early Sayyid Atā'ī tradition emphasized natural descent from Sayyid Ata himself, rather than his somewhat tenuous *silsila* ties to Aḥmad Yasavī, as the key source of its spiritual legitimacy and social authority, and while the descendants of Sayyid Jamāl al-Dīn in India seem to have become known as Naqshbandī shaykhs (a development presaged, in some respects, in the *Manāqib al-akhyār*),[11] the community gathered around Sayyid Jamāl al-Dīn himself, and presumably his father as well, clearly regarded itself as being affiliated with the Yasavī *ṭarīqa.*

Sayyid Pādshāh Khwāja, we are told, was martyred during "the *fitna* of Shāh Ismāʿīl," referring to the Ṣafavid occupation of Khwārazm following the defeat and death of Muḥammad Shībānī Khān, when Sayyid Jamāl al-Dīn was only four months old;[12] this allows us to date the latter's birth to approximately 916/1510-11. From the work's account of Sayyid Jamāl al-Dīn's upbringing, we learn of the activity of other Sayyid Atā'ī descendants in Khwārazm; after his father died, Sayyid Jamāl al-Dīn was raised by a certain "Khwāja Bābā," identified as a disciple of Sayyid Pādshāh Khwāja, as a descendant of Sayyid Ata (though his specific lineage is not indicated), and as a native of Khwārazm. Despite his link, by kinship and by *silsila*, with the Sayyid

---

Catalogue of the Persian Manuscripts in the Library of the India Office, I (Oxford, 1903), cols. 268-270], ff. 14b, 31a; MS Rampur, *Sulūk fārsī* No. 724/*Tadhkirahs*, No. 2378 [not described in a published catalogue], ff. 18b, 39a).

[11] On the Naqshbandī influences evident in the *Manāqib al-akhyār*, see my "Neglected Source," pp. 41, 45, 49-50. Sayyid Jamāl al-Dīn himself, and a son and a grandson, are portrayed in late Indian sources as Naqshbandī shaykhs, in a Jūybārī lineage (clearly reflecting Jamāl al-Dīn's meetings with Jūybārī figures as mentioned in the *Manāqib al-akhyār* ["Neglected Source," pp. 46-47]); see Arthur F. Buehler, *Sufi Heirs of the Prophet: The Indian Naqshbandiyya and the Rise of the Mediating Sufi Shaykh* (Columbia: University of South Carolina Press, 1998), p. 65.

[12] MS India Office, ff. 14b-15a, 31a; MS Rampur, ff. 18b, 39a.

Atāʾī lineage that is the focus of the *Manāqib al-akhyār*, Khwāja Bābā also sought training in Sufism with the Naqshbandī shaykh Khwāja Aḥrār; he was joined in his service to Khwāja Aḥrār by his younger brother, Sayyid Muḥammad. When the two brothers were sent back by Khwāja Aḥrār to Sayyid Pādshāh Khwāja in Khwārazm, the account says, Sayyid Muḥammad attended to the training of his own disciples in an unidentified town of Khwārazm, while Khwāja Bābā sought seclusion in the desert. It was Khwāja Bābā, however, who raised Sayyid Jamāl al-Dīn, and Sayyid Muḥammad is not heard of again.

The account of Sayyid Jamāl al-Dīn's own career in the *Manāqib al-akhyār* focuses more on his travels elsewhere in Central Asia and India than it does in his time in Khwārazm. The work does mention, however, two figures from among the 'kings' or 'princes' of Khwārazm, referring to the 'ʿArabshāhid' dynastic clan of Chinggisid rulers, who were associated with Sayyid Jamāl al-Dīn. One was ʿAlī Sulṭān, identified as "among the kings (*mulūk*) of Khwārazm and Marv;" he is mentioned in connection with a campaign led against him, in the Dasht-i Khāvarān in Khurāsān, by "Imām Qulī Jūlāq," an *amīr* of Shāh Ṭahmāsb.[13] Sayyid Jamāl al-Dīn is credited with blessing ʿAlī Sulṭān, and with thwarting the surprise attack planned by the Qïzïlbash, thereby ensuring ʿAlī Sulṭān a decisive victory.

The ʿAlī Sulṭān mentioned in this account is clearly to be identified with the son of Avānish Khān (by a daughter of a Manghït *mīrzā*) who is mentioned prominently in the account of the Khwārazmian dynasty in the the Turkic *Shajarah-i Turk* by the Khwārazmian *khān* Abū'l-Ghāzī (d. 1074/1663).[14] When his father was killed in the course of the seizure of Urgench by the Shïbānid ruler of Mavarannahr, ʿUbaydullāh Khān, in 945/1538-39, ʿAlī Sulṭān took refuge with his elder brother Dīn Muḥammad in Khurāsān, in the region of Durūn, Nisā, and Abīvard, and remained there after ʿUbaydullāh's puppet-ruler in Urgench was driven out; he appears to have been based in the region of Nisā, indeed, for nearly twenty years, until, after siding with the victor in a later succession struggle that brought Ḥājjim Khān to power in 965/1558, he

[13] MS India Office, ff. 72a-b; MS Rampur, ff. 88a-89a.

[14] Abū'l-Ghāzī, *Histoire des Mongols et des Tatares par Aboul-Ghâzî Béhâdour Khan*, ed. & tr. P. I. Desmaisons (St. Petersburg, 1871-72; repr. Amsterdam: Philo Press, 1970), ed., pp. 212-213, 223-224, 230, 235, 243-248, 255; transl., pp. 228-229, 239-240, 246, 252, 260-265, 273. Cf. Muʾnis, *Firdaws al-iqbāl*, ed. Bregel, pp. 112-113, 120-122; tr. Bregel, pp. 32, 36-37.

was given Urgench as his appanage, and evidently moved there. Abū'l-Ghāzī also recounts the victory over Shāh Ṭahmāsb's forces to which the *Manāqib al-akhyār* evidently refers; his chronology is unfortunately unclear (since it is given in terms of the equally uncertain date of ʿAlī Sulṭān's death), but Ḥasan Rūmlū and Iskandar Munshī recount the same battle, dating it to 965/1557-58 (and place ʿAlī Sulṭān's death in 973/1565-66).[15] "Imām Qulī Jūlāq," however, is not mentioned by Abū'l-Ghāzī or by the Ṣafavid sources that mention this battle.

The other figure linked with the Khwārazmian rulers who is closely associated with Sayyid Jamāl al-Dīn is Shāh Qulī Sulṭān (from among the "*abnā-yi mulūk-i Khwārazm*"); this figure, portrayed as an actual disciple of the Sayyid Atā'ī shaykh, is said to have been in the service of the noted Yasavī master Qāsim Shaykh of Karmīna (d. 986/1579) before becoming a follower of Sayyid Jamāl al-Dīn, but his identification is complicated by the *Manāqib al-akhyār*'s affirmation that this Shāh Qulī Sulṭān was present at his shaykh's death, which occurred in Sūrat, in India, in 1016/1607.[16] The only "Shāh Qulī Sulṭān" mentioned in Abū'l-Ghāzī's work was a son of Īsh Sulṭān b. Būchughā Khān (Būchughā was a brother of Avānish Khān). Abū'l-Ghāzī says that Shāh Qulī and a brother were sent to Bukhara after their father was killed in the struggle for the throne with Ḥājjim Khān in 965/1558; he adds that both sons of Īsh Sulṭān died in Bukhara, but does not say when.[17] On the one hand Abū'l-Ghāzī's testimony lends credence to the association of Shāh Qulī with Qāsim Shaykh, whose activity was centered in Miyānkāl, but would seem to accord less well with the move to India implied for Shāh Qulī in the *Manāqib al-akhyār*. It is possible that his move was temporary, and that he did die in Bukhara after his return; or

[15] Ḥasan Rūmlū, *Aḥsanu't-tawārīkh*, ed. and tr. C. N. Seddon (Baroda: Oriental Institute, 1931-34; Gaekwad's Oriental Series, Nos. LVII, LXIX), vol. I (text), pp. 401-404, 429-430; vol. II (transl.), pp. 176-177, 186-187. Cf. Eskandar Monshi, *History of Shah ʿAbbas the Great*, tr. Roger M. Savory, I (Boulder, Colorado: Westview Press, 1978), pp. 179-181. On the chronological problems, see *Firdaws al-iqbāl*, tr. Bregel, p. 556, n. 201.

[16] MS India Office, ff. 55b, 119b; MS Rampur, ff. 69b-70a, 139a (in the second passage he is said to have been in Sayyid Jamāl al-Dīn's *khānqāh* just before his death, and to have been among the shaykh's disciples who performed the vocal *dhikr* on that occasion).

[17] Abū'l-Ghāzī, *Histoire des mongols et des tatares*, ed. Desmaisons, p. 236; tr., p. 253.

we might suppose that Abū'l-Ghāzī was simply unaware of the details of Shāh Qulī's fate after his departure from Khwārazm. On the other hand, it is also possible that the disciple of Sayyid Jamāl al-Dīn was another, even more obscure, member of the Khwārazmian Chinggisid dynastic clan.

The *Manāqib al-akhyār*, naturally, follows the Sayyid Atāʾī tradition that is its focus away from Khwārazm. Its value lies not only in the specific information it provides on Sayyid Atāʾī groups in Khwārazm and elsewhere, but in its portrayal of an essentially hereditary Sufism, with a combined natural and spiritual descent line in the Sayyid Atāʾī lineage, that was nevertheless taking on the trappings of a more typical, non-hereditary, *silsila*-based *ṭarīqa*. A similar picture—of genealogy and *silsila* coinciding, though with considerably less evidence of the institutional or organizational aspects of hereditary Sufism—is presented in a somewhat earlier source, from Bukhara, to which we may now turn.

SAYYID VILĀYAT KHWĀJA AND THE LINEAGE OF SAYYID ʿUTHMĀN

Additional information on Sayyid Atāʾī shaykhs of Khwārazm from the 16th century is found in the *Adhkār al-azkiyā*, a little-known hagiographical compendium produced some 40 years before the *Manāqib al-akhyār*; completed in 993/1584 by Mīr Sayyid Muḥammad, known as Mīr Sivinchī al-Sāmānī (d. 1024/1615), and dedicated to ʿAbdullāh Khān b. Iskandar, the work is an especially important source on Yasavī, Kubravī, and ʿIshqī shaykhs from a period marked by the increasing dominance of Naqshbandī groups.[18]

The *Adhkār al-azkiyā* includes entries focused on a father and son of Sayyid Atāʾī lineage, clearly linked to Khwārazm. The father, Sayyid Vilāyat Khwāja Bāqïrghānī,[19] is portrayed as a contemporary of the Shïbānid ruler ʿUbaydullāh Khān (r. 940-946/1534-1539), and the account of him includes an anecdote noting ʿUbaydullāh's contrition (and

[18] The *Adhkār al-azkiyā* is described only in *SVR*, XI, pp. 364-365, Nos. 7567-7568; citations are to MS IVANRUz No. 7582/III (ff. 84b-244b [Cat. No. 7568]), a full copy completed in 1168/1755. The work was discussed in the introduction to M. A. Salakhetdinova's translation of the principal history of ʿAbdullāh Khān, the *Sharaf-nāmah-i shāhī* of Ḥāfiẓ Tanïsh Bukhārī (Khafiz-i Tanysh Ibn Mir Mukhammad Bukhari, *Sharaf-nama-ii shakhi (Kniga shakhskoi slavy)*, tr. M. A. Salakhetdinova, I [Moscow: Nauka, 1983], pp. 6-7).

[19] *Adhkār al-azkiyā*, MS IVANRUz No. 7582, ff. 137a-138a.

suitable supplicatory offering) after initially snubbing the shaykh; another anecdote tells how Sayyid Vilāyat Khwāja exerted his spiritual powers, while in contemplation at a local shrine, to induce the chief of a band of thieves who had plundered the *sayyid*'s property to return his things; when the chief relented, Sayyid Vilāyat Khwāja forgave him, but the damage was already done, and within a week the man, his wife, and his children all died.

Both these wonders, we are told, increased the devotion and discipleship of "the people of that region" to Sayyid Vilāyat Khwāja. Unfortunately, despite the Khwārazmian *nisba* assigned to him—Bāqïrghānī—the "region" in question is not identified, and we cannot be certain where this Sayyid Atā'ī shaykh was active. The story involving ʿUbaydullāh Khān might suggest that Sayyid Vilāyat Khwāja had moved to the Shïbānid domains in Mavarannahr; on the other hand, as noted, ʿUbaydullāh campaigned in Khwārazm in 945/1538-39, defeating Avānish Khān and briefly installing his own son ʿAbd al-ʿAzīz as ruler, and it is possible that the anecdote—which offers no details of when or where the encounter occurred—might refer to ʿUbaydullāh's time in Khwārazm. The account in the *Adhkār al-azkiyā* offers only two other clues: it says that Sayyid Vilāyat Khwāja dwelled in Khwārazm "at the beginning," implying that he did move elsewhere at some point; and it affirms that he was buried in "Qïshlāq," a seemingly generic designation that in all likelihood, however, refers to the locality known as "Qïshlāq-i Kalān," near Bukhara, which as we will see is described, as early as the latter 17th century, as the hereditary burial ground of a particular Sayyid Atā'ī lineage. The mention of Sayyid Vilāyat Khwāja's burial place is also of some significance in connection with a story from the *Manāqib al-akhyār*, discussed below, explaining the origins of the Sayyid Atā'ī 'diaspora,' outside Khwārazm; in any case, while it seems clear that he ended his life outside Khwārazm, we are left unable to judge even approximately when Sayyid Vilāyat Khwāja might have moved from Khwārazm to Bukhara.

The *Adhkār al-azkiyā* says that Sayyid Vilāyat Khwāja left as his posterity "many Sayyid Atā'ī *sayyid*s." It names only one of them, however, his son Sayyid Hidāyat Khwāja Bāqïrghānī, who still appears to have been closely linked with Khwārazm.[20] The account of Sayyid Hidāyat Khwāja declares that he enjoyed the complete confidence and

[20] *Adhkār al-azkiyā*, MS IVANRUz No. 7582, ff. 214a-215b.

devotion of "the people of Khwārazm and Manghïshlāq," suggesting the well-attested pattern of communal affiliation linking both nomadic and sedentary communities with hereditary shaykhs. One anecdote relates his aid in finding property lost by a person from Manghïshlāq, and affirms that the people of that region were his devoted disciples; another anecdote, about a devotee of the *sayyid* from Bāvard, makes it clear that Sayyid Hidāyat Khwāja maintained a *khānqāh* in Manghïshlāq. The latter comment is important for confirming the Sufi activity of Sayyid Hidāyat Khwāja, in addition to his purely hereditary function as leader of his Sayyid Atāʾī lineage; the *Adhkār al-azkiyā*, indeed, explicitly states that Sayyid Hidāyat Khwāja was a disciple of his father, and that he "maintained the *ṭarīq* of his ancestors" for nearly 50 years. The account cites comments by Qāsim Shaykh of Karmīna (the chief Yasavī shaykh of the time, mentioned above), in praise of him, and affirms that someone who lived as Sayyid Hidāyat Khwāja did for 50 years—steadfast in prayer, with his sanctity clear to everyone—"would certainly not have been without a connection to sainthood, even though the status of saint (*manṣab-i vilāyat*) was hereditary for him." The comment highlights the presumed tension between hereditary shaykh-hood and the spiritual qualities expected of an authentic shaykh; it not only implies that the two can be combined, but insists that they were in the person of Sayyid Hidāyat Khwāja.

The account of Sayyid Hidāyat Khwāja Bāqïrghānī in the *Adhkār al-azkiyā* gives his natural lineage, starting with his father, as follows: Sayyid Vilāyat Khwāja < Sayyid ʿUthmān Khwāja < Sayyid ʿUmar Khwāja < Sayyid Muḥammad Shahīd < Sayyid ʿAlāʾ al-Dīn Pārsā < Sayyid ʿAbdullāh Zarbakhsh < the holy *quṭb al-aqṭāb* Sayyid Aḥmad, known as the holy Ata; "and the holy Sayyid Ata goes back to the holy Prophet through 23 intermediaries." The lineage thus 'branches' from the one claimed by Sayyid Jamāl al-Dīn, and recorded in the *Manāqib al-akhyār*, already with the grandsons of Sayyid Ata: both share descent from the latter's son Sayyid ʿAbdullāh Zarbakhsh, but the lineage leading to Sayyid Vilāyat Khwāja and Sayyid Hidāyat Khwāja stems from Sayyid ʿAlāʾ al-Dīn Pārsā, while the lineage traced in the *Manāqib al-akhyār* stems from another Sayyid Vilāyat Khwāja.[21]

[21] In this case the coincidence of this name's appearance in both lineages should most likely not lead us to assume a conflation of genealogies, since the Sayyid Vilāyat Khwāja known from the *Adhkār al-azkiyā* must have been a contemporary of Sayyid Jamāl al-Dīn's father, Sayyid Pādshāh Khwāja, who is shown as a great-grandson of that lineage's 'Sayyid Vilāyat Khwāja;' however, it is likely that the genealogy reflected in the *Manāqib al-akhyār* has been telescoped, with some generations omitted

The information provided on these two saints of Bāqïrghān in the *Adhkār al-azkiyā* is relatively sparse, but is nevertheless valuable for providing a key link with two other isolated references to the lineage of Sayyid Vilāyat Khwāja in sources from the 16th and 17th centuries.

One of these references appears in the *Mudhakkir-i aḥbāb*, the poetic *tadhkira* of Sayyid Ḥasan 'Nithārī' Bukhārī, completed in 974/1566; at the end of this work, Nithārī includes brief notices on members of his own family, who traced their ancestry through Zangī Ata—the saint usually shown as Sayyid Ata's master in the Yasavī *silsila*—back to Aḥmad Yasavī's enigmatic 'patron,' Bāb Arslān. In this section Nithārī mentions that one of his cousins, Mīrim Khwāja (the son of Nithārī's paternal uncle Shaykh ʿAlī Khwāja), was, on his mother's side, among the grandsons (*aḥfād*, a term that might also mean simply 'descendants') of "the exemplar of the *sayyid*s, Sayyid ʿUthmān Khwāja Sayyid Atāʾī;" Nithārī does not give us a clear idea of where Mīrim Khwāja lived (several members of the family discussed by Nithārī dwelled in Khurāsān, near Nisā, in the south of present-day Turkmenistan, while others were active in and around Bukhara), but in any case he affirms that Mīrim Khwāja was buried "near his maternal uncle, Sayyid Vilāyat Khwāja."[22] Nithārī's comment corroborates the genealogical presentation from the *Adhkār al-azkiyā*, affirming Sayyid ʿUthmān Khwāja as the father of Vilāyat Khwāja, with the latter's sister, and ʿUthmān's daughter, marrying Shaykh ʿAlī Khwāja; that marriage is of further interest as the union of the natural lineages of Sayyid Ata and Zangī Ata.[23] It is unfortunate that Nithārī does not indicate *where* Mīrim

---

after Sayyid ʿAbdullāh Zarbakhsh (most likely the earlier generations), leaving the possibility that the two lineages branched somewhat later.

[22] See the older edition, *Mudhakkir-i-Aḥbāb ("Remembrancer of Friends") of Khwāja Bahā al-Dīn Ḥasan Nithārī Bukhārī*, ed. Syed Muhammad Fazlullah (Hyderabad: Osmania University, Da'iratu'l-Maʿarif Press, 1969), pp. 513-514; and the new edition, Sayyid Ḥasan Khwāja Naqīb al-Ashrāf Bukhārī, "Nithārī," *Mudhakkir-i aḥbāb (Adab va farhang-i fārsī dar qarn-i dahum-i hijrī)*, ed. Najīb Māyil Haravī (Tehran: Nashr-i Markaz, 1377/1999), p. 308.

[23] According to Nithārī, moreover, Shaykh ʿAlī Khwāja was also descended himself, on his mother's side, from "Sayyid Mīr Jalāl al-Dīn Gurlānī" (both editors of the *Mudhakkir-i aḥbāb* [ed. Haravī, p. 304; ed. Fazlullah, p. 503] have opted for "Kirmānī" as the proper reading of this figure's *nisba*, with Fazlullah alone noting the variant "*k.r.lānī*" as a variant appearing in two manuscripts, including the oldest, that he consulted; the reading "*k.r.lānī*," however, reflects the name of the Khwārazmian locality now known as Gürlen, and is clearly to be preferred). This Jalāl al-Dīn is of interest for several reasons. His name and *nisba* clearly recall the name of a Ḥanafī

Khwāja and Sayyid Vilāyat Khwāja were buried, but his account is in accord with the chronological indications of the *Adhkār al-azkiyā*, placing Sayyid Vilāyat Khwāja in the early 16th century, and his father, Sayyid ᶜUthmān Khwāja, roughly at the end of the 15th century and the beginning of the 16th.

The other reference is not to Sayyid Vilāyat Khwāja himself, but to the figure identifiable as his father on the basis of both the *Adhkār al-azkiyā* and the *Mudhakkir-i aḥbāb*, and comes from the *Manāqib al-akhyār.* The latter work occasionally refers to Sayyid Atāʾī figures outside the lineage claimed by Sayyid Jamāl al-Dīn, and includes one story involving two such figures, portrayed as brothers, one of whom is called Sayyid ᶜUthmān; the story is told without any chronological indicators, but the likely identity of Sayyid ᶜUthmān's brother likewise points to the late 15th century, and the beginning of the 16th.

The story is told with the aim of explaining the establishment of Sayyid Atāʾī lineages outside the ancestral homeland of Khwārazm; it is of special importance in connection with our later genealogical accounts of the lineages traced to Sayyid Ata, focused on his descendants active in Mavarannahr. According to the account,[24] two brothers among the descendants of Sayyid Ata, Sayyid ᶜUthmān and Sayyid Ḥusām al-Dīn, fell into discord and contention with one another, leading Sayyid Ḥusām al-Dīn to declare to his brother that "henceforth your descendants will

---

jurist of Khwārazm who died in the early 14th century, and who is portrayed, in a Khwārazmian 'family history' from the 18th century, as having married the daughter of a Yasavī saint known as Sharaf Ata, whose Sufi tradition he also transmitted ("*Nasab-nāma-i Qāżī Khwāja Khān maᶜa barādarānish,*" MS IVANRUz No. 8707 [*SVR*, VI, pp. 59-60, No. 4202], ff. 197a-201a); the appellation "Sharaf Ata" is essentially the same, semantically, as that of "Sayyid Ata." From the union of Gurlānī and the daughter of Sharaf Ata was born a figure who is assigned, in that family history, the *nisba* "Manzilkhānī," and this in turn recalls the name of "Jalāl al-Dīn of Manzilkhāna," who is portrayed in the *Ḥakīm Atā kitābï* as the *mujāvur* at Ḥakīm Ata's shrine in Bāqïrghān who was in effect ousted upon Sayyid Ata's arrival there (Zaleman, "Legenda," pp. 119-121, narrative 11; on the Khwārazmian toponym "Manzilkhān," see *Firdaws al-iqbāl*, tr. Bregel, p. 608, n. 593). The Ḥanafī jurist Jalāl al-Dīn Kurlānī is also cited in a Yasavī source from the early 17th century (the *Lamaḥāt min nafaḥāt al-quds*) as a proponent of the legitimacy of the vocal *dhikr*, the hallmark of Yasavī (and, according to the *Manāqib al-akhyār*, of Sayyid Atāʾī) Sufi practice. Nithārī also notes that his uncle Sayyid ᶜAlī Khwāja inherited, through his mother, a *khirqa* that had belonged to the Prophet himself, and that the *sulṭān*s and *khān*s of his time used to come to see the holy relic.

24 *Manāqib al-akhyār*, MS India Office, Ethé 644, f. 19b; MS Rampur, ff. 24a-b.

not be allowed at the hill (*pushta*) of Bāghïrghan Ata." And since then, the account continues, "whenever they buried one of the descendants of Sayyid ʿUthmān on that hill, the earth would cast out his bier, so that after repeated attempts, they despaired of that ground, and, choosing exile, took up residence in every abode and country."

The story does not appear to be reflected in other sources. In general, of course, it highlights the importance of the ancestral shrine in the communal cohesion of a descent group such as the Sayyid Atāʾī *sayyids*; but whether we assume that the story was developed to account for a move by some Sayyid Atāʾī lineages away from Khwārazm, or we assume instead that it reflects the emergence of rival familial claimants, in different localities, to the Sayyid Atāʾī legacy, it masks these social developments through a reported conflict between two separate lineages, one traced through Sayyid ʿUthmān—whose descendants, we are told, eventually had to be buried elsewhere—and the other traced through Sayyid Ḥusām al-Dīn—whose descendants, presumably, maintained their connection with Bāqïrghān.

If the "Sayyid ʿUthmān" of this story is indeed the father of Sayyid Vilāyat Khwāja, as seems likely, we have in the narrative an explanation for the 'expulsion,' in effect, of Sayyid ʿUthmān and his lineage from the ancestral Sayyid Atāʾī homeland. This seems to be borne out, on the one hand, by what little information we have regarding Sayyid ʿUthmān's son and grandson; even though the *Adhkār al-azkiyā* continues to assign both Vilāyat Khwāja and his son Hidāyat Khwāja the *nisba* "Bāqïrghānī," it also confirms, as we have seen, that Vilāyat Khwāja was buried outside Khwārazm, and that Hidāyat Khwāja maintained a *khānqāh* in Mangïshlāq, far to the west of Bāqïrghān (as for Sayyid ʿUthmān himself, we have no early information regarding his burial place, but it may be significant that a shrine known as that of "Usman-Seid-bobo" is found near the town of Gurlen—in Khwārazm, to be sure, but well to the southeast of Bāqïrghān[25]).

Of perhaps greater significance is the genealogical tradition reflecting the lineage of Sayyid ʿUthmān. The Sayyid Atāʾī genealogy given in the *Adhkār al-azkiyā* is reflected quite clearly (though in 'updated' form, to include subsequent generations) in two later

[25] Man'kovskaia and Bulatova, *Pamiatniki zodchestva Khorezma*, p. 156, with illustration [p. 155]; cf. L. Iu. Man'kovskaia, "Neizvestnye pamiatniki arkhitektury Khorezma," *Stroitel'stvo i arkhitektura Uzbekistana*, 1970, No. 10, pp. 32-34.

hagiographical compendiums, the *Thamarāt al-mashā'ikh*, from the late 17th century (where it is drawn from a *nasab-nāma* belonging to a great-great-great grandson of Sayyid ʿUthmān who was a contemporary of the *Thamarāt*'s author), and in the *Tadhkira-i Ṭāhir Īshān* from the middle of the 18th century. Both these accounts reflect the Bukharan Sayyid Atāʾī lineages that gained prominence in the Shībānid and Ashtarkhānid courts, as well as in Sufi circles, in the 16th and 17th centuries; the work of Ṭāhir Īshān links the Sayyid Atāʾī lineage its genealogical outline follows with the Bukharan locality of Qïshlāq-i Kalān—the toponym echoed, as we have seen, in the *Adhkār al-azkiyā*, already, as the site of Sayyid Vilāyat Khwāja's grave—while the *Thamarāt*, in addition to mentioning several representatives of this lineage buried in Qïshlāq-i Kalān, explicitly affirms that Qïshlāq-i Kalān is well-known for "the shrines (*mazārāt*) of the descendants of the holy Sayyid Ata."[26]

These two sources say nothing about a Sayyid Ḥusām al-Dīn, the ancestor of the lineage that remained, as the *Manāqib al-akhyār* implies, in Khwārazm. Somewhat later accounts, however, do include such a figure in their genealogical presentations of the Sayyid Atāʾī family, portraying him not as a brother, but as an uncle, of Sayyid ʿUthmān; they appear in the hagiographical compendium of Mīr Musayyab Bukhārī, referred to above, from the mid-19th century, and in the *Tuḥfat al-zāʾirīn*, a guide to the shrines of Bukhara compiled by Nāṣir al-Dīn Töre b. Amīr Muẓaffar al-Dīn in 1324/1906. These works cite, in turn, two apparently independent, and now evidently lost, genealogical works on Sayyid Atāʾī lineages compiled in the late 18th century and the early 19th.[27] These sources, while late, attest not only to an apparently

[26] Sayyid Zindah-ʿAlī al-Muftī b. ʿAzīzān Khwāja Mīr al-Ḥusaynī al-Qāsimī al-Bukhārī, *Thamarāt al-mashā'ikh*, MS IVANRUz No. 2619/II (*SVR*, III, p. 353, No. 2669), ff. 201b-202b, 571a-b; *Tadhkirah-i Ṭāhir Īshān*, MS IVANRUz No. 855 (*SVR*, III, pp. 364-365, No. 2694), f. 67b.

[27] Mīr Musayyab, ff. 473a-b; Nāṣir al-Dīn Töre, *Tuḥfat al-zāʾirīn* (lithograph, Bukhara, 1328/1909), p. 88. Mīr Musayyab cites a treatise by one of Sayyid Ata's descendants written in 1200/1785-86, and later mentions Sayyid ʿAbd al-Raḥīm, the son of Sayyid Hāshim Khwāja Naqīb (who served as *naqīb* in Bukhara during the reign of the Ashtarkhānid Abū'l-Fayż Khān [r. 1123-1169/1711-1747]), as the author of a "*Risālah-i ansāb-i Sayyid Atā*" (Mīr Musayyab, ff. 473a, 474a). In the *Tuḥfat al-zāʾirīn* we find mention of a work referred to as the "*Favāʾid-i muntaja*," and later called the "*Manāqib-i Ḥażrat-i Sayyid Atā*," said to have been compiled in the time of Amīr Ḥaydar (r. 1215-1242/1800-1825) "on the order of Sayyid Aḥmad Khwāja Naqīb" (lith., pp. 85, 90; on this Sayyid Aḥmad Khwāja, see my "Descendants of Sayyid Ata," pp. 623-624). Mīr Musayyab, further, explicitly states that Sayyid ʿUthmān, the ancestor of the lineage reflected in the Sayyid Atāʾī genealogy that served

ongoing tradition of genealogical texts produced within Sayyid Atāʾī lineages (at least within those based by then in Bukhara), but also to much the same bifurcation of the Sayyid Atāʾī lineage that is reflected in the story from the *Manāqib al-akhyār*, with the descendants of Sayyid Ḥusām al-Dīn remaining in Khwārazm, in Bāqïrghān, and those of his brother, or nephew, Sayyid ʿUthmān, establishing themselves in Bukhara.

THE LINEAGE OF SAYYID ḤUSĀM AL-DĪN

The Khwārazmian side of this purported familial schism is unfortunately less fully known from genealogical and hagiographical sources identified to date, but we do have some information that accords well with the anecdote from *Manāqib al-akhyār*, and with the brief 'Bukharan' genealogies recorded near the end of the 18th century. The Sayyid Ḥusām al-Dīn mentioned in the story from the *Manāqib al-akhyār* is clearly suitable, by name and chronology and location, for identification with a prominent Sayyid Atāʾī shaykh, called "Ḥusām al-Dīn Qattāl," mentioned in Abū'l-Ghāzī's *Shajara-i Turk*. There we learn of the pivotal role played by this Ḥusām al-Dīn in establishing a separate Uzbek dynasty in Khwārazm and ending the region's occupation by troops of the Ṣafavid Shāh Ismāʿīl.[28]

According to Abū'l-Ghāzī, following the death of Muḥammad Shïbānī Khān in the battle with Shāh Ismāʿīl at Marv in 916/1510, the victorious Ṣafavids installed governors in several Khwārazmian localities, and the governor sent to the town of Vazīr arranged a great feast to win over the local elite; the *qāżī*, a certain ʿUmar,[29] however,

---

as his source, was buried in Qïshlāq-i Kalān, and that "most of his descendants" are taken there for burial as well.

[28] Abū'l-Ghāzī, *Histoire des mongols et des tatares*, ed. Desmaisons, pp. 195-197, tr., pp. 209-212; cf. my "Atāʾīya Order," and "Neglected Source," p. 44. Ḥusām al-Dīn Qattāl is mentioned by Muʾnis as well (*Firdaws al-iqbāl*, ed. Bregel, p. 106; tr. Bregel, pp. 27-28), in a much-abbreviated account.

[29] This Qāżī ʿUmar is not identified more fully by Abū'l-Ghāzī, and is never actually linked in any way with Ḥusām al-Dīn Qattāl Sayyid Atāʾī (beyond the two figures' participation, at different phases, in the events leading to the ouster of the Qïzïlbāsh from Khwārazm). It is worth noting, however, that the Sayyid Atāʾī genealogy presented in Mīr Musayyab's work, which casts Sayyid ʿUthmān as a *nephew* of Sayyid Ḥusām al-Dīn, calls Sayyid ʿUthmān's father (and Sayyid Ḥusām al-Dīn's brother) "Sayyid ʿUmar," and ascribes *him* the epithet "Qattāl-Qūl," explaining that Sayyid ʿUmar received this appellation after accidentally killing his father with a

declined to attend, and when the other notables of Vazīr spoke with him privately, Qāżī ʿUmar startled them by congratulating them on the fine clothes presented by the new governor, and on "your new religion." When they asked what he meant by the latter comment, Qāżī ʿUmar explained that their new *pādshāh*, Shāh Ismāʿīl, and their new governor adhered to a corrupt *madhhab*, and that although they were now weak in number, they would eventually require the people of Khwārazm, beginning with the notables, to curse the Companions of the Prophet, thus turning them into infidels.

The notables of Vazīr agreed with Qāżī ʿUmar's words, the account continues, but were unable to do anything for "a year or two;" then, however, several of them went to Bāqïrghān and appealed to Ḥusām al-Dīn Qattāl, who we are told was "a good man" (*bir yakhshï kishi*) from the lineage of Sayyid Ata, saying, "We shall make you *pādshāh* and crush the Qïzïlbāsh." Ḥusām al-Dīn declined their offer, citing the vagaries of public support—the people might consent to his rulership today, he said, but might well change their minds later. "If you want to do this properly," he continued, "I will find a good *pādshāh* for you, of royal lineage." The men from Vazīr asked whom he had in mind, and "the *khwāja*" (i.e., Ḥusām al-Dīn)—who we are told had traveled in the Dasht-i Qïpchāq[30] in order to gather offerings among the Uzbeks—told them about Īlbārs Khān (who belonged to a Chinggisid lineage that branched from the line leading to the 'Shïbānids' of Mavarannahr two generations before the latter group's ancestor, Abū'l-Khayr Khān); then two men from Vazīr accompanied one of Ḥusām al-Dīn's followers, who bore a letter from the Sayyid Atāʾī *khwāja*, to present their appeal to Īlbārs Khān himself. Īlbārs and his younger brother Bālbārs accepted the offer and came to Vazīr, where the local people, learning of their

stray arrow shot, and that his descendants were therefore referred to collectively as the "*khwājagān-i padar-kush*," i.e., "the patricidal *khwājas*" (Mīr Musayyab, ff. 473a-b). The account preserved by Mīr Musayyab gives no basis for identifying the same Sayyid ʿUmar as a *qāżī*, but it is possible that Abū'l-Ghāzī's narrative might echo a memory of the involvement of both 'sides' of the Sayyid Atāʾī familial schism in Khwārazmian politics during the early 16th century; it seems certain, in any case, that the genealogical tradition preserved in Mīr Musayyab's work reflects the same familial schism reflected also in the *Manāqib al-akhyār*, but with a somewhat different 'explanation,' implicitly, of the origin of the antagonism.

[30] The account says literally that he had traveled "to the *ārqā*," using the common name for the northerly region from which the Uzbeks had moved south; cf. B. Kh. Karmysheva and Dzh. Kh. Karmysheva, "Chto takoe Arka-iurt? (K istoricheskoi geografii Kazakhstana)," *Onomastika Vostoka* (Moscow: Nauka, 1980), pp. 108-114.

arrival, massacred the Qïzïlbāsh garrison and acknowledged their submission to Īlbārs; the latter was proclaimed *khān*, and soon seized Urgench and the other towns of Khwārazm as well, driving out the Ṣafavid forces.

Abū'l-Ghāzī tells us no more about Ḥusām al-Dīn Qattāl Sayyid Atāʾī, and we know nothing of his fate following the expulsion of the Qïzïlbāsh; unfortunately we have no other unequivocal references to this figure in any other early source,[31] and we cannot yet trace the familial legacy, in Khwārazm, of the Sayyid Ḥusām al-Dīn who is mentioned in the late Bukharan genealogical works with the same detail as is possible for the Bukharan Sayyid Atāʾī lineages. Those same late sources, however, do mention that Sayyid Ḥusām al-Dīn had a son named

[31] It is possible that the Ḥusām al-Dīn Qattāl mentioned by Abū'l-Ghāzī may be identified further with a "Ḥusāmī" or "Ḥusāmī Dīvāna," mentioned sporadically, in sources from the 16th century to the 19th, as a poet linked with the region of Khwārazm. Nithārī, already, includes an account of "Ḥusāmī Dīvāna," affirming that he was a native of Khīvaq and was buried in Qarākūl (*Mudhakkir*, ed. Fazlullah, pp. 160-163; ed. Haravī, pp. 86-87); Nithārī includes an anecdote illustrating this Ḥusāmī's disdain for worldly power, and adds that he was suspected of Shīʿism but praised the four Caliphs in his verse (this detail might seem to conflict with Abū'l-Ghāzī's account of Ḥusām ad-Dīn Qattāl's hostility to Qïzïlbāsh Shīʿism, but the mere accusation of Shīʿite sympathies may show simply that Ḥusāmī had enemies willing to level that charge against him). We find scattered references to the poet Ḥusāmī in 17th-century Central Asian sources, but the fullest account of his life comes only in the 19th-century *Riyāż al-ʿārifīn* of Riżā Qulī Khān "Hidāyat;" this work affirms that "Ḥusāmī Khwārazmī" died in Qarākūl in 923/1517, and that he was also known as Ḥusāmī Qarākūlī because of his long residence there. The account also stresses his poverty and disdain for worldly power, and ascribes to him an encounter with "Muḥammad Khān Shïbānī" (Riżā Qulī Khān "Hidāyat," *Riyāż al-ʿārifīn*, ed. Mihr-ʿAlī Garkānī [Tehran: Kitābfurūshī-i Maḥmūdī, 1344/1965], p. 307). A 19th-century manuscript of a poetic *Dīvān* of "Mawlānā Ḥusāmī Khīvaqī," preserved in Tashkent (MS IVANRUz No. 159/IV, ff. 31a-62a, described at *SVR*, II, p. 195, No. 1212), unfortunately contains no helpful historical allusions that might support or preclude an identification with Abū'l-Ghāzī's Ḥusām al-Dīn. We need not insist that Abū'l-Ghāzī's portrayal of Ḥusām al-Dīn residing in Bāqïrghān, in northern Khwārazm, necessarily precludes activity on his part with Khīvaq (in southeastern Khwārazm) or even Qarākūl (near Bukhara), but the failure of any of our sources on the poet Ḥusāmī even to hint at his Sayyid Atāʾī lineage suggests that two separate figures were intended; on the other hand, his descent might well have been ignored in the poetic venues that led to Ḥusāmī's occasional mention in other sources. In the end we cannot be sure that the brief accounts of the poet Ḥusāmī allude to the same "good man" whom Abū'l-Ghāzī calls "Ḥusām al-Dīn Qattāl" and identifies as a descendant of Sayyid Ata.

"Sayyid Nāṣir," and assuming that the father is indeed to be identified with Abū'l-Ghāzī's "Ḥusām al-Dīn Qattāl," the son is undoubtedly to be identified with the "Sayyid Nāṣir Khwāja Sayyid Atāʾī" of Khwārazm mentioned in several 16th century sources.

Two works from the early 16th century register the intercession of Sayyid Nāṣir Khwāja Sayyid Atāʾī for a Khwārazmian town besieged by Muḥammad Shībānī Khān in 891/1486 (well before his successful conquest of Khwārazm some 20 years later); the town had been surrounded shortly after the *khān* was compelled to withdraw from his attempt on Urgench itself by the news that Sulṭān Ḥusayn Bāyqarā had dispatched a large army to deal with the threat to his Khwārazmian territories. According to the Turkic *Tavārīkh-i guzīda-i nuṣrat-nāma*, the people of the besieged town, called Būldūm Sāz,[32] appealed to Sayyid Nāṣir Khwāja, a descendant of Sayyid Ata (*sayyid atā ʿalayhi'l-raḥma-ning oghlï sayyid nāṣir khwāja*), prepared gifts, including the horses belonging to the town's Timurid governor and "the falcons that Sulṭān Ḥusayn Mīrzā had sent from Khwārazm," and sent them to the *khān*, thereby saving themselves and their town.[33] According to the shorter account found in a Persian history of the *khān*'s conquests written by Kamāl al-Dīn Bināʾī, Sayyid Nāṣir, one of the descendants of Sayyid Ata (*az awlād-i sayyid atā*), was sent out to the *khān* bearing "suitable gifts and one falcon" (*pīshkash-hā-yi lāʾiq va yak shunqār*), and the town was thus spared.[34]

The Sayyid Atāʾī "Sayyid Nāṣir" mentioned in these accounts as an intercessor is almost certainly to be identified with the "Sayyid Nāṣir Khwāja Sayyid Atāʾī" who is mentioned, in a quite different light, in the *Jāddat al-ʿāshiqīn*, the hagiography, cited earlier, devoted to the Kubravī shaykh Ḥusayn Khwārazmī; Sayyid Nāṣir Khwāja is mentioned there in connection with what was clearly a quite bitter conflict between the Sayyid Atāʾī shaykh and Ḥusayn Khwārazmī, and the account offers a

[32] On the two sites in Khwārazm known by this designation, see *Firdaws al-iqbāl*, tr. Bregel, p. 604, n. 529.

[33] See the facsimiles published by A. M. Akramov, *Tavarikh-i guzīda-Nuṣrat-nāme* [*sic*] (Tashkent: Fan, 1967), pp. 278-279, and the translation in *Materialy po istorii kazakhskikh khanstv XV-XVIII vekov (Izvlecheniia iz persidskikh i tiurkskikh sochinenii)*, ed. S. K. Ibragimov, N. N. Mingulov, K. A. Pishchulina, and V. P. Iudin (Alma-Ata: Nauka, 1969), p. 23.

[34] Bināʾī, '*Shaybānī-nāma*,' MS IVANRUz No. 844 (*SVR*, I, p. 62, No. 139), f. 15b; translated in *Materialy po istorii kazakhskikh khanstv*, p. 114.

remarkable illustration of the social and political influence entailed by the hereditary shaykh-hood of the Sayyid Atāʾī tradition not merely with *khāns* and *amīrs*, but among nomadic tribal communities as well. The story, indeed, provides an excellent illustration, from the 16th century, of the kinds of communal ties between nomadic groups and Sufi shaykhs—described in terms of discipleship, and quite solid regardless of the 'depth' of Sufism entailed thereby—that I have discussed elsewhere in connection with the 14th and 15th centuries.[35]

According to the account,[36] the people of Manghïshlāq had formerly been *murīds* and devotees of a person named Nāṣir Khwāja, who was "among the Sayyid Atāʾī *sayyids*." After Ḥusayn Khwārazmī came to the region, however, "group after group, of every kind, came and entered *his* path (*ṭarīq*)," and Sayyid Nāṣir Khwāja grew so disturbed by this loss of followers that he gathered an "army" of those who remained loyal to him and led it against Ḥusayn Khwārazmī and his dervishes.

The account shifts at this point to the words of Ḥusayn Khwārazmī himself. When Nāṣir Khwāja had come to attack him and his followers, he related, there had been no more than 18 of the "Manqïshlāqīs" with the party; "everyone had scattered to his own home." The rest of the group consisted of "a few dervishes from Khwārazm, who had come out [to Manghïshlāq] with us," but the shaykh's words implicitly acknowledge the different talents of the two types of supporters present with him: according to Khwārazmī, these dervishes—who we may assume were regularly engaged in the Sufi struggle against the carnal soul—"had no training or weapons for external warfare" (*ba-ānhā istiʿdād va ālāt-i ḥarb-i ẓāhirī nabūd*).

[35] See my "Yasavī Šayḫs in the Timurid Era: Notes on the Social and Political Role of Communal Sufi Affiliations in the 14th and 15th Centuries," in *La civiltà timuride come fenomeno internazionale*, ed. Michele Bernardini [= *Oriente Moderno* (Rome), N.S., 15 (76), No. 2 (1996)], pp. 173-188.

[36] *Jāddat al-ʿāshiqīn*, MS Aligarh, ff. 202b-204a; MS Hyderabad, Andhra Pradesh Government Oriental Manuscripts Library, Pers. MS *tadhkira* No. 168, pp. 251-254; MS Islamabad, Iran-Pakistan Institute of Persian Studies, No. 764 (described in Aḥmad Munzavī, ed., *Fihrist-i nuskhahā-yi khaṭṭī-yi Kitābkhāna-i Ganjbakhsh*, vol. IV [Islamabad, 1982], pp. 2100-2102, Title No. 2492, MS No. 5820), pp. 317-319. The story (which reflects some textual differences in the available manuscripts) is recounted in several voices: it is told in the words of Shaykh Artūq Manqïshlāqī, one of Ḥusayn Khwārazmī's successors; in Khwārazmī's own words as reported by Shaykh Artūq; and in Khwārazmī's words as heard directly by the author of the *Jāddat al-ʿāshiqīn* (Khwārazmī's son).

All through the night before the attack was expected, Khwārazmī's own account continues, the Manqïshlāqīs prepared for the battle; they came before the shaykh, having sharpened their spears,[37] to offer up their lives in his defense, and one by one they received a blessing from him. What follows at this point is a remarkable comment by Khwārazmī that offers a succinct encapsulation of the character of such communal affiliations, highlighting the depth of loyalty that could be engendered by the bonds between a Sufi shaykh and his 'disciples' among nomadic groups; the shaykh's words are especially interesting insofar as he had just acknowledged that only 18 of these devoted defenders remained with him, the rest of the newfound followers whom he had lured away from the Sayyid Atā'ī shaykh having scattered before the fight. As he gave his "Manqïshlāqī" devotees his blessing, Khwārazmī said,

> The thought occurred to me, "What have these fellows yet seen of dervish-hood, that they are offering up their lives?" Yet no one has taken note of the devotion and steadfastness of the Turks of Manqïshlāq, man and woman alike, who are renowned for the perfection of their discipleship and of their humble self-sacrifice.[38]

In order to spare these willing defenders, the shaykh resolved to go out by himself to face the enemy the next morning, because he himself was the cause of the conflict; the odds did not favor Ḥusayn Khwārazmī's supporters, since, we are told, the "enemy" that had come against them numbered over 200, while there were no more than 50 supporters with Ḥusayn Khwārazmī, "and most of them were not armed."

The next morning, however, one of Ḥusayn Khwārazmī's disciples who had come with him to Manghïshlāq—Shaykh Artūq, himself a native of the region—saw ʿAlī in a vision affirming that he would be with Ḥusayn Khwārazmī; when Shaykh Artūq told his master about the vision, both realized that Sayyid Nāṣir Khwāja, even with his multitudes, would be unable to stand against Khwārazmī. The shaykh indeed rode out ahead of his followers (on a horse, we are told, that even the

[37] I am indebted to Ron Sela for pointing out this reading.

[38] *Īnhā hanūz az darvīshī cha dīda bāshand ki sar-ū-tan-rā īthār mīkunand; va ba-ṣidq-ū-ikhlāṣ-i atrāk-i manqishlāq az zan-ū-mard ki ba-kamāl-i irādat va niyāz maʿrūf-and dar hīch jā kas nishān namīdahad.*

nomadic "Manqïshlāqīs" praised), and threw himself into the enemy ranks, shouting, "I am the one who is the cause of this fight;" and because ʿAlī was with him, no one among the enemy could withstand him (the mention of ʿAlī's aid, of course, undercuts the legitimacy of Sayyid Nāṣir Khwāja, who is symbolically deprived even of his own ancestor's support). The account concludes noting Ḥusayn Khwārazmī's own description of his attack's effect: wherever he rode, the enemy 'soldiers' were so terrified that the swords they were brandishing, and the arrows they were holding ready at their bows, simply fell from their hands.

The story is interesting in several regards, not least of which is the Kubravī shaykh's evaluation of his nomadic followers. He implicitly evokes the expectation that these nomads would lack constancy in religion, and in loyalty to the shaykh (an expectation that is still very much with us even today, in attitudes toward the depth or strength of Islam among nomadic peoples in Central Asian history), but dismisses it; instead, he affirms that these 'Turks of Manghïshlāq' were every bit as devoted to the success of his community as his intimate Sufi disciples, even though the nomads knew little of the Sufi path. The latter point is perhaps the most important, insofar as it cautions us against misconstruing the character and content of the nomads' attachment to Ḥusayn Khwārazmī, and formerly, we may assume, to Sayyid Nāṣir Khwāja; it reminds us that, in Khwārazmī's view at least, the 'Turks of Manghïshlāq' were indeed unschooled in Sufi doctrine and, presumably, practice, but that this had no bearing on the fact, or on the depth, of their personal and communal commitment to the shaykh.

We might object, that is, in a perhaps laudable effort to avoid stereotyping the Sufism, or the Islam, of the nomads as deficient or substandard, that these few devoted followers among the 'Manghïshlāqīs' *did* know, and *were* committed to, the teaching and practice of their shaykh; but here the shaykh himself affirms that this was not the case, and, by extension, that Sufi teaching and practice were not what these nomads of Manghïshlaq had *sought* from the shaykh. Khwārazmī's point is that these particular nomads' unfamiliarity with the intellectual aspects of the Sufi path was in effect unrelated to, and ultimately less important than, their affective attachment to the path itself, as embodied in the shaykh, and as expressed in terms of the Sufi notion of 'discipleship' (*irādat*). For our purposes, the lesson perhaps most worth drawing from this story is that any attempt to understand the influence of Sayyid Atāʾī or other shaykhs among nomadic communities in Central Asia, or to understand more broadly the nature of the bonds between those communities and Sufi shaykhs, will fail so long as we continue to privilege the intellectual 'content' of Sufism (or of Islam) over other aspects, whether affective or thaumaturgical or aesthetic, or over the totality of Sufism as directly and immediately embodied in the person of the shaykh.

As noted, we may in fact doubt the constancy of these Turks of Manghïshlāq, insofar as, if we believe the account, they had only recently abandoned their communal attachment to Sayyid Nāṣir al-Dīn and taken up with Ḥusayn Khwārazmī, and many of them had abandoned the latter in the face of their former master's threat. In any case, the story attests to the bonds that linked nomadic communities in Manghïshlāq to a particular Sayyid Atāʾī shaykh—bonds that were understood in terms of the structures and terminology characteristic of Sufism and Sufi circles—and to the shifting communal alignments that could result from rivalries that were also couched in terms of Sufi communities, whether rooted in hereditary transmission or *silsila*-based succession.

Two more concrete aspects of the account of these 'Turks of Manghïshlāq' also deserve comment. First, the date of this encounter is difficult to establish. The story would appear to reflect a time before Ḥusayn Khwārazmī's move from Khwārazm to Samarqand in 923/1517, but it is clear that he returned often to Khwārazm in subsequent years, and the narrative may reflect a later time (down to Ḥusayn Khwārazmī's departure from Central Asia, to perform the *ḥajj* during which he was to die, in 956/1549). That he was accompanied on this journey to Manghïshlāq by Shaykh Artūq Manqïshlāqī would seem to suggest a time later in this range, since there is some indication that Shaykh Artūq attached himself to Ḥusayn Khwārazmī relatively late in the latter's career.[39] On the other hand, an earlier date certainly fits better with Sayyid Nāṣir's involvement in Muḥammad Shïbānī Khān's campaigns in Khwārazm.

Second, in addition to the account's chronological imprecision, we are also unable to identify with certainty the 'Turks' of Manghïshlāq

[39] Shaykh Artūq is portrayed as a 'replacement,' in effect, for another disciple who had angered Khwārazmī by going off to the town of Vazīr without his master's permission and establishing himself there as an independent shaykh (*Jāddat al-ʿāshiqīn*, MS Aligarh, f. 73b).

whose steadfastness Ḥusayn Khwārazmī praises; the account itself gives no clues, and the *Jāddat al-ʿāshiqīn* elsewhere refers only in the most general terms to "Ūzbakistān" and the lands of the "Manghït-Uzbeks" as the chief nomadic environments in which Ḥusayn Khwārazmī and his successors were active—suggesting, of course, that the 'Turks' of Manghïshlāq were recognized as *not* being of the same ethnic stock as the peoples of the Dasht-i Qïpchāq to whom were applied, in the middle of the 16th century, the appellations "Uzbek," "Manghït," and "Qazaq" (as well as combinations of these). That the 'Turks' of Manghïshlāq who had been followers of Sayyid Nāṣir Khwāja, and became disciples of his Kubravī rival, were most likely Türkmens is suggested by an important clue found in the earlier hagiography written about Ḥusayn Khwārazmī, the *Miftāḥ al-ṭālibīn*, compiled during the shaykh's lifetime. As noted already by Bartol'd,[40] this work mentions one of Ḥusayn Khwārazmī's journeys to "Manqïshlāq," and identifies this region as the dwelling place of the Sālūr tribe (*īl-i sālūr*) of the Türkmens; one group of these people, called the Inner (*īchkī*) Sālūr, "great and small, men and women, were all disciples and companions" of Ḥusayn Khwārazmī.[41]

The name "Sālūr" appears to have been applied, during the 16th century, to a loose tribal confederation of Türkmen groups that included the Sālūr tribe itself as well as the Ersarï, Teke, Sarïq, and Yomut. This 'Sālūr confederation' inhabited the region along the eastern shore of the Caspian Sea from the Mangïshlāq peninsula south to the region of the Balkhān mountains; the phrase "Outer (*tashqï*) Sālūr" seems to have referred to the tribal union as a whole, or to the tribes other than the Sālūrs themselves, with the Sālūr tribe itself known as the "Inner (*ichki*) Sālūr."[42] Given both the specific echo of Ḥusayn Khwārazmī's

40 See V. V. Bartol'd, "Otchet o komandirovke v Turkestan," in his collected *Sochineniia*, VIII (Moscow, 1973), p. 148.

41 Jānī Maḥmūd Ghijduvānī, *Miftāḥ al-ṭālibīn*, MS Aligarh, ff. 137a-144a. The anecdote in which this passage appears involves the fate of Ḥusayn Khwārazmī's dog, Bābā Qoldāsh, who was accidentally killed during the visit to Manghïshlāq, and whose grave became a pilgrimage site for the people there; I have discussed this story in "Dog Saints and Dog Shrines in Kubravī Tradition: Notes on a Hagiographical Motif from Khwārazm," *Miracle et karāma: Hagiographies médiévales comparées*, 2, ed. Denise Aigle (Turnhout, Belgium: Brepols, 2000; Bibliothèque de l'école des hautes études, sciences religieuses, vol. 109), pp. 459-497.

42 On the so-called Sālūr confederation, see the discussion in Bartol'd, "Ocherk istorii turkmenskogo naroda," *Sochineniia*, II/1, pp. 547-623 [pp. 593-594], and the English translation, "A History of the Turkman People," in [V. V. Barthold], *Four Studies on the History of Central Asia*, tr. V. and T. Minorsky, vol. III (Leiden:

communal disciples among the 'Inner Sālūrs,' and the region—Manghïshlāq—reflected in both sources, it is quite likely that precisely the same people, of the Sālūr tribe, were intended by the references in the *Jāddat al-ʿāshiqīn* to the communal followers of Ḥusayn Khwārazmī and, previously, of Sayyid Nāṣir Khwāja Sayyid Atāʾī.

The story, of course, does not dwell on the identity of the people who remained loyal to Sayyid Nāṣir Khwāja, a group that was acknowledged to have been significantly larger than the group attached to Ḥusayn Khwārazmī (even though we were first told that Sayyid Nāṣir Khwāja's following had been severely reduced by 'defections' to Ḥusayn Khwārazmī's side); perhaps they should be understood as representing the non-Sālūr members of the 'Sālūr confederation,' or some other group altogether. It is perhaps significant, moreover, that the story does not end with explicit mention of a large-scale, or total, shift of Sayyid Nāṣir Khwāja's followers to the side of Ḥusayn Khwārazmī. It is not unlikely, however the story is told in the *Jāddat al-ʿāshiqīn*, that the Sayyid Atāʾī shaykh's reputation and following among the 'Turks of Manghïshlāq' were diminished very little, or not at all, by whatever confrontation inspired the hagiographical account that survives; that account, clearly composite, bears obvious internal contradictions (e.g., on the question of each group's size), signaling the development and circulation of parts of the story at different times and for different purposes. In any case, we can only speculate about the specific fate of Sayyid Nāṣir Khwāja Sayyid Atāʾī; the story simply ends with the defeat of his supporters, and nothing more is said of him.

The 19th-century genealogy given in the work of Mīr Musayyab Bukhārī and in the *Tuḥfat al-zāʾirīn* traces ten more generations after

---

E. J. Brill, 1962), pp. 75-170 [pp. 131-133]; cf. Yu. Bregel, "Nomadic and Sedentary Elements among the Turkmens," *Central Asiatic Journal*, 25 (1981), pp. 5-37 [p. 18], A. Dzhikiev, "K istorii rasseleniia turkmen-salyrov v XVI-nachale XX v.," *Issledovaniia po ètnografii turkmen*, ed. S. G. Agadzhanov and A. Orazov (Ashkhabad: Turkmenistan, 1965), pp. 3-24, and the survey of William Wood, "Turkmen Ethnohistory," in *Vanishing Jewels: Central Asian Tribal Weavings* (Rochester, New York: The Center, 1990), pp. 27-44 [pp. 32-33]. The "inner" and "outer" Sālūrs are both explicitly mentioned (and the tribes comprising the "outer" Sālūrs listed) in Abū'l-Ghāzī's *Shajara-i Turk* (*Histoire des mongols et des tatares*, ed. Desmaison, text, pp. 208-210; tr., pp. 223-224), but only the phrase "Ichki Sālūr" appears in his *Shajara-i tarākima* (*Rodoslovnaia turkmen: sochinenie Abu-l-Gazi Khana Khivinskogo*, ed. & tr. A. N. Kononov [Moscow/Leningrad: Izd-vo AN SSSR, 1958], pp. 73-74 [tr.], 70-71 [text]; cf. Ebulgazi Bahadır Han, *Şecere-i Terākime (Türkmenlerin Soykütüğü)*, ed. Zuhal Kargı Ölmez [Ankara: Mehmet Ölmez/Şafak Matbaacılık, 1996], pp. 215-217).

Sayyid Ḥusām al-Dīn, through the "Sayyid Nāṣir" shown there as his son:[43] Ḥusām al-Dīn > Nāṣir > ʿAbdullāh > Qūch Khwāja Naqīb > Qul-Muḥammad Khwāja Naqīb > ʿAbd al-Qāhir Khwāja Naqīb > Jaʿfar Khwāja Naqīb > ʿAbd al-Raḥmān Khwāja > ʿAbd al-Fattāḥ Khwāja the *ṣadr* > ʿUmar Khwāja the *ūrāq*;[44] the latter figure is ascribed four sons—Ibrāhīm, Zakarīyā Khwāja the *ūrāq*, Sulaymān Khwāja, and ʿAbd al-Jabbār Khwāja the *ḥāfiẓ*—and is said to have married a woman from the lineage of Sayyid ʿUthmān Khwāja (from whom she was a ninth-generation descendant), thus reuniting these Sayyid Atāʾī lineages.

The Sayyid Jaʿfar Khwāja Naqīb who appears as the sixth generation after Ḥusām al-Dīn, however, is identified in the *Tuḥfat al-zāʾirīn* as the figure responsible for the construction of several prominent 'religious buildings' (*buqʿāt-i khayrāt*) in Bukhara; to judge from a rough generational chronology, moreover, he is suitable for identification with the Jaʿfar Khwāja Naqīb Sayyid Atāʾī who was active in Bukhara at the end of the 17th century and the beginning of the 18th.[45] It is thus evident that this descendant of Sayyid Ḥusām al-Dīn, at least, had established himself in Mavarannahr; we cannot determine whether, or when, any earlier members of this lineage moved from Khwārazm to Bukhara, but it seems clear that we know even the names of the generational links in this lineage stemming from Sayyid Ḥusām al-Dīn only because this lineage too eventually became established in Mavarannahr, to be included in our Bukharan sources on Sayyid Atāʾī genealogy.

[43] Mīr Musayyab, ff. 473a-b; *Tuḥfat al-zāʾirīn*, lith., p. 89 (the title "*sayyid*" is given in the texts for each individual, but is omitted here).

[44] On this title as borne by Sayyid Atāʾī figures, see my "Descendants of Sayyid Ata," pp. 623, 629 (n. 97), with further references.

[45] He is mentioned in the court history of the Ashtarkhānid ʿUbaydullāh Khān; see Mir Mukhammed Amin-i Bukhari, *Ubaidulla-name*, tr. A. A. Semenov (Tashkent: Izd-vo AN UzSSR, 1957), pp. 43-44. To judge from the account in the *Tuḥfat al-zāʾirīn*, the Jaʿfar Khwāja whose name is borne by a *madrasa* and neighborhood in Bukhara (see O. A. Sukhareva, *Kvartal'naia obshchina pozdnefeoldal'nogo goroda Bukhary* [Moscow: Nauka, 1976], pp. 256-258, 315) is this Sayyid Atāʾī figure.

OTHER SAYYID ATĀʾĪ DESCENDANTS IN KHWĀRAZM, 16TH-17TH CENTURIES

The *Jāddat al-ʿāshiqīn* mentions three other Sayyid Atāʾī figures in its account of Ḥusayn Khwārazmī, and the brief accounts of them make it clear that the Kubravī shaykh's hostile relations with Sayyid Nāṣir Khwāja did not entail any general hostility toward the Sayyid Atāʾī legacy. Two of these other Sayyid Atāʾī figures established marital ties with the Kubravī shaykh: the *Jāddat al-ʿāshiqīn* notes that Ḥusayn Khwārazmī gave one of his daughters in marriage to Māmāq Khwāja Sayyid Atāʾī, and that after the latter died, the same daughter was married to Khwāja Ismāʿīl Mīrzā, who is identified as the son of Māmāq Khwāja's sister (and hence also a Sayyid Atāʾī).[46] In addition, a certain "Sayyid Niʿmat Khwāja Sayyid Atāʾī" is mentioned among the Sufi disciples and successors of Ḥusayn Khwārazmī "who are not well-known among the people;" this figure, we are told, was licensed by Ḥusayn Khwārazmī and sent off to "Ūzbakistān" (suggesting perhaps some effort by the master to capitalize on his disciple's hereditary respect among the nomadic inhabitants of that country).[47]

These other Sayyid Atāʾī descendants may have been active in Khwārazm, but we cannot know for certain in view of Ḥusayn Khwārazmī's long residence in Samarqand; and in any case, we have no further information on their genealogical place in any Sayyid Atāʾī lineage. The same holds true in the case of several other Sayyid Atāʾī *sayyids*, mentioned in sources from the 16th and 17th centuries, who *can* be placed in Khwārazm, or linked with the Khwārazmian ruling house; none of them can yet be connected with the lineage stemming from Sayyid Ḥusām al-Dīn, or indeed with any lineage reflected in the genealogical sources that have so far come to light.

One is a certain "Sayyid Pādshāh Ḥājjī Sayyid Atāʾī," of whom we hear in connection with a Chaghatay Turkic translation, which he

[46] *Jāddat al-ʿāshiqīn*, MS Aligarh, f. 214b; Māmāq Khwāja is mentioned also at ff. 108b and 123a. The Islamabad copy cited above (note 36) appears to spell his name, instead of "Māmāq," first "Bābātā" and then twice "Mābātāq" or "Bābātāq," with the element "*-tā-*" written above the line in both cases; the first spelling (and perhaps as well the apparent confusion signaled by the other forms) suggests this figure's possible identification with the "Bābā Khwāja" known from the *Manāqib al-akhyār* as the Sayyid Atāʾī guardian of the orphaned Sayyid Jamāl al-Dīn.

[47] *Jāddat al-ʿāshiqīn*, MS India Office, Ethé 1877, f. 117a; he is mentioned also, as "Sayyid Niʿmatullāh Sayyid Atāʾī," in the *Thamarāt al-mashāʾikh*, f. 97b.

evidently sponsored or prepared himself, of Mawlānā Yaʿqūb Charkhī's *tafsīr*, completed in 993/1585 (he is thus too late, clearly, to identify with the father of Sayyid Jamāl al-Dīn, called "Sayyid Pādshāh Khwāja," known through the *Manāqib al-akhyār*).[48] The introduction to this translation notes that because the *tafsīr* had originally been written in Persian (here, "*tājīklär tili*," and "*tājīk tili*"), Turkic dervishes were deprived of its benefits because they did not understand that language (*türk faqīrlar ol tilgä tüshünä almay fāyda-dïn maḥrūm érmishlär*); therefore, during the time of Sanjar Muḥammad Sulṭān, who ruled in Nisā (spelled here "*nīsāy*"), a group of sincere and pious Turks[49] asked "their *pīr*," Sayyid Pādshāh Ḥājjī, to have the work translated into Turkic. Sayyid Pādshāh Ḥājjī is identified as a Sayyid Atāʾī, is called "the repository of the post of *naqīb*" (*niqābat dastgāhï*) and "the jewel of the ocean of *sayyid*-ship" (*siyādat baḥrï-nïng gawharï*), and is further described as one who has "turned his heart cold to the world, kept to a corner away from the people, filled his bosom with the remembrance of God, forgotten everything other than God, and soothed his heart with the remembrance of the lord."[50] The allusion to this shaykh's Turkic disciples is unfortunately vague, but it may suggest the kind of communal affiliation with a Sayyid Atāʾī figure who, we may presume, was at least formally regarded as a Sufi shaykh and as a preceptor in the study of the Qurʾān.

In this case, to be sure, the text itself suggests the region of Nisā, in Khurāsān, and not Khwārazm, as the scene of Sayyid Pādshāh Ḥājjī's activity among his Turkic disciples; in this era, however, this region was closely linked, politically and socially, with Khwārazm, and the "Sanjar Muḥammad Sulṭān" mentioned in the work clearly must refer to the "Sanjar Sulṭān" whom Abū'l-Ghāzī identifies as a son of ʿAlī Sulṭān b.

[48] A single manuscript of this work, which runs to 193 ff. and was copied most likely in the 19th century, is preserved in Tashkent: MS IVANRUz No. 7180 (*SVR*, VII, pp. 353-354, No. 5516), ff. 2a-b for the passage cited from the introduction.

[49] They are described as "*ṣādiq al-qawl türklär*," "with their livers bound [i.e., with their emotions under control] and their eyes moist [with tears], who have shunned the people of this world, alighted in the realm of divine unity, resisted the poison of Satan through the remembrance of God, and submitted to the merciful lord" (*baghrï baghlïgh közi yashligh dunyā ahlïndïn iʿrāż qïlghan vaḥdat ʿālamïnda qonghan allāh yādï birle shayṭān zahrin yarïp raḥmān édhigha boyun sunghan*).

[50] *dunyā-dïn könglin savutghan khalāʾiqdïn gūsha tutghan allāh yādï birle kögsi tolghan mā-savā'llāh-dïn unutghan édhi dhikri birlä könglin āvutghan.*

Avānish Khān—who, as noted, was portrayed in the *Manāqib al-akhyār* as the beneficiary of Sayyid Jamāl al-Dīn's blessing.[51] It may thus be reasonable to suppose a Khwārazmian origin for Sayyid Pādshāh Ḥājjī.

Another echo of a Sayyid Atāʾī descendant apparently active in Khwārazm appears in the *Maṭlab al-ṭālibīn*, a 17th-century Jūybārī hagiography, which mentions a visit to Tāj al-Dīn Ḥasan Jūybārī (d. 1056/1646) by Jaʿfar Khwāja Sayyid Atāʾī, who came from Khwārazm with a large retinue and lavish gifts.[52] The same work mentions two brothers, Tīmūr Khwāja and Shādmān Khwāja, as "servants" of Khwāja Saʿd Jūybārī (d. 997/1589), and as representatives

[51] According to Abū'l-Ghāzī (*Histoire des mongols et des tatares*, ed. Desmaisons, tr. pp. 265-266, text p. 248), ʿAlī Sulṭān left two sons, Iskandar and Sanjar. The former died just six months after his father, while Sanjar, despite (or because of) the fact that he was *dīvāna* (i.e., "insane," but perhaps implying also an inclination toward dervish-hood), was installed by a Nāymān tribal chieftain named Qul Muḥammad Bīy as a figurehead ruler in Nisā. The tribal chieftain, says the account, would bring out Sanjar Sulṭān once a week for a public audience (*körünüsh*), intending through this limited access to conceal his real state; and Sanjar 'ruled' in this fashion for 25 years, a period that, if we date ʿAlī Sulṭān's death to 973/1565-66, leaves him reigning until 998/1590, well in accord with the date mentioned in the translation of the *tafsīr*. The translation, incidentally, is not explicitly dedicated to Sanjar Sulṭān, but it is interesting to note the literary activity associated with his father, ʿAlī Sulṭān; the latter was the patron of Sālār Bābā b. Qul-ʿAlī," who produced a Turkic translation of part, at least, of Rashīd al-Dīn's *Jāmiʿ al-tavārīkh* (in 963/1556), and who copied a manuscript of the *Zubdat al-āthār* (see my "A Note on Manuscripts of the *Zubdat al-āthār*, a Chaghatay Turkic History from Sixteenth-Century Mavarannahr," *Manuscripts of the Middle East*, 6 [1992], pp. 96-100 [p. 100]).

[52] *Maṭlab al-ṭālibīn*, MS Berlin, Staatsbibliothek Preussischer Kulturbesitz, MS Or. Oct. 1540 (described in *Verzeichnis der orientalischen Handschriften in Deutschland*, Bd. XIV/1, *Persische Handschriften*, ed. Wilhelm Eilers and Wilhelm Heinz [Wiesbaden: Franz Steiner Verlag, 1968], No. 158), f. 113b. Clearly an earlier Jaʿfar Khwāja Sayyid Atāʾī is intended in the same work's affirmation that a figure by this name was a disciple of Khwāja Muḥammad Islām Jūybārī (d. 971/1563), and participated in preparing his body for burial (*Maṭlab al-ṭālibīn*, MS Berlin, f. 68a]). The name "Jaʿfar Khwāja Sayyid Atāʾī" is fairly common in Sayyid Atāʾī genealogies and in historical references: one figure by that name was active at the very beginning of the 16th century in Bukhara (he was mentioned, for instance, by Nithārī [*Mudhakkir-i aḥbāb*, ed. Fazlullah, p. 505; ed. Haravī, p. 304], and in the *Manāqib al-akhyār* [MS India Office, f. 17b; MS Rampur, ff. 21b-22a]; another was evidently the father of Sayyid Ḥasan Khwāja, the *naqīb* of ʿAbdullāh Khān b. Iskandar (on whom see my "Descendants of Sayyid Ata," pp. 621-622), and was most likely the one linked to Khwāja Muḥammad Islām Jūybārī; and another, as noted, was active in Bukhara in the late 17th and early 18th centuries.

of "the *sayyid*s of Khwārazm;"[53] they are not explicitly identified as Sayyid Atāʾī descendants, however, while two Sayyid Atāʾī figures mentioned in 16th-century sources who bear the same name as one of these brothers appear to have been active outside Khwārazm.[54]

Our most extensive account of the activity of a Khwārazmian Sayyid Atāʾī shaykh in the early 17th century appears in Abū'l-Ghāzī's history, and is decidedly hostile (for evident reasons).[55] The context for the events narrated in this account is the succession struggle of 1031/1622, after ʿArab-Muḥammad Khān, Abū'l-Ghāzī's father, had been deposed, blinded, and finally put to death following a revolt led by two of his own sons (and Abū'l-Ghāzī's half-brothers) Īlbārs and Ḥabash, who were eventually challenged by Isfandiyār (Abū'l-Ghāzī's full brother); Isfandiyār was gaining support among the troops that had been loyal to

[53] *Maṭlab aṭ-ṭālibīn*, MS Berlin, f. 79a. The phrase "*sayyid*s of Khwārazm" is nowhere explicitly explained as referring to descendants of Sayyid Ata, and I have not yet found any instance of the phrase's use to refer to a specific figure who is clearly identifiable, on some other basis, as a Sayyid Atāʾī; a parallel to this 'geographical' usage is found, however, in the phrase "*sayyid*s of the Dasht-i Qïpchāq," which *can* be linked with an identifiable Sayyid Atāʾī figure (as in the case of the Sayyid Jaʿfar Khwāja mentioned by Khwāndamīr in connection with his agitation in Khurāsān on behalf of Muḥammad Shïbānī Khān, in 909/1502-03 [*Ḥabīb al-siyar*, ed. Jalāl al-Dīn Humāʾī (Tehran: Khayyām, 1333/1954; repr. 1362/1983), IV, pp. 294-296; cf. the translation of Wheeler M. Thackston, Khwandamir, *Habibu's-siyar, Tome Three* (Cambridge, Massachusetts, 1994; *Sources of Oriental Languages and Literatures*, 24), Part 2, pp. 498-499]).

[54] The chief court history of ʿAbdullāh Khān b. Iskandar mentions a Timūr Khwāja Sayyid Atāʾī, who met with the *khān* at Āq Tepe, near Samarqand (see my "Descendants of Sayyid Ata," p. 621, n. 47); and an earlier Jūybārī hagiography mentions a *sayyid* of Marv, Tīmūr Khwāja, who was a descendant of Sayyid Ata but was best known for his wine-drinking and derisive attitude toward dervishes (Ḥusayn Sarakhsī, *Saʿdīyah*, MS IVANRUz No. 4514 [uncatalogued; see the descriptions of the other known copies of the work in *SVR*, III, p. 324, Nos. 2591-2593], f. 48b).

[55] Abū'l-Ghāzī, *Histoire des mongols et des tatares*, ed. Desmaisons, text pp. 288-290, tr. pp. 309-311. The revolt of Īlbārs and his brother against their father, and the eventual victory of Isfandiyār, are recounted briefly by Muʾnis (*Firdaws al-iqbāl*, ed. Bregel, pp. 128-131; tr. Bregel, pp. 40-41), but without any mention of Naẓar Khwāja Sayyid Atāʾī; this may signal a reluctance on the part of Muʾnis, who is quite respectful of Sayyid Ata and his legacy, even to allude to such an unflattering account of Naẓar Khwāja (Abū'l-Ghāzī, by contrast, seems to relish recounting the Sayyid Atāʾī shaykh's misdeeds, and it is undoubtedly not mere coincidence that Abū'l-Ghāzī's works offer not even a hint of the story of Sayyid Ata's role in the Islamization of the Dasht-i Qïpchāq).

his father, and the Sayyid Atāʾī descendant, a supporter, and father-in-law, of the patricide Īlbārs, sought to prevent Isfandiyār from coming to the throne.

"At the shrine (*āstāna*) of Bāqïrghān," the account explains, there was a man named Naẓar Khwāja, from among the descendants of Sayyid Ata; he was a liar and was devoted to worldly things, but had some experience in military affairs, and had given his daughter in marriage to Īlbārs. This Naẓar Khwāja sent word to Isfandiyār promising to come to his side, but instead went among the tribal communities he knew were well-disposed toward Īlbārs, in order to gather troops; meanwhile, the account explains, the populace was rallying to Isfandiyār, disgusted with Īlbārs' murder of his own father. Naẓar Khwāja thus went with three or four hundred men and took up a position at a river crossing, astride the road by which those wishing to join Isfandiyār would have to pass; there he harangued the Uzbek tribesmen who came intending to support Isfandiyār, declaring that the latter, if he should succeed in taking control of the country, would kill them all, with their children, and order the Türkmens of the Balkhān mountains and Manqïshlāq to carry off their wives and daughters. Naẓar Khwāja swore by the Qurʾān, to each person, that what he said was true, and the account suggests that many were swayed both by respect for the venerable *sayyid*, and by the threats to their lives and property of which the *sayyid* warned; word of Naẓar Khwāja's success, moreover, induced many troops who had joined Isfandiyār to desert him.

At this point in the account, unfortunately, we lose sight of Naẓar Khwāja, as the focus turns toward the eventual victor. Isfandiyār was in fact defeated in his first campaign against the supporters of Īlbārs, but regrouped in Manghïshlāq, where a large number of Türkmens strengthened his forces; he then marched on Urgench, fighting for 22 straight days, and finally put his enemies to flight on the 23rd day. Īlbārs was captured and put to death, and Isfandiyār assumed the throne in 1032/1623; Abū'l-Ghāzī does not tell us of Naẓar Khwāja's fate. Nevertheless, the account depicts Naẓar Khwāja as a typical 'communal' shaykh of this period—that is, a figure with a substantial reputation (and strong persuasive ability) among the nomadic tribal population, in this case Uzbek rather than Türkmen, on whom the Chinggisid rulers depended for their military and political power; his influence among the tribes was undoubtedly no small factor in making marital relations with his family attractive to an ambitious Chinggisid prince. In any case,

Abū'l-Ghāzī's hostile account attests to the influence of this Sayyid Atāʾī shaykh among the Uzbek tribes of Khwārazm in the early 17th century; Isfandiyār's reliance on Türkmen support in defeating Īlbārs, indeed, may further highlight the effectiveness of Naẓar Khwāja in aligning the Uzbek tribes against Isfandiyār (ironically, the eventual champion of Uzbek tribal interests, who would set out to crush the Türkmens of Khwārazm, was Abū'l-Ghāzī himself).

It is unfortunately impossible to judge whether the Naẓar Khwāja mentioned by Abū'l-Ghāzī might be the same Sayyid Atāʾī figure mentioned, as "Naẓar Khwāja b. ʿAlāw Khwāja," in another source from the same period, the *Baḥr al-asrār*. As discussed elsewhere,[56] the latter source affirms this Naẓar Khwāja's Sayyid Atāʾī descent as well as his service as *naqīb*—involving active involvement in military campaigns—under the Ashtarkhānid ruler of Balkh, Nadhr Muḥammad Khān; while it is clear that this Naẓar Khwāja spent at least the latter part of his life in the region of Balkh, the *Baḥr al-asrār* affirms that when he died (in or shortly before 1044/1634), Naẓar Khwāja Sayyid Atāʾī was taken to Khwārazm for burial, upon his own instructions, in "Urgench." It is quite reasonable to suppose that Abū'l-Ghāzī's Naẓar Khwāja left Khwārazm after his candidate's defeat in the succession struggle of the early 1620s, and entered the service of the Ashtarkhānids in Balkh, but it is equally plausible that Abū'l-Ghāzī and the *Baḥr al-asrār* are dealing with two entirely different figures. We thus cannot be certain whether Naẓar Khwāja's burial in Khwārazm reflects his own earlier life there, or merely a general tradition of the Sayyid Atāʾī ancestral burial ground in Khwārazm; even in the latter case, however, we have an additional indication of an ongoing Sayyid Atāʾī presence in Khwārazm in the first half of the 17th century.

CONCLUSION

The evidence we have considered here suggests that the development of the Sayyid Atāʾī legacy in Khwārazm followed a course quite different from what we find in Mavarannahr, and that, despite the presence of Sayyid Ata's shrine in Khwārazm, and the development of traditions affirming Sayyid Ata's close association with that region (at least toward the end of his life), the Sayyid Atāʾī legacy was in some respects less

[56] See my "Descendants of Sayyid Ata," pp. 622, 626-627.

prominent in Khwārazm than it became in Mavarannahr. It is entirely possible that this situation is simply an artifact of the sources: we have far fewer sources dealing with Khwārazm for the 15th-18th centuries than we have in the case of Mavarannahr, and we might argue that it is only natural for our information on a specific descent group in Mavarannahr to be correspondingly richer than what we can learn about that group in Khwārazm. It is also possible, however, that the seeming disparity in the prominence of Sayyid Atāʾī descendants in Khwārazm and of those in Mavarannahr reflects real differences, and that the descendants of Sayyid Ata in the two regions did indeed play different roles, rooted perhaps in different relationships with the respective Chinggisid dynasties that held power in the two regions.

That the Sayyid Atāʾī descendants played substantially different institutional roles in the two polities seems clear. As noted at the outset of this article, sources produced in Shībānid and Ashtarkhānid circles offer ample evidence of prominent Sayyid Atāʾī functionaries in Bukhara and Balkh, and affirm their close relationship with the important institution of the *niqābat*, while available sources from the Chinggisid state of Khwārazm provide no substantive confirmation of a similarly close link between the descendants of Sayyid Ata and the post of *naqīb*;[57] only in the 18th and 19th centuries, indeed, do we find evidence of Sayyid Atāʾī figures involved in the administrative structures of the Khwārazmian state (though Abū'l-Ghāzī is credited—by Muʾnis, in the early 19th century—with allocating a specific post—*not* that of *naqīb*—to the descendants of Sayyid Ata). We might even suggest that the genealogical texts noted here testify, in effect, to a steady 'drain' of Sayyid Atāʾī descendants away from Khwārazm and toward Mavarannahr; whether this might reflect primarily a greater 'market' for Sayyid Atāʾī 'talent' in Mavarannahr, or tensions (either incidental, or 'structural') with the Chinggisid elite in Khwārazm, remains unclear.

In the latter regard, however, the information reviewed here on the Sayyid Atāʾī legacy in Khwārazm might be construed as indicating a

[57] "Descendants of Sayyid Ata," pp. 624-626. Of the specific Sayyid Atāʾī figures discussed here, only the Sayyid Pādshāh Ḥājjī Sayyid Atāʾī who is mentioned in connection with the Turkic translation of Charkhī's *tafsīr* is assigned epithets indicating a connection with the title "*naqīb*;" he is described as a reclusive shaykh, however, and is not expressly linked with the Chinggisid Sanjar Muḥammad Sulṭān, except chronologically (it is not impossible, moreover, that the epithets linking this figure to the *niqābat* might reflect the 19th-century date of the surviving copy rather than the 16th-century lifetime of Sayyid Pādshāh Ḥājjī).

fundamentally different focus of Sayyid Atāʾī power and prestige in Khwārazm, concentrated not at the Chinggisid courts, but among the nomadic tribal populations; this, in turn, might naturally have contributed, as often as not, to an adversarial stance, on the part of Sayyid Atāʾī descendants, with respect to certain Chinggisid rulers, and would help to explain why Sayyid Atāʾī groups were handled differently, in connection with state administration, in Mavarannahr and Khwārazm. Assuming a different focus of Sayyid Atāʾī influence, indeed, would perhaps place the Sayyid Atāʾī 'monopoly' on the instititution of the *niqābat* in Mawrannahr in a different light, as marking, in effect, one strategy for 'co-opting' Sayyid Atāʾī influence in an effort to limit potential alliances between the Sayyid Atāʾī family and tribal forces.

Such an interpretation is perhaps most clearly warranted in the case of Naẓar Khwāja,[58] depicted by the Chinggisid Abū'l-Ghāzī as a rabble-rousing demagogue, and in the case of Sayyid Nāṣir Khwāja, whose prominence rested in large measure on his support among the nomadic population of Manghïshlāq (or did, at least, until Ḥusayn Khwārazmī lured his followers away); but the popularity of Sayyid Vilāyat Khwāja and his son Sayyid Hidāyat Khwāja among the people of Manghïshlāq also suggests the importance of the same kind of tribal nomadic following (perhaps their apparent departure from Khwārazm was itself a sign of tensions with the Khwārazmian Chinggisids, rather than evidence of a quarrel between two branches of the Sayyid Atāʾī family).

It is also reasonable to assume, further, that the "Turkic *faqīr*s" who requested the translation of Yaʿqūb Charkhī's *tafsīr* from their Sayyid Atāʾī *pīr* represented much the same social environment. Even the case of Sayyid Ḥusām al-Dīn, as recounted by Abū'l-Ghāzī, may reflect some

[58] As suggested, the marital ties established between Naẓar Khwāja and the Chinggisid Īlbārs may have been rooted in the latter's wish to cultivate Naẓar Khwāja's constituency among the nomadic Uzbeks; in this connection it is interesting that although we have evidence of Timurid princes marrying into Sayyid Atāʾī families in the late 15th century, we find almost no instances—after sporadic indications of marriages between the Sayyid Atāʾī and Abū'l-Khayrid families down to the early 16th century—of any marital connections established with descendants of Sayyid Ata by the Shïbānid or Ashtarkhānid rulers who accorded *institutional* recognition to the descendants of Sayyid Ata. Our data is not sufficient to allow any firm conclusion posing marital and administrative relationships between the Chinggisid rulers and the Sayyid Atāʾī descent groups as alternating models, but it is quite possible that they do reflect complementary ways of addressing the social and political influence of the Sayyid Atāʾī family.

tension between the Sayyid Atāʾī legacy and the prerogatives of the Chinggisids he is credited with bringing to the rulership of Khwārazm: while Abū'l-Ghāzī's account can be read as respectful of Ḥusām al-Dīn for his role in installing the 'ʿArabshāhid' dynastic clan in the region, we might equally argue that the most significant point made in the story is not the Sayyid Atāʾī shaykh's sanction of the new rulers, but his wisdom, and example, in *declining* actual power for himself. Only in the case of Sayyid Jamāl al-Dīn and the two figures linked to him within the Khwārazmian dynasty, ʿAlī Sulṭān and Shāh Qulī Sulṭān, do we find any hints of closer connections between a Sayyid Atāʾī lineage and Chinggisid rulers in Khwārazm. In the latter case, however, the Chinggisid prince was clearly no longer a player in political or military affairs, while in the case of ʿAlī Sulṭān, we hear of the Sayyid Atāʾī shaykh's aid and blessing, but not of the prince's actual discipleship or any long-standing relationship, much less any administrative or ceremonial role on the part of the Sayyid Atāʾī shaykh; indeed, considering the Khwārazmian locus of Sayyid Jamāl al-Dīn's early career, the *Manāqib al-akhyār* in fact refers quite sparingly—and never with any mention of the post of *naqīb*—to the Sayyid Atāʾī shaykh's links with the Khwārazmian Chinggisid dynasty.[59]

By the 19th century, at least, some evidence suggests that the Khwārazmian descendants of Sayyid Ata had in many respects 'caught up' with those in Mavarannahr in terms of their respect and formal recognition at court (by then no longer Chinggisid). It may have been this more even regard for the Sayyid Atāʾī legacy, for instance, that led Mīr Musayyab Bukhārī to include Khwārazm in the domain supposedly marked by longstanding administrative recognition of Sayyid Atāʾī prerogatives; as he affirms, one indication of Sayyid Ata's greatness is the fact that, "down to the present time, which is the year 1261/1845, most important posts and positions in Bukhara and Khwārazm, including the *naqīb* and *ūrāq-i kalān* and *fayżī*, and others, belong exclusively to the descendants of Sayyid Ata."[60] Mīr Musayyab's account is quite late,

[59] The *Manāqib al-akhyār* is, of course, our earliest source to affirm a connection between the lineage of Sayyid Ata and the post of *naqīb* (see "Descendants of Sayyid Ata," p. 613); despite this work's focus on a Khwārazmian Sayyid Atāʾī lineage, however, it clearly reflects its author's familiarity with practices and traditions in Mawarannahr, and offers no evidence that any of the Sayyid Atāʾī figures known personally by the author held the rank of *naqīb*, or any other post, under the Chinggisid rulers of Khwārazm.

[60] Mīr Musayyab, ff. 474b-475a.

of course, and is suspicious, moreover, for expanding the number of ranks supposedly reserved for the descendants of Sayyid Ata; his expansion of the geographical and political range of the Sayyid Atāʾī 'monopoly' on these posts may be equally suspicious.

In any event, we have insufficient evidence with which to decide these questions; the kind of evidence we do find tends to support the supposition that differences more substantial than a mere disparity in the availability of sources are at work, but the relative sparseness of sources for the period in question is nevertheless real, and undermines the solidity of any conclusions drawn from them. In the end, the status and roles of Sayyid Atāʾī families in Khwārazm will have to be illuminated through the discovery of additional sources; these may come from established manuscript repositories, but a more likely venue for the discovery of such material is the surviving Sayyid Atāʾī communities of Khwārazm themselves. These communities no doubt preserve traditions, oral and perhaps written, that would illuminate their familial history, and perhaps fill in the genealogical gaps left by the sources noted here, of primarily Bukharan provenance; these traditions will inevitably reveal multiple layers in the formulation and adjustment of genealogical and narrative material, and it will be important to analyze them in the light of traditions that can be fixed, chronologically, with somewhat greater precision. It is hoped that the present review of evidence on the Khwārazmian Sayyid Atāʾī communities of the 16th and 17th centuries may facilitate the study and evaluation of such sources, as they are brought to light.

ON SOME 16TH- AND 17TH-CENTURY DOCUMENTS CONCERNING NOMADS

Jürgen Paul

Martin-Luther-Universität Halle-Wittenberg

Yuri Bregel recently remarked that "[t]he study of Central Asian history, especially post-Mongol history, in the West . . . became one of the casualties of the cold war;" and while he stated that there are some signs of a change for the better as far as the Timurid period is concerned, he observed that "[f]or the later period, from the 16th century and on, one can indicate only one major work of high quality"[1] written by a Western scholar in the last decades. Indeed, the history of Central Asia from ca. 1500 to the eve of the Russian conquest in the 19th century is one of the most glaring gaps in the field.

Of course, this paper cannot and does not aim in any way at filling that gap; it will be a long time before this period is as well served historically as the Timurid 15th century. Its very modest purpose is to draw attention to some untapped (or nearly untapped) sources, and it is concerned with only one factor in the region's history: nomads.[2] In fact, as is often stated, nomads provided the military power for each appanage-holder (and for the paramount *khān* also).[3] The general

[1] Y. Bregel, "Notes on the Study of Central Asia," *Papers on Inner Asia*, No. 28 (Bloomington, Indiana, 1996), pp. 28 and 58. The study Bregel has in mind is that of R. D. McChesney, *Waqf in Central Asia: Four Hundred Years in the History of a Muslim Shrine, 1480-1889* (Princeton, 1991).

[2] I am quite aware of the fallacies this term comports. In the course of the argument, it will appear that I am convinced that 'full-time' nomadism was rather the exception in Mavarannahr, and that all possible forms of mixing agriculture and stock-breeding prevailed, leading to more or less extended migrations of a given group in its entirety, or of parts thereof. For an introduction to the problem, see Yuri Bregel, "Nomadic and Sedentary Elements among the Turkmen," *Central Asiatic Journal*, 25 (1981), pp. 5-37.

[3] McChesney, *Waqf in Central Asia*, p. 57. The terminology used for 16th century Mavarannahr has been coined in a large measure by M. Dickson; see the (very brief) discussion in his "Uzbek Dynastic Theory in the Sixteenth Century," *Trudy XXVogo Kongressa Vostokovedov* [Moscow, 1960] (Moscow, 1963), III, pp. 208-216.

impression is that the Uzbeks were a "military stratum."[4] However, the ties linking the *khān* and the appanage rulers to these nomads have not yet been elucidated. This, of course, is due to the fact that the narrative sources (and the documentary sources as well) tend to take a sedentary perspective,[5] so that all information concerning nomads has to be pieced together in a rather painstaking process.[6] This research has yet to be done for 16th century Mavarannahr (and for the following periods as well). Moreover, the relationship between rulers and nomads tends to be obfuscated by the way both are frequently lumped together into a 'tribal confederation;' for, even if the tribes who later came to be known as "Uzbeks,"[7] mostly in hostile sources, had formed a confederation of sorts at some point in their history,[8] the ruling clan was not part of it; it was Chinggisid and therefore above all tribal differentiations.

Thus, even if new studies show how the system of combining appanage rule and tribal military forces contributed to the weakness of the Mavarannahrid states in the 16th century,[9] the problem of the nomads and their influence on possible state- or empire-building

[4] Bregel, "Nomadic and sedentary elements," p. 28.

[5] This was noted by Dickson, "Uzbek Dynastic Theory," p. 208.

[6] An example of what can be achieved in such a process is B. Manz, *The Rise and Rule of Tamerlane* (Cambridge, 1988).

[7] That the term "Uzbek" was not banned from official language, but on the contrary was used to denote the tribes that formed the military basis of the Mavarannahrid states in the 16th century, will be evident from several quotations from documents given below (e.g., notes 44 and 50).

[8] For the early history of these people see B. A. Akhmedov, *Gosudarstvo kochevykh uzbekov* (Moscow, 1965). This book, however, is marred not only by Soviet historical ideology ('nomadic feudalism' and so on), but also by its polemics against all those who put a question mark behind claims that settled economy was not only extant, but in fact central along the Syr Darya (i.e., the chapter on "Social-economic relations and state structure among the Uzbek nomads," pp. 71-108), and therefore it must be used only with caution for details (for the backgound of these polemics, see Bregel, "Notes," pp. 12-17, and also his discussion in "Nomadic and sedentary elements"); for an outline of the debate over 'nomadic feudalism' and its political implications, see Gellner's preface to A. Khazanov, *Nomads and the Outside World* (Cambridge, 1984). As for the 'tribal confederation' that supported Abū'l-Khayr Khān in his bid for power, see Akhmedov, *Gosudarstvo*, p. 46.

[9] R. D. McChesney, "The Conquest of Herat 995-6/1587-8: Sources for the Study of Ṣafavid/Qizilbāsh–Shībānid/Ūzbak relations," *Etudes Safavides*, ed. Jean Calmard (Paris/Tehran, 1993), pp. 69-107.

processes or on the political structures prevailing in the region still remains to be analyzed. This question is all the more important since the decline of Central Asia as a major player in international politics has been ascribed to the Uzbek nomadic invasion and subsequent minor ones following in its wake.[10]

A note is in order regarding the sources. Basically, I use two collections of "original" documents and one of *inshā*ʾ; in addition, several documents published by R. N. Nabiev (see note 12), as well as letters preserved in the *Rawżat al-riżvān*, have been consulted.

The first collection is the series published by O. D. Chekhovich and A. Egani in three consecutive issues of *Pis'mennye pamiatniki Vostoka*.[11] Only a few of these documents had been published previously, and apart from a few pieces that seem to form a small series, they are apparently unconnected. They cover a period from the second half of the 15th century down to the very end of the 18th (which was the margin the editors set themselves). This series is a mixture of official (issued mostly by appanage rulers) and judiciary documents (elaborated at *qāżīs*' courts).

The second collection, presently preserved in Kazan, contains documents concerning primarily the Farghana valley and the Andijan region in particular.[12] These documents are mostly in Persian, but a

[10] Yu. Bregel, "The Role of Central Asia in the History of the Muslim East," *Afghanistan Council Occasional Papers*, No. 20 (New York, 1980).

[11] A. A. Egani and O. D. Chekhovich, "Regesty sredneaziatskikh aktov (s fotoproizvedeniem publikuemykh vpervye," in *Pis'mennye pamiatniki Vostoka* (hereafter *PPV*), 1974 [published 1981], pp. 47-57, and plates, pp. 305-336; *PPV*, 1975 [1982], pp. 32-51, plates, pp. 266-317; *PPV*, 1976-1977 [1984], pp. 105-110, plates, pp. 321-362. The documents are numbered consecutively; the first issue has documents 1-35, the second issue docs. 36-100, and the third issue docs. 101-110. References given here are to the numbers of the documents. Most of the original pieces are (or, at least, were) kept in Dushanbe, and thus have a strong regional bias. The publications were intended as a first step toward an "overall catalogue of documentary sources in the Soviet Union," but, as far as I know, nothing more has been published.

[12] They are housed at the Tsentral'naia Nauchnaia i Publichnaia Biblioteka (TsNPB) in Kazan. I am using a transcript made at Bamberg University by Eckart Schiewek, Farzin Atefi, and Christoph Werner; the publication of this collection is being prepared in Bamberg (thanks to the Bamberg colleagues and Professor Bert Fragner who kindly let me see the preliminary results of their work). To this collection one might add the documents used by R. N. Nabiev in his "Istochniki po istorii krepostnogo prava v Srednei Azii," *Arkheograficheskii ezhegodnik*, 1963, pp. 87-105. In this article, Nabiev has reproduced and translated six documents; information

substantial number is in Turkic; they span a period from the last quarter of the 15th century down to the last third of the 17th, with one piece dated 1799, the bulk of them being dated to the 16th and 17th centuries.

The third source is a volume of *inshāʾ* kept in St. Petersburg.[13] The manuscript was dated by Volin "not later than the middle of the 16th century, judging by the paper and the script," and on internal evidence, he concluded that it must have been written during the lifetime of ʿAbd al-ʿAzīz Khān (d. 957/1550).[14] The structure of this manuscript is,

concerning the series of which these documents form a part can at best be termed scanty (p. 90). There is, however, no information on nomads in the published texts.

[13] Sankt-Peterburgskii filial Instituta vostokovedeniia Rossiiskoi Akademii nauk (SPFIVRAN), MS A210; see N. D. Miklukho-Maklai, *Persidskie i tadzhikskie rukopisi Instituta Narodov Azii: Kratkii alfavitnyi katalog* (Moscow, 1964), I, p. 567, No. 4246. The manuscript is characterized as "a collection of official documents and private correspondence as well as of specimens for the redaction of the latter. Excerpts are included from the *Ruqaʿāt* of Jāmī and from Khwāndamīr's *Nāma-i nāmī*." Two documents from this collection have been published, translated, and commented upon by S. L. Volin in his "K istorii sredneaziatskikh arabov," *Trudy Vtoroi sessii assotsiatsii arabistov* (Moscow, 1941; Trudy Instituta vostokovedeniia, vyp. 36), pp. 111-126. The manuscript has remained largely unknown, and it is not included in McChesney's list of sources for the Shībānid century in his article "Shībānids," *EI*[2], IX, pp. 428-431, probably because of the imprecise description in the catalogue. Miklukho-Maklai evidently did not use Volin's publication.

[14] Volin, "K istorii," p. 117. This is too simple. Volin evidently had in mind the appanage ruler of Bukhara, ʿAbd al-ʿAzīz b. ʿUbaydullāh Khān; ʿAbd al-ʿAzīz died in 1549 (according to Audrey Burton, *The Bukharans: A Dynastic, Diplomatic and Commercial History, 1550-1771* [Richmond, Surrey, 1997], p. 8). He never was supreme ruler of the Abū'l-Khayrid family, even if he is called "*khān*" in our manuscript and in Iranian sources as well (e.g., the popular history, by an anonymous author, *ʿĀlam-ārā-yi Shāh Ṭahmasp*, ed. Īraj Afshār [Tehran, 1370/1991]). The references in Volin's article are wrong; the name of this ruler occurs not on ff. 83b and 186b, but on ff. 85a and 189a. His name is mentioned once—Volin is right so far—with a formula indicating that the person is alive (*ṭawwala'llāhu ʿumrahu*, [f. 85a, last line]). This document is a *darubast* for ʿAbd al-ʿAzīz; he receives Mashhad province (in Khurāsān) as appanage from his father ʿUbaydullāh Khān. Thus, this document not only must have been written during ʿAbd al-ʿAzīz's lifetime, but can be dated more precisely to the second half of the 1520s, when ʿUbaydullāh made a bid, at first successful, for Khurāsān. In the second instance, it is not ʿAbd al-ʿAzīz himself who is meant in the corresponding formula, but his son ʿUmar-i ʿAbd al-ʿAzīz; the text reads ". . . *Abū'l-Muẓaffar ʿUmar-i ʿAbd al-ʿAzīz ṭawwala'llāhu ʿumrahu fī sarīr al-ʿizz wa'l-iqbāl wa khallada'llāhu dawām salṭanat[ihi] fī masnad al-khilāfa wa'l-ijlāl*" (f. 189a). From the context it is clear that this is a newborn child (the document in fact announces his birth, names the province of Qarākūl as the infant's appanage and names

however, much more complex than one would gather from Volin's information. It is in fact made up of numerous parts (ten or more); two of these are quotations from earlier collections, and for one of these, a source is given in the manuscript when reference is made to the *munsha'āt* of Mullā Ghiyāth al-Dīn, known as Khwāndamīr (f. 150a).[15] In the other case, the quotation is taken from ʿAbdullāh Marvarīd's *Sharaf-nāma*,[16] without the compiler acknowledging his source.

The St. Petersburg manuscript clearly deserves a careful new analysis. At first sight, most of the documents seem to stem from 16th-century Mavarannahr, but some of them certainly belong to late Timurid Khurāsān (some of these being quoted from earlier authors), and at least one bears the name of Shāh Ismāʿīl Ṣafavī (f. 172).[17] Many of the

---

an *atalīq* for him). ʿAbd al-ʿAzīz Sulṭān in fact had a son called ʿUmar-i ʿAbd al-ʿAzīz (see Burton, *Bukharans*, genealogical table, p. 545). Bregel mentions that ʿAbd al-ʿAzīz at another point was appointed as appanage ruler in Khwārazm ("Nomadic and sedentary elements," p. 28), as is evident also from the aforementioned popular history on Shāh Ṭahmasp (pp. 26 ff.). Other instances where easily identifiable persons are mentioned seem to indicate that in fact a relatively large part of the documents can be attributed to the Bukharan appanage and be linked to ʿAbd al-ʿAzīz. For instance, on f. 185a-b, reference is made to the *sulṭān*'s deceased brother, Muḥammad Raḥīm Sulṭān (ʿAbd al-ʿAzīz had a brother called thus; see Burton, *loc. cit.*). It is curious that in this case as well as in some other instances the promulgating ruler's father is styled "Jān Bābā Mīr" (or, if we take into account that the formula was written without any diacritical dots, "Khān Bābāmīz"?); in these instances, ʿUbaydullāh Khān must be meant. On the other hand, the manuscript includes texts that must be later than this, e.g., a *darubast* deed in favor of Khwāja Muḥammad Islām (Jūybārī) who is mentioned with a formula indicating that he was still alive (*adāma'llāhu taʿālā ẓilāl jalālihi'l-ʿālī* [f. 183b, last line]); this document may stem from the Jānībegid line and must have been written before 971/1563.

15 This, therefore, is the *Nāma-i nāmī* treated by G. Herrmann in his Ph.D. dissertation, "Der historische Gehalt des *Nāmä-yi nāmī* von Ḫōndamīr," (Göttingen, 1968; unpublished), as already noted by Miklukho-Maklai. A comparison of Herrmann's work with the St. Petersburg manuscript reveals that the part taken from the *Nāma-i nāmī* contains most of the appointment documents (but none of the letters and other pieces) from f. 150a to f. 177b.

16 Edited and translated by H. R. Roemer as *Staatsschreiben der Timuridenzeit: Das Šaraf-nāmä des ʿAbdallāh Marwarīd in kritischer Auswertung* (Wiesbaden, 1952). Roemer rightly assumed that Volin had worked with another copy of this text (p. 25, and p. 177, note 1), although it is evident that he had not seen Volin's article. Volin also noted that quite a few of the documents in A210 are to be found also in the *Sharaf-nāma* (of which he used a copy in St. Petersburg, MS SPFIVRAN C333).

17 Taken from Khwāndamīr (see Herrmann, doc. 22, German translation, p. 156, Persian text. p. 87).

documents are incomplete, and some are clearly 'only' stylistic exercises (e.g., how to address holders of certain offices). I counted 257 entries in all, in 217 folios; it must be left for further research how many of these have been taken from earlier sources. The manuscript under study thus seems to point at rather close links between Timurid and Shībānid administrative practice.[18]

The letters inserted into the hagiography on the Jūybārī shaykhs called *Rawżat al-riżvān* represent another source that needs to be taken into account. Even if the authenticity of these letters is not easily established, it may be assumed that they shed some light on fundamental questions. These letters have been used by Akhmedov (without source-critical treatment) and by McChesney; McChesney has shown that these letters fit in very well with the information found in narrative sources.[19] These texts are a selection of letters written to the Jūybārī shaykhs and kept in their archives where the compiler found them. This man, author of the hagiography in question, claims that there were 550 letters written by *khān*s, appanage rulers, and other rulers alone, not to mention those written by important persons including queens and princesses, scholars, and Sufis, but presumably also men of modest means; of those there were more than a thousand,[20] but it apparently did not serve the author's purposes to include any of them into his selection. Thus, the selection process the letters underwent seriously diminishes the collection's value as a historical source; we may assume that his choice was informed by his desire to let his masters, the Jūybārī *khwāja*s, appear as de facto overlords of the appanage rulers.

When reading the documents in question, the first observation one makes is that nomads are mentioned infrequently. Even smaller is the

[18] McChesney rightly pointed out that this subject has not been dealt with so far; see his article "Shībānids," in *EI*[2].

[19] Badr ad-Dīn Kashmīrī, *Rawżat al-riżvān*, MS Tashkent, Institute of Oriental Studies of the Academy of Sciences of the Republic of Uzbekistan, Inv. No. 2094, ff. 306-366. Cf. B. Akhmedov, "Rol' dzhuibarskikh khodzhei v obshchestvenno-politicheskoi zhizni Srednei Azii XVI-XVII vekov," *Dukhovenstvo i politicheskaia zhizn' na blizhnem i srednem vostoke v period feodalizma* (Moscow, 1985), pp. 16-31, and McChesney, "The conquest of Herat." The recent *kandidatskaia* thesis of Saidakhmedov gives an overview over the letters included in the work, but has no source-critical reflections, either; see Ibragim Saidakhmedov, "Pis'ma Shaibanidov - vazhnyi istoricheskii istochnik," Avtoreferat kandidatskoi dissertatsii (Tashkent 1994).

[20] *Rawżat al-riżvān*, f. 366a.

number of documents addressing nomads and questions related to nomads directly. Of these, two (or three, counting the piece taken from ʿAbdullāh Marvarīd) have been treated by Volin.[21]

Nomads are mentioned in some cases in the *inscriptio*, mostly as "desert-" or "steppe-dwellers" (*ṣaḥrā-nishīnān*). Whether nomads are mentioned in a document or not depends to a certain degree on the subject matter treated: they appear above all in appointment deeds. It is, however, noteworthy that nomads are mentioned in appointment deeds not only for offices dealing in some way with military affairs or whose incumbents may be expected to have something to do with nomads.[22] When mentioned, though, in most cases, they occupy the last place among all groups enumerated, after the peasants. Not too much should probably made out of the position they occupy; but sometimes, a hierarchy seems to be implied. Thus, the nomads would be relegated to an inferior position in society (in the authors' view).[23] As an example (chosen nearly at random): "The village elders and other important people in Balkh province generally, and the peasants, tillers, and settled people, as well as the bedouins and nomads of Nahr-i Iṣfahān should know" (that a certain person has been appointed *muḥtasib*).[24] As an exception to this rule, one might quote a document written in Turkic,

[21] See note 16. Volin gives part of a document installing a *mīrākhūr* (p. 117; MS A210, f. 25b), the complete text of a *nishān-i mīr-hazārī-yi aʿrāb* (appointing a leader over a given group of Arabs [p. 118; MS A210, ff. 124a-b]), and the document taken from the *Sharaf-nāma* (p. 122; MS A210, ff. 97a-98b, without what remains of the protocol, *arenga* included; Roemer, *Staatsschreiben*, p. 94, facs., f. 38b). However, Roemer's text breaks off shortly before Volin's begins; Roemer has the *arenga*, whereas Volin starts with the *narratio*.

[22] A number of examples: MS A210, f. 28b, appointment for a *shaykh al-islām*; f. 33a, appointment of a *muḥtasib* at Marghīnān; f. 33b, appointment of a *ṣadr* in the same town; f. 34a, appointment of a *qāżī* at an unnamed place; f. 195b, appointment of a commander of night sentinels (*mīr-i shab*). Military affairs: f. 100b, appointment of a governor whose responsibility includes warriors for the faith (*ghuzāt*) [here, nomads are evoked in the *adhortatio*]; f. 151b, appointment for a governor and *dārūgha* over Andkhūd province (taken from Khwāndamīr; cf. Herrmann, doc. 4); ff. 193b-195b, appointment of a military commander, "Lord of Attack" (*mīr-i ghaṣab*).

[23] Nomads are placed at the same spot in some documents adduced by Khwāndamīr.

[24] MS A210, f. 28a: *arbāb va kalāntarān-i sarkār-i Balkh ʿumūman raʿāyā va muzāriʿān va muqīmān va aʿrāb va aḥshām va ṣaḥrā-nishīnān-i Nahr-i Iṣfahān . . . bidānand ki . . .*

where the addressed groups are dealt with on an equal footing: ". . . especially the *sayyids*, *mullās*, and notables in each town, the leaders and important people in each nomadic tribe, the commanders of thousands and tens of thousands should know that . . ."[25] It certainly is not by accident that the document written in Turkic offers a slightly different view from those written in Persian, even if the number of Turkic documents is too small to use them as quantitative evidence.

Another point worth mentioning about the document just quoted is that it refers to "commanders of thousands and tens of thousands." In general, formulas like "the commanders of hundreds of the [Turkic] tribes and the commanders of thousands of the [Arabic] bedouins" are used.[26]

Documents directly concerned with nomads fall into several categories. There are some appointments (to posts giving the incumbents some form of authority over the nomads in question), and some cases of litigation as well as petitions. Another case—addressed in letters—is mediation between nomads and rulers, with Sufi shaykhs appearing as mediators. A last group are documents where the offices of "military judge" (*qāżī-yi ʿaskar*) and "military *muḥtasib*" (*muḥtasib-i ʿaskar*) are mentioned. Among the questions addressed by the documents, taxes due take a prominent place.

An appointment to the office of *mīrākhūr* ("chief equerry") shows that these persons were responsible for, among other things, collecting taxes from nomads, including those who practiced some agriculture. They are ordered to take what is due from summer and winter pastures (*ʿamal az yaylāqāna va qishlāqāna*), and the document stipulates that "those who, in their summer pastures, have cultivated the soil, must give what is due to the aforementioned person as has long been common practice."[27]

It is not evident whether in a legal case the parties are peasants who also practiced some stockbreeding, nomads, or anything in between;

25 MS A210, f. 35a: *sayyid va sādāt mavālī va ahālī va ashrāf va aʿyānlar bile kent kent aymāq aymāq ṣaḥrā-nishīnān illärning arbāb va kalāntarläri bile ming begi va on ming begi bile vāżiḥ va lāʾiḥ bolsun kim . . .*

26 MS A210, f. 26a: *yūzbakīyān-i aymāqāt va mīr-hazārān-i aʿrāb*. For traces of the Mongol decimal organization, see Volin, who thinks that it was still practiced (for sedentary people) in peripheral regions.

27 MS A210, f. 26a: *va har kas dar yaylāqhā zirāʿat namūda bāshad māl-i ān-rā ba-dastūr-i qadīm ba-mushār ilayhi dahand.*

the question is whether a given group of people that has had access to summer pastures (where also some agriculture can take place) and has paid its dues in full can deny access to this place to another group who has come there.[28]

A conflict between nomads and sedentary people (how sedentary?) seems to underly another document: two Qïrghïz leaders and their people are told not to interfere with lands whose owner is privileged in the decree.[29] Conflict between nomads and sedentary people is more in evidence in a document adduced by Semenov (dated, with a question mark, to 1106-07/1695); here, a group of nomads (called "Uzbeks") are admonished not to disturb a given shaykh and his people.[30]

In another appointment of a *mīrākhūr*, the incumbent is to gather horses for *sūqūm*;[31] this expression is used for cattle and other animals which are kept and fattened for later consumption.

Appointments for *amīr*s are more frequent. One example refers to the "Chaghatays" in Dīzaq province (east of Samarqand). The people living there are styled "all the Chaghatays in that region, the notables, and village elders" (or "tribal chiefs"?) (*jamāʿat-i chaghatāyān-i qalamraw va arbāb va kalāntarān*), and in the *inscriptio*, they are called, in more detail, ". . . and all the other followers of this palace, the abode of the world, and everyone else, the bedouin, the nomads and the commanders of hundreds of the tribes, the notables, and village elders" (or "tribal chiefs"?), "all the settled people living in Samarqand

[28] Egani and Chekhovich, doc. 12, dated not before 1012/1603. The text is a *rivāyat*, a narrative expounding a legal case, leading to a corresponding decision (*fatwā*). The answer to the question is yes, the first group has an exclusive right to this summer pasture (including agricultural possibilities?), because the other group belongs to another place; the fact that it is the petitioners who pay the taxes seems to earn them this right. The people are called *mardum-i dah manāra*, and this place in turn is styled a "*qarya*." Must we conclude from this that the people in question are peasants? What do they do in the *yaylāq*? There is no information on this.

[29] Egani and Chekhovich, doc. 37, dated 1669-70. I would say that the phrase "*mardum-i qirqizīya-i Ulchika va Naẓar Bī*" is not very well rendered by the translation "*sluzhilye liudi iz Kirgizov - Uldzhaka i Nazar Bi*;" there is no information that these Qïrghïz were "officials" in any way.

[30] A. Semenov, *Ocherk pozemel'no-podatnogo i nalogovogo ustroistva b. Bukharskogo khanstva* (Tashkent, 1929), p. 15.

[31] MS A210, f. 76b.

province."[32] They are to give certain dues to the incumbent, and the Chaghatays are more specifically told to hand their "dead and absent" (animals?) over to the governor. All courtiers are admonished not to accept these Chaghatays in *ḥimāyat* ("protection").[33]

Another decree, concerning the governorship of Samarqand province, also mentions nomads, but the focus is on the fee the governor is to receive.[34]

A third appointment deed is literally called "Appointment to the office of Chaghatay *amīr*;" the incumbent is one Yār Bābā Beg. First, this man's military qualities and loyalty are praised. In the following, all the Chaghatay warriors (*sipāhīyān-i chaghaṭāy*) are told to obey him, and all the other *amīr*s are warned not to take any Chaghatays as followers and not to accept them in *ḥimāyat*.[35] In this case, the "governor" also is to take care that nobody loses all his animals; if such a situation should arise, he may take animals from the well-to-do.

Another appointed governor clearly has military tasks (cf. note 21 above), but we do not learn where the warriors come from, or whether they are tribal levies or not.[36]

There is a short decree appointing a certain Mubāriz ad-Dīn *fulān* Bī as chief of one hundred in Ḥiṣār-i Shādmān province, but no nomads are evident in the text.[37]

Two features seem to characterize offices designed to control nomads, if we follow these appointment deeds. First, there are some taxes the appointees are to collect, and there may be other dues the nomads have to give, services to render, horses to deliver, and so forth. But second, and probably first of all, appointments of officials over nomads are serving the purpose of organizing loyalties. The rulers who issued these decrees were interested in establishing links of loyalty

[32] MS A210, f. 26a: *va sā'ir-i mulāzimān-i dargāh-i ʿālam-panāh va ghayr dhālik va aʿrāb va aḥshām va yūzbakīyān-i aymāqāt va arbāb va kalāntarān va jumhūr-i sakana va ʿumūm-i mutawaṭṭina-yi wilāyat-i Samarqand.*

[33] For this way of changing masters, cf. J. Paul, *Die politische und soziale Bedeutung der Naqšbandiyya in Mittelasien im 15. Jahrhundert* (Berlin, 1991).

[34] MS A210, f. 26a.

[35] MS A210, f. 84a.

[36] MS A210, f. 99a.

[37] MS A210, f. 130b. The *ṣada* is called KNKURD, if I am not mistaken. For the time being, I cannot tell whether this is a local or a tribal designation.

between certain persons and certain tribal groupings; the persons appointed may or may not have close (among them: genealogical) ties to their constituencies, but at any rate, the relationship is meant to be exclusive. No other person, and above all, no highly placed person, is to interfere; no one has the right to constitute a following out of nomads, and the nomads are denied the right to choose whom they want to follow.

The two or three decrees analyzed by Volin confirm this result, above all the text included in both the *Sharaf-nāma* and in MS A210. This is a petition by nomads (probably of Arab stock) who are asking for "protection" (*ihtimām* in this case); that is, they want the ruler to name somebody who "cares for them."[38] Even if this decree clearly stems from Timurid Khurāsān (probably late 15th century), the system had not really changed.

Mediation is apparent in one of the letters inserted into the *Rawżat al-riżvān*.[39] The Tülkichi tribe had not given what the ruler—ʿAbdullāh Khān—thought they owed (12,000 head of sheep per year); and since they had allowed three years to lapse without paying, he had resolved to punish them. Then, however, he had learned that only some of them were guilty, so he had planned to punish only those. But now, since the *khwāja* had asked that they be spared, he had decided to do so. "But these people have greatly wronged me. They owed me a *muqarrarī* (a fixed amount of something, in this case, animals), but to the present day, they have not given my officials anything. In the time of Pīr Muḥammad Khān, they gave 12,000 head of sheep every year together with the *ashlugh* (provisions for the royal kitchen)."[40] These nomads evidently thought that their dues could be negotiated anew when a new *khān* ascended the throne. That nomads were at least sometimes treated on the same lines as other taxpaying subjects appears from the series of documents quoted in the same source; in these, the Jūybārī *khwāja*s are

[38] Volin, "K istorii," pp. 122-123, and see note 21 above. Volin remarks that *ihtimām* was something the nomads had to pay for; he believes that it involved bringing all kinds of cases and petitions to the ruler's attention.

[39] *Rawżat al-riżvān*, ff. 308b-309a; cf. a Russian translation in Akhmedov, "Rol'," p. 25.

[40] *Fa-ammā ān mardum ba-mā bisyār ihānat karda būdand muqarrarī-yi mā dar dhimma-i īshān būd tā īn zamān ba-kasān-i mā nadāda būdand va dar zamān-i Pīr Muḥammad Khān har sāl ba-ʿadad-i davāzdah hazār gūsfand ba-ghayr az āshlūgh mīdādand.*

endowed with manpower (presumably corvée labor) in order to dig a canal. The commandeered men are to be chosen among others from the *aymāqāt* ("tribes").[41]

Mediation between rulers and nomads was nothing new; another case is documented in the late Timurid *Sharaf-nāma*.[42]

Some nomads were exempt from taxes—but not because they were nomads. This is documented in the way a petition was answered. A certain Sulṭān Muḥammad claimed to be a descendant of Aḥmad Yasavī, but since he could not produce a document proving this—apparently he said that it had been lost—he had been put on the list of *aymāqāt* (this term thus should mean "tax-paying tribes" in the given context; see the preceding paragraph about their being subject to forced labor). However, after awhile he had found the document again, and he had shown it to competent persons who stated that it was real proof of the petitioner's claim, because it had been confirmed by Khwāja Naṣīr ad-Dīn ʿUbaydullāh (this, then, must be Khwāja Aḥrār). This document had been accepted as legal proof by ʿAbd al-ʿAzīz Khān, who had issued a decree that this man's name should be deleted from the tax roll (*daftar-i yasāq*: a register for tax-paying nomads?), that he should be registered among the descendants of Aḥmad Yasavī (who evidently were exempt from taxes), and that he not be molested any longer with demands for various taxes.[43] In this case, we cannot tell what kind of taxes the *aymāqāt* had to give, whether animals (sheep or horses?), money, or services.

It is interesting to ask whether the military—and did this category include all the nomads?—were subject to a separate judicial administration represented by the "military judge" (*qāżī-yi ʿaskar*). This office is mentioned in several instances, and sometimes it is explicitly stated that this official should not occupy himself with anything but the "Uzbeks and Chaghatays."[44] In another document (undated), it is stated that

[41] *Rawżat al-riżvān*, f. 316b (an inserted document dated Jumādā I 993/May 1585).

[42] Roemer, *Staatsschreiben*, pp. 115 ff. The mediator in this case is Khwāja Aḥrār.

[43] MS A210, ff. 181b ff. As taxes, the text mentions *yasaq*, *ikhrājāt*, *sar-shumār*, and, as general terms, *kull-i ḥavālāt-i dīvānī* and *tavajjuhāt-i ḥukmī*.

[44] TsNPB Kazan 285, dated 1009/1601, line 10: *va qāżī-yi ʿaskar-i humāyūn ba-ghayr az Ūzbak va Chaghaṭāy ba-chīzī dakhl nakunad*.

certain lands are what amounts to private tax-free property (*milk-i khāliṣ*) belonging to a certain Khwāja Hāshim-i Aḥrārī (obviously a descendant of Khwāja Aḥrār).[45] It had been established by a *qāżī-yi ʿaskar* that this property was tax-free, in a document drawn up to this purpose.[46] The last instance where the office of *qāżī-yi ʿaskar* is mentioned occurs in an appointment deed dated 992/1584. Those persons who before did not fall under the *qāżī-yi ʿaskar*'s jurisdiction are not subject to him in future; he and his deputies are to occupy themselves only with affairs concerning the military and the tribes.[47] It is not evident, however, that this document is an appointment for a *qāżī-yi ʿaskar*: the office is called *mansab-i rafīʿ al-qadr qażā-yi balada-yi maḥfūẓa-yi Samarqand*, and the duties of the incumbent are the same as those habitually ascribed to a judge. There is another instance where offices demanded by Islamic law are doubled, one for 'civilians' and another for the 'military' (and 'military' may mean, as the document just quoted states explicitly, the *aymāqāt*, that is, the tribes). This is an appointment deed for Mullā Shihāb; he is appointed as *muḥtasib*, and it is specified that *iḥtisāb-i ʿaskar* is to be understood.[48] But this difference probably was not always made, as is evident from those appointments where both groups are included.[49] The way these offices functioned is not apparent from the documents themselves and thus, the question must be left open at this point.

That "Uzbeks and Chaghatays" were viewed as belonging to a military stratum to the exclusion of all "Sarts and Tajiks" is hinted at in some phrases describing the entire population in binary pairs: "No

45 On Khwāja Hāshim-i Aḥrārī, a Naqshbandī descendant of Khoja Aḥrār active in Samarqand in the early 17th century, see R. D. McChesney, "The 'Reforms' of Bāqī Muḥammad Khān," *Central Asiatic Journal*, 24 (1980), pp. 79-80 (with further references).

46 MS A210, f. 178a. This type of document is called a *thubūt-nāma*.

47 Egani and Chekhovich, doc. 105. The text is not easily read due to the poor quality of the reproduction. I take it to read: *mardumī ki az qadīm qāżī-yi ʿaskar dakhl nakarda va nāʾibān-i ū dakhl nakunand va juz jundī va aymāqāt dar qażāyā-yi dīgar dakhl* (or: *madkhal*) *nanamāyand*.

48 MS A210, f. 105a. This document is unfortunately transmitted only as a fragment, so that the portion indicating the way in which other groups of people are to act (*sabīl* or *adhortatio*) is not extant.

49 As for instance in MS A210, f. 165b, on the appointment of a judge in Shapūrghān; nomads are explicitly mentioned as forming part of his responsibility.

one, no creature, no Uzbek or Sart, no Turk or Tajik, no military or other" (should dare to ignore the decree).[50] Similar binary oppositions are taken up in a later decree: "Everyone, humble and noble, small and great, military and other, who had suffered from him and did not want him to be governor any longer" (came to the *khān* in order to seek redress).[51] It is not clear, however, whether these binary pairs reflect any real cleavage in society or whether they corresponded to the view the authors had of society.

[50] TsNPB Kazan No. 243, issued by Nawrūz Aḥmad Khān in 942/1535; this decree is in Turkic, but the fomula is in Persian: *hīch afrīda ūzbīk va sārt turk va tājīk sipāhī va ghayrihi*.

[51] TsNPB Kazan No. 252, a decree issued by Imām Qulī Khān in 1042/1632-33.

MUSLIM SACRED HISTORY AND THE 1905 REVOLUTION IN A SUFI HISTORY OF ASTRAKHAN

Allen J. Frank

Takoma Park, Maryland

INTRODUCTION

At the turn of the 19th and 20th centuries, Muslim society in Russia's Volga-Ural region began a fundamental and long-term shift toward secularization in its intellectual and political life. Until that time, at least on an intellectual level, this Muslim society was largely isolated from Russian society as a whole, in the sense that it sustained an internal discourse whose framework of reference was essentially an Islamic one. As in most traditional Islamic societies, social and political discourse remained the realm of the *ʿulamā*, which by its very existence served to define the community as Islamic. In his recent study of the Islamic intellectual history of the Volga-Ural *ʿulamā* under Russian rule, Michael Kemper has labeled this discourse "Islamic discourse," and has demonstrated that within the realm of such areas as Sufism, law, and theology various social and political issues, as well as issues relating to the latter Islamic fields of study, were actively addressed and debated among Volga-Ural Muslims.[1] In a similar vein, the role and development of locally-produced historiography in this Islamic discourse have been addressed in a number of recent works.[2]

[1] Michael Kemper, *Sufis und Gelehrte in Tatarien und Baschkirien, 1789-1889: Der islamische Diskurs unter russischer Herrschaft* (Berlin, 1998; Islamkundliche Untersuchungen, Bd. 218); Michael Kemper, "Šihābaddīn al-Marǧānī als Religionsgelehrter," *Muslim Culture in Russia and Central Asia from the 18th to the Early 20th Centuries*, ed. Michael Kemper, Anke von Kügelgen, and Dmitriy Yermakov (Berlin, 1996; Islamkundliche Untersuchungen, Bd. 200), pp. 129-166; Michael Kemper, "Entre Boukhara et la Moyenne Volga: ʿAbd an-Naṣīr al-Qursāwī (1776-1812) en conflit avec les oulémas traditionalistes," *Cahiers du monde russe*, 37/1-2 (1996), pp. 41-52.

[2] Allen Frank, "The Development of Regional Islamic Identity in Imperial Russia: Two Commentaries on the Tavārīx-i Bulġārīya of Ḥusāmaddīn al-Muslimī," *Muslim Culture in Russia and Central Asia from the 18th to the Early 20th Centuries* (Berlin,

Previous studies, which have focused on the rise of secularism, Islamic modernism, and romantic nationalism among Volga-Ural Muslims, have proceeded from the a priori assumption that meaningful social and political discourse was impossible in an Islamic society dominated by traditional institutions until the rise of secularism and nationalism; in these studies, the assumption is that traditional discourse, when even mentioned, was arcane, esoteric, and essentially meaningless in a modern context, and served to retard the 'national' progress of Muslim society. For these historians the only meaningful intellectual activity before the rise of secularism involved those members of the *ʿulamā* whose works anticipated the rise of secularism, and foretold the eclipse of the influence of Islam among Volga-Ural Muslims. In these studies the twin processes of the rise of secularism, and the rejection of Islam's religious influence on society, are identified as 'the Tatar enlightenment.' Secularists are often labeled 'jadīdist' and those who opposed 'jadīdism' are called 'qadīmists.'[3] This interpretation emerged already before 1917 and has endured, and even thrived, up to the present. It was expressed by Tatar exiles in the 1920s and 1930s,[4] as well as by Tatar and Russian writers throughout the Soviet period;[5] it

1996), pp. 113-128; Allen J. Frank, *Islamic Historiography and 'Bulghar' Identity among the Tatars and Bashkirs of Russia* (Leiden, 1998).

[3] For critical approaches to this issue, see the recent article by Stéphane Dudoignon "Qu'est-ce-que la «*qadîmiya*»? Éléments pour un sociologie du traditionalisme musulman, en Islam de Russia et en Transoxiane (au tournant des XIXe et XXe siècles)," *L'Islam de Russie: Conscience communautaire et autonomie politique chez les Tatars de la Volga et de l'Oural depuis le XVIIIe siècle* (Paris, 1997), pp. 207-225; Galina M. Yémelianova, "The national identity of the Volga Tatars at the turn of the 19th century: Tatarism, Turkism and Islam," *Central Asian Survey*, 16/4 (1997), pp. 543-572.

[4] Cf. G. Baṭṭāl, *Qazān tūrkleri* (Istanbul, 1926); Gaiaz Iskhaki, *Idel-Ural* (Kazan, 1991).

[5] This interpretation is evident both in Soviet historical works and in literary criticism; some representative samples of the many works that fall into this category include: Liutsian Klimovich, *Islam v tsarskoi Rossii* (Moscow, 1936); A. I. Kharisov, *Literaturnoe nasledie bashkirskogo naroda* (Ufa, 1973); Z. A. Ishmukhametov, *Sotsial'naia rol' i evoliutsiia islama v Tatarii* (Kazan, 1979); M. Kh. Iusupov, *Shigabutdin Merdzhani kak istorik* (Kazan, 1981); *Tatar ädäbiyatï tarikhï*, I-II (Kazan, 1984-1986); *Obshchestvennaia i filosofskaia mysl' v Tatarii nachala XX veka* (Kazan, 1990). This approach is succinctly related in the article by Reshat M. Amirkhanov, "Islam and the Tatar Social and Ethical Thought," *Central Asian Survey*, 9/2 (1990), pp. 103-108.

persists in post-Soviet Tatarstan,[6] and has been adopted, with a particularly lamentable absence of critical analysis, among many historians in the West.[7] One of the most remarkable characteristics of this approach has been its lack of nuance in evaluating the supposed secular-religious conflict within Volga-Ural Muslim society. Depending on the ideological allegiances of the specific observer, essentially all figures are categorized as enlightened or obscurantist, progressive or reactionary, reasoned or fanatical, jadidist or qadimist, etc.

In retrospect, it is clear that during the first decades of the 20th century, at least at the intellectual level, secularism, modernism, and nationalism were beginning to displace the older Islamic intellectual traditions. However, the scale of this displacement was certainly limited, and the internal debate preceding the 1917 Revolution probably did little to effectively secularize the Tatar and Bashkir peasantry, to say nothing of the *ʿulamā*; indeed Soviet historians are in all likelihood correct in claiming the secularization of Tatar and Bashkir society as a Soviet 'achievement,' even if they conceal the fact that the physical extermination of the *ʿulamā*, of whom perhaps thirty thousand were executed or perished in the Gulag, was an important element of this 'achievement.'[8]

In fact, before 1917 many members of the *ʿulamā* may not have perceived a conflict between secular education and political reforms on the one hand, and, on the other hand, the more enduring features that consciously defined the community as traditionally Islamic; such features included the tombs of Muslims saints, Sufi shaykhs, and the histories of

[6] The post-Soviet interpretations of Tatar cultural history are presented very succinctly in a semi-official 'guide' to Tatar history published in the Republic of Tatarstan: R. M. Mukhametshin (ed.), *Tatary i Tatarstan: spravochnik* (Kazan, 1993), pp. 110-133. Cf. Yahya Abdoulline, "Histoire et interprétations contemporaines de second réformisme musulman (ou djadidisme) chez les tatars de la Volga et de Crimée," *Cahiers du monde russe*, 37/1-2 (1996), pp. 65-82.

[7] See especially A. Rorlich, *The Volga Tatars: A Profile in National Resilience* (Stanford, California, 1986).

[8] A. A. Alov and N. G. Vladimirov, *Islam v Rossii* (Moscow, 1996), p. 60; for a brief case-study of Soviet anti-Islamic policies in the city of Omsk cf. N. I. Lebedeva, "Zakrytie Omskikh mechetei," *Islam, obshchestvo i kul'tura: meterialy mezhdu-narod-noi nauchnoi konferentsii 'Islamskaia tsivilizatsiia v preddverii XXI veka (k 600-letiiu islama v Sibiri)'* (Omsk, 1994), pp. 96-97.

local mosques and of the local *ʿulamā*.[9] With this in mind, the present article seeks to explore how the rise of secular education and the political changes brought about by the 1905 Revolution in Russia are reflected in a Turkic historical treatise, devoted to typically traditional historical themes—the work includes a sacred history of the city of Astrakhan, a catalogue of shrines in the city, and a biographical dictionary of Sufis active there—as well as to the consequences and significance for Muslims of the 1905 Revolution and political reform.

This historical treatise in question is entitled *Tārīkh-i Astarkhān* ("The History of Astrakhan"), and was written by a certain Ḥāfiẓ Jahānshāh b. ʿAbd al-Jabbār al-Nīzhghārūṭī al-Ḥājjītarkhānī, and was published in Astrakhan in 1907.[10] The book is an interesting example of local historiography that became very popular among the Muslims of Russia proper at the beginning of the 20th century, and is an important source in its own right for the religious history of Astrakhan, which at the turn of the 19th and 20th centuries boasted one of the largest Muslim populations in Russia proper.[11] It is the single most extensive biographical source for the *imāms*, and especially for the Sufi shaykhs, of Astrakhan province, and also contains what is certainly the most detailed discussion of Muslim hagiolatry in the Lower Volga region, an aspect of Muslim life of considerable historic importance in Volga-Ural region as a whole.[12]

[9] The political activities and debates of the Volga-Ural *ʿulamā* in Revolutionary Russia remain to be studied. Nevertheless, the proceedings of the first meeting of the Union of *ʿulamā* convened in Moscow in June of 1917 reveal both a strong attachment to political and educational reform in general, and a similar attachment to traditional religious education and existing local religious institutions; cf. *ʿUlamā ittifāqï: birinchi nadvasï* (Kazan, 1917). Although this organization claimed to be 'All-Russian,' the overwhelming majority of the 270 delegates listed were from the Volga-Ural region. Of these, nine are listed as being from Astrakhan province.

[10] Jahānshāh b. ʿAbd al-Jabbār al-Nīzhghārūṭī al-Ḥājjītarkhānī, *Tārīkh-i Astarkhān* (Astrakhan, 1907), 52 pp.

[11] Unfortunately, Astrakhan is excluded from the most complete study to date of Tatar historical demography, D. M. Iskhakov's *Istoricheskaia demografiia tatarskogo naroda (XVIII-nachalo XX vv.)* (Kazan, 1993). According to a publication of the Ministry of Internal Affairs, in 1883 there were 4,508 Muslims in the city of Astrakhan with fourteen mosques; see *Alfavitnye spiski armiano-grigorianskikh tserkvei i magometanskikh mechetei v imperii* (Moscow, 1883).

[12] Cf. Allen J. Frank, "Islamic Shrine Catalogues and Communal Geography in the Volga-Ural Region: 1788-1917," *Journal of Islamic Studies*, 7/2 (1996), pp. 265-286.

But the *Tārīkh-i Astarkhān* also stands out within the genre of the Tatar local history for its author's willingness to venture beyond a discussion of purely local concerns into the larger realm of recent and distant Russian history. Writing during the Revolution of 1905-1907, Jahānshāh addresses issues that concerned the Muslims of Imperial Russia as a whole, such as the meaning for Muslims of the end of autocracy (as it seemed at the time), and the significance for Muslims of "progress" (*taraqqīyāt*) and "freedom" (*ḥurrīyat*). His narrative deserves attention because as a Sufi historian he is expressing his own views on the issues of modernism, 'freedom' and 'progress,' and educational reform. His views, and the biographical and historical material he presents, are interesting in their own right, but Jahānshāh's perceptions and explanations of 'progress' and 'freedom' call into question the usefulness of the reformist-traditionalist dichotomy underpinning the works of many Western, Soviet, and post-Soviet Tatar historians.

THE WORK AND ITS AUTHOR

The author of the *Tārīkh-i Astarkhān* identifies himself at the end of his book as Ḥāfiẓ Jahānshāh b. ʿAbd al-Jabbār al-Ḥājjītarkhānī; in ethnic terms it is likely that he was a Mishar, since on the title page he uses the additional *nisba*s of al-Nīzhghārūṭī Shūbīlī, suggesting that he was originally from the village Shubino in Nizhnii Novgorod province. In addition to this, we know only that he was a Sufi, since he identifies a prominent local Sufi shaykh, ʿAbd al-Vahhāb Ḥājjī b. ʿAlī (d. 1899) as his master (*ustādh*).[13] It is unlikely that Jahānshāh was himself an *imām*, since his narrative on the *imām*s and mosques of Astrakhan is rather short for a city that boasted fourteen mosques as early as the 1880s, and it is possible that he was a merchant, since he seems well acquainted with Astrakhan's economic life and its wealthier Muslim citizens, but I have unfortunately been unable to find any information of Jahānshāh's subsequent activities or his ultimate fate. His work was published in Astrakhan in 1907, but Jahānshāh tells us in the introduction that the published version was an abridgement of a larger work:

> This poor humble [author] had offered to compose a treatise [entitled] "the History of Astrakhan," with the intention of being of humble service, through this publication, to his

[13] *Tārīkh-i Astarkhān*, p. 40.

> countrymen. Although I, the humble [author], did not sufficiently complete this treatise as I would have wished, nonetheless, for the sake of my dear countrymen, to some degree, I shifted my endeavors and energies toward this direction in order to compile a treatise on Astrakhan. This is because, upon reading [the first draft of] the treatise, regret or boasting was entering into it.[14]

Although the *Tārīkh-i Astarkhān* includes various essays on the larger issues of historical, educational and cultural issues of interest to a general audience of Muslims in Russia, the work is primarily concerned with local history, and is especially a sacred history of the city of Astrakhan and Astrakhan province, with considerable space devoted to the histories of mosques and saints' tombs, biographical sketches of prominent *imāms*, Muslim saints, and Sufis, and the establishment of a sacred geography, with an enumeration of important shrines, saints' tombs, and mosques. As a result of Jahānshāh's focus on religious history, the *Tārīkh-i Astarkhān* corresponds rather closely to the wider historiographic genre of the Tatar local history, which by 1907 had become quite popular among Volga-Ural Muslims.

The origins of this highly popular genre are unclear, at least for the Volga-Ural region,[15] but probably emerged from several earlier genres; these include tribal and village genealogies (*shajara*s)[16] that were widespread among both Bashkirs and Tatars, as well as narratives recounting the corporate relationships of specific Muslim communities with the Russian authorities.[17] In these sorts of works the community was described and defined, and the history of its relationship with Russia was similarly recounted. By the turn of the 19th and 20th centuries village histories had evolved into a number of styles, all sharing a

[14] *Tārīkh-i Astarkhān*, p. 2.

[15] For a discussion of this genre, see R. Shaikhiev, *Tatarskaia narodno-kraevedcheskaia literatura XIX-XX vv.* (Kazan, 1990).

[16] Cf. R. G. Kuzeev, *Bashkirskie shezhere* (Ufa, 1960); M. A. Usmanov, *Tatarskie istoricheskie istochniki XVII-XVIII vekov* (Kazan, 1972), pp. 167-195; Marsel' Akhmetzianov, *Tatarskie shedzhere* (Kazan, 1991), Marsel' Äkhmätjanov, *Tatar shäjäräläre* (Kazan, 1995).

[17] For examples of these sorts of documents, see Iu. G. Mukhametshin, "Materialy po istorii dereven' Permskikh tatar," *Permskie tatary* (Kazan, 1983), pp. 155-163.

primarily religious institutional focus. Among printed works, for example, the *Tārīkh-i Isterlībāsh* addressed the history of a Sufi dynasty and its madrasa in Ufa province;[18] Riżā al-Dīn Fakhrutdinov's *Saʿīd* addressed the history of Seitovskii Posad, or Qarghalï, a famous center for Islamic learning located near Orenburg, listing its mosques and *imāms*;[19] and the *Īskī Qïyïshqī Tārīkhi* of Muṭahhir b. Mullā Mīr Ḥaydar addresses the history of a mosque and *madrasa* near the city of Ufa.[20] Village, or even city histories, were also inserted into larger historical works, such as a history of Kazan's New Tatar Quarter (the Novaya Tatarskaya Sloboda) in Ḥusayn Amīrkhānov's *Tavārīkh-i Bulghārīya*.[21] Many Tatar village histories were printed, but by far the largest number of village histories are preserved in uncatalogued manuscripts, located in various manuscript collection in the cities of Kazan and Ufa.[22]

REVOLUTION AND MODERNISM

Jahānshāh's political and historical commentaries are of particular interest since they were written during an especially fluid and optimistic period in the social and intellectual history of Imperial Russia's Muslims. Furthermore, while both Soviet and pro-modernist Western historians have generally underscored the support shown by Muslim intellectuals and reformers for the 1905 Revolution, Jahānshāh's treatise shows that the revolution, and specifically the end of autocracy, was well received by a portion of the *ʿulamā* connected with an important religious center such as Astrakhan.

The work's social and political commentaries concern two basic themes. The first is the deleterious effects of autocracy on the Russian empire's subjects through history, as well as the advantages of "freedom" (*ḥurrīyat*), specifically for Muslims and Islam. The second,

[18] Muḥammad Shākir Makhdūm Ṭūqāyef, *Tārīkh-i Isterlībāsh* (Kazan, 1899).

[19] Riżāʾ al-Dīn Fakhrutdinov, *Saʿīd* (Kazan, 1897).

[20] Muṭahhir b. Mullā Mīr Ḥaydar, *Īskī Qïyïshqī Tārīkhi* (Orenburg, 1911).

[21] Ḥusayn Amīrkhānov, *Tavārīkh-i Bulghārīya* (Kazan, 1883), pp. 72-88; this section is entitled *Bayān al-ʿulamā maʿālim al-mażīyat fī khuṣūṣ al-Qazān maʿa manāqibihim*. For a discussion of this work see Frank, *Islamic Historiography and 'Bulghar' Identity*, pp. 125-138.

[22] Cf. Shaikhiev, *Tatarskaia narodno-kraevedcheskaia literatura* (*passim*); it should be noted that many of Shaikhiev's manuscript citations are incorrect.

related, theme concerns the need for education among Muslims, but especially traditional Islamic education, which Jahānshāh sees as essential to maintaining a genuinely Islamic community; to this end, he is especially proud of communicating to the reader how Astrakhan is an important center for training in Qurʾān recitation (*qirāʾat*). In this respect he depicts European culture as having certain benefits, but at the same time, notes that enlightened European culture ultimately originated with the ʿAbbāsid Caliphate and its preservation and translation of the ancient Greek classics.

Following his introduction, Jahānshāh begins his treatise with a history of the Russian conquest of Tatar lands and of serfdom in Russia. He depicts the two processes as closely linked, and as the result of autocracy, although he is especially quick to lay a share of the blame for their conquest by the Russians at the feet of the Tatar *khāns*, who were disorganized politically, and were later co-opted by the Russian autocrats.[23] He is especially critical of the Russian Orthodox Church, which he depicts as a cipher for the interests of the Muscovite rulers, as intentionally keeping the Russian people in ignorance, and as violating the fundamental moral laws of Christianity.[24] In discussing serfdom, Jahānshāh concentrates on legislation beginning in the 16th century leading to the immobilization of the peasantry, and the alliance between the landowners and the imperial government. He chronicles the gradual erosion of the peasants' rights during the 18th century, especially under Catherine II. He mentions Tsar Alexander II's reforms, but adds that the abolition of serfdom in 1861 did not bring freedom to the Russian people, and that by the end of the 19th century the only countries without "freedom" were Russia and Turkey. Indeed, the Russian government continued to impede "progress" among its people by trying to limit literacy; yet, he concludes, "Now the time of freedom has arrived, and the people have begun requesting their rights."[25]

Jahānshāh is especially concerned with how the "progress" and "freedom" brought about by the 1905 Revolution will benefit the Muslim people (*Islām millati*). He sees the lifting of autocratic rule as allowing

[23] *Tārīkh-i Astarkhān*, pp. 3-6. Here Jahānshāh uses the term "Tatar" to refer to Chinggisid dynasts, and not as an ethnonym. Jahānshāh refers to his own community as "Muslims" or "Russian Muslims."

[24] *Tārīkh-i Astarkhān*, pp. 5, 8.

[25] *Tārīkh-i Astarkhān*, pp. 8-11.

Muslims the unimpeded ability to develop their own educational institutions, and he describes education, and especially Islamic education, as the best way to improve the Islamic consciousness of Muslims, and thereby to accelerate their "progress." He encourages the teaching of both religious and secular subjects, and explains China's recent defeat in the Boxer Rebellion as the result of an inflexible attachment on the part of Chinese officials to Confucian dogmas, especially concerning military training.[26] He devotes an entire chapter to proving that modern European ideas and "culture" (*madanīyat*) are ultimately of Islamic origin. In the chapter entitled "the movement of culture from Islam to Europe," Jahānshāh writes that during ʿAbbāsid times, Europe was not only culturally far behind the Islamic world, but classical Greek culture only reached Europe because it had been preserved by the ʿAbbāsids and translated into Arabic. As a result, he sees modern culture and progress as not exclusively European, but Islamic in its origins, and states that modern education and its fruits, while of Islamic origin, are the shared property of all humanity. He calls on Muslims to claim their share of this property, and specifically calls on Muslims in Central Asia (*Turkistānlīlar*) to study both secular and religious subjects; at the same time he calls for the improvement of local *madrasas*.[27]

Nowhere, however, does Jahānshāh suggest that Muslims dilute their traditions to become more European, or suggest that Muslims abandon traditional practices that many Tatar modernists actively attacked. That Jahānshāh's support for secular education is far from unqualified is clearly demonstrated by two chapters in which he highlights the distinctions between the Qazaqs and Polish Muslims in terms of their Islamic consciousness. In these chapters, he contrasts the model Islamic piety and behavior of the Qazaqs with the illiteracy and ignorance of things Muslim among the Polish Tatars, in effect reversing the modernist view that admired the Europeanness of the assimilated Polish Tatars and decried the "savagery" and alleged semi-animism of the Qazaq nomads. Jahānshāh partially credits the high Islamic consciousness of the Qazaqs to the presence among them of Russian missionaries, who, while persecuting the Qazaqs, honed these nomads' awareness of the need to give their children proper Islamic education. Specifically, he notes that this awareness came about because

[26] *Tārīkh-i Astarkhān*, pp. 31-32.

[27] *Tārīkh-i Astarkhān*, pp. 36-38.

these missionaries would tell the Qazaqs they could not be Muslims because they practiced customary law rather than the *sharīʿa*, and this encouraged the Qazaqs to learn and implement the *sharīʿa*. Thus, to resist the missionaries, the Qazaqs would send their children to *madrasa*s in Kazan and Bukhara, and also hire Tatar teachers to instruct them in the *sharīʿa*, and Jahānshāh adds that one of the benefits of the 1905 Revolution is that it will strengthen the position of the *sharīʿa* among the Qazaqs.[28]

In contrast to the Qazaqs, Jahānshāh insists, the piety of the Polish Tatars is very weak. Their knowledge of Islam is weakened by the fact that they speak only Polish and Russian, and that they are unable to read Turkic books. He suggests that had they had missionaries among them, they might have reacted in the same way as the Qazaqs, and strengthened their knowledge of Islam. He also notes that they share with Russians many of the prejudices held against the Muslims of Kazan, considering Kazan Tatars to be savages and fearing to go among them. He points out that some Polish Muslims are currently studying in various *madrasa*s, but that "great efforts will be needed to raise them up."[29] While he praises the cultured qualities of Poles in general (including their supposed reluctance to allow missionary activity among Polish Muslims), he points out that members of the Polish Muslim elite are not engaged in commerce, but rather earn their livelihood as bureaucrats; Jahānshāh thus depicts the assimilation of the Polish Muslims into a European society as being ultimately deleterious to their status as Muslims. His critique of the Polish Muslims can be summarized as follows: regardless of the emotional or historical attachment of Polish Muslims to Islam, Jahānshāh decries their assimilation into Russian and Polish culture, an assimilation that manifests itself in Polish Muslims' ignorance of Islamic traditions and Turkic languages, and in their adoption of the Russians' stereotypes of the Volga Tatars; and he especially faults the Polish Muslim elite for working primarily as "bureaucrats" (*chīnovnīkī*).[30]

[28] *Tārīkh-i Astarkhān*, pp. 26-28.

[29] *Tārīkh-i Astarkhān*, pp. 30-31.

[30] In a recent monograph on the Polish Muslims, Iakov Grishin has noted that at the beginning of the 20th century the Polish Tatar peasantry was for the most part illiterate, while the Polich Muslim elite was primarily urban, was firmly integrated in Polish Catholic society, and was in fact quite isolated from rural Muslims; see Iakov Grishin, *Pol'sko-litovskie tatary: nasledniki Zolotoi Ordy* (Kazan, 1995), pp. 159, 161.

Jahānshāh also devotes space to Astrakhan's two principal benevolent educational societies, the *Jamʿīya Islāmīya* and the *Shūrā-yi Islāmīya.* In keeping with the reformist-conservative dichotomy that supposedly existed in Volga-Ural Muslim society, A. Rorlich has categorized the former society as "conservative" and the latter society as "reformist," and states that conflicts between these two societies came to harm the prospects of reform in Astrakhan.[31] Yet Jahānshāh makes no mention of any conflict. Rather, he writes the following:

> In recent days, when the spark of freedom is spreading, our co-religionists have somewhat raised their heads, and have begun to follow the path of progress. In particular, two associations have been opened in our city, with the desire of spreading the light of knowledge and learning, the *Shūrā-yi Islām* and the *Jamʿīyat-i Islāmīya.* They are expending the pure exertions of their gentlemen members, and they are saving our co-religionists from darkness and ignorance; they are opening finely arranged *maktab*s and *madrasa*s, and they serve the sons of the fatherland.[32]

The first of these societies was the *Jamʿīya Islāmīya*, which opened a *madrasa* in 1907, and brought from the Anatolian city of Bursa [*b.rūsa*] a certain Dāmullā Ṣāliḥ Efendī to serve as *mudarris.*[33] Yet Jahānshāh provides considerable biographical information on the founder of the *Shūrā-yi Islāmīya* as well, Muṣṭafā Luṭfī Ṣadr al-Dīn oghlï Ismāʿīlof. He was born in 1873 in the town of Shemakha (Shamāḥī) in Baku province, in a family descended from a line of *ʿālim*s. He studied in two local *madrasa*s; one of these was founded by his ancestors, and the other was run by his cousin. His education was both intensive and traditional. In 1900 he received his attestation, and went to the town of Troitsk, in Orenburg province, where he studied *ḥadīth* under Shaykh

---

See also Tamara Bairašauskaitė, "Politische Integration und religiöse Eigenständigkeit der litauischen Tataren im 19. Jahrhundert," *Muslim Culture in Russia and Central Asia from the 18th to the Early 20th Centuries*, vol. 2, ed. Anke von Kügelgen, Michael Kemper, and Allen J. Frank (Berlin, 1998; Islamkundliche Untersuchungen, Bd. 216), pp. 313-334.

[31] Rorlich, *The Volga Tatars*, pp. 78-79.

[32] *Tārīkh-i Astarkhān*, p. 15.

[33] *Tārīkh-i Astarkhān*, p. 21.

Zaynullāh Rasulev.[34] He then went briefly to Astrakhan, where his father had opened a trading house, before continuing his studies in Istanbul. In November of 1905 he returned to Astrakhan, where he founded and ran the Dār al-Adab *maktab*.[35]

THE ISLAMIC HISTORY OF ASTRAKHAN AND ASTRAKHAN PROVINCE

Although political and social commentary forms an important part of the work, Jahānshāh's history remains essentially a local history, with an emphasis on the region's mosques and prominent Muslims. However, unlike other areas that were the subjects of local histories, Astrakhan, as the center of the former Astrakhan Khanate, could also boast its own political history, which Jahānshāh addresses. Like the authors of other Tatar local histories, Jahānshāh expresses local pride in his community, and naturally this pride derives from the Islamic qualities of the community.

> And since Astrakhan has been a Muslim city since long ago, it has very many great shaykhs and mighty saints (*mashā'ikh al-kirām wa'l-awliyā' al-ʿiẓām*) buried in its environs. If God will it, at the end of this treatise I will relate the names, burial places, biographies, and dates of death of each one of them. The Astrakhan Muslims are very mild and kind to everyone. They are especially pure to the learned scholars who come from elsewhere. As far as possible, according to each one's rank, they show respect. As a result, learned scholars come from everywhere and they visit our city. While compared to [people of] other cities, our Astrakhan Muslims are not cultured, nevertheless in these areas they are ahead of the Muslims of other cities.[36]

Thus, he describes Astrakhan as provincial city, but nonetheless a very old Muslim city sanctified by the tombs of "great shaykhs and

[34] On this figure see Hamid Algar, "Shaykh Zaynullah Rasulev: the Last Great Naqshbandi Shaykh of the Volga-Urals Region," *Muslims in Central Asia: Expressions of Identity and Change*, ed. Jo-Ann Gross (London and Durham, 1992), pp. 112-133.

[35] *Tārīkh-i Astarkhān*, pp. 21-23.

[36] *Tārīkh-i Astarkhān*, p. 16.

mighty saints," and second to none in their treatment of Muslim scholars.

Jahānshāh traces the origins of Astrakhan as a Muslim city to the foundation of the Astrakhan Khanate, which he places after Timur's destruction of the Golden Horde at the end of the 14th century,[37] and provides a list of the *khāns* of Astrakhan.[38] Jahānshāh claims to have compiled his list "from various histories," although he does not provide us with any titles. It appears that his main source was Shihāb al-Dīn Marjānī's *Mustafād al-akhbār fī aḥwāl Qazān wa Bulghār*, but his list is not entirely derived from Marjānī's; some of the names he provides differ from those listed by Marjānī, and Jahānshāh also cites additional numismatic information. Concerning the fall of Astrakhan, he places it within the context of the fall of the Tatar states in general to Russia; he briefly, and rather laconically, describes Ivan IV's conquest of Astrakhan in 1554, resulting in the end of Astrakhan's existence as an Islamic state.[39]

Thematically, Jahānshāh's discussion of the modern Islamic history of Astrakhan province corresponds closely with the major themes of Tatar local historiography, including the relation of geographic, economic, and ethnographic information on the region at hand, as well as a central focus on the history of local Islamic religious institutions, specifically mosques, *imāms*, and *madrasas*. In terms of ethnographic information, Jahānshāh supplies a brief essay on the Astrakhan region's original inhabitants, the Astrakhan Noghays. He describes them as a separate and distinct people, whose ancestors ruled as the *khāns* of Astrakhan. Concerning their origins, the author tells us that the Astrakhan Noghays are descended from the Khazars, who originally came from Turkistān, and notes their lack of a written historical tradition. He also discusses the Russians' role in sedentarizing the nomadic Noghays, and the prominence, in his time, of the Noghays' activity as fruit and vegetable gardeners, noting that their produce is famed throughout Russia. Of particular interest is his depiction of the Noghays as an alien and savage, albeit Muslim, people. He notes their strange clothing (which he assures us is seen only in villages, and no longer in cities), and the role of Kazan Tatars and Mishar settlers in

[37] *Tārīkh-i Astarkhān*, p. 11.

[38] *Tārīkh-i Astarkhān*, pp. 17-18.

[39] *Tārīkh-i Astarkhān*, p. 12.

weaning the Noghays from their "savage Mongol customs" (*vakhshī mūghūl ʿādatlarï*) and "Noghayisms" (*nūghāylïqlar*).[40]

Jahānshāh also discusses the Noghays' Islamic institutions, including the so-called Noghay Mosque, which was built in 1825 by the patron Ākhūn-Jān Qāżī Niyāzōf. The first *imām* at that mosque was Ḥājjī Ḥamza b. Murtażā, known as Ḥamza Ākhūn, who was supposedly a descendant of the *khāns* of Astrakhan. This mosque, and its *imāms*, seem to have served primarily the Noghay population, and Jahānshāh tells us how Ḥamza Ākhūn would nomadize with the Noghays, and would carefully interpret official Russian documents for them.

In addition to the Noghay Mosque, Jahānshāh discusses five other mosques among the fourteen that were located in the city of Astrakhan; in each instance, he identifies the *imām*, and the way in which funds were raised for building the mosque. In most cases, the construction of a new mosque was paid for by a wealthy notable. For example, we read that the Kazan merchant Shākir Qazāqof built two mosques around the turn of the 19th and 20th centuries. The account also mentions two stone mosques, including the ʿAbd al-Vahhāb mosque, named after Jahānshāh's own Sufi master, who was also the *imām* of the mosque, ʿAbd al-Vahhāb b. ʿAlī. One of the earliest mosques to be built in Astrakhan was the so-called White Mosque; according to Jahānshāh, this mosque was built in 1810 by the patron Dāwūd Āghā. To judge from his mention of the "Noghay Mosque," mosques and their *maḥalla*s also seem to have been divided to some degree along ethnic lines.[41]

The *imāms* whom Jahānshāh discusses came from a variety of backgrounds, but with the exception of Ḥamza Ākhūn and ʿAbd al-Vahhāb, both of whom were native to Astrakhan, all of them were Mishars or Kazan Tatars by origin. The *imām* of the stone mosque, Fayżullah Ḥażrat, was from Penza province, and Nūr Muḥammad Isfandiyār oghlï, the *imām* of the Krivish [*k.rīv.sh*] Mosque, was from Nizhnii Novgorod Province. ʿAbd al-Laṭīf, the *imām* of the White Mosque, had come from the city of Kazan, and another *imām*, ʿAbd al-Raḥīm, is reported to have

[40] *Tārīkh-i Astarkhān*, pp. 13-14.

[41] The separation of Muslim communities into 'ethnic' congregations is documented elsewhere in the Volga-Ural region. For example, in western Ufa province (today eastern Tatarstan) a number of villages had separate mosques and *maḥalla*s; for these villages' respective 'Tatar' and Teptiar-Bashkir communities, see Radik Salikhov and Ramil Khayrutdinov, *Tatar khalqïnïng tarikhi häm mädäni häykälläre* (Kazan, 1995), pp. 180, 223.

come to Astrakhan from the city of Kronstadt (*Qrānshtānt*). A number of *imāms* were also Sufis, most notably ʿAbd al-Vahhāb and Farīd, Ḥamza Ākhūn's successor. This Farīd himself had studied under one of the Sterlibashevo *īshāns*, Ḥārith Tukaev.[42]

Several *imāms* were educated in Astrakhan, such as ʿAbd al-Vahhāb and his student Fayżullāh; but more often *imāms* studied elsewhere in the Russian empire, or even beyond its borders. Nūr Muḥammad Isfandiyār oghlï was educated in Kazan, while Ḥamza Ākhūn studied in a well-known *madrasa* in the village of Maskara, in Vyatka province. ʿAbd al-Raḥīm, the *imām* from Kronstadt, is said to have studied in Egypt. Among these figures, Jahānshāh identifies Nūr Muḥammad Isfandiyār oghlï, ʿAbd al-Raḥīm of Kronstadt, Muṣṭafā Luṭfī, and the Noghay *imām* Farīd as supporters of "today's progress" and "current events."

SUFIS, SAINTS, AND SHRINES IN ASTRAKHAN PROVINCE

Jahānshāh discusses thirteen Sufi shaykhs who were active in the city of Astrakhan, and in his biographical sketches he also included elegies (*marthīyas*) devoted to these figures. It should be noted that Jahānshāh's is the most extensive biographical sources for Sufism in Astrakhan.[43] The main figure is of course ʿAbd al-Vahhāb b. ʿAlī, the *imām* of a mosque in Astrakhan and the author's master. In 1849 he succeeded ʿAbd al-Raḥīm as *imām*. As for this ʿAbd al-Raḥīm, he is also mentioned in the biographical dictionary of Riżā al-Dīn Fakhrutdinov, where his name appears as ʿAbd al-Raḥīm b. ʿĀshūr al-Ḥājjṭarkhānī,[44] and where he is said to have trained ʿAbd al-Vahhāb in Qurʾān recitation. ʿAbd al-Vahhāb, however, studied Sufism under a different figure, Maḥmūd al-Dāghistānī. This figure appears in the biographical dictionary of Muḥammad Murād al-Ramzī as "Shaykh Maḥmūd b. Muḥammad al-Dāghistānī al-Shirvānī."[45] Concerning ʿAbd al-Raḥīm, Riżā al-Dīn Fakhrutdinov tells us that he died in Astrakhan in

[42] On this figure see the *Tārīkh-i Isterlībāsh* (Kazan, 1899), *passim.*

[43] Several Sufis from Astrakhan are also discussed in Riżā al-Dīn Fakhrutdinov's biographical dictionary, *Āthār* (2 vols., Ufa-Orenburg, 1900-1908).

[44] Fakhrutdinov, *Āthār*, II, p. 188.

[45] Muḥammad Murād al-Ramzī, *Talfīq al-akhbār wa talqīḥ al-āthār fī waqāʾiʿ Qazān wa Bulghār wa mulūk at-Tatār*, II, (Orenburg, 1908), p. 475; I thank Dr. Michael Kemper for bringing this reference to my attention.

1848 and was known as Shabātālī Mullā. He studied in Qarghālī with ʿAbd al-Raḥmān b. Muḥammad Sharīf al-Kirmānī, and later went to Cairo to study, and he was licensed (*murakhkhaṣ*) there in Qurʾān recitation by a certain Muṣṭafā Efendī al-Miṣrī. Fakhrutdinov also mentions ʿAbd al-Vahhāb b. ʿAlī as one of his students.[46]

Another Sufi in Jahānshāh's list is ʿUbaydullāh b. Subḥānqul of Kazan, who, we are told, died in 1853 and was *imām* and *mudarris* in a nearby village.[47] ʿUbaydullāh also appears in Fakhrutdinov's biographical dictionary under the name ʿUbaydullāh b. Sapqul. Fakhrutdinov writes that ʿUbaydullāh was the *imām* in Astrakhan's Seventh Mosque; he had studied in Bukhara, and returned to Astrakhan in 1829, when he married the daughter of the *imām* of the Mūlṭān Sarāy *maḥalla*, Fatḥullāh b. Ūrāzmat, and subsequently was appointed *imām* there.[48]

Yet Jahānshāh also discusses a number of other Sufis active in the late 19th and early 20th centuries who are not incluided in the works of Fakhrutdinov and Ramzī. One apparently important figure is Najm al-Dīn b. Shaykh Aḥmad al-Bulghārī al-Bālṭāyī (d. 1895). He is said to have been a well known Sufi, as well as a healer (*ṣāḥib-i nafas*) and miracle worker (*ṣāḥib-i karāmat*). He was also a *khalīfa* of Jaʿfar b. Ṣāliḥ b. Muḥammad-ʿAlī al-Qūlātqī al-Bulghārī, popularly known as "Jaʿfar al-Thānī" (as distinguished from Jaʿfar b. ʿAbdī, or Jaʿfar-i Avval). This Jaʿfar al-Thānī (d. 1862) was a major Naqshbandī figure in Saratov province, and indeed throughout the Volga-Ural region; among his pupils was Bahāʾ al-Dīn Vaysī, founder of the Vaysī brotherhood, an important anti-Muftī movement among Volga-Ural Muslims in Imperial Russia.[49] Another *murīd* of Jaʿfar al-Thānī in Astrakhan was ʿAbd al-Nāṣir b. Murād ʿAlī Shaykh (d. 1874). He reportedly taught the *ṭarīq-i Naqshbandīya* in Astrakhan for many years.[50] Najm al-Dīn al-Bulghārī's successor (*khāṣṣ khalīfa*) was ʿAbd al-Hādī b. Shaykh ʿAbd

[46] Fakhrutdinov, *Āthār*, II, p. 188.

[47] *Tārīkh-i Astarkhān*, pp. 43-44.

[48] Fakhrutdinov, *Āthār*, II, pp. 236-237.

[49] *Tārīkh-i Astarkhān*, p. 42. On the relationship between Jaʿfar al-Thānī and Bahāʾ al-Dīn Vaysī, see Kemper, *Sufis und Gelehrte*, pp. 400-403.

[50] *Tārīkh-i Astarkhān*, p. 47 (the text gives the name of ʿAbd al-Nāṣir's father as "*Lurād* ʿAlī Shaykh," clearly a misprint).

al-Jabbār b. ʿAbd al-Mannān al-Qazānī (d. 1905), who was himself a saint.[51]

Jahānshāh lists a total of twenty shrines located in and around Astrakhan, and elsewhere in Astrakhan province. His is the only known shrine catalogue for the Lower Volga region, and as such is an important source for hagiolatry and Muslim sacred geography in this region. Shrine catalogues and historiography are closely linked in the Volga-Ural region, and their role in establishing a sacred geographical outline of a Muslim community has been established for the Middle Volga region and Bashkiria for the 19th century.[52] However, Jahānshāh's catalogue, while perhaps influenced by this tradition, shows no sign of being directly inspired by it. Nonetheless, the presence of the shrine catalogue clearly demonstrates that such a shrine-centered conception of the community's geography not only persisted in the lower Volga region, but that it was so deeply rooted that an author like Jahānshāh, who considered himself a partisan of political freedom and progress, would include it as a central part of a work devoted to commentary on current political events. In fact, the shrine catalogue—and with it the entire work—concludes with Jahānshāh's brief discussion of the uses of hagiography, and the benefits afforded to the Muslim community by the spirits of the saints.

Concerning the city of Astrakhan, Jahānshāh notes that after the Russians took over the city, they expelled the Noghays, who were forced to abandon the saints' tombs in the city proper, and as a result, these tombs now lie underneath buildings and cannot be located. Nevertheless, he does discuss the shrines located elsewhere in the province, and notes that while the Noghays were forced by the Russians to live in swampy and reedy places, they made their cemeteries on low hills, and most of the shrines he lists are located on such hills.[53]

The importance of these cemeteries for their communities should not be underestimated. The spirits of the saints were thought to protect individuals as well as the community as a whole, and the graves of the saints were important pilgrimage sites. The center of the cemetery, both physically and spiritually, was usually the tomb of a saint, and it is these saints whom Jahānshāh lists. Especially pious or devoted people were

[51] *Tārīkh-i Astarkhān*, p. 43.

[52] Cf. Frank, "Islamic Shrine Catalogues," *passim.*

[53] *Tārīkh-i Astarkhān*, p. 19.

buried as close to the main saint as possible. For example, we are told how the Sufi Maḥmūd al-Dāghistānī was buried next to the powerful saint Shaykh Zamān in the Qāz Qaryasï cemetery.[54] Similarly, the Sufi Ḥabībullah b. Murtażā Zimnīchawī was buried in Yārlī Tūbā cemetery next to another powerful Sufi, Iskandar al-Dāghistānī;[55] and Būkāy Khān, the ruler of the Qazaq Inner Horde, who migrated into Astrakhan province at the beginning of the 19th century, was buried at Krasnyi Iar at the shrine known as *Sayyidlär Ziyārati*.[56]

Although most of the catalogue is essentially an enumeration of names and places, at least a few saints and shrines are documented in other sources. The tomb of a certain "Jigit Āzī Ḥażrati," located, according to Jahānshāh, in the village of Selitrennoe, is mentioned in an 18th century source; according to the Polish nobleman Jan Potocki, who visited the site of Selitrennoe in 1797, the ruins of the old Mongol capital of Sarāy were located here, and the local Muslims called the site "Dzhid-Khadzhi," considering the ruins to have formerly been a Muslim city.[57] In a later Russian ethnographic source, we are told that within the ruins of an old Tatar city here, there was a Tatar cemetery held in great respect by the local Kundrov Tatars (i.e., the Noghays), and that they call this cemetery "Dzhigit Khadzhi."[58] Jahānshāh tells us that in the cemetery of Qāzāchī Būghïr there is the tomb of Shaykh Ḥājjī ʿAbd al-Raḥmān, better known as Tūklī Bābā. This is, of course, a reference to the legendary Islamizer of the Golden Horde, Bābā Tükles. As Devin DeWeese has recently shown, Bābā Tükles figures prominently in the folklore and oral history of many Muslim peoples of western Inner Asia,

54 *Tārīkh-i Astarkhān*, p. 45.

55 *Tārīkh-i Astarkhān*, p. 45.

56 *Tārīkh-i Astarkhān*, p. 48. Currently Būkāy Khān's tomb has itself come to be venerated as a shrine; cf. V. M. Viktorin, "Muzhavirat i kul't sviatykh mest—'aul'ia' v nizhevolzhskom variante islama (tsivilizatsionnyi, formatsionnyi i ètnicheskii podkhody k izucheniiu)," *Islam, obshchestvo i kul'tura: materialy mezhdunarodnoi nauchnoi konferentsii 'Islamskaia tsivilizatsiia v preddverii XXI veka (k 600-letiiu islama v Sibiri)'* (Omsk, 1994), p. 41.

57 "Puteshestvie grafa Ivana Pototskogo v Astrakhan' i okrestnyia strany v 1797 godu," *Astrakhanskii sbornik* (Astrakhan, 1896), pp. 325-326.

58 K. N. Malinovskii, "Otchet o poezdke v selo Selitriannoe (Kniazhevskoi volosti, Enotaevskogo uezda) letom 1888 goda," *Sbornik trudov chlenov Petrovskogo obshchestva izsledovatelei Astrakhanskogo kraia* (Astrakhan, 1892), pp. 8, 11-12.

not least of which are the Noghays.[59] The presence of Bābā Tükles' tomb at "Kazachii Bugor" was noted already in 1842 by Alexander Chodzko.[60] In a Soviet anti-religious monograph from 1929, the tomb of "Tukli-baba" is said to be located near the settlement of Mashaikovo,[61] and this identification is further confirmed in a recent ethnographic source, which identifies Mashaikovo as a Noghay settlement, and as a major and still-functioning pilgrimage site for local Muslims.[62]

Another shrine documented in other sources is the tomb of Shaykh Zamān, whose full name appears as Shaykh Muṣliḥ al-Dīn Bukhārālī.[63] According to Jahānshāh, this saint came to Astrakhan already before the Russian conquest; legends concerning Shaykh Zamān appear in the anti-religious work from 1929, and the shrine, today known as that of "sheikh Masletdin Uzaman-khadzhi Bukharly" (according to the Russian equivalent spelling) is still visited by Muslim pilgrims.[64] Jahānshāh also mentions the tomb of a saint located at the cemetery of Barāqlī Tūbā.[65] This saint is named Khiżr Ātā, and is known among the Noghays as Qïdïr Ātā; he is said to have come to Astrakhan from Bulghār (that is, the Middle Volga region). Jahānshāh cites as his source a work entitled *Tārīkh al-Dāghistān.* However, Jahānshāh's account corresponds verbatim with a description of the same saint in a work entitled *Tavārīkh-i Bulghārīya*, written by the Kazan *imām* Ḥusayn Amīrkhānov,

59 Devin DeWeese, *Islamization and Native Religion in the Golden Horde: Baba Tükles and Conversion to Islam in Historical and Epic Tradition* (University Park, Pennsylvania, 1994), pp. 451-453 and *passim.*

60 Alexander Chodzko, *Specimens of the Popular Poetry of Persia, as found in the Adventures and Improvisations of Kurroglou, the Bandit-Minstrel of Northern Persia; and in the Songs of the People Inhabiting the Shores of the Caspian Sea* (London, 1842), p. 355.

61 N. Matorin, *Religiia u narodov Volzhsko-Kamskogo kraia prezhde i teper'* (Moscow, 1929), p. 88.

62 L. Sh. Arslanov and V. M. Viktorin, "Astrakhanskie tatary," *Materialy po istorii tatarskogo naroda* (Kazan, 1995), pp. 340-341; cf. Viktorin, "Muzhavirat i kul't sviatykh mest—'aul'ia'," pp. 40-42.

63 *Tārīkh-i Astarkhān*, p. 47.

64 Matorin, *Religiia u narodov Volzhsko-Kamskogo kraia*, p. 88; Viktorin, "Muzhavirat i kul't sviatykh mest—'aul'ia'," p. 41.

65 *Tārīkh-i Astarkhān*, p. 48.

and published in 1883; in his account Amīrkhānov cites the same mysterious *Tārīkh al-Dāghistān*.[66]

The best documented shrine in the Astrakhan region that Jahānshāh mentions is the tomb of Ḥājjī Nūr-Muḥammad Ḥażrati, better known as Ūrdāk Ajī.[67] This shrine is located near the Mishar village of Yango Asker, and, along with the tomb of Bābā Tükles, remains one of the most important and frequented shrines in the Astrakhan region.[68] Although the village of Yango Asker has been populated by Mishars since the early 19th century, the village was intitially populated by Noghays. The tomb and the nearby lake are both considered sacred, and are the site for an annual pilgrimage ritual for the Muslim inhabitants of surrounding villages.[69]

Among the saints mentioned in the shrine catalogue is at least one who is known as a historical figure. Jahānshāh mentions Ākhūn Khwāja among the saints buried at Khān Tūbā. This figure, Jahānshāh tells us, originally came from Bukhara and established himself as an *imām* and *ākhūn* in Astrakhan.[70] Indeed, Riżā al-Dīn Fakhrutdinov's biographical dictionary mentions an Ākhūn Khwāja b. Māhīm Khwāja (d. 1169/1755-56) as a Yasavī shaykh resident in Khān Tūbā.[71]

CONCLUSION

The contents of the *Tārīkh-i Astarkhān* demonstrate the uselessness of the conventional 'reformist vs. traditionalist' categorization of Jahānshāh al-Ḥājjītarkhānī's views on modernism, Russian history, and Islamic culture, and raises doubts concerning the suitability of such categorization, at least for the period immediately following the 1905 Revolution. Jahānshāh is a firm supporter of educational reform, political integration, and the immediate political consquences of the 1905

66 Amīrkhānov, *Tavārīkh-i Bulghārīya*, p. 33; cf. Frank, *Islamic Historiography*, p. 132.

67 *Tārīkh-i Astarkhān*, p. 49.

68 Arslanov and Viktorin, "Astrakhanskie tatary," pp. 340-341.

69 R. K. Urazmanova, "Prazdniki i obriady Astrakhanskikh tatar," *Astrakhanskie tatary* (Kazan, 1992), pp. 94-95.

70 *Tārīkh-i Astarkhān*, pp. 48-49.

71 Fakhrutdinov, *Āthār*, II, pp. 44; cf. Kemper, *Sufis und Gelehrte in Tatarien und Baschkirien*, p. 85, n. 26.

Revolution. His analogies and direct statements to that effect make this plain. Furthermore, he lists numerous *imāms* and Sufis who share his outlook, suggesting that among the *ʿulamā* of Astrakhan, at least, support for political and educational reforms was broadly based. Yet while supporting the 1905 Revolution and educational reform, Jahānshāh questions modernist and pro-European ideas; in fact, he explicitly rejects them as harmful to Muslims, but portrays European-style education as something ultimately derived from an Islamic source, the ʿAbbāsid Caliphate. His conception of his community, both local and 'national,' is a religious and sacred one. He refers to his people as "Russian Muslims" (*Rūsīya musulmānlarī*), and notes early in the treatise that "We Russian Muslims *have been given* the name Tatar"[72] [italics mine], suggesting that *ʿālims* viewed national designations such as "Tatar" as originating outside their community, and hence as essentially foreign. While he speaks well of "culture" or "sophistication" (*madanīyat*), his contrast of the Qazaqs with the "cultured" Polish Muslims makes it clear that this "culture" is of little use to the Polish Muslims when they lack basic knowledge of Islamic precepts, and entirely lack the energy and devotion to Islamic learning that is evident among the Qazaqs.

Perhaps the best evidence of Jahānshāh's unwavering commitment to traditional Islamic conceptions of a sacred community, however, is his unapologetic inclusion of a biographical dictionary of saints and Sufis, and a shrine catalogue, in his work. Shrine catalogues (not to mention Sufis) appear, as a rule, to have confused Tatar nationalist scholars, who have tended to ignore them, or to treat them as literary or historiographic non-sequiturs. But the fact that they appear in the *Tārīkh-i Astarkhān* demonstrates that the conceptions and worldview reflected in such traditional genres were very deeply rooted, even among the partisans of reforms. Indeed, Jahānshāh sees fit to include a section explaining the importance of saints and shrines for the community.[73]

The *Tārīkh-i Astarkhān* thus reveals a 'traditional' Muslim society that was not crisis-ridden, rigid, or dogmatic, but self-conscious, sophisticated, and flexible. Jahānshāh, indeed, believes that it is Russian society, not his own, that is truly in need of reforms. In this sense, the work is an informative antidote to earlier treatments of reformism, focused on modernism and *jadīdism*, and provides a more nuanced—and more accurate—indigenous view of Muslim society in Imperial Russia.

[72] *Tārīkh-i Astarkhān*, p. 3.

[73] *Tārīkh-i Astarkhān*, pp. 49-51.

THE SOCIAL STRUCTURE
OF THE NOMADS OF ASIA AND AFRICA

G. E. Markov

Moscow University

For thousands of years, the history of humankind and human culture has been in large measure determined by the interaction of agricultural and pastoral peoples. In historical scholarship, however, significantly greater attention was devoted in the past to the study of settled agricultural societies than to the study of mobile, pastoral societies. Increased interest in nomads typically emerged either in the course of discussions about general questions of theory, or—as in recent decades—in connection with practical problems in the transition of mobile pastoral populations to sedentary life.[1]

The study of nomadism in Russia differs somewhat, in terms of direction, from that in the West. Western scholars have been interested chiefly in questions of the history and economy of nomads, and their culture, and have devoted less attention to their social relations, which were long approached as a distinct 'socio-technological system.' Russian investigators of nomadism, in addition to considering these questions, have given special importance, since the 1920s, to the study of the genesis of nomadism and of the social structure and societal organization of nomads. However, down to the 1960s, attempts to resolve these problems through formal, dogmatic Marxist positions predominated, as expressed, in particular, in the tendency to discover among nomads a society based on class antagonisms and feudal relations. In connection with the study of the social relations of nomads, discussions repeatedly

[1] Cf. G. E. Markov, "Osedanie kochevnikov i formirovanie u nikh territorial'nykh obshchnostei," *Rasy i narody*, 1974, No. 4, pp. 27-44; *Nomaden und ihre Umwelt* (*Der Tropenlandwirt* [Witzenhausen], Beiheft 38, 1989); Catherine Butter, "Extension and Pastoral Development: Past, Present and Future," *Network Paper* (Pastoral Development Network, Overseas Development Institute), No. 37-d (London, 1994); C. Kerven, "Review of Planning and Policies on Extensive Livestock Development in Central Asia," *Network Paper*, No. 38 (London, 1995).

arose regarding the applicability of socio-economic categories such as 'social-economic formations,' 'means of production,' 'statehood,' and 'class society,' in their Marxist understanding.

In general terms the history of the emergence of nomadism has been clarified in the works of Russian and foreign scholars, although many questions remain the subjects of discussion still today.[2]

Judging from archeological data, and to some extent from written materials, the sources of mobile pastoralism must be sought in the processes of the emergence of productive economies, processes that were unfolding in the so-called 'primary centers' of the sub-tropical foothill regions of western Asia and North Africa. The result of these processes was the beginning of a major differentiation of labor, which manifested itself in the partial separation of pastoralism from agriculture. The fundamental reason for this lies in the difference of natural conditions in the primary centers of the cultivation of plants and of the domestication of animals. Some turned out to be more suitable for the development of agriculture, and others for pastoralism, as the dominant type of economic activity. In time, groups of primarily agricultural people abandoned the foothill regions, in which were located the primary centers of the emergence of the productive economy, and migrated to the alluvial valleys along the banks of rivers, where they established early agricultural settlements. In the primary centers that were poorly suited for agriculture, pastoralism began to emerge, from the Aeneolithic and the Bronze Age, in the form of extensive pastoral stock-herding, still not fully differentiated from agriculture. Later processes, which were the consequences of natural and man-made events, contributed in many arid regions to an increase in the mobility of pastoral groups, their isolation from agricultural oases, and the emergence of nomadism as a special economic and cultural type.

The result of these extended processes was the emergence of independent societies, distinct one from another, of settled agriculturalists and nomads, whose viability and productive capacity were based upon different means of production and, accordingly, different social systems.[3]

[2] G. E. Markov, "Teoreticheskie problemy nomadizma v sovetskoi ètnograficheskoi literature," *Istoriografiia ètnograficheskogo izucheniia narodov SSSR i zarubezhnykh stran* (Moscow, 1989), pp. 54-75.

[3] G. E. Markov, *Istoriia khoziaistva i material'noi kul'tury v pervobytnom i ranneklassovom obshchestve* (Moscow, 1989).

Accounts of the mobile stock-herding peoples who inhabited the frontiers of the 'civilized' world appeared with the origin of written language. Pastoral peoples and, later, nomads are mentioned in the inscriptions of the Persian kings; they are referred to in the Bible and in the works of scholars and travelers from antiquity down to medieval and more recent times.

From antiquity, the relationships between settled and pastoral peoples developed in different ways. They traded with each other, and fought each other. It must be noted that in a significant majority of older scholarly works and descriptions, the mobile pastoralists were portrayed as inveterate aggressors, inspiring terror in their settled neighbors and sowing devastation and death around themselves. In fact, the mobile, dynamically organized, armed, and united masses of nomads often successfully withstood settled societies, less mobile because of their attachment to the land. However, quite a few occasions are known when settled peoples themselves attacked nomads, in order to ensure peace on the borders of their lands, and in order to take nomads into captivity for use as slaves. Not infrequently, in retaliation for such attacks, masses of horsemen would fall upon oases and states, bringing great devastation upon the agricultural peoples. Many pages of history are filled with descriptions of the wars between settled and nomadic peoples. Wars with the Hsiung-nu, Turks, Mongols, Arabs, and other pastoral peoples in Europe, Asia, and Africa caused the settled population enormous and at times irreplaceable losses. Some societies, swept away by waves of nomads, did not recover from their defeat, but disappeared from the face of the earth, absorbed by other peoples. The clash of nomadic and settled populations originated, as a rule, from concrete economic and political causes, and for internal and external reasons. In the history of these relationships, one should not lose sight of the fact that the nomads themselves often sought to avoid conflicts with their settled neighbors. For instance, ethnology knows numerous instances when pastoralists tried to avoid violating, with the routes of their nomadizing, the borders of lands possessed by agriculturalists, so as not to disturb their fields, seeking in this way to avoid any disadvantageous contacts or armed confrontations with the settled population.[4]

[4] G. E. Markov, *Ocherk istorii formirovaniia severnykh turkmen* (Moscow, 1961); K. P. Kalinovskaia, *Skotovody Vostochnoi Afriki v XIX-XX vv.: Khoziaistvo i sotsial'naia organizatsiia* (Moscow, 1989); *idem*, *Ocherki ètnologii Vostochnoi Afriki* (Moscow, 1995).

Centuries passed, and in the course of time the relationships between nomads and their settled neighbors changed. While the economy and the entire cultural complex of the latter developed relatively rapidly and underwent significant changes, the nomadic resources for economy and culture changed little. With the progress of productive forces in agricultural societies and the growth of their technical and military prowess, unavoidable rivalries for living space grew more intense. Nomads could no longer withstand organized armies and new methods of warfare, against which their cavalry and primitive arms proved to be powerless. As a result, the nomads withdrew ever further into the uninhabited, marginal regions. And although the nomadic peoples resisted this onslaught into their native territories, through which had passed, for centuries, the routes of their migrations with their animals, the historical nomads were nonetheless doomed.

In modern times nomadic populations that found themselves part of modern states were inevitably drawn not only into the political life of these countries, but into their systems of industrial economy and social relations as well. The latter led to an acceleration of the decay of nomadism, which in our times is preserved only in isolated desert regions of Asia and Africa. Even there, however, it is being supplanted by agriculture and other occupational forms, and is also threatened as a result of the organization of preserves and protected natural zones in the form of national parks.[5] To be sure, in recent years, since the attainment of independence by a series of states of Inner Asia, including Mongolia, certain elements of a revival of nomadism have been noted. However, such phenomena are still not clear in many respects, and require further investigation.

In Soviet scholarship, problems of the social structure of nomadic peoples became the subject of sharp discussion already in the 1920s, when a series of scholars, moving toward Marxist positions, quite rightly rejected the notion of the primitive character of social relations in societies of nomads. At the same time, however, there emerged a tendency to overstate, without justification, the modernization of the level and condition of their social structure, as a result of the fulfillment of a specific social directive of the party and state leadership. The extreme politicization of the problem was evoked by the tendency to declare nomadic societies to be 'classist' and 'antagonistic,' thereby

[5] G. E. Markov, *Kochevniki Azii: Struktura khoziaistva i obshchestvennoi organizatsii* (Moscow, 1976); *idem*, "Osedanie kochevnikov."

giving the party leadership an ideological basis for the struggle against 'kulakism' ('*bay*-ism') and the traditional democratic institutions of the nomads, which were unacceptable for the Soviet system. The politicization of the idea of the historical and cultural equality of all peoples of the Soviet Union, regardless of the real level of their development and their economic and cultural type, led to the creation and consolidation, among the most politically 'engaged' scholars, of the doctrine, and myth, about the dominance of 'feudal relations' among nomads. In spite of the real historical facts, nomadic societies came to be defined as feudal, with the antagonistic class relationships corresponding to this historical type; the presence of such relationships made it necessary, supposedly, to conduct the class struggle among the nomads, which led to tragic consequences for many peoples of the USSR.[6]

Though agreeing in the evaluation of nomadism not as a primitive social order, but as one with a higher social development, differentiated in terms of ownership and social status, Soviet researchers differed in their identifications of the essence of this social structure, and differed on the question of which means of production were most fundamental among nomads. Some found the development of feudalism already among the nomads of ancient times; others affirmed the existence of a specifically 'nomadic feudalism,'[7] while still others proposed that feudal relations among nomads were combined with strong patriarchal survivals, and thus identified their social structure as 'patriarchal-feudal.'[8] At the same time, the basis of feudalism among nomads was interpreted differently. Some considered it to be feudal property in

[6] See, for example, K. P. Kalinovskaia and G. E. Markov, "Dinamika khoziaistvenno-kul'turnykh tipov i sotsial'nykh otnoshenii v turkmenskom obshchestve v pozdnem srednevekov'e," *Problemy srednevekovoi istorii Turkmenistana (Materialy respublikanskoi konferentsii 1989 g.)* (Ashgabat, 1993), pp. 33-40; K. P. Kalinovskaia and G. E. Markov, "Nogaitsy: Ètnokul'turnye problemy i mezhnatsional'nye otnosheniia," *Vestnik Moskovskogo universiteta*, Seriia 8, Istoriia, 1991, No. 4, pp. 59-70.

[7] B. Ia. Vladimirtsov, *Obshchestvennyi stroi mongolov: Mongol'skii kochevoi feodalizm* (Leningrad, 1934).

[8] L. P. Potapov, "O sushchnosti patriarkhal'no-feodal'nykh otnoshenii u kochevykh narodov Srednei Azii i Kazakhstana," *Voprosy istorii*, 1954, No. 6, pp. 73-89.

animals,[9] others property in land.[10] Along the way each side so convincingly criticized the assertions of their opponents, on the basis of the citation and interpretation of reliable factual material, that, in the final analysis, the conclusions of both sides not only were left in doubt, but were refuted altogether. The argumentation of the rival scholars, moreover, was based as a rule on quite late material, in chronological terms, belonging to the beginning of th 20th century—that is, a historical period when, in the regions under consideration (for the most part, in Kazakhstan), nomadism had nearly completely decayed as an independent, self-supporting economic and social system. Thus, the existence of feudal relations among nomads was supposedly confirmed by the presence of 'feudal' titles among the leaders of the tribal structures of nomads, titles that were in fact no more than borrowings by the nomads from the settled population, and did not reflect real social relations. Similarly, if a source mentioned a local term in connection with rulers, an arbitrary translation from the language of the source into Russian would be used as the desired 'proof' of the term's feudal character (many examples of this sort may be found, and some have made their way into dictionaries). As a result, many authors would write that "princes" *(kniaz'ia)*, "*khān*s," or "*sulṭān*s" existed among nomads, supposing that they had thereby 'proven' the existence of feudalism among mobile stock-herders. In all these 'feudal' constructions, the most important issue was disregarded—namely, that feudalism, as a social structure, was not just a set of separate, incidental indicators, but a system of specific economic and social components, the basis of which was formed by the monopolized, hereditary ownership, on the part of the feudal estate, of the basic means of production, together with societal relations, forms of dependence and exploitation, and a particular mentality that resulted therefrom.[11]

[9] S. E. Tolybekov, "O patriarkhal'no-feodal'nykh otnosheniiakh u kochevykh narodov," *Voprosy istorii*, 1955, No. 1, pp. 75-83; V. F. Shakhmatov, "K voprosu o sushchnosti i spetsifike patriarkhal'no-feodal'nykh otnoshenii v Kazakhstane," *Vestnik AN KazSSR*, 1951, No. 7, pp. 18-36.

[10] A. E. Erenov, "K voprosam prava feodal'noi sobstvennosti v dorevoliutsionnom Kazakhstane," *Vestnik AN KazSSR*, 1953, No. 5, pp. 35-48; S. Z. Zimanov, "O patriarkhal'no-feodal'nykh otnosheniiakh u kochevnikov-skotovodov," *Voprosy istorii*, 1955, No. 12, pp. 63-67.

[11] Markov, *Kochevniki Azii*, pp. 288 ff.

The entire aggregate of factual material that provides evidence on economic and social relations among nomads, and also the convincing mutual criticism of the partisans of scholars from various schools of thought, who tried, despite the facts, to prove the existence of feudalism among nomads, attest to the erroneous character of the 'feudal' hypothesis. It should also be noted that all the partisans of the notion that feudalism existed among nomads undertook efforts to rely, in their theoretical postulates, upon the views of Marx and Engels, which supposedly confirmed their hypothesis. Political accusations of 'anti-Marxism,' extremely dangerous in the conditions of the Soviet regime, were often advanced against those who did not agree with this sort of 'argumentation.' The paradox here is that the founders of Marxism not only never spoke in their works about the existence of feudal relations among nomads, but, on the contrary, proposed the existence in such societies of a special *means of production.*[12] In spite of this, partisans of the 'feudal' theory would frequently cite documents of the Communist Party, and the resolutions of party congresses, which had nothing to do with scholarly argumentation.

The restoration of scholarly objectivity required a rejection of the politicization of the problem and investigation of actual historical facts. Beginning from the 1960s, detailed research began on the stock-herders of Asia, who inhabited the enormous expanses of steppe and desert rangeland, where nomadism had developed long ago.[13]

Such research showed that the system of social relations among the nomads of Asia, and many aspects of their economy and culture, were also characteristic of nomads of East and North Africa, though with certain special features evoked by the particularities of economic and cultural types in regions of the tropical and subtropical zones. Special features of social structure among pastoralists of the tropics (though not the entire system of social relations) may be explained through not only natural, but also political conditions and traditions, as well as, possibly, through certain survivals of the period when the process of the decay of primitive communal relations had not yet come to an end. Thus, specific distinctions existed in the nature and level of social development, which are also explained by certain particularities of tropical

[12] See, for example, K. Marks and F. Èngel's, *Sochineniia* (Moscow, 1958), XII, p. 724.

[13] Markov, *Kochevniki Azii*.

pastoralism. However, despite specifics of region and stage in the lives of the relevant societies of Asia, East Africa, and North Africa, the essence of their social relations is the same, and changed little up until the time of sedentarization.

As a result of a comparative analysis of ethnographic data on stock-herding societies of different regions, a new theoretical conception was formulated in 1967, the essence of which is that a special, independent means of production is characteristic for nomads.[14] Within the framework of this conception, nomadism, as a historical notion, is considered as a special economic and cultural type, and as a method whereby people obtain the necessities of life primarily through extensive, mobile, pastoral stock-herding, for which quite vast resources of pasturage are essential. Its fundamental marker is that stock animals comprise the freely disposable property of indi-vidual families, while land and water sources are a communal, tribal possession.

Because of the specific features of the extensive stock-herding economy, it had a relatively primitive productive base. The technical means of managing the economy, the implements of production, and the qualitative structure of the herds were marked by stagnation, and in practical terms were improved little. This explains why the division of labor among nomads did not undergo substantial development, but remained at a low level for centuries. Craft production, too, did not become a separate field. Nomads did not establish cities. The so-called 'cities of the nomads' were in fact either settlements of colonists from agricultural regions, or towns, seized from a sedentary agricultural population, in which a small number of nomads settled. Stock-herders who moved to a sedentary way of life were no longer nomads, and their economic and cultural type changed completely. Examples of this are the oasis-cities of the Kurds, the Berber towns of North Africa, and many cities of Inner Asia in which dynasties established by emigrants from nomadic societies ruled.

Among nomads there was no monopoly of an elite or some other social stratum over the means of production, as a result of the special character of the extensive nomadic economy. At the same time, private ownership of livestock, as well as the spoils of war, engendered a significant stratification in terms of property. The tasks of those who directed economic activity, the necessary centralization and military

[14] G. E. Markov, "Kochevniki Azii" (*Avtoreferat dissertatsii na soiskanie uchenoi stepeni doktora istoricheskikh nauk*, Moscow, 1967), p. 30.

leadership in times of wars and conflicts, and stratification in terms of property led to the social stratification of the community—which, however, did not create a monopoly over the means of production, and did not lead to the development of estates or classes, once again owing to the peculiarities of the nomadic economic and cultural type. The entire people was armed, comprising a military-tribal 'militia,' and the military leaders and elders did not have at their disposal an armed force capable of creating coercion outside the economic context. Naturally, property differentiation, and to some degree social differentiation, provided the basis for the emergence of exploitation of the poor by the rich; however, down to recent times the poor and the rich comprised only an insignificant part of nomadic societies. The majority of nomads were self-sufficient stock-herders, of average prosperity. What in Soviet literature prior to the 1960s was often called exploitation was in fact more often mutual aid among kinsmen or neighbors. Real exploitation began to emerge in the nomadic environment only in the course of its decay, beginning at the end of the 19th century, or in fact even in the 20th. It should also be noted that in the context of the economic and military instability of nomadic life, notions of wealth and poverty were only relative. Yesterday's rich man could become a poor man today, while a poor man could acquire a higher status. As a result of the lack of hereditary monopolistic rights over the means of production and power, a once-rich nomad who became impoverished would lose the privileges he had formerly held. Abrupt changes in property-relations and societal relations occurred only when nomads were either forcibly converted to sedentary life, or drawn into socioeconomic relations with neighboring states. But on a broad scale this process unfolded only from the time when capitalism, and socialist countries, emerged. In conditions of settled life, the former nomads were inevitably deprived of the great bulk of their livestock, for which there was no longer sufficient pasturage, and were forced to change to other, more intensive occupational forms.[15]

A few decades have passed since the time of the bitter discussions in Soviet literature about problems relating to the level of the social structure of nomads, and on the whole, at present, in Russian

[15] Markov, *Kochevniki Azii*; B. V. Andrianov and G. E. Markov, "Khoziaistvenno-kul'turnye tipy i sposoby proizvodstva," *Voprosy istorii*, 1990, No. 8, pp. 3-15.

ethnological and historical scholarship, the interpretation of nomadic societies as an economic and cultural type, and, in accordance therewith, a means of production based on extensive, mobile pastoral stock-herding as the chief means of obtaining the necessities of life (though not excluding other auxiliary forms of work as well, including agriculture), has become firmly established.[16]

Gradually, by far the greater number of Russian authors has begun to reject the earlier interpretation of nomadic societies as feudal. Some authors have undertaken efforts toward the further elaboration of problems in the social history of nomads, contributing greater precision to definitions and specific positions. On the whole such an approach may be welcomed. However, the tendency of some researchers, in publications of the 1980s and 1990s, toward original conclusions has not in all cases turned out to be justified, and has entered into contradiction with historical facts; and one cannot agree in all cases with the arrangement of scholarly priorities. Thus, some authors, denying that nomadism constitutes a special means of production, propose to regard it as merely a separate form of economic activity.[17] Others, without denying that nomadism is a special means of production, refer to it with the barely intelligible term "exopolitarian."[18] In both cases, however, the authors attempt to determine the *formational* affiliation of nomadism, a shortsighted effort in view of the vagueness of the very notion of 'formation.'

Also worth noting is yet another issue raised in the above-mentioned studies. One can scarcely agree with assorted attempts to describe the

[16] Iu. I. Semenov, "Kochevnichestvo i nekotorye obshchie problemy teorii khoziaistva i obshchestva," *Sovetskaia ètnografiia*, 1982, No. 2, pp. 48-59; N. È. Masanov, *Problemy sotsial'no-èkonomicheskoi istorii Kazakhstana na rubezhe XVIII-XIX vekov* (Alma-Ata, 1984); V. M. Viktorin, "Potestarno-politicheskie i pravovye otnosheniia u kochevykh narodov (vzaimosviaz' vnutrennikh i vneshnikh faktorov)," *Filosofskie problemy gosudarstva i prava: Mezhvuzovskii nauchnyi sbornik*, vyp. 5 (Saratov, 1988), pp. 123-135; V. A. Popov, *Ètnosotsial'naia istoriia akanov v XVI-XIX vekakh: Problemy genezisa i stadial'no-formatsionnogo razvitiia ètnopoliticheskikh organizmov* (Moscow, 1990); S. I. Vainshtein, *Mir kochevnikov tsentra Azii* (Moscow, 1991); N. N. Kradin, *Kochevye obshchestva: Problemy formatsionnoi kharakteristiki* (Vladivostok, 1992); Ch. Iazlyev, *Turkmenskaia sel'skaia obshchina* (Ashkhabad, 1992); V. V. Matveev, *Srednevekovaia Severnaia Afrika: Razvitie feodal'nykh otnoshenii v VI-IX vv.* (Moscow, 1993); and others.

[17] A. M. Khazanov, *Nomads and the Outside World* (Cambridge, 1984), p. 193.

[18] Kradin, *Kochevye obshchestva*, pp. 189, 191 ("èkzopolitarnyi").

social structure (and means of production) of all nomadic societies, throughout the course of their existence, based on data concerning the so-called 'nomadic empires.' Epochs of 'nomadic empires' are only isolated episodes in the history of nomadism. Over the millenia of nomadism's existence, the overwhelming number of stock-herders did not form and did not become part of the ephemeral 'nomadic empires,' but carried on their traditional way of life, uniting in communities and tribes according to the principle of *genealogical kinship*. And indeed, those nomadic groups and tribes that temporarily became part of such 'empires' returned, once again, after the empires' disintegration, to traditional life. For this reason, an attempt to find, for 'nomadic empires,' some sort of special 'innate formational tendency,' ignoring the social structure of the basic mass of nomads, can hardly be fruitful.[19] In actuality, the social structure of nomadic communities has remained unchanged since the time of nomadism's emergence, down to the period of its decay, as data from Asia, East Africa, and North Africa attest.[20]

In the end, the fundamental marker of societies of mobile stock-herders is tribal structure, ideologically based upon legendary genealogical kinship. At the same time, the social organization of nomads was neither a repetition nor a continuation of the social structure of societies that stood at the developmental level of primitive communities. The vital activities of nomads, conducted under conditions of large-scale mobility and instability of life, led to the emergence of a quite durable social organization, based on a specific system of social relations.

Various forms of social relations are combined in the social structure of nomads: blood-kinship, familial, economic, genealogical, military, cultural, linguistic, religious, and others. The system-defining type, however, is that of kinship relations. In the absence of firm territorial and economic connections, these alone could ideologically bind groups of nomads into a single organism, and allow the possibility of once again uniting communities and tribes after the military catastrophes that were so frequent in the history of nomadism.

[19] See K. P. Kalinovskaia's review of Kradin, *Kochevye obshchestva*, in *Ètnograficheskoe obozrenie*, 1994, No. 4, pp. 151-155.

[20] Markov, *Kochevniki Azii*; Andrianov and Markov, "Khoziaistvenno-kul'turnye tipy;" Kalinovskaia, *Skotovody Vostochnoi Afriki*; Matveev, *Srednevekovaia Severnaia Afrika*; K. P. Kalinovskaia, "O kochevnichestve v sviazi s knigoi V. V. Matveeva 'Srednevekovaia Severnaia Afrika' (M., 1993)," *Ètnograficheskoe obozrenie*, 1996, No. 4, pp. 153-158.

As a rule it was considered that this or that people or major tribe of nomads originated from a single progenitor. His sons, grandsons, and so forth were considered the ancestors of subdivisions of tribes and of smaller nomadic groups, down to the level of communities and separate families. In the event of the defeat of a nomadic group, and its dispersion, the need to reconstitute its social structure would arise; in this process, weaker families and communities would join larger ones, 'joining' their own 'ancestors' to the genealogies of those larger groups. As a result, genealogical 'kinship' was established, and societal connections emerged. At the same time, nomads distinguished quite plainly—and often terminologically—between genealogical kinship and blood kinship, which existed in reality only at the lowest levels of tribal structure, between closely related families and in small nomadic communities. For this reason, communal and tribal structure as a whole was a fundamentally historical phenomenon, and its principles were preserved unchanged over the course of centuries and millenia.[21]

It has been suggested that the structure of social and tribal organization among nomads may be envisioned within two aggregate conditions: 'communal-nomadic,' characteristic of nomads in relatively peaceful times, when their tribal structure was amorphous and nomadic communities were quite independent and autonomous; and 'military-nomadic' (including 'nomadic empires' as well), when out of necessity a temporary centralization emerged, and families and nomadic communities joined together within a more or less strict system of military subordination. It is in this regard that attempts to consider the temporary and ephemeral unions of nomads, the 'nomadic empires,' to be states are unconvincing. These 'empires' did not have any economic basis of their own, and existed chiefly through plundering settled agriculturalists and other nomadic tribes. They were composed of tribal

[21] Markov, *Kochevniki Azii*; *idem*, "Nekotorye problemy obshchestvennoi organizatsii kochevnikov Azii," *Sovetskaia ètnografiia*, 1970, No. 6, pp. 74-89; *idem*, *Problemy razvitiia obshchestvennoi struktury kochevnikov Azii* (Moscow, 1973; IX Mezhdunarodnyi kongress antropologicheskikh i ètnograficheskikh nauk); G. E. Markov and N. È. Masanov, "Znachenie otnositel'noi kontsentratsii i dispersnosti v khoziaistvennoi i obshchestvennoi organizatsii kochevykh narodov," *Vestnik Moskovskogo universiteta*, Seriia 8, Istoriia, 1985, No. 4, pp. 86-96; G. E. Markov, "Problems of Social Change among the Asiatic Nomads," *The Nomadic Alternative: Modes and Models of Interaction in the African-Asian Deserts and Steppes*, ed. W. Weissleder (The Hague, 1978), pp. 305-311.

groups organized by tens, hundreds, thousands, and so on, and were active structures only so long as military conquests or migrations continued. After their completion, the 'empires' split up into tribes; some warriors settled among the rural and urban population, others returned to traditional nomadic stock-herding, and in one form or another, communal tribal structure was revived.[22]

In support of this presentation, let us turn to factual data on the social organization of the Mongols, Turkmens, Qazaqs, Arabs, and the mobile stock-herders of East Africa, which confirm the presence of overall patterns within their social organization. Historical evidence on the social organization of ancient stock-herders, such as the Scythians, Huns, and others, is quite limited. There is significantly more evidence for medieval and modern times.

Little is known about the Mongols and their social organization in the period preceding the establishment of the 'nomadic empire' of Chinggis Khān; what is known, moreover, is not always reliable, insofar as only relatively late sources offer evidence about that period, especially Chinese sources that reflect the worldview and political traditions of the Chinese empire, through which the ancient writers understood the world around them, including the nomads. The chroniclers originated from agricultural regions, and described societies of nomads from the standpoint of the system of social, economic, and political relations to which they themselves were accustomed.

It is known that before the 13th century, the Mongols had a tribal structure. Tribes and their subdivisions were for the most part economically and politically independent, and had their own leaders. Internecine strife often developed between tribes, but there were often unions of tribes as well. For the realization of Chinggis Khān's policy of conquest, the creation of a centralized military and administrative system was required. The tribes of the Mongols and their subdivisions came to be included—in some cases in whole, in other cases in part—in a military organization built on the decimal principle. Each nomadic group supplied levies, in accordance with its numerical size, of ten, 100, or 1000 warriors. The tribes allied to Chinggis Khān entered into the structure of his army in the form, usually, of entire large tribal unions, amounting to a thousand or ten thousand. Warriors from among the

[22] Markov, *Kochevniki Azii*.

conquered peoples were distributed among different military units.[23] At the same time, Chinggis Khān did not concern himself with, and did not violate, the most basic principle of tribal organization. The system of social-genealogical connections was preserved, as is evident above all from the fact that after the collapse of the 'empire,' the majority of the Mongols themselves, and of the nomads subdued by the Mongols, who had become part of their army and had not remained in the conquered countries, once again returned to nomadism, preserving tribal structure. As B. Ia. Vladimirtsov noted, the Mongols, after the collapse of the empire, "again fell into the same situation in which they had existed before the birth of their brilliant chief," since "civilization cannot be combined with nomadic life."[24] From Vladimirtsov's words it is clear that he did not regard the 'empire' of Chinggis Khān as a *civilization*, and that by "nomadic life" he meant the communal-nomadic condition of nomads—that is, their traditional way of life, with intermittent wars and temporary political unifications at a level above the tribe.

The emergence of the 'nomadic empire' of Chinggis Khān, and his campaigns of conquest, introduced major changes into the lives of the Mongols. All of Mongolia was turned into a military camp. Some groups of Mongols stayed in the conquered oases, others continued to nomadize in the steppes of Eastern Europe, while some remained in Mongolia. For the most part it was young men who entered the army; the remainder of each tribe—women, children, and older men—remained in their nomad camps and preserved the traditional way of life. When the warriors returned home from the campaigns, they were once again included into their tribal organization and the nomadic system of social relations.

Aside from plunder, which comprised a significant portion of the means of subsistence for the army of Chinggis Khān, the army itself had substantial herds of livestock in its rear, which supplied the troops and their leaders with all necessities. Nevertheless, the means of production was the very same mode of livestock herding in extended pasture lands—that is, the nomadic mode—and on the whole the 'nomadic empire' did

[23] Vladimirtsov, *Obshchestvennyi stroi mongolov*; S. A. Kozin, tr., *Sokrovennoe skazanie: Mongol'skaia khronika 1240 g. pod nazvaniem Mongγol-un niγuča tobčiyan. Iuan' chao bi shi. Mongol'skii obydennyi izbornik*, vol. 1, *Vvedenie v izuchenie pamiatnika, perevod, teksty, gloassarii* (Moscow/Leningrad, 1941), pp. 133, 186, 218.

[24] B. Ia. Vladimirtsov, *Chingis-khan* (Berlin/Peterburg/Moscow, 1922), p. 160.

not create any kind of special means of production, besides the nomadic one (in the 'military-nomadic' condition).

As the sources attest, with the collapse of the empire, beginning approximately in the 15th century, the fundamental 'cellular unit' of the social organization of the Mongolian stock-herders came to be the community or group known as the *ail-otog*. Several *otog*s formed an *aimag*. Social relations in this case served economic interests. *Otog*s and *aimag*s united into tribal groups (*ulus*, *tümen*). Once again the typical tribal structure of the nomads, based ideologically on patriarchal genealogical relationships, was revived.

In the 17th century, China conquered Mongolia, and a new administrative system was introduced, turning Mongol chieftains into state officials who assisted the Manchu administration in exploiting the population. In other words, the Chinese military-administrative system supplanted, under new conditions, the upper levels of the tribal organization of the nomads, and the earlier traditional patriarchal-genealogical relations began to be replaced by new, territorial relations. Only the lower elements of tribal social organization, whose existence was determined by the conditions of nomadizing and by economic necessity, continued to function. From the end of the 17th century, permanent settlements around monasteries and the headquarters of leaders began to emerge. At the same time, among portions of the Mongols who did not fall under the yoke of China, and especially among the western groups, their tribal organization and the system of patriarchal-genealogical relations were preserved down to quite recent times.[25] This shows that the changes in the social organization of the Mongols under Chinese power were not the result of internal development, but a consequence of a political system imposed from outside.[26] One may suggest, as a hypothesis, that at the present time, in connection with the revival of certain features of nomadism among some groups of Mongols, elements of communal-tribal organization will again emerge.

Let us now consider another formerly nomadic people, the Türkmens. Their historical development attests to the gradual weakening of intertribal relations. From late medieval times, the sources note that the Turkmens were disunited territorially, politically, and economically, and virtually none of the major tribes (at the beginning of

[25] Vladimirtsov, *Chingis-khan*.

[26] Markov, *Kochevniki Azii*.

the 20th century there were as many as 19 larger and smaller tribes) formed a compact whole. Tribal structure was amorphous, and the nomenclature of tribal subdivisions was not well-defined.[27] In relatively peaceful periods of the history of the Türkmen people, the major tribal groups and subdivisions lost socio-political and economic significance, and property-based divisions and the social stratification of society gradually deepened, leading to the separation of individual wealthy families.[28] At the same time, in the nomadic society of the Türkmens, notions about genealogical tribal structure and genealogical 'kinship' were firmly preserved, and in time of necessity this structure would again begin to function as a military-political tribal organization, quickly uniting the tribes and their subdivisions into the hierarchically coordinative structure of an army.

Memory of genealogical tribal structure—chiefly in the spheres of ideology, daily life, and ceremony—remains quite strong in our time as well, even though the mass sedentarization of the Türkmens began in the 18th century. In any case, even today virtually every Türkmen man and woman knows his or her tribal affiliation.[29]

Regarding the social organization of the Qazaqs down to the 17th century little is known, aside from the fact that their tribes were united in 'hordes' (*zhüz*).[30] By the 18th century, with the profound social and economic changes after the incorporation of Kazakhstan into the structure of the Russian empire, the social organization of the Qazaqs lost its military function, which had been very important for it in the past. Higher-order tribal groupings no longer had their former significance, and were preserved by the Tsarist administration only initially—and, even then, already in the form of units of administrative-territorial structure.

[27] G. E. Markov, "Skotovodcheskoe khoziaistvo i obshchestvennaia organizatsiia severobalkhanskikh turkmen v kontse XIX—nachale XX v.," *Vestnik Moskovskogo universiteta*, Istoriko-filologicheskaia seriia, 1958, No. 4, pp. 165-177; Markov, *Ocherk istorii formirovaniia severnykh turkmen*; *idem* ["G. E. Martov"], "The Turkmen Population of the Khorezm Oasis," *Asian Review* (London), 50 (1954), No. 184, pp. 307-316.

[28] Markov, "Skotovodcheskoe khoziaistvo i obshchestvennaia organizatsiia severobalkhanskikh turkmen."

[29] G. E.Markov, "Obraz zhizni turkmen v XIX—nachale XX veka," *Voprosy istorii*, 1983, No. 12, pp. 84-98.

[30] V. V. Vostrov and M. S. Mukanov, *Rodoplemennoi sostav i rasselenie kazakhov (konets XIX-nachalo XX v.)* (Alma-Ata, 1968), p. 10.

The situation was different with lower-order tribal subdivisions, which were united by real economic interests, by the joint use of pastures, and by more or less intimate kinship ties.[31]

Toward the end of the 19th century, nomadic groups became ever more mixed in composition, and the kinship principle of their organization was ever more frequently violated, with 'neighborhood' bonds, based on territorial proximity, replacing it. A weakening of social-genealogical ties occurred. The socio-economic stratification of society grew deeper, and the local elites of the wealthy *bay*s grew stronger. Some of the poorer stock-herders were eventually forced to shift to settled life and to a different economic-cultural type.[32]

At the end of the 19th century and the beginning of the 20th, these processes began to develop even more precipitously. The mass devastation of stock-herders forced them to settle on the land, and territorial bonds took precedence over communal-nomadic bonds, though even now, in the spheres of ideology and daily life, tribal affiliation still plays a quite substantial role.[33]

Tribal organization is preserved among the nomadic Arabs, as well as among the settled Arabs, though to a lesser degree. At the very least, every Arab knows his or her tribal affiliation. Among the Arabs, as among other current or former nomads, tribal structure and its nomenclature differ from group to group, and the practical significance of the individual elements of tribal structure varies in specific cases. Individual families and nomadic communities of differing social composition may enter into, or unite with, any tribe, whether temporarily or permanently, with the aim of obtaining protection from a strong tribe; in the process, an adaptation and unification of genealogies may occur.[34]

The social structure of the Arabs was formed by tribal sub-divisions of two levels. The first, of higher order, consisted of confederations and tribes. These were political unions, based on military-administrative

[31] N. P. Rychkov, *Dnevnye zapiski puteshestviia kapitana Nikolaia Rychkova v Kirgiz-Kaisatskoi stepi, 1771 goda* (St. Petersburg, 1772), pp. 20, 23.

[32] A. I. Levshin, *Opisanie kirgiz-kazach'ikh ili kirgiz-kaisatskikh ord i stepei* (St. Petersburg, 1832), ch. 3, pp. 24, 25.

[33] S. I. Rudenko, "Ocherk byta kazakov rek Uila i Sagyza," *Kazaki: Antropologicheskie ocherki*, ed. S. I. Rudenko (vyp. 1, Leningrad, 1927), pp. 7-32.

[34] E. Bräunlich, "Beiträge zur Gesellschaftsordnung der arabischen Beduinenstämme," *Islamica*, 6 (1934), pp. 68-111, 182-229 [pp. 78-81].

relations. In the past their significance rose sharply in times of military conflict and during migrations; in peaceful times, their significance in the lives of the nomads was negligible. To the second level belonged families, groups of families or nomadic communities, small tribal subdivisions, and tribes united by common economic interests and by conceptions of common origin. In times of warfare and major migrations, nomadic groups united in a general army of tribes and confederations, and tribal structure facilitated the activization of the mechanism of the nomads' military organization. In relatively peaceful times, the organizational bonds within confederations and tribes grew weaker, though they did not lose their significance altogether, despite the autonomy of tribal subdivisions.[35]

Study of the mobile stock-herders of Africa has revealed the regional particularity of this way of life, and allows us to distinguish two forms of nomadism in the eastern part of the continent: 'Asiatic' and 'African.'[36]

The 'African,' seminomadic form of nomadism, the most widespread in East Africa, is found among the Boran, Gabra, Suk, Nandi, Masai, and others. The means of conducting this type of stock-herding economy differ little from those of the 'Asiatic' form.[37] Its distinctive features are manifested in the social sphere—in the presence, in the societal organization of these seminomadic pastoralists, of social bonds based on age. Among the 'African' nomads, unlike the 'Asiatic' groups, there exists a dual social affiliation. The first is horizontal and local, in the system of patriarchal-genealogical ties (as among 'Asiatic' nomads). It arranges members of the society in a hierarchical sequence, in the order of proximity to the common forebear—that is, in a genealogical chain beginning with the 'ancestor' of the tribe. This indicator is stable, and never changes.[38] The second social affiliation of the 'African' nomads is vertical, and lies in the system of age-based social relations. This is a moveable indicator, insofar as its indicator—the social age of each member of society—exists, together with its age-class, in the process of successive increase (growth), since

[35] Markov, *Kochevniki Azii* (Chapter 5 [pp. 236-277], "Arabs").

[36] Kalinovskaia, *Skotovody Vostochnoi Afriki*.

[37] Kalinovskaia, *Ocherki ètnologii Vostochnoi Afriki*, pp. 146-148.

[38] Kalinovskaia, *Ocherki ètnologii Vostochnoi Afriki*, pp. 146-148.

each age-class and all its members are moving in the direction of aging.[39]

The totality of the 'genealogical' and 'age-based' systems of relations creates a special type of moveable tribal and social organization for the seminomads representing the 'African' form of nomadism. The points of intersection of these two systems of relations supplies a structure of affiliation, for every nomad, to the general social structure; in these same points of intersection lies the mechanism for the rapid reaction of the social organization of African nomads to any sort of radical shifts in the political or natural conditions of the environment they inhabit. While living in a dispersed state during relatively peaceful times, nomadic communities, for all their autonomy, display, during times of crisis, a unique mobility and precision in restructuring from a communal-nomadic condition to a military-nomadic condition. And this is possible only through the knowledge, on the part of each member of the society, of his or her tribal affiliation. The structure described here is relatively stable, and does not change so long as nomadic society exists in reality, reproducing itself in the framework of tradition.

Only a few groups, not numerous, that conduct a mobile stock-herding economy may be ascribed to the 'Asiatic' form of nomadism; these are the northern Somali, Afar, Saho, Adal, and, with certain reservations, the Beja (since among them the remains of an age-based social system are weak, but detectable). Nomadism of the 'Asiatic' form represents, apparently, a more developed and later stage in the history of nomadic societies. Several social and cultural features that go back to the epoch of primitive communal relations, or the time of their decay, are preserved among seminomads representing the 'African' form of nomadism; they relate, above all, to the system, widely encountered in these societies of East Africa, of age-based classes, a system representing a way of actualizing the principle of the social division of labor that took shape long ago.[40] Such a system of division of labor has a more strictly regulated, and more primitive, character than is found among nomads of the 'Asiatic' form, whose societies either bypassed altogether, or already passed through this stage of social development,

[39] K. P. Kalinovskaia, "Kategoriia 'vozrast' v predstavleniiakh nekotorykh narodov Vostochnoi Afriki," *Afrikanskii ètnograficheskii sbornik*, 12 (1980; = Trudy Instituta Ètnografii AN SSSR, Novaia seriia, t. 109), pp. 49-80.

[40] K. P. Kalinovskaia, *Vozrastnye gruppy narodov Vostochnoi Afriki: Struktura i funktsii* (Moscow, 1976).

when the life-activity of the social group was strictly subordinated to the normative functioning of the principle of division of labor according to gender and age. Among 'Asiatic' nomads, age-group affiliation has no social significance; their system of social relations, in the structure of societal organization, is more flexible and free of limitations.

With all the local and historical-cultural differences among the nomads of Asia and Africa, the markers of property in livestock, water sources, and pastures, of forms of economic activity, and of the tribal organization of society remain common for all of them. This too is not accidental, insofar as our understanding of 'nomadism' implies not only the economic characteristics of society, but the social characteristics as well, with nomads constituting social organisms separate from those of agriculturalists. The extensive pastoral stock-herding foundation engenders a corresponding social structure and a tribal form of societal organization.[41]

The comparative analysis of data regarding the nomadic peoples of Asia and of East and North Africa reveals a similarity in the patterns of constructing social organization among different groups of nomads. Tribal structure and the principles of its organization were the most serviceable pattern, and, apparently, the only one that was possible in conditions of mobile life and frequent wars; when certain tribes fell apart, others emerged anew, forming ideologically- as well as formally-genealogical communities. Tribes and their subdivisions were in reality often complex ethnic organisms, a situation often encountered among nomads. At the level of the lowest levels of societal organization, communities and subgroups linked by kinship, and others not linked by kinship, united 'genealogically,' bound by concrete economic and military interests. The highest levels of the social organization of nomads, meanwhile, were, apart from this, chiefly politically- and militarily-based communities, bound together by legendary genealogical kinship, and maintaining significance so long as they served the ideological formulation of real political, military, economic, and other bonds. Their violation, and the emergence of new nomadic formations, led to the appearance of new 'genealogical' structures in the form of tribes.

[41] K. P. Kalinovskaia and G. E. Markov, "Skotovody Azii i Afriki: Problemy istoricheskoi tipologii i periodizatsii," *Vestnik Moskovskogo Universiteta*, Seriia 8, Istoriia, 1983, No. 5, pp. 59-72.

The constituent elements of the societal organization of nomads, and their interaction, worked differently in various social and political circumstances. The communal-nomadic condition of the tribal organization of nomads underwent significant influence from neighboring states, especially in the period of the development of capitalistic relations. This influence hastened the decay of nomadism, which turned out to be a historical 'dead-end' as an economic and social form. Nevertheless, even after the sedentarization of nomads, distinct notions about tribal affiliation have been preserved, in the spheres of ideology and daily life, among many of them (Turkmens, Arabs, Qazaqs, Qïrghïz, Oromo, and many others); this phenomenon, in many cases, shows no tendency toward disappearance, and indeed tribal self-identification may even grow stronger under certain conditions.

In years of warfare and major migrations conducted by nomads, the most extreme consequence of the strengthening of centralized military organization was the emergence of the so-called 'nomadic empires,' as a regular expression of the idea of the military organi-zation of nomads. But these 'empires' did not have their own distinctive economic foundation, and existed only so long as military expansion, or nomadic migrations, continued. After the inevitable collapse of the ephemeral 'empires,' there would occur a quite rapid shift in nomadic social organization from the 'military-nomadic' to the 'communal-nomadic' condition. Through this 'reversibility' of social organization, nomads differ fundamentally from settled agricultural societies, whose states can disappear only as a result of the physical annihilation of their populations.

Following the disintegration of the ephemeral 'nomadic empires,' in the agricultural regions conquered by them, either the previous state structure would be preserved, or there would emerge new formations (which would nevertheless be governmental formations). In places of traditional habitation by nomads, communal-nomadic organization was revived in one form or another, and aside from oral legends, no trace remained of the 'empires.' This is why amorphous tribal formations were to be found afterwards, in place of the old 'nomadic empires.' The communal-nomadic social structure did not decompose in the 'empires' of nomads, but continued to function as long as nomadism itself did not disappear.[42]

[42] Markov, *Kochevniki Azii*, p. 313.

Together with the general nature of the social structure of various groups of nomads, it is essential to strictly distinguish the elements of it that are connected with the genealogical-tribal, economic, military, and political organization of society. Such an approach allows us to uncover the essence of social relationships and the character of the social organization of nomads. The emergence of class relations in the society of nomads signals its death as an economic and cultural type and as a social organism.

In conclusion we must pose one additional problem—namely, what was the social influence of the nomadic peoples on the agricultural peoples conquered by them, or on the peoples with whom they were in close contact (for instance, on the formation of feudalism among the Germanic tribes, the Turks, and other peoples)? This problem requires further detailed investigation.

THE CONCEPT OF REGIONALISM IN HISTORICAL RESEARCH ON CENTRAL ASIA AND IRAN (A MACRO-HISTORICAL INTERPRETATION)

Bert G. Fragner

University of Bamberg

I. INTRODUCTION

In some respects, this contribution may be perceived as a 'position paper.' It aims at the application of some concepts of macro-history to the historical study of Central Asia and Iran. These concepts can be found in abundance in other areas of historical and cultural research, but were hitherto less often taken into consideration with regard to Western and Central Asia. What I have in mind is the concept of 'regionalism,' closely connected to what nowadays is often called 'mental mapping' in literary criticism and cultural sciences. 'Regionalism' refers to the idea that the modes employed by human beings, by virtue of extended history, to organize their social embeddedness are not limited to imaginations of socio-political realms and orders within which they may identify their own position (albeit fictitiously or only partially related to reality); rather, premodern as well as contemporary concepts of imagination, identification, and consciousness of one's 'self' cover not only aspects of social embeddedness, but also notions of space (and, together with space, time necessarily figures as well). This notion developed in the context of the growing acceptance and importance, on a world-wide basis, of concepts such as the 'history of mentalities,' caused by what became famous as the so-called 'cultural turn' in social sciences, in the late 1970s and 1980s.

Regionalism deals with human perceptions of space, relativized by the dimension of time. In cultural history, it is important to understand that regional consciousness—i.e., consciousness of space as an embedding category of self-identity, and/or consciousness of the spatial significance of the alien, the strange, the 'other'—is a long-term but inevitably changing matter. Regionalism attempts to reconstruct spatial orders of the world, from locality to sub-region, with the sub-region to be understood as part of 'the region,' per se, that determines extended identities and helps frame an understanding of the 'self' as a collective category. Conversely, the 'region' may also be conceived as part of a 'mega-region,' which may serve to identify that part of the universe where these collective 'selves' may meet other 'selves' that are signified by neighbouring regions, thus shaping a 'world' that resembles by and large a kind of playground where one's history takes place. This onion-like concept of spatial units embedded in numerous larger and wider units or, alternatively, bearing within themselves smaller regional units, like a Russian *matrioshka*-doll, must be understood as a long-lasting but ultimately changing pattern. In order to serve the maintenance of identities, the concept of region must also serve the requirements of maintaining collective memory. There can be no doubt that concepts of regionalism do change, eventually, but it is inevitable that such changes of regionalism take place very slowly, and, even more important, that these changes never occur simultaneously at all levels (from localism to mega-regionalism). This is an important observation; otherwise the concept of regionalism could no longer support collective and historical memory, or thereby support also a subjective or even biased imagination of continuity on the side of the 'self,' disregarding the fact that there may have occured major changes in collective perception, as seen from a dispassionate and objective point of view.

This is, undoubtedly, one of the important mechanisms in processes producing nationalist ideology. Nationalism deals with language and territoriality (among other important, if not to say constituent, elements). Territoriality is the subject of a highly ideologized variety of regionalism. In our times, regionalist thinking is to be found all over the world, thus arguing in favor of nation-states—whether effective or would-be nation-states—defending and supporting their claim for what they assume to be their 'traditional national territory.'

According to my concept of the importance of regionalism in history as presented above, such nationalist claims for 'the everlasting and sacred territory of a nation' will in many cases be inevitably unveiled as historicist fakes, often manufactured consciously by intellectuals, and/or based on the ground of a changing understanding, on any given level, of my regionalist categories ranging from 'micro' to 'mega.'

To a historian, moreover, and particularly to anyone dealing with cultural history, it might be important to be consciously aware that contemporary concepts of space and regionalism must not be transferred uncritically into any phase of the historical past, but should always be understood as phenomena that have come into existence at a given time, have changed gradually at any given level, and will, at these levels, gradually come to an end.

It is worthwhile to consider, in this sense, the long-term and slowly changing concepts of space and regionalism in the history of Central Asia and Iran—the "Lands of the Eastern Caliphate," as Guy Le Strange worded it, or 'Western and Central Asia,' as a cultural materialist might prefer to say, or '*Īrān-u-Tūrān*,' as might sound smoother to the ears of a romanticist scholar devoted to the fields of Central Asian and Iranian Studies.

In premodern history, the meaning of 'region' is in many cases closely connected to natural conditions. This may mislead us to the assumption that regions reflect primarily the acceptance, by human beings, of natural *a priori* categories, and may consequently be understood as indicators of man's conscious inferiority to nature, in early history. This assumption is an obvious misunderstanding, at least according to my model: the intention of regionalism is not to subordinate physical nature to a structured spatial order, but to express and define human cultural and social conditions by means of space. From this perspective, nature will be interpreted by human consciousness. A river, a mountain range, even a desert or an ocean can therefore serve as a delimitating border line or a border region, but also as a connecting element in terms of traffic, commerce and travel, communication and transfer. The Roman *limes* may serve as a striking example for my point: the limits of Roman imperial presence in Germany did not follow any 'natural' borders, but obeyed ultimately the priority of security. In other words, by having maintained imperial power in southern Germany and adjacent territories, the Romans nourished numerous aspects of regionalism in medieval history up to modern times, many centuries after their own breakdown in late antiquity.

It is the rich tradition concerning the Achaemenid empire—whether 'emic' or 'etic'—that supplies us with indications of early regionalism; or, to phrase it more precisely, after their own political realm had vanished, the Achaemenids eventually turned out to have established regionalism. It is obvious, moreover, that they had already followed traditions of regionalism that had been established much earlier. Media,

Elam, Persis, Karamania, Hyrcania, and others in the west, Margiana, Areia, and Bactria in the east, and Khwārazm and Sogdia in Western Central Asia—all of these were regions already existing and accepted prior to the rise of Achaemenid power, having been taken over in the guise of Achaemenid satrapies, and ultimately survived for a long time, some of them down to the present. They were by no means mere 'natural' regions, but, once established, they survived (even though changing their names in some cases), in various shapes reflecting additional aspects of spatial embeddedness, for very long a time.[1]

I shall now focus on conditions immediately prior to the Muslim conquest of Iran and Western Central Asia and shall then try to offer an overview on changing aspects of regionalism in this part of the world.

II. AN EMPIRE VANISHES

Iran—or, more precisely, *Eran-shahr*—was the official designation of the Sasanian empire. The concept of this political entity was invented by the early founders of this empire; the invention has been analyzed masterfully by Gherardo Gnoli in his book *The Idea of Iran.*[2] In accordance with what I postulated above, this invention was not created out of nothing; the idea of *Eran-shahr* reflected much older Zoroastrian patterns that were thus bundled together in order to give the then-new empire some kind of sacred legitimacy. Following the Sasanian breakdown, the designation '*Eran-shahr*,' or, more conveniently 'Iran,' fell into oblivion, since there was no longer a political or administrative entity resembling the Sasanian empire in its territoriality. On the other hand, the Muslim Arabs did not hesitate to take over the 'lands' of the vanished empire, whose provinces and regions had been taken over by the Sasanians themselves from earlier times, such as some of the already mentioned territorial creations of the Achaemenids, or, further, Azerbaijan—which was conceived as a specific part of Media under Alexander the Great (i.e., 'Media Atropatene,' Alexander's supporter Atropates having then served as the eponym of this important entity in

[1] Various references to the topic treated in this article may be found in Bert G. Fragner, *Die "Persophonie:" Regionalität, Identität und Sprachkontakt in der Geschichte Asiens* (Halle/Berlin: Das Arabische Buch, 1999; ANOR, No. 5).

[2] Gherardo Gnoli, *The Idea of Iran: An Essay on its Origin* (Rome, 1989).

West Asian regionalism)—or Parthia, in present-day Turkmenistan. Parthia was of particular attraction to the Sasanians, since it was the home of their early enemies and counterparts, without whose conquest the origin of Sasanian power would have been entirely different from what history tells us. Perhaps the most important Sasanian contribution to Iranian regionalism, however, was the creation of Khurāsān, made up from a number of more ancient regions and former provinces: Hyrcania (Jurjān/Gurgān), Margiana (Marv), Areia (Herat), and eventually Bactria (Balkh). Shapur I's new metropolis in the eastern part of the empire, Nev-Shapur (Nīshābūr), was to symbolize the center of this then newly-conceived region.

This particular Sasanian invention, Khurāsān, was supposed to shape the frontier toward Transoxiana and its adjacent areas, a region—sometimes in the political shadow of the Sasanians—that continued to exist, in politics and in minds, in a form similar to that which it had already in Achaemenid and Alexandrian times: Khwārazm, south of the Aral Sea along the lower Oxus; Transoxiana (Sogdia) proper, marked by the Zarafshan valley and its ancient urban centers; and Farghāna, along the upper Jaxartes.

Since early antiquity, these three regions shaped a chain of the principal cultivated areas along what became well-known as the 'Great Silk Road.' What seems to have been rather marginal to the Sasanians was of high centrality as seen from the Silk Road perspective.

It is not surprising that, as the Arabs approached *Eran-shahr* from the west, or from the southwest respectively, Khurāsān attracted their attention, in mental mapping, more than did the lands beyond, in the first stage of the conquest. But already under the early ʿAbbāsid caliphs, a new concept of mapping Western and Central Asia came into existence which successfully superseded the idea of *Eran-shahr*: while the western areas—Media together with Azerbaijan, Shīrvān, Ṭabaristān, Qūhistān and Fārs—were gradually conceived to be the coherent *hinterland* of Baghdad, Khurāsān was seen, rather, as the corresponding area in the East. In the 10th century at the latest, under the rule of the Sāmānid kings who had their residence in Bukhara, it became clear that the Oxus—the Amu Darya—was no longer an alienating and separating border line. On the contrary, the Oxus connected Transoxiana (henceforth, under Islamic rule, known as Mavarannahr), i.e., the former Sogdia, as well as Farghāna, closely to Khurāsān. Even Khwārazm was perceived as being close to western Khurāsān: the Parthian deserts, crossed and mastered by merchants, soldiers, and robbers, connected Jurjān (Gurgān) tightly to Urganj, especially under Sāmānid rule. This close connection between western Central Asia and Khurāsān, as expressed by the political rule of the Sāmānids and, partially, that of their successors, the Ghaznavids, was and still is sometimes referred to as '*Khurāsān-i buzurg*,' i.e., 'Greater Khurāsān.'

This concept of 'Greater Khurāsān' stood in sharp contrast to the western lands of the former *Eran-shahr*, which used to be conceived as '*ʿIrāq-i ʿajam*' (brought together with Mesopotamia, '*ʿIrāq-i ʿarab*,' as the '*ʿIrāqayn*'), based on the idea of the centrality of ancient Media, connected to the Persis of antiquity. It was quite clear that the Khurāsān-ʿIrāq opposition decisively superseded the pre-Islamic concept of Iran. Even Firdawsī seems not to have been entirely confident in re-evoking the former lands of Iran, which had passed away in a political sense centuries earlier; his intention, when he spoke about 'Iran,' was clearly to refer to the Sasanian empire. But is not his idea of 'Īrān and Tūrān,' beyond its contradictory content, also a significant marker of ʿAbbāsid geopolitics, so that it might also be understood as an allusion to the then-existing and accepted model of visualizing 'ʿIrāq' (presumably '*ʿIrāq-i ʿajam*,' at least) in the west and (Greater) 'Khurāsān' in the east, shaping together what was then mapped as the *mashriq* or, in the words of Guy Le Strange, "The Lands of the Eastern Caliphate"? And within this *mashriq*, the Amu Darya did not at all mark a delimiting border line, but was much more a connecting line along which the two sub-regions, Khurāsān and Mavarannahr, were brought closely together, during the period of the caliphate.

There is much evidence for a strong and deep acceptance of this way of mapping the eastern part of the *Dār al-Islām*, albeit in terms of territorial politics, or even in intellectual discourse, all over the area where the Persian, and later Turkic, languages became dominant, first beneath and then, gradually, instead of Arabic.

When the early Saljūqs approached the lands of ʿIrāq, coming from the east, they aimed politically at dominance over the caliphate and its center, Baghdad, but even with extensive research we may not find any argument that the Saljūqs would have perceived their lands as anything that could be characterized as 'Iran.' Even Niẓām al-Mulk, who repeatedly referred to the strong Sasanian background of his own idea of the 'World of Islam' (*Dār al-Islām*), was never struck with the idea of designating his lords' lands by the term 'Iran,' notwithstanding the fact that the Great Saljūqs' territory covered by far the greater part of the soil of the former Sasanian empire. On the contrary, under Sulṭān Sanjar it became evident that the 'Khurāsān-versus-ʿIrāq' model had become dominant: by separating his own part of his realm—Khurāsān, with its center, Marv—from the west, Sanjar strongly supported this 'non-Iranian' concept that prevailed throughout the period of the ʿAbbāsid caliphate. He had left the rest of the realm (the western part) to his nephew, whereby the so-called 'ʿIrāqī Saljūqs' came into existence, to rule there, at least formally, until the beginning of the 13th century.

If we observe the following intermezzo of the Khwārazmshāh's rule first superseding Sanjar's realm in Khurāsān, and then aiming at the conquest of the west, and thereby absorbing former Saljūq territories in a strategy that might be categorized as a reflection of regionalism, we might be inclined to find an indication of the Khwārazmshāh's intention to recreate ancient—and vanished—Iran; or we might argue that he had simply tried to repeat the early Saljūqs' strategy of gaining Baghdad and thus eventually holding sway over the caliphate. We are left unable to decide between these alternatives, however, owing to the most striking external phenomenon, which cut down any continuity in Islamic geopolitics of that period: the Mongol invasion under the leadership of Chinggis Khān.

III. 'ULŪSISM'—A NEW REGIONALIST CONCEPT IN CENTRAL AND WESTERN ASIA

This is not the place to deal with the Mongol expansion usually associated with the rulership of Chinggis Khān, in the 12th and 13th centuries. In the context of the quest for regionalism, it is not the ideal concept of a homogeneous Mongol World Empire that ought to be regarded as the Mongol conquerors' great innovative contribution to world history. This contribution is, much more, to be found in what is usually disparaged by historians as an indication of the political weakness and instability of Mongol rulership: the partition of power, after the death of Chinggis Khān, in accord with a dynastic as well as regionalist concept, i.e., the system of the so-called 'four *ulūs*es.' In Chinggisid terminology this meant that, under the supervision of one 'Great Khān,' power should be divided in terms of territory, and the results of this division were then given not so much to Chinggis Khān's four legal sons, but to their lineages. Subsequently, it would turn out that the territorial concept might be even stronger than the lineage principle, as can be shown in the case of the '*ulūs* of Chaghatay,' comprising Transoxiana, the region of Semirechye (Zhetisu), Kashgharia ("T'ien-shan nan-lu", in Chinese), and Turfan together with Dzungaria ("T'ien-shan pei-lu"). In this sense also, the '*ulūs* of Jöchi' came into existence and succeeded, dynastically, for a considerable time in Russia, as the rule of the famous 'Golden Horde' indicates; but even after the breakdown of Chinggisid rule in the territory of the *ulūs* of Jöchi, the regional concept of this *ulūs* survived, as evidenced by the emergence of the Russian Tsardom, which followed perfectly the territorial concepts of the former Golden Horde—despite later historicist interpretations of the 'Kievan Rus,' which, as its designation indicates, was in fact different from the realm of Ivan Groznyi, the latter appearing as none other than a perfect carry over of a regionalist concept that was invented by the Mongols' rule.

There is no particular need to deal with *ulūs* of Ögödey, which vanished already in the 13th century in favour of the territorial claims of Chaghatay and Toluy. The *ulūs* of Toluy, as it was conceived by Chinggis Khān, resembled by far the Mongolian heartlands and comprised the smallest *ulūs* territory, at the time of Chinggis Khāns' death. But later on, the lineage of Toluy's descendants would turn out to be the most actively expansionist of the Chinggisid sub-dynasties. China in the east, then ruled by Toluid emperors shaping the so-called Yüan dynasty, was complemented by another territory ruled by Toluids in the west—the lands of the so-called 'Ilkhans,' corresponding closely to the area that had once been ruled by the Sasanians, some 700 years earlier. As the official designation of this 'neo-Toluid' territory, the ancient name of 'Iran'—which had been out of use since the breakdown of the Sasanian empire in the 7th century—came into use again, sometimes, even, in an obvious imitation of the Sasanians' term '*Eran-shahr*,' in the form of the phrase '*Īrān-zamīn*' (as used repeatedly, for example, by the geographer Ḥamdullāh Mustawfī in the 14th century). Ghāzān Khān proclaimed himself formally as "*pādshāh-i Īrān va Islām.*" It seems evident that the Ilkhans' empire may therefore be interpreted as a re-birth, or better, a re-invention, of pre-Islamic Iran, in the sense of regionalism.[3] As seen through the Ilkhans' political and regionalist perspective, the Oxus (Amu Darya) was again conceived as their border

[3] Bert G. Fragner, "Iran under Ilkhanid Rule in a World History Perspective," *L'Iran face à la domination mongole*, ed. Denise Aigle (Paris/Tehran, 1997; Bibliothèque iranienne, 45), pp. 121-131.

line in the northeast, just as under the Sasanians before the Muslim conquest. But from the perspective of the *ulūs* of Chaghatay, things were seen quite differently, as far as the Oxus was concerned: from the 13th century, there were outspoken Chaghatay claims to the region of Khurāsān, and it goes without saying that these claims were raised at the expense of the Ilkhans' realm. Moreover, there were Chaghatay claims also for Khwārazm, which had fallen under the rule of the *khān*s of the Golden Horde.

In terms of regionalism, we witness therefore a clear change of paradigms in the early 14th century: Ilkhanid ('Hülegüid') Iran was a somewhat reestablished and reanimated concept of what Sasanian *Eranshahr* had once been. In terms of ideology, then, it is hardly surprising that, among other effects, a strong tendency toward propagating and distributing Firdawsī's *Shāhnāma* can be observed, retrospectively, specifically under the Ilkhans. Moreover, it was under late Ilkhanid rule that the already mentioned Ḥamdullāh Mustawfī, after having produced a new redaction of the *Shāhnāma*, also wrote his so-called *Ẓafarnāma*, which was the first attempt to adopt Firdawsī's style and concept to write a versified history of a contemporary and then still-ruling dynasty. This *Ẓafarnāma* offered the pattern along which numerous *Shāhnāma*-like texts were written in praise of living rulers, from the Ottoman Empire down to the western reaches of the Himalayas, down to the 20th century. It is also clear, moreover, that with regard to Khurāsān, a deep controversy between defenders of the Chaghatayid and Ilkhanid concepts can be observed, over generations and centuries.

Amīr Temür, the famous Central Asian conqueror, followed clearly the intentions of the *ulūs* of Chaghatay, and in fact we may realize that his first conquests beyond the western Chaghatayid heartlands reflected the claims maintained by this *ulūs*: Khurāsān was incorporated to the south of Transoxiana, and Khwārazm was added from the side of the Golden Horde. Temür, moreover, also laid claim to the heritage of the Ilkhanid realm, thus adding the central and western parts of Iran to his empire; this led his chronicler and geographer Ḥāfiẓ-i Abrū to portray Temür and his successors as the lords of '*Īrān-u-Tūrān*,' signaling once more the usage of an ancient expression in a new regionalist context, and thus in an alienated meaning: the phrase '*Īrān-u-Tūrān*' refers, in the 15th century, to nothing less than the political unification of the *ulūs*es of Chaghatay and Hülegü, and therefore it gradually came to be used as the semi-official or even official designation for the Timurid empire, as abundant evidence in various chronicles confirms. Concerning the issue of Khurāsān, Ḥāfiẓ-i Abrū, a convinced follower of Amīr Temür and thus a defender of the Chaghatayid concept, differs clearly from his professional colleague Ḥamdullāh Mustawfī.

But at the same time (the 15th century), whenever the rulers belonging to the Türkmen dynasties of Bahārlū (Qara-Qoyunlu) and Bāyïndïrīya (Aq-Qoyunlu), originating from Anatolia, approached western Iran, and particularly Azerbaijan, moving eastwards from Asia Minor, and succeeded in conquering Tabrīz, they would install themselves officially as '*pādshāh-i Īrān*' or as '*kisrā-yi Īrān*,' as shown by various chancery documents and royal decrees pertaining to these dynasties; they thus claimed the Ilkhanid heritage, including the metropolitan capital, Tabrīz. And in the 16th century, the Ṣafavids did the same, despite their quite different religious aims. The spatial orientation of their conquests followed clearly the Hülegüid concept of the Ilkhans, which led subsequently into a century-long fight for supremacy in Khurāsān, at that time no longer against the Timurids, but against the so-called Uzbek tribal confederation led by the Jöchid *khān*s of the Shïbānid dynasty.

IV. ULŪSIST REVISIONISM AFTER THE BREAKDOWN OF TIMURID RULE IN KHURĀSĀN AND CENTRAL ASIA (16TH TO 18TH CENTURIES)

In terms of 'ulūsism,' the Uzbek conquest of Transoxiana and Khwārazm meant first of all something like revisionist revenge for Amīr Temür's take-over of Khwārazm in the 14th century; Khwārazm had been claimed as belonging to the *ulūs* of Jöchi since the early stages of Chinggisid rule. But there was more to it: the Shïbānid rulers of the Uzbek confederation claimed also the heritage of the Timurids, which meant the *ulūs* of Chaghatay, or at least its western part (i.e., Transoxiana and, according to Chaghatayid and later, also, Timurid interpretations, Khurāsān). If we consider that the Ṣafavid dynasty (with Shāh Ismāʿīl I) had come into power roughly at the same time as the Shïbānid *khān*s, the military contest for rule over Khurāsān seems to have been inevitable, in retrospect: while the Shïbānid *khān*s followed the Chaghatayid concept with respect to Khurāsān, the Ṣafavids perceived themselves, in terms of *realpolitik*, first and foremost as the immediate successors of the Aq-Qoyunlu rulers, following the former

Ilkhanid concept of '*Īrān-zamīn*' (which included Khurāsān, as had been the case under the Ilkhans). This makes it clear that the fight for Khurāsān between the Ṣafavids and the Uzbeks throughout the greater part of the 16th century is not only to be interpreted as a fight between Shīᶜites and Sunnīs. It was, perhaps, much more a fight between two different versions of 'ulūsist' patterns within the regionalist discourse I have sought to trace since the collapse of the Sasanian empire.

A late Ṣafavid geographer, Muḥammad-i Mufīd (late 17th century) provides evidence of this regionalist understanding of rulership: he praises the founder of 'his' rulers' dynasty, Shāh Ismāᶜīl, as the legitimate heir to both the Aq-Qoyunlu and the Timurid rulers, having thus been the one who 'reunited' the lands of Iran (i.e., the Türkmen west and the Timurid east of Iran).[4] About 1600, it was clear that the Hülegüid concept of 'Iran' had succeeded at the expense of the Uzbek khanates (at that time still ruled by Chinggisids): Iran's border with Transoxiana was then shaped by the Amu Darya, and Khurāsān, perhaps with the exception of the left bank of the upper Oxus, was basically understood as being ruled by the Ṣafavids, and thus as belonging to Iran.

The history of Iran in the 18th century offers evidence that this solution was still not yet stable. Structurally, it seems that Nādir Shāh shifted at least partially from the Hülegüid understanding of '*Īrān-zamīn*' toward somewhat Chaghatayid concepts; fostering the position of his own native region, Khurāsān—the *yūrt* of his own tribal community, the Afshārs—he clearly displayed an inclination to follow in the footsteps of Temür (not only in adopting Temür's title, '*ṣāḥib-qirān*,' but also in following Temür's programs in warfare and in proclaiming himself as the overlord of Transoxiana). This may be interpreted as an indication of some kind of regionalist revival of the 15th-century Timurid concept of '*Īrān-u-Tūrān*,' which was obviously given up by the Shībānids when they confined themselves to the struggle for Khurāsān—thus accepting the Ṣafavids' rule over central and western Iran.

The military and political history of 18th-century Iran (and, from 1747 onwards, Afghanistan as well) is much too complicated to be fitted into this pattern of regionalism with just a few words, and would therefore surpass the limits of this article, but I argue that it may be worthwhile to analyse the development of territorial rulership in this area in the context of the regionalist discourses to which I refer. But even in

[4] Seyfeddin Najmabadi, ed., *Moḫtaṣar-e Mofīd des Moḥammad Mofīd Mostoufī* (Wiesbaden, 1991; 2 vols.), I, pp. 4 ff.

the early 19th century there were attempts on Iranian soil to visualize the then-ruling dynasty, the Qājārs, as a family with not only Qājār but also Ṣafavid and even Timurid roots, dating still further back to Hülegü.[5] There is striking evidence of continuity in the regionalist understanding of the concept of 'Iran,' leading directly from the Ilkhanid idea of '*Īrān-zamīn*' down to the Qājār idea of the '*mamālik-i maḥrūsa-i Īrān*'—lands that were then reinterpreted, step-by-step throughout the 19th century, by early forerunners of modern Iranan nationalism (whose activities may be witnessed from the late 1820s onward), as the legacy of the ancient Sasanians. In terms of regionalism, modern Iran is simply the direct heir to the territorial concept that had been invented by the Ilkhans and their servants. It was by external force alone that Iranian authorities agreed, reluctantly, to their own renunciation of the greater part of Khurāsān, thus favoring Afghanistan (on the basis of British pressure) and the Türkmens, and later on to Russian rule on the soil of present-day Turkmenistan. In any case, by comparison with other countries of the Near and Middle East, the modern state of Iran shows a convincing continuity in its territorial self-understanding, the nationalist version being no more than an ideological and historicist reinterpretation of a given territorial concept that was invented by the Ilkhans about 1300. Nationalist ideologists of the countries neighboring Iran have much greater difficulties in bringing together nationalist and historicist territorial claims with their territorial reality, which was in many cases created no earlier than in the 20th century.

Since we may recognize in modern Iran's territorial physiognomy late traces of Hülegüid 'ulūsism,' it is worthwhile to search for the destiny of 'ulūsist' concepts in neighboring Central Asia.

Chinggisid rule vanished gradually in the 'khanates.' The ruling families of Jöchid *khāns* (the Shībānids, followed by their cousins the Jānids—also called Ashtarkhānids—in Transoxiana/Bukhara, and the ᶜArabshāhids in Khwārazm, also of Jöchid origin) were replaced by leading lineages of two Uzbek tribes, the Manghïts in Bukhara (late 18th century) and the Qongrats in Khwārazm. While both ruling families still referred to some kind of Chinggisid descent, it turned out that their

[5] Rich corroboration for this phenomenon can be found, for example, in the work (from the early 19th century) of Rustam al-ḥukamā Muḥammad-Hāshim b. Muḥammad-Ḥusayn Iṣfahānī, *Rustam al-tavārīkh*, ed. Muḥammad Mushīrī (Tehran, 1348-49/1969-70).

regionalist understanding of their territory concentrated more and more on the traditional—'pre-ulūsist'—regions of Khwārazm and Sogdia/ Transoxiana/Mavarannahr. An interesting example of the process of transition from 'ulūsism' to traditional regionalism in Central Asia can be found in the case of the establishment of the so-called Ming rulers in Farghāna, the founders of what became famous as the khanate of Qoqand; they too were Uzbek tribal leaders, and in this sense comparable to their Qongrat and Manghït colleagues, but they claimed Chinggisid and Timurid genetic origin. This, nevertheless, is an indication of the continued high esteem for descent from these past ruling houses, rather than of the survival of 'ulūsism' as a regionalist concept; although the Ming rulers from Qoqand continued to challenge the *amīr*s of Bukhara militarily and politically, their territorial concept was bound to the three great and ancient regions of this area as they were already defined in antiquity: Khwārazm, Sogdia/Transoxiana, and Farghāna. Thus, in the 19th century, political entities in western Central Asia referred, in terms of territories, largely to these three traditional units. With the end of the 18th century, 'ulūsism' had come to an end in Central Asian history, as an imaginative tool for conceptualizing history.

Russian colonial rule in Central Asia accepted widely this reestablished and 'de-ulūsized' concept of regionalism in Central Asia, until the establishment of the Soviet Union. The heartlands of Khwārazm and Transoxiana remained, in the shape of two puppet states, until 1920 (or 1924, respectively), while Farghāna was conceived as a territorial administrative unit, after the dissolution of Ming rulership. The Transcaspian area consisted broadly of the northern part of traditional Khurāsān, and the Governor-Generalship of the Steppe included the northern banks of Syr Darya and Semirechye. None of these traditional regions remained solely within one of the so-called national republics that were established under Soviet rule: Khwārazm belongs to Turkmenistan and Uzbekistan (and also Kazakhstan), the same republics have their share of Transoxiana, with Tajikistan joining them, and Farghāna is possessed by Uzbekistan, Kyrgyzstan, and Tajikistan. It is interesting that Uzbekistan holds important shares of all three regions, while the other republics have parts of only two of them, or even only one (Kazakhstan—Khwārazm and Transoxiana; Kyrgyzstan—Farghāna; Tajikistan—Transoxiana and Farghāna; Turkmenistan—Khwārazm and Transoxiana).

Old Khurāsān, like Transoxiana, is also tripartitioned: its west belongs to Iran, bearing the traditional designation; northern Khurāsān—ancient Margiana—shapes the greater part of Turkmenistan; and Afghanistan contains most of the Khurāsānian east, i.e., Areia and Bactria.

In the West, Azerbaijan endured a similar fate.

* * *

I refrain from contingent and stringent conclusions and prognostications. Perhaps modernity has brought these traditional concepts of regionalism to an end in the area under discussion in this contribution. Or perhaps aspects of historical regionalism will find some kind of revival in the future. It seems, after all, that the contemporary countries of this area, while separated and, in some cases, even isolated from each other, still have many common features, structurally considered. In 1999, the popular American magazine *National Geographic* published a thematic map under the title "The Caspian Region," thus presenting a new geostrategic 'mega-region,' comparable to the so-called 'Gulf Region' or the 'Horn of Africa' (not to forget the good old 'Near East'). In any case, the 'Caspian Region' contains all the relevant areas under discussion in my paper; this might be an indication of the continuing importance of my regionalist concept. And, last but not least, one should not forget that there is a quite respectable number of intellectuals in contemporary Iran, Tajikistan, and Afghanistan who are obviously fascinated by discussing vigorously the question of revitalizing the idea of '*Khurāsān-i buzurg*,' thus still stressing the old Timurid concept of '*Īrān-u-Tūrān*,' and memorializing traditions dating back to early Islamic times.